The Patriot's Toolbox

One Hundred Principles for Restoring Our Freedom and Prosperity

The Heartland Institute

The Patriot's Toolbox

Fourth Revised Edition
Copyright ©2017
The Heartland Institute

Published by The Heartland Institute
3939 North Wilke Road
Arlington Heights, Illinois 60004
phone 312/377-4000
fax 312/277-4122
www.heartland.org

Additional copies of this book
are available from The Heartland Institute
at the following prices:

1-10 copies	$8.95 per copy
11-50 copies	$7.95 per copy
51-100 copies	$6.95 per copy
101 or more	$5.95 per copy

Printed in the United States of America
ISBN-13 978-1-934791-62-2
ISBN-10 1-934791-62-8

Manufactured in the United States of America

Contents

Preface to the Fourth Edition

The November 2016 election sent a strong message that "business as usual" was no longer acceptable to the American people. Voters resoundingly rejected the policies of the ruling and largely liberal political class. They don't want economic stagnation, racial and class division, and socialism. *They want economic prosperity, harmony, and freedom.*

Donald Trump campaigned for president of the United States as a political outsider promising to undo much of his predecessor's legacy. President Trump moved quickly to keep his campaign promises, using his executive authority and appointments to advance his agenda when Democrats and some Republicans in Congress blocked legislation needed to implement it. The president's "coattails"—mostly Republican victories down the ballot in Congress and in state capitols across the country—are ensuring political change will occur regardless of whether the Trump administration is successful.

State and national policymakers, both Democrats and Republicans, are busy formulating, articulating, and implementing an agenda that will help freedom rise in America again. With their help, and the help of nearly a score of contributors from many of the country's leading think tanks and advocacy groups, we have collected 100 bold steps policymakers can take, and some already are taking, to move the country in this new direction.

This new edition of *The Patriot's Toolbox*, the fourth since the first edition was released in 2010, is completely rewritten and thoroughly updated to reflect the events of 2016 and so far in 2017. It offers an agenda for incumbent office holders, a platform for candidates for public office, and a report card for civic and business leaders and journalists following the policy moves of the Trump administration, Congress, and state lawmakers.

The word "patriot" appears in the title of this book because the principles we recommend would return the country to government based on the ideals of the Founders who led the American Revolution: liberty, limited taxation, and limited government. The word "toolbox" appears because the principles can be used as tools to fix what is wrong with the country's politics and public policies. Just as not every tool in a toolbox is used for every project, we don't expect every reader to find every chapter and every principle useful to his or her effort.

The book consists of ten chapters. Eight of them significantly update topics covered in the third edition while two chapters—on firearms policy and constitutional reform—are new to this edition. Together, they provide a comprehensive collection of practical, evidence-based principles in the major fields of legislation. Additional research and commentary, including nearly all the sources identified in the references sections at the end of each chapter, can be found on The Heartland Institute's website at www.heartland.org.

Attentive readers will notice some controversial topics are missing. Immigration, foreign policy, religion, and policies regarding race and gender—what has come to be called "identity politics"—are not addressed at all. This is in keeping with the decision we made when writing the first edition. These topics are just as important as the ones we chose to include but differences of opinion are based on values, personal experience, and interpretations of history that divide rather than unite conservatives, libertarians, and other members of the freedom movement. We therefore leave them to others to address.

We extend our sincere thanks to the following policy experts who contributed to this volume:

Vicki E. Alger	Leonard Gilroy	Publius
Timothy Benson	Matthew Glans	Justin Strehle
Roman Buhler	Hance Haney	Austill Stuart
Joshua Distel	Adrian Moore	James Taylor
Peter J. Ferrara	Isaac Orr	Steven Titch
George Gilder	Dan Pilla	Richard Vedder

Their bios appear at the end of the book. We also thank everyone who helped edit and proofread this new edition, including especially Diane Bast as well as Jessica Chen, Edward Hudgins, S.T. Karnick, Barbara Liang, and Arianna Wilkerson. Thank you, too, to the donors who make this book and all of the work of The Heartland Institute possible.

Herbert J. Walberg   Joseph L. Bast
Chairman   Chief Executive Officer
The Heartland Institute   The Heartland Institute

Introduction

Herbert J. Walberg

Americans want new leadership and substantial change. As this was written, in August 2017, President Donald Trump, who previously had not held political office, was using executive orders and appointments to repeal some of the policies adopted by his predecessor, Barack Obama. He and the new Congress were promising to go much farther, cutting and abolishing taxes, repealing costly regulations, and changing priorities to "put America first" and "make America great again."

Of course, not all of Obama's legacy is bad and not all of Trump's ideas and plans are good. Still, the need for a change in direction was clear even before the November 2016 elections. The past eight years witnessed mounting frustration over the political, economic, and cultural direction of the country.

Americans suffered through an economic crisis and then stagnation—the longest economic recovery on record never to surpass 2 percent per year in GDP growth. Millions of people grew frustrated by the lack of jobs and opportunities for advancement and simply dropped out of the workforce (or never entered it after high school or college) and became dependent on new or expanded government entitlement programs.

The country experienced unprecedented fiscal irresponsibility. The national debt increased more over an eight-year period than the increase in the entire history of the United States prior to 2009. A war on manufacturing jobs and affordable energy was waged in the name of stopping "global warming," a quest that seemed to take on quasi-religious meaning even as traditional religion was disrespected and mocked by elites.

Average Americans lost control over their local public schools as a result of federal policies leading to the adoption of a *de facto* national curriculum, the so-called "Common Core State Standards," despite the long tradition of local control and despite laws outlawing such federal intervention. Similarly, millions of Americans lost their private health insurance attributable to a new national program referred to as "Obamacare," despite health insurance having always been the domain of state and not national regulators, and despite presidential promises that "if you like your current insurance plan, you can keep it."

Not all of these problems and disturbing developments were attributable to policies adopted or supported by Obama. Many are the results of trends predating his administration and bipartisan actions going back many decades. The Founding Fathers' vision of a republican form of government—of divided and limited powers in the service of protecting individual liberty rather than bestowing privileges—has been under attack almost since the Constitutional Convention of 1787 came to a close.

What is truly new today, in 2017, is not the change from one political party to another in the White House, but the opening of a window of opportunity to redirect both national and state public policies toward less reliance on government and more reliance on free-market solutions. How long that window will remain open is unclear. Developments in both foreign and domestic policy could lead to a return to Obama-era policies and attitudes.

For now, however, freedom-loving patriots have an opportunity to help change the course of the country. Nearly a decade after the Tea Party Movement popularized the slogan "take back our country," we are once again at a moment in history when the need and opportunities for doing so are probably greater than at any time in recent memory. We have the best ideas, the most carefully thought-out roadmap, the support of the public, and sympathetic elected officials ready to act. It's time to open the toolbox and get to work!

Overview of the Book

This book is not a treatise, a collection of reflections or opinions, or a memoir. It is definitely not a campaign book written to support or oppose the election of any candidate or the candidates of any political party.

The Patriot's Toolbox was written by specialists with extensive backgrounds in state and national public policy. They worked closely with elected officials who either have successfully implemented the policies they recommend or who know first-hand the challenges of getting them adopted. Here are a few of the recommendations from each chapter:

■ **Chapter 1: Health Care** shows how we can attain better health care at lower cost by repealing Obamacare, reforming Medicaid and Medicare, reducing reliance on third-party payers, and repealing unnecessary regulations.

■ **Chapter 2: Energy and Environment** explains the errors of global warming alarmists and radical environmentalists who want to paralyze America's economy and return the country to the living standards of third-world countries. It recounts the success of past efforts to protect human health and the natural environment, and it documents how America's natural resources can be safely developed with tremendous benefits for everyone.

■ **Chapter 3: Elementary and Secondary Education** documents the continuing failure of too many public schools to prepare the next generation for the duties of citizenship and self-sufficiency. It presents evidence of the success of school choice programs, such as vouchers and charter schools, and the promise of education savings accounts and programs that reward achievement and improvement.

■ **Chapter 4: Higher Education** explains the crisis in higher education as the quality of instruction is falling even though costs are rising out of control and students are facing ever-higher levels of debt. Many colleges and universities fail to graduate half their entering classes and are replacing solid instruction with liberal indoctrination. This chapter recommends a series of reforms that make higher education more affordable and more efficient.

■ **Chapter 5: Privatization** explains how governments at all levels can save taxpayers money and improve the quality of public services by contracting with private firms, using vouchers to encourage competition and empower consumers. The chapter further explains "load-shedding"; that is, ending the public provision of some services (such as operating golf courses) altogether.

■ **Chapter 6: Firearms** explains why the Founding Fathers thought private ownership of firearms was an essential protection of all the other rights guaranteed by the Constitution. It presents the overwhelming evidence that private ownership of firearms contributes positively to public safety.

■ **Chapter 7: Telecommunications** describes how the internet and modern communications technologies are producing great value, both economically and culturally. It points out ways governments interfere with the spread of affordable broadband and cellphone service by imposing so-called "net neutrality" rules, discriminatory taxes, and unnecessary regulations.

■ **Chapter 8: State Fiscal Policy** presents the latest evidence on how states compete with one another and with governments in other countries to attract and keep investment assets and productive citizens. The most successful states are those that keep taxes low, create transparent and accountable budgets, privatize public services to maximize competition, avoid corporate welfare, and protect state employees from politics.

■ **Chapter 9: Federal Tax Policy** describes the abuses and unfairness of the current national tax system, with its thousands of pages of tax code, crippling compliance costs, and perverse incentives for investors and workers. It offers policymakers ways to adhere to sound constitutional and economic principles when levying taxes.

■ **Chapter 10: Constitutional Reform** confronts the fact that the constitutional restraints the Founding Fathers thought they had imposed on the national government have been weakened or avoided over time, creating a need for constitutional amendments. This chapter refutes concerns of a "run-away convention," explaining how a convention of states could be convened and the rules under which it would operate. The chapter also proposes some crucial amendments.

Each chapter presents ten principles, which we intend to be understood as enduring insights or key facts necessary for a solid understanding of a topic area. Every principle is succinctly presented, carefully documented, and accompanied by specific policy recommendations for turning the principle into real-world public policy. The result is 100 principles, all told, enough to fill even the most ambitious patriot's toolbox! They are summarized at the end of this introduction.

I urge our fellow patriots to at least skim this list of principles, and then read at least those chapters addressing topics of particular interest to you, your organization, or your family. Treat this book as a reference work, something to be returned to over time as issues arise and opportunities present themselves.

Most readers will recall the famous exchange between Benjamin Franklin and an anxious person outside the Constitutional Convention of 1787. Franklin was asked, "Well, doctor, what have we got, a republic or a monarchy?" He replied, "A republic, if you can keep it." The republic is at risk today. This book is filled with tools to keep it safe, for ourselves and for future generations. I hope it is put to good use.

One Hundred Principles
for Restoring Our Freedom and Prosperity

Chapter 1: Health Care
1. Repeal and replace Obamacare.
2. Reform Medicaid and Medicare.
3. Repeal existing regulations.
4. Expand health savings accounts.
5. Expand high-risk pools.
6. Encourage price transparency.
7. Expand the use of direct primary care programs.
8. Expand access to prescription drugs.
9. Remove regulatory barriers to medical innovation.
10. Reduce malpractice litigation expenses.

Chapter 2: Energy and Environment
1. Global warming is not a crisis.
2. End the war on fossil fuels.
3. Hydraulic fracturing ("fracking") is safe and beneficial.
4. National security requires affordable energy.
5. Energy self-sufficiency is achievable.
6. Air pollution is a fading challenge.
7. End subsides to alternative energy producers.
8. Biofuels cannot replace oil.
9. Corporate Average Fuel Economy standards sacrifice lives for oil.
10. Replace the Environmental Protection Agency.

Chapter 3: Elementary and Secondary Education
1. The rising tide of mediocrity.
2. Common Core was not the answer.
3. Allow parents to choose.
4. School choice programs work.
5. Avoid new regulations.
6. School choice benefits teachers.
7. Design guidelines for voucher programs.
8. Design guidelines for education savings accounts.
9. Design guidelines for charter schools.
10. Digital learning: The future of education?

One Hundred Principles
for Restoring Our Freedom and Prosperity
(continued)

Chapter 4: Higher Education
1. Higher education in the United States isn't working.
2. Make students foot a larger share of the bill.
3. Promote free expression of ideas.
4. Increase transparency of costs and results.
5. Promote alternatives to college.
6. Emphasize instruction and raise academic standards.
7. Restructure university ownership and governance.
8. Revamp or eliminate federal student financial aid.
9. End destructive government regulation.
10. Reform or eliminate accreditation.

Chapter 5: Privatization
1. Identify privatization opportunities.
2. Prepare a business case evaluation.
3. Create a privatization center of excellence.
4. Choose contractors on best value, not lowest price.
5. Use performance-based contracting.
6. Provide effective monitoring and oversight.
7. Bundle services for better value.
8. Prepare a real property inventory.
9. Divest non-core assets.
10. Make the case to the public.

Chapter 6: Firearms
1. Americans have an individual right to keep and bear arms.
2. Bans on "assault weapons" are incoherent and self-defeating.
3. An increase in the number of guns does not lead directly to more gun crime.
4. Firearms possession among law-abiding citizens deters crime.
5. Defensive gun use saves lives.
6. Right to carry laws do not increase crime and may generate social benefits.
7. "Stand Your Ground" laws have been the historical norm in the United States.
8. The risk of firearms accidents is low and falling.

One Hundred Principles
for Restoring Our Freedom and Prosperity
(continued)

9. Large-scale illegal gun-running is a myth.
10. International experience does not support gun control in the United States.

Chapter 7: Telecommunications
1. Don't mandate net neutrality.
2. Eliminate rules left over from the monopoly era.
3. Avoid municipal broadband projects.
4. Reform carrier of last resort and build-out obligations.
5. Reform regulation of inter-carrier access charges and interconnection fees.
6. Repeal discriminatory taxes and fees on telecom services.
7. Prohibit the collection of sales taxes on online purchases that cross state lines.
8. Strengthen privacy and Fourth Amendment protections.
9. Prohibit government regulation of content.
10. Don't thwart expansion of Internet applications and e-commerce.

Chapter 8: State Fiscal Policy
1. Keep taxes low.
2. Avoid progressive income taxes.
3. Reduce reliance on excise taxes.
4. Create transparent and accountable budget processes.
5. Stop corporate welfare.
6. Remove regulatory barriers to prosperity.
7. Reform public pension and health care programs.
8. Fund school children, not schools.
9. Fix, don't expand, Medicaid.
10. Cap taxes and expenditures.

Chapter 9: Federal Tax Policy
1. Tax codes should be simple and understandable.
2. Collect taxes in the least invasive manner.
3. Make tax collection efficient.
4. Make the tax code stable and predictable.
5. Taxes should not be hidden from taxpayers.

One Hundred Principles
for Restoring Our Freedom and Prosperity
(continued)

   6. The tax code should be neutral.
   7. Taxes profoundly affect economic growth.
   8. The broader the tax base, the better.
   9. Everyone should pay the same income tax rate.
  10. Perhaps it is time to repeal the income tax.

Chapter 10: Constitutional Reform
   1. The national government is out of control.
   2. Constitutional reform is the solution.
   3. Fear of a runaway convention is unfounded.
   4. Choose amendments carefully.
   5. Agree on convention procedures ahead of time.
   6. Require Congress to balance its budget.
   7. Consider the Compact approach.
   8. Require congressional approval of major regulations.
   9. Require due process for all administrative law proceedings.
  10. States can refuse to enforce federal laws.

I hope this brief overview whets the reader's appetite for the chapters that follow. Even more, I hope the principles recommended and the discussion and readings prove useful in developing legislation to help the country's patriots succeed in their goal of expanding and preserving American freedom and prosperity.

Chapter 1
Health Care

Joseph L. Bast and Matthew Glans

---

10 Principles of Health Care Policy

1. Repeal and replace Obamacare.
2. Reform Medicaid and Medicare.
3. Repeal existing regulations.
4. Expand health savings accounts.
5. Expand high-risk pools.
6. Encourage price transparency.
7. Expand the use of direct primary care programs.
8. Expand access to prescription drugs.
9. Remove regulatory barriers to medical innovation.
10. Reduce malpractice litigation expenses.

Introduction

Waste and inefficiency are easily identified in our hospitals, government programs, and private insurance markets (Bisu 2013). We see it in the number of people who lack health insurance, the lack of price transparency in much of the health care system, the high rate of medical mistakes in hospitals, and the massive transfers of income—often from the poor and uninsured to the well-to-do and insured—the current system generates.

A good health care system would not employ armies of gatekeepers to stand between doctors and their patients, wouldn't require lawsuits to ensure victims of malpractice get adequate compensation or incompetent providers lose their licenses, and wouldn't require patients to wait eight to 10 years for potentially life-saving drugs.

There are two paths to reforming health care in the United States. The first is to double-down on the mistakes made in the past by adding more regulations, more subsidies, and more barriers to innovation and consumer choice. The second is to learn from past mistakes, repeal ineffective and often deadly regulations and subsidies, and start fresh (Bast, Rue, and Wesbury 1993). Sadly, beginning in 2010 policymakers opted for the first path by passing the Patient Protection and Affordable Care Act (more popularly known as "Obamacare").

The good news is that policymakers can make health care more affordable and higher quality without increasing state budgets or the national debt, and without violating the freedoms of patients or health care providers. Enlightened legislators across the country are embracing parts of this "fresh start agenda." They offer guidance and leadership for elected officials elsewhere and for everyone interested in improving health care in the United States.

Recommended Readings: John C. Goodman, *Priceless: Curing the Health Care Crisis* (Oakland, CA: Independent Institute, 2012); Rituparna Bisu, *The Broken State of American Health Insurance Prior to the Affordable Care Act: A Market Rife with Government Distortions* (Irvine, CA: Ayn Rand Institute, 2013).

1. Repeal and replace Obamacare.

> Health care reform cannot proceed unless the Patient Protection and Affordable Care Act (Obamacare) is repealed and replaced.

Health care reform cannot proceed unless the Patient Protection and Affordable Care Act (Obamacare) is repealed and replaced.

President Barack Obama and Democrats campaigned for passage of Obamacare claiming it would reduce health care spending, expand insurance coverage, and preserve choice and innovation. Seven years later, it is clear Obamacare achieved none of these objectives. Instead, by destabilizing private insurance markets it has come close to paving the way for single-payer health care.

By 2017, Obamacare had caused average individual market premiums to more than double from $2,784 per year in 2013 to $5,712 on Healthcare.gov in 2017—an increase of $2,928 or 105%, according to a report by the U.S. Department of Health and Human Services (HHS 2017). According to the report, "All 39 states using Healthcare.gov experienced an increase in individual market premiums from 2013–2017. Sixty-two percent of states using Healthcare.gov had 2017 premiums double what was measured in 2013. Three states—Alaska, Alabama, and Oklahoma—saw premiums triple from 2013–2017."

Today, more than one thousand counties in the nation had just one insurer participating on an exchange (CBS News 2017). Obamacare caused at least 4.7 million policies in the individual market—possibly more than 6 million—to be canceled (Associated Press 2013). Up to 16.6 million people in the small-group market and 102.7 million people in the large-group market could lose their plans because they violate Obamacare's stringent "grandfather" regulations (Hogberg 2014a; Conover 2013; Gabel *et al.* 2012; OFR 2010).

With President Donald Trump and the GOP intent on repealing and replacing Obamacare, a health care disaster has been averted (perhaps). The ball will soon be back in the hands of state legislatures, where it should have been all along.

Over-reliance on Third Party Payers

The principal reason Obamacare failed is that it did not challenge the current system's biggest flaw: its over-reliance on third-party payers. Tax policy, entitlement programs, and regulations all encourage people to secure health insurance rather than pay cash or self-insure. Obamacare tilted the balance even further by encouraging reliance on two specific types of health insurance: that purchased via government health insurance exchanges; and that provided via Medicaid, the nation's health care entitlement program previously available only to the poor.

As Milton Friedman explained many years ago, when we spend our own money on ourselves, we try to get the most value for our money. When we spend other people's money either on ourselves or on others, we are far less diligent about the cost (in the first case) or the benefits (in the second case) (Friedman 2004). Most health care in the United States today is paid for with "other people's money."

Federal tax policies have long encouraged third-party prepaid medical care over individual insurance or direct payment. Under current tax law, employers can deduct the cost of health insurance premiums from their employees' pre-tax income, so one dollar of earned income buys one dollar's worth of health insurance.

People without employer-provided health insurance, and people with insurance but paying out-of-pocket for expenses below the deductible or for required copayments, typically must use after-tax dollars. This means one dollar of earned income may buy only 50 to 75 cents' worth (depending on a person's tax bracket) of health insurance or medical services. This encourages over-reliance on employer-provided insurance with low deductibles and copayments (Goodman and Musgrave 1992).

Government health care programs for the poor and elderly add greatly to the number of people who depend on third parties to pay for their health care. According to one study, the creation of Medicare and Medicaid caused about half of the increase in health expenditures nationwide since 1965 (Finkelstein 2007).

As a result of tax policy and the expansion of Medicaid and Medicare, the amount Americans pay out-of-pocket for health care has fallen precipitously. In 1970, Americans paid about 40 percent of their medical bills out-of-pocket. By 2012, less than 12 cents of every dollar was paid out-of-pocket (CMS 2012).

Obamacare doubled-down on past mistakes, imposing a mandate on individuals to buy insurance, expanding government subsidies for those buying private insurance from government insurance exchanges, and expanding enrollment in Medicaid. The number of uninsured fell, but only because Medicaid rolls were expanded. Obamacare caused insurance premiums to increase by close to 25 percent in 2016, making it unaffordable for millions of families (Alonso-Zaldivar 2016).

Confusing Insurance Coverage with Health Care

Obamacare's second major flaw was to confuse health insurance coverage with health care. The former is one method of financing access to the latter, but it is not the only or often the best way. Sometimes, having health insurance does not deliver access to quality health care.

While health insurance is obviously beneficial for many people and in many situations, so long as there are safety nets for the uninsured (and there are, described below), its main benefit is protecting people's assets in the event of a major or "catastrophic" medical incident. People without assets and people with sufficient assets to self-insure against the cost of a major medical incident do not benefit much from health insurance and may pay much more than it is worth.

Advocates of universal health insurance point to a series of studies produced by Families USA, an advocacy group for single-payer health care, claiming a lack of health insurance causes 45,000 deaths in the United States per year. But those reports were expertly debunked by Linda Gorman (2008), John Goodman (2009), and others. Better research by Steven Asch et al. (2006) and Helen Levy and David Meltzer (2008) found little evidence of a consistent relationship between health insurance and health outcomes.

In 2016, 27 million nonelderly people lacked health insurance coverage. According to the Kaiser Family Foundation, roughly 11.7 million of those uninsured were eligible for financial assistance to gain coverage through either Medicaid or subsidized marketplace coverage (Garfield *et al.* 2016). Many of these individuals do not bother enrolling because they can always do so *after* they become sick.

At the other end of the income spectrum, many people are uninsured but could plainly afford insurance. According to the Kaiser Family Foundation, 47 percent of the nonelderly uninsured come from households with income greater than 200 percent of the federal poverty level (KFF 2015). Forty percent, or 19 million, of the uninsured are between the ages of 18 and 34 (DeNavas-Walt *et al.* 2013). These young people realize they probably will not incur any medical expenses in the coming year, making health insurance (especially at prices inflated by government regulations) a poor investment.

Finally, the uninsured on average receive care at a level similar to patients insured by Medicare, managed care, and fee-for-service (Asch *et al.* 2006). They receive less care than those on Medicaid but have no worse health outcomes (Baicker *et al.* 2013). Federal and state governments spend more than $300 billion annually on public health insurance, such as Medicaid and state children's health insurance programs (SCHIP). Government and private charity spending on uninsured people total about $1,000 per full-time uninsured individual (Thorpe and Goodman 2005).

By confusing or conflating health insurance with actual health care, Obamacare failed to target the real reason access to health care is too often limited: over-reliance on third-party payers resulting in high prices, a lack of price transparency, laws that try to limit spending by restricting supply and limiting competition, and more.

Repeal and Replace Obamacare

As of the time of this writing, the U.S. Senate had failed to adopt legislation to repeal or replace Obamacare. Liberal Senate members insisted on keeping some of the regulations and entitlement provisions of Obamacare, making repeal of other provisions (such as the individual mandate and taxes to pay for the "risk corridor" program) difficult or impossible. Conservative and libertarian members of the Senate wanted more than partial or cosmetic reforms and feared a compromise would result in an Obamacare 2.0 rather than real reform.

While the details are difficult to work out in the political arena, the broad outline of reform is relatively easy to see. National legislation to repeal and replace Obamacare should include the following provisions:

- Eliminate the individual mandate to purchase insurance and the financial penalties associated with it.

- Replace the current tax exclusion of employer-provided health insurance and the tax deduction for individuals with high medical expenses with an age-adjusted individual tax credit large enough to make private health insurance affordable.

■ Repeal burdensome insurance regulations (community rating, guaranteed issue, and "essential benefits") of Obamacare while giving the Department of Health and Human Services Secretary leeway to alleviate the burden of other regulations.

■ Abolish the nearly one trillion dollars per decade in taxes that are part of Obamacare.

■ Abolish Obamacare's risk corridor program, which was intended to transfer funds from profitable insurers to unprofitable ones during the first three years of the insurance exchanges.

■ End the Medicaid expansion program, either all at once or by gradually reducing the federal subsidy from 100 percent of medical bills to no more than the federal matching percentage for every other category of recipients, and then excluding nonpoor adults.

■ Block grant Medicaid to the states through a per-capita allotment, giving states options to improve the efficiency of the program and control enrollment as local voters and policymakers see fit.

Some of these changes can begin without congressional action. The Affordable Care Act gives the Health and Human Services Secretary considerable latitude in how or even whether to implement many provisions. The Heritage Foundation's Robert Moffit observed, "state officials can take advantage of Obamacare's Section 1332, and apply to the secretary of health and human services for a five-year waiver from 11 statutory requirements of the national health law" (Moffit 2017).

Recommended Readings: Peter Ferrara, *The Obamacare Disaster* (Chicago, IL: The Heartland Institute, 2010); Association of American Physicians and Surgeons, "White Paper on Repeal/Replacement of the Affordable Care Act," January 6, 2017.

2. Reform Medicaid and Medicare.

America's health care system cannot be improved without changing Medicaid and Medicare.

America's health care system cannot be improved without changing Medicaid and Medicare, the nation's two largest government-run health care finance systems. Neither program provides health care directly. Instead, they pay hospitals, physicians, nursing homes, managed care plans, and other health care providers for covered services they deliver to eligible patients.

Both programs insulate the insured from the cost of medical services, contributing to over-utilization of services and rising spending without commensurate benefits. By using price controls to under-pay providers, both programs result in cost-shifting to privately insured individuals and businesses that provide health insurance. The good news is that reforms being discussed in Washington, DC would dramatically change these programs for the better.

Why Medicaid Fails

Medicaid is the national health care entitlement program for the poor, including low-income children, parents, women who are pregnant, and seniors. Taxpayers finance Medicaid through a formula whereby the federal government picks up about 60 percent of the cost and states pay the rest. Obamacare used a higher reimbursement rate (100 percent, dropping to 90 percent over time) to reward states that expanded Medicaid to cover all individuals whose income is equal to or less than 138 percent of the federal poverty level ($16,642 for individuals and $33,948 for a family of four in 2017, higher in Alaska). Thirty-two states chose to expand their Medicaid enrollment.

Unsurprisingly, federal spending on Medicaid soared from $200 billion in 2008, the last year of President George W. Bush's term, to $376.6 billion in 2017. By 2024, spending is expected to reach $552 billion due to enrollment expansions encouraged by Obamacare. State spending is soaring as well.

National restrictions on how states can use Medicaid dollars have resulted in a system that insulates patients from the cost of the care they receive, making them insensitive to prices and inclined to over-utilize services. Policies as simple and promising as allowing Medicaid recipients to have health savings accounts or imposing a work requirement on able-bodied recipients are prohibited. Physicians and other care providers are limited in how they can innovate to deliver care by a rigid system of price controls and eligibility rules.

The perverse incentives extend to the government agencies administering Medicaid, which would rather tolerate waste and fraud than invest in the kinds of fraud detection and prevention systems that private insurers use routinely. One consequence: $36 billion in improper payments by Medicaid in 2016, up from $29.1 billion in fiscal year 2015 (GAO 2017).

Medicaid attempts to remain financially sustainable despite perverse incentives, waste, and fraud by imposing low reimbursement rates on providers, typically 40 percent less than what doctors and hospitals charge private insurers and individuals without insurance. According to Scott Gottlieb, then of the New York University School of Medicine and now commissioner of the Food and Drug Administration, "In some states, they've cut reimbursements to providers so low that beneficiaries cannot find doctors willing to accept Medicaid. ... Dozens of recent medical studies show that Medicaid patients suffer for it. In some cases, they'd do just as well without health insurance" (Gottlieb 2011).

Once again, Obamacare doubled down on a problem rather than solve it. Cuts to Medicaid promised in the Obamacare legislation would reduce payment rates to doctors and hospitals to just one-third what is paid by private insurance and only half what is paid by Medicare (Shatto and Clemens 2010). This would have catastrophic effects for people who rely on Medicaid for their health care.

One more problem facing Medicaid is how middle-income and even upper-income families use the program to pay for nursing home care. "Medicaid long-term care benefits do not require impoverishment," wrote retirement benefits expert Stephen Moses (2017). "Virtually unlimited income does not obstruct eligibility if medical and long-term care expenses are high enough, as they usually are for people in need of formal, paid long-term care." He concludes: "Easy access to Medicaid after care is needed has caused most of long-term care's problems."

Why Medicare Fails

Medicare is the nation's health care entitlement program for the elderly, disabled, or individuals with end-stage renal disease. It is projected to provide health insurance to 58 million individuals and to cost $709 billion in 2017. Medicare spending, like Medicaid, is soaring: Spending in 2008 was $469 billion. Obamacare was projected to cut Medicare spending by $716 billion over 10 years versus forecasts, mostly by cutting payments to doctors and hospitals, but experts almost unanimously believe Congress would act to prevent such draconian cuts.

Like Medicaid, Medicare tolerates waste and fraud. According to the Government Accountability Office (GAO), improper payments reached an estimated $60 billion in fiscal year 2016 (GAO 2017).

Medicare is not insurance, at least not the kind of insurance one would find in a real marketplace for health care. As Dr. Jane Orient writes, "Premiums are not risk-based, and benefits are determined by the discretion of the managers, not an indemnity table agreed to by contract. The payment and delivery systems are commingled. The system benefits by restricting service. With the passage of MACRA (the Medicare Access and CHIP Reauthorization Act), our single-payer system for seniors—Medicare—is being turned into the equivalent of a giant, capitation-based HMO. Physicians are gatekeepers who profit by rationing care and are punished for providing too much" (AAPS 2017).

According to Medicare's Office of the Actuary, the Obamacare cuts to Medicare would result in payment rates to doctors and hospitals being only one-third what is paid by private insurance and half what is paid by Medicaid (Shatto and Clemens 2010). It goes on to say, "the large reductions in Medicare payment rates to physicians would likely have serious implications for beneficiary access to care; utilization, intensity and quality of services; and other factors."

Such draconian Medicare cuts would wreak havoc in health care for seniors. Doctors, hospitals, surgeons, and specialists providing critical care to the elderly—surgery for hip and knee replacements, sophisticated diagnostics through MRIs and CT scans, and even treatment for cancer and heart disease—will either have to withdraw from serving Medicare patients or eventually go into bankruptcy.

Reform Agenda

Medicaid and Medicare can be reformed to make them part of the solution to, rather than the problems facing, health care in America today. One model for Medicaid reform is the State Health Flexibility Act of 2016. The Congressional Budget Office (CBO) scored it to save nearly $2 trillion over 10 years.

A comprehensive reform agenda for Medicaid would include:

■ End the Medicaid expansion program that is part of Obamacare.

■ Replace the federal matching formula with fixed, finite block grants. Each state would be free to use the funds for its own redesigned health care safety net program for the poor.

■ States could replace insurance with vouchers that would allow the poor to help pay for the private health insurance of their choice in the competitive marketplace.

■ Medicaid vouchers should be subject to a work requirement for the able-bodied. Each state could set work requirements as it prefers.

- States could have the authority to establish health savings accounts (HSAs) for the poor, which maximize consumer choice over their own health care and consumer control over the funds.

- States could experiment with different ways to pay for care, such as the direct primary care model (see Principle 7) and payment bundles for all the costs of a procedure.

- States should implement enhanced eligibility checks, possibly including drug tests for able-bodied patients and increased asset recovery efforts directed at those seeking aid for long-term care.

A reform agenda for Medicare would include the following steps:

- Allow workers under age 55 today to choose when they retire a private plan competing alongside traditional Medicare. Medicare would provide these seniors with a voucher they could use to pay for or offset some of the premium of the private plan they choose.

- Seniors should be free to choose health savings accounts (HSAs) for their Medicare coverage, maximizing the control they have over their own health care.

- Workers should be free to put the Medicare payroll taxes they and their employers currently pay into own personal retirement accounts, similar to what is in place in Chile and has been proposed for reforming Social Security (Ferrara 2015, Goodman and Cordell 1998).

- Patients and physicians alike should be allowed to opt out of Medicare and Medicaid *on a per-service basis*, just as participants in other entitlement programs can.

- The Centers for Medicare and Medicaid Services could issue a new regulation directing insurance carriers to reimburse Medicare beneficiaries—patients, not "providers"—who receive services from a nonenrolled or disenrolled physician and submit their own claim with an itemized bill, without imposing any claims submission requirement on the physician.

- Repeal the rules that people cannot leave Medicare Part A without losing their Social Security benefits, and that enrolled providers must file claims for all covered services rendered to Part B beneficiaries.

- Expand the current "opt out" provision to allow physicians to work outside the system on a patient-by-patient basis without an all-or-none opt-out.

- Institute a *patient-value-based* system by repealing the Resource-Based Relative Value Scale for nonparticipating physicians.

Recommended Readings: Chris Jacobs, "States Need Freedom From Washington To Transform Their Medicaid Programs," *The Federalist*, June 29, 2017; Association of American Physicians and Surgeons, "White Paper on Repeal/Replacement of the Affordable Care Act," January 6, 2017.

3. Repeal existing regulations.

Many existing federal and state laws should be repealed before implementing any new laws and programs.

Obamacare, Medicaid, and Medicare do more to disrupt and damage health care in America than any other government program or regulation, but myriad other federal and state laws also contribute to the problem. Policymakers should repeal such laws and programs *first,* before implementing any new laws and programs.

Mandated Benefits

In the United States, there are 2,271 laws mandating insurers cover specific health providers, procedures, or benefits (Bunce 2013). These laws often are billed as being pro-consumer, but they mostly benefit the special-interest groups that lobby for them. They needlessly raise the cost of health insurance premiums by as much as 24 percent (Gohmann and McCrickard 2009). On average, each state-mandated benefit causes an increase in the number of uninsured by .25 percent (Graham 2008). Repealing these mandates would lower the cost of premiums and allow millions of people to get back into the private insurance marketplace.

Mandated benefit laws disproportionately affect those who are self-employed or unemployed, or who work for companies too small to afford insurance benefits for their employees. Big businesses typically self-insure and are exempt from such regulations.

Guaranteed Issue Laws

Guaranteed issue laws require insurance companies to provide insurance to anyone who seeks it. The 1996 Health Insurance Portability and Accountability Act (HIPAA) required insurers to offer guaranteed issue policies in the small group (2–50 insured persons) market. Some states also try to impose guaranteed issue on their individual markets, with disastrous effects (Meier 2005a). Obamacare made guaranteed issue a requirement for any insurance offered through state insurance exchanges.

Guaranteed issue drives up the price of health insurance by creating an incentive for people to wait until they are sick before buying insurance. Insurance companies raise premiums to guard against the larger claims of the insured population that tends to be less healthy at any given time. Each round of premium increases causes a new group of healthy people to drop its coverage, causing the insured population to become still more expensive to insure. The results are soaring premiums and rising numbers of uninsured people (Bast 2004).

Community Rating Laws

Community rating laws require insurers to charge similar rates to all members of a community typically without regard to age, lifestyle, health, or gender. Because an insurer cannot adjust its premiums to reflect the individual health risks of consumers, the healthy majority see their premiums rise.

Community rating means insurance premiums paid by young and healthy individuals are higher than the benefits they are likely to receive, encouraging them to drop their coverage. Like guaranteed issue, this results in an insured population with higher health care expenses than the average population, requiring higher insurance premiums. Once again, premiums increase because more healthy people choose to go without health insurance.

States that have adopted guaranteed issue and community rating have higher premiums and fewer insurers competing for customers than states that have not. Guaranteed issue and community rating laws have been especially harmful in states where they have been applied to the individual insurance market (Meier 2005a; NAHU 2005).

Other Regulations to Repeal

Mandated benefits, guaranteed issue, and community rating are the three most destructive regulations states impose on health insurance companies. Other regulations on insurers and health care providers that limit competition and consumer choices and ought to be repealed or reformed include:

■ *Certificate of need.* Thirty-five states require health care providers to obtain certificates of need before expanding facilities or opening new centers (Glans 2014b). Extensive research demonstrates certificate of need laws reduce competition and result in higher prices (Barnes 2006; Conover and Sloan 1998; Cordato 2005).

■ *Clean claims and prompt pay laws.* Some states mandate health insurers pay 95 percent or more of all claims within a certain amount of time after receipt of the claim by the insurer. Such laws can be reasonable, but if the percentage of claims is set too high or the time period too short, compliance costs can soar (Bunce 2002).

■ *Impediments to interstate competition.* Consumers are unable to purchase insurance from out-of-state companies because of the McCarran-Ferguson Act of 1945, which grants states the right to regulate health plans within their borders. The patchwork of 50 different sets of state regulations makes it costly and time-consuming for insurers to enter new states (Bast 2005; Flowers 2007).

■ *Prohibitions on exclusionary waivers.* Some states prohibit insurers in the individual health insurance market from offering policies with either temporary or permanent medical waivers for pre-existing conditions. Such waivers enable insurers to offer affordable coverage for all but one or two known conditions that would otherwise require much higher premiums (Wieske and Matthews 2007).

■ *Rate reviews and bands.* Most states regulate the rates insurers charge for insurance products in the small group market either by requiring prior approval of rates or by prohibiting insurers from offering rates more than 25 percent above or below a base rate. Rate reviews and narrow bands stifle innovation and competition (Wieske 2007).

■ *Unnecessary licensing standards.* Restrictions on what nurse practitioners, dental therapists, and midwives are allowed to do, and whether they can operate without a medical doctor present, unnecessarily restrict the supply of medical services and consequently raise the price (Hamilton *et al.* 2016).

■ *Overregulation of dental service organizations.* First launched in the late 1990s, dental service organizations (DSOs) allow dentists to focus on patients by providing, on a contract basis, routine office operations such as accounting, insurance, scheduling, and purchasing equipment and supplies. State Dental Boards often oppose DSOs and try to over-regulate them (Glans 2017c; Palmieri Heck 2017).

■ *Maintenance of certification (MOC) requirements.* While a certain degree of certification will always be necessary, physicians should not be required to pass through a quagmire of costly and expensive tests that may be unnecessary (Glans 2016b). Oklahoma provides a model other states can follow: It forbids the requirement of MOC as a condition of licensure, reimbursement, employment, or admitting privileges at a hospital in the state (Hamilton 2016a).

■ *Interstate licensure reciprocity.* Reciprocity laws would allow a physician in one state to use his license in another state without needing to reapply. According to the Mercatus Center at George Mason University, reciprocity laws are "the easiest and least controversial ways for states to minimize restraints on physicians, yet a substantial number of states do not allow reciprocity" (Bryan *et al.* 2016).

Recommended Readings: Matthew Glans, "Certificate of Need Reform," *Research & Commentary*, The Heartland Institute, November 13, 2014; J.P. Wieske and Merrill Matthews, *Understanding the Uninsured and What to Do About Them* (Washington, DC: Council for Affordable Health Insurance, 2007); Conrad F. Meier, *Destroying Insurance Markets: How Guaranteed Issue and Community Rating Destroyed the Individual Health Insurance Market in Eight States* (Washington, DC: Council for Affordable Health Insurance and Chicago, IL: The Heartland Institute, 2005).

4. Expand health savings accounts.

Health savings accounts (HSAs) are the key to reducing reliance on third-party payers.

Health savings accounts (HSAs) are the key to reducing reliance on third-party payers. They level the tax treatment of dollars used to pay directly for health care and dollars used to purchase health insurance.

They also can (but do not yet) level the tax treatment of dollars spent by businesses on health insurance for their employees and dollars spent by individuals for their own health insurance (Emanuel 2008).

HSAs, similar to 401(k) retirement plans, are privately owned savings accounts funded with pre-tax dollars used to pay for future medical expenses. By law, HSAs must be paired with high-deductible health plans (HDHPs). Since those policies cost much less than the usual comprehensive insurance provided by employers, the premium savings can be deposited into the account and used to pay routine medical bills up to the deductible. Any money left in the account at the end of each year "rolls over" to the next year.

The number of people enrolled in HSA plans continues to increase over time. As of January 2016, 20.2 million people were enrolled in HSA/HDHP plans (AHIP 2017). HSAs held more than $37 billion in assets in 2016 and the average account balance was $14,971 (American Funds 2017).

Benefits of HSAs

HSAs primarily benefit people who pay income taxes, since they generate tax savings. Low-income people therefore do not stand to benefit from the accounts unless their employers (or the government) contribute to them. The higher deductibles that come with an HSA can be difficult for some individuals and families to cope with, at least until enough money has accumulated in their HSAs to help cover the expenses.

Premiums for HSA plans cost about 17 percent less for a family and 14 percent less for a single person compared to the next cheapest alternative (Claxton *et al.* 2013). Surveys, including one conducted in 2014 by the Employee Benefit Research Institute, find people with HSA/HDHP plans have lower satisfaction rates than those with traditional insurance plans, but the gap is not large and is narrowing with time. Forty-six percent of HSA/HDHP enrollees said they were extremely or very satisfied with their overall health plans, while 61 percent of traditional-plan enrollees said the same of their plans (Employee Benefit Research Institute, 2015).

Because they spend their own money, patients with HSAs shop more wisely for medical care than do people with conventional low-deductible insurance coverage. Two surveys have found people with HSA plans are about twice as likely to ask about drug costs and 50 percent more likely to inquire about the overall cost of care (Agrawal *et al.* 2005; Blue Cross and Blue Shield Association 2005). HSA patients were 20 percent more likely to manage chronic conditions and 25 percent more likely to use preventive care and engage in health and wellness programs.

National Reform Agenda

The American Health Care Act (AHCA), passed by the U.S. House of Representatives in May 2017 but not approved by the Senate, would have abolished several taxes on HSAs. It also would have expanded the contribution limits for HSAs to $6,550 for individuals and $13,100 for families, so they could cover more medical costs. The bill also allowed more flexibility by allowing spouses to make catch-up contributions to HSAs and allowing HSAs to cover certain medical expenses incurred before the savings account has been established. These are all good reforms that policymakers should consider.

Health savings accounts would be even more successful if federal laws allowed unlimited contributions to HSAs and permitted such accounts to wrap around third-party insurance—paying for any expense the insurance plan does not pay. Other national reforms that would improve HSAs include:

- Allow people over the age of 65 and eligible for Medicare to have HSAs.

- Allow people who do not have employer-sponsored health insurance to pay for health insurance with funds from their HSAs.

- Let insurers offer a portable, nationally regulated HSA high-deductible health plan.

- Permit insurers to design plans with different deductibles and copayments for different medical services: high deductibles for services where patient discretion is possible and low or no deductibles where patient discretion is inappropriate.

State Reform Agenda

States can help expand HSAs by adopting policies recommended by the Council for Affordable Health Insurance (2007):

- Ensure the state's definition of income conforms to the Internal Revenue Code for HSA purposes. Among the states that do not accept or follow the federal tax treatment for HSAs are Alabama, California, and New Jersey (HSA for America 2017).

- Adopt laws exempting HSA high-deductible health plans from state-mandated benefit requirements. States with mandated benefits that conflict with HSAs include California, Illinois, Maine, Missouri, New York, and Ohio.

■ Add an HSA option for persons who buy insurance through the state's high-risk pool (12 states have done so already), for state and municipal employees (13 states have done so already), and for Medicaid (until the Obama administration shut it down, Indiana had a very successful Medicaid program that included HSAs).

Recommended Readings: Jeff Emanuel, "Health Savings Accounts," *Research & Commentary*, The Heartland Institute, May 15, 2008; John Goodman, "Making HSAs Better," *Brief Analyses* No. 518, National Center for Policy Analysis, 2005.

5. Expand high-risk pools.

High-risk pools serve people with pre-existing conditions and help stabilize the rest of the health insurance marketplace.

High-risk pools offer affordable health insurance to people with pre-existing conditions who otherwise could not find affordable health insurance in the private marketplace. They offer a safety net narrowly targeted to those who need public assistance. By removing from the insurance pool people with very high known health care costs, high-risk pools help stabilize the rest of the marketplace and lower premiums for healthy people.

High-risk pools are state-chartered, nonprofit associations offering health insurance through the private sector. Premiums range from 125 percent to 200 percent of the premiums charged for standard coverage. Under the provisions established in 2002 by the Trade Adjustment Assistance Act (TAAA), which provided modest federal funding for high-risk pools, a state must cap the premium at 150 percent of standard in order to qualify for federal funding.

It is inherent in the design of a risk pool that it will lose money. It simply is not feasible to pool a group of individuals known to have major health problems and expect their premium contributions to cover the entire cost of their care. For this reason, risk pools need some form of subsidy, often an assessment charged to insurance carriers in the state.

Risk pools are overseen by appointed boards of directors usually including representatives from the insurance industry, consumers, and medical professionals. The pools often are supervised by the state insurance departments. A private third-party administrator typically handles day-to-day claims and administrative operations.

A Proven Solution

In 2011, the most recent year for which statistics are available, "the top 1 percent of health care spenders accounted for 23 percent of overall spending, and the top 20 percent were responsible for 82 percent of the total," according to Pew Trusts (Ollove 2017). These people are difficult to insure by private insurers, since their inclusion in a group of generally healthy insureds can result in rate increases for all members of the group in order to cover the expense, causing the healthier insureds to search for cheaper insurance, i.e., a group without a high-cost person in it.

One proven solution for covering patients with pre-existing conditions is the creation of high-risk pools. Risk-pool insurance exists in 35 states. Prior to passage of Obamacare, high-risk pools covered more than 222,000 uninsurable people nationwide. This seemingly small number is actually a large part of the total population of "uninsurable" individuals in the 35 states with high-risk pools.

High-risk pools give the insurance industry and the general public a way to share and spread out the costs of insuring medically risky people on a broad and predictable basis. Studies of the individual insurance market have found states with risk pools have had more success in keeping their individual health insurance markets competitive, keeping insurance rates affordable, reducing Medicaid enrollments, and increasing private coverage (Meier 1999).

Better than Obamacare

According to Curtis Dubay, a research fellow with The Heritage Foundation, "The problem of providing access to individuals with pre-existing conditions, while very real, did not necessitate the massive changes in America's health care system included in Obamacare" (Dubay 2013). While the Obama administration claimed as many as 129 million Americans with pre-existing conditions were "at risk" and "could be denied coverage" unless Obamacare were adopted, Dubay notes the real number of people truly uninsurable due to pre-existing conditions was vastly smaller.

Individuals with employer-sponsored coverage are not subject to pre-existing condition exclusions, and since they amount to approximately 90 percent of the people with private insurance, the number of people genuinely "at risk" could not be greater than 10 percent of those with private insurance. Only 134,708 individuals have enrolled in the supplemental federal high-risk pool program since it was created under Obamacare to cover individuals with pre-existing conditions, a good indication of how small the problem actually is.

Whereas Obamacare attempted to transform the entire health care financing system in the name of helping the uninsured, high-risk pools tailor the solution to the needs of the small number of people with real problems, thereby helping the rest of the insurance system work the way it should, covering individuals whose future medical needs are generally unknown.

Reform Agenda

Embracing high-risk pools and encouraging them to thrive would allow states to abandon guaranteed issue and provide health insurance to a vulnerable population while helping to keep health insurance prices down. During the debate over how to repeal and replace Obamacare, House Republican leaders proposed a national $15 billion high-risk pool, an idea with considerable merit.

Recommended Readings: Conrad F. Meier "Extending Affordable Health Insurance to the Uninsurable," *Heartland Policy Study* No. 91, The Heartland Institute, August 27, 1999; Matthew Glans, "State High-Risk Pools for Health Insurance," *Research & Commentary*, The Heartland Institute, May 25, 2017.

6. Encourage price transparency.

> Over-reliance on third-party payers means providers have little incentive to be transparent about prices for their services and consumers have little incentive to ask.

Over-reliance on third-party payers for health care has resulted in a system in which health care providers have little incentive to advertise or even share prices for their services. Most health care consumers, insulated from price considerations by private insurance, Medicaid, or Medicare, simply do not care about prices: They pay the same copay regardless of the services they choose and are not penalized for ineffective choices.

This system might seem to work well most of the time since no one wants to be shown a menu of prices during a health emergency, and the absence of price transparency helps create the illusion that much of the health care we consume is "free." But upon closer inspection it does not work well at all.

Lack of Transparency

Consumers seeking price estimates for basic medical services often have great difficulty obtaining any information from providers in a timely manner. The Pioneer Institute, a think tank in Pennsylvania, surveyed 54 hospitals in six metropolitan areas across the United States and found consumers seeking a price estimate for a routine medical procedure face a "difficult and frustrating task" (Pioneer Institute 2016).

Pioneer researchers contacted hospitals in and around Dallas-Ft. Worth, Des Moines, Los Angeles, New York City, Orlando, and Raleigh-Durham to request price information for a fictional patient looking to receive an MRI. Their results show in 57 percent of the hospitals, "it took more than 15 minutes to get a complete price that included the radiologist's fee for reading the MRI," said the study's authors. "Two-thirds of the time, researchers had to call a separate number or organization to obtain an estimate for the reading fee."

A poll conducted in 2006 by the Council for Affordable Health Insurance (CAHI) found 84 percent of consumers would like to see health care prices published, and 79 percent said they would use this information to "shop for the best price" (as reported by McKeown 2011). As use of the internet, smart phones, and apps used for finding the lowest prices for all sorts of goods and services has expanded dramatically since then, one can assume nearly everyone today would respond positively to such a poll.

The lack of price transparency results in dramatic variation, from practice to practice and hospital to hospital, in prices for identical tests and procedures (Ungar 2013). Even someone with generous insurance would benefit from knowing at least some prices before choosing a doctor or hospital for non-emergency care. For the uninsured, such information could mean the difference between a minor financial setback and bankruptcy.

Why Prices Are Important

Lulled by the illusion of "free health care," many patients over-utilize medical services. This imposes unnecessary costs on health care providers, which ultimately are paid for by others either directly (through insurance premiums, direct payment, or taxes) or indirectly (by having to wait for a service or even be denied access altogether). It can also endanger the lives of patients who ask for and receive multiple prescriptions for drugs, unnecessary invasive tests, and even unnecessary surgeries.

Many consumers are shocked to receive bills for costs not covered by their insurance—the part they are responsible for up to their deductible, and then through copays for higher amounts. People without insurance are exposed to the entire cost of services. Patients often are not told how much they owe until weeks and even months after the services have been delivered. In the case of even a routine hospital visit, a dozen bills or more arrive in the patient's mail weeks or months after a procedure, all of them describing charges that were not made known at the time they were incurred.

The lack of price transparency also hurts health care providers. Hospitals, clinics, and private practices need consumer feedback to prices in order to know if they are less efficient than other providers at producing a particular service and therefore need to find ways to reduce inefficiency and waste. Similarly, providers cannot discover their comparative advantage—what they do better or at a lower cost than other providers—without a real price system in place (Azar II *et al.* 2006).

Finally, the lack of transparency does not work for taxpayers who must bear the increasingly heavy burden of paying for Medicaid and Medicare programs whose costs are skyrocketing because consumers act as if their health care were free.

Price Transparency Legislation

A July 2016 "report card" on state price transparency laws produced by the Health Care Incentives Improvement Institute and Altarum Institute said: "State laws mandating health care price transparency for consumers can help fix the mystery surrounding health care prices, unbolting the door between consumers and the information they need to shop for and buy high-quality, affordable health care" (deBrantes and Delbanco 2016).

The report card found "too many states still fall far short of requiring and implementing thorough, useable transparency resources. Dozens of states have laws that refer to price transparency, but provide little to help consumers shop for and choose care, and offer little potential to move the health care delivery system toward quality and affordability" (*Ibid.*).

While many current price transparency laws need to be improved, research shows they do work. In a 2013 "census of state health care price transparency websites" published in the *Journal of the American Medical Association*, researchers looked at the medical claims paid by employers after a price transparency tool was made available (Kullgren *et al.* 2013). The study covered 500,000 individuals in 253,000 households between 2010 and 2013 and examined three types of medical services: laboratory tests, advanced imaging services, and clinician office visits.

The results were positive: Costs for consumers using the price transparency tool were "14 percent lower for lab tests and 13 percent lower for imaging services compared to those who did not use the tool. Costs associated with office visits declined by 1 percent." The amount of money saved by the patients was also noteworthy. For instance, consumers using the price transparency tool for imaging services saw an average reduction of $124.74 per service.

Tools for discovering prices and choosing lower-priced service providers are emerging, especially online (see Herrick and Goodman, 2007) but progress is slow because too few consumers benefit personally from being smart consumers. New Hampshire was one of the first states post hospital prices online, starting in 2007. According to a Government Accountability Office report, the state proves "that while providing complete cost information presents challenges, it can be done" (GAO 2011, p. 14).

In 2016, the Missouri legislature considered a health care bill that would require the state Department of Health and Senior Services to create an online web portal where hospitals and health care providers would share service costs for 100 common health care procedures. This is one way to empower consumers and creating real competition in the health care market.

Reform Agenda

Ultimately, the only way to restore prices to health care is to reduce reliance on third-party payers. Without increased consumer demand for prices, hospitals and other providers have no incentive to post prices, or even discover them for internal purposes. The reforms recommended earlier in this chapter would help reduce reliance on third-party payers, and therefore are an essential part of an agenda to increase price transparency.

Price transparency promotes competition and improves the quality of health care. When consumers are able to shop and compare prices, market pressures encourage providers to produce a more affordable, high-quality product. If they do not, they risk losing out to their competitors. State legislators should work to promote health care price transparency to help empower consumers and lower health care costs.

Recommended Readings: Alex M. Azar II *et al.*, "Transparency in Health Care: What Consumers Need to Know," speech delivered at The Heritage Foundation, October 3, 2006; Pioneer Institute, "National Survey Finds Limited Access to Price Estimates for Routine Hospital Procedure," February 21, 2016.

7. Expand the use of direct primary care programs.

> Insurance is necessary and appropriate for expensive and unexpected care, but direct payment by patients is more appropriate for relatively routine and inexpensive treatments.

Direct primary care (DPC) programs require patients to pay a monthly membership fee, typically ranging from $50 to $80, to receive a more generous allocation of appointments than they would under most traditional health insurance plans. Some plans even allow for same-day appointments or house calls. Individuals enrolled in a DPC program often supplement their DPC coverage with a wraparound catastrophic insurance policy for all services not specific to primary care.

The guarantee of a set monthly fee removes the layers of regulation and bureaucracy created by the traditional insurance system and allows physicians to spend more time with patients. Routine tests and procedures are included in most DPC plans at prices considerably less than what would be charged to patients with traditional insurance (Makla and Glans 2016). Alabama recently became the 22nd state to pass legislation clarifying how DPC is regulated.

The Direct Payment Option

Insurance is necessary and appropriate for expensive and unexpected care, but nearly half of all health care spending is for relatively routine and inexpensive treatments best paid directly by patients. Recognizing this, many doctors have arranged their practices to encourage direct payment. These practices accept only cash, checks, credit cards, or debit cards for health savings accounts. Because they no longer require large staffs to process complex insurance claims or comply with price controls imposed by government programs, they are able to offer prices 25 to 50 percent less than the reimbursement paid by Medicare and other insurers.

Direct payment for health care services also reduces the need for claims reviewers and "gatekeepers" who make up the bureaucracy created by managed care programs. Under a system of direct payment, doctors and patients are once again allowed to determine appropriate care without third-party interference.

Additionally, direct payment ends the injustice present in the current system whereby households with the highest incomes, and therefore in higher tax brackets, get the largest tax benefits for employer-provided health insurance. John Goodman estimates families in the wealthiest quintile get an annual tax subsidy of $1,560 a year, whereas families in the poorest quintile get only $250 (Thorpe and Goodman 2005).

Dr. Maura McLaughlin, a family physician and DPC provider in Charlottesville, Virginia, says DPC saves her patients more than 20 percent for some services. "[One] patient was due for four needed tests, which I drew for $38 total with our discounted cash pricing," McLaughlin told reporter Emma Vinton. "He told me those exact same four tests last year had cost him $1,300 with insurance" (Vinton 2017).

McLaughlin also reported, "In Washington state, the large DPC group Qliance worked with Medicaid to provide primary care through its DPC clinics to patients with Medicaid and demonstrated a savings of 20 percent for Medicaid while improving patient satisfaction. If a similar program were implemented in Virginia, we would be able to expand Medicaid in a cost-neutral manner. Imagine how many more people could be covered with the 20 percent savings in the Medicaid budget." (*Ibid.*)

Union County, North Carolina, expects to save $1 million in the first year of its contract with DPC provider Paladina Health (Restrepo 2016). A pilot program enrolling 2,400 Medicaid beneficiaries in Michigan in a DPC program is expected to save millions of dollars in its first year. The hope is eventually to expand DPCs to all 2.4 million Medicaid enrollees in the state, which could generate potential savings to the state of $3.4 billion (Glans 2016a).

More information about DPC, including directories of physicians who are part of the movement, is available on websites hosted by Docs4PatientCare, DPC Frontier, and the Association of American Physicians and Surgeons.

Reform Agenda

Direct primary care and other direct payment arrangements will expand only if policies that encourage over-reliance on third-party payers are repealed, the focus of previous principles presented in this chapter. Specific steps states and the national government can take to help promote the movement to DPC-type arrangements between patients and physicians include the following:

■ Congress can pass legislation specifying DPC is an acceptable form of payment under Medicaid and Medicare and fund pilot programs testing the concept.

■ Congress can pass legislation, such as the Primary Care Enhancement Act (H.R. 365), that clarifies DPC arrangements are not health plans for the purposes of the tax code, and defines fees paid to primary care providers in periodic fee arrangements as qualified health expenses paid from HSAs.

■ States should pass legislation stating DPC is not a form of insurance.

■ States can integrate DPC into their Medicaid systems with or without waivers from the national government to help reduce costs and improve care.

■ States can also incorporate DPC programs into health benefits for state and local employees.

Recommended Readings: Michael Hamilton, "Policy Diagnosis: Direct Primary Care Helps Patients, Doctors, and the Health Care System," interview with Hal Scherz, M.D., founder of Docs4PatientCare, *Health Care News,* April 6, 2016, Daniel McCorry, "Direct Primary Care: An Innovative Alternative to Conventional Health Insurance," The Heritage Foundation, August 6, 2014.

8. Expand access to prescription drugs.

Prescription drugs are too heavily regulated, restricting patient access to new drugs in a timely manner and making them more expensive than they need to be.

Prescription drugs are an essential component of the modern medical system, extending life, reducing suffering, and making surgery less necessary. New technologies for discovering and testing drugs promise to make them an ever-growing part of the health care system, leading to concerns over their cost. Drug treatments tailored to an individual's genetic makeup are especially promising.

Thoughtful policymakers can make prescription drugs more affordable by encouraging price transparency, speeding the approval of generic drugs and new drugs by the Food and Drug Administration (FDA), and preserving the market-based provisions of Medicare Part D.

Drug Price Controls Are No Answer

While high drug prices sometimes make headlines in newspapers, drugs represent only about 9.4 percent of total U.S. health care spending. Drug therapy is often the most efficient method of caring for patients: A dollar of drug expenditure reduces hospital costs by more than $3.50 on average (Lichtenberg 2007). Among Medicare beneficiaries, each additional prescription filled lowers hospital costs by $104 (Stuart *et al.* 2009).

Newer drugs work even better than older ones. A reduction in the age of prescription drugs reduces other health care expenditures 7.2 times as much as it increases spending on prescription drugs (Lichtenberg 2007).

Consumers can often reduce the amount of money they spend on prescription drugs by 30 percent to 50 percent, and sometimes more, simply by comparison-shopping. Requesting a generic substitute for an expensive brand-name drug can cut prices as much as 90 percent. With a physician's permission, buying larger-dose tablets and an inexpensive pill splitter can cut drug costs in half (Herrick 2006c).

State Medicaid programs and the U.S. Veterans Benefits Administration attempt to control spending on drugs by allowing access only to those on lists of preapproved drugs, called drug formularies. In order for their drugs to appear on the lists, drug companies must offer discounts or pay rebates to the states. Formularies are used in the private sector, too, but when used to limit the cost of public entitlement programs, formularies often act as crude and ineffective price controls. Politicians rather than consumers dictate spending, resulting in pressure on plan administrators to substitute older or generic drugs for new or expensive drugs requested by doctors.

Drug Piracy and Direct Negotiation

Those who lament high drug prices often advocate lifting the ban on importing drugs from other countries. Such a policy makes drugs vulnerable to counterfeiting, contamination, and improper handling (Giuliani Partners 2005; Meier 2005b; Pitts 2006). And to what end? Countries with pharmaceutical price controls produce too few drugs to provide more than a small fraction of what the U.S. market needs (Goodman 2005a).

Pirating for sale in the United States drugs manufactured for price-controlled markets amounts to importing price controls. The availability of cheaper drugs from abroad would make it more difficult for drug companies to charge prices high enough to finance research and development, leading to less investment in new drugs in America (Turner and Meier 2004).

Another proposal for limiting spending on drugs is to allow the national government to negotiate prices with drug manufacturers under Medicare Part D, the prescription drug benefit for seniors. Part D, implemented in 2006, was designed to ensure low-income seniors and those with extremely high prescription drug costs receive coverage. To avoid the hazard of government price controls, Part D prohibits direct negotiation of drug prices between the government and drug companies, through what came to be called the "non-interference clause."

The non-interference clause has been extremely effective. Today, Part D is one of the rare entitlement programs that target the truly needy and cost less than what was originally budgeted, and that cost does not even include an offset for expenses involving surgery and hospitalization avoided by the availability of drugs (Neuman *et al.* 2007; Medicare Board of Trustees 2013, 2007).

Unfortunately, advocacy groups have launched a campaign against Part D's effective approach. Instead of allowing market forces to determine drug prices, these groups want the government to negotiate directly with drug companies and impose taxes (called "rebates") on drugs made available through the program. These changes would hurt seniors and raise the risk of rationing drugs for Medicare patients.

Need for Food and Drug Administration Reform

Instead of price controls, a better way to reduce the price of new drugs is to reform the costly and time-consuming approval process used by the Food and Drug Administration (FDA). Since 1962, FDA has required new drugs to pass effectiveness and safety trials, causing the new drug approval process to take approximately eight years. Many drug developers cannot afford the substantial fees or wait that long for revenue from drug sales to begin. Further, FDA often defines "efficacy" in subjective ways—for example, "economic efficacy," which involves its view of whether a drug is needed in the market.

A promising way to reform FDA regulation of new drugs is Free to Choose Medicine, a dual-track system whereby patients and their doctors can choose either to wait for FDA-approved drugs or use drugs that have passed Phase I safety trials but still are undergoing clinical trials for effectiveness (Madden and Conko 2010). Patients choosing early access to new drugs agree to post information about side effects to a publicly accessible Tradeoff Evaluation Database.

The Goldwater Institute has developed a similar but more limited model it calls Right To Try. The program allows access to experimental drugs by terminal patients who have exhausted other available treatments (Corieri 2014). Participating patients must provide informed consent, limiting legal exposure for the drug's manufacturer (Glans 2014a).

Reform Agenda

Policymakers who wish to expand access to prescription drugs should:

- Support policies that increase price transparency, such as creating state websites that report the price of prescription drugs sold by different chains of drug stores and the availability of generic alternatives.

- Support efforts underway at FDA to speed up the approval of generics and new drugs and the Free to Choose Medicine plan allowing drugs to reach patients without going through FDA's time-consuming and largely obsolete series of efficacy trials.

- Oppose efforts to restrict access to new drugs by imposing restrictive formularies on public programs. While hard decisions must sometimes be made, the prevailing policy ought to be to respect the decisions of doctors and favor newer drugs.

- Continue to oppose efforts to legalize the importation of drugs from other countries. The public health hazards created by allowing drugs from countries outside the highly secure U.S. drug supply chain are simply too high to merit relaxing the current ban.

Recommended Readings: Bartley J. Madden and Gregory Conko, *Free to Choose Medicine: Better Drugs Sooner at Lower Cost* (Chicago, IL: The Heartland Institute, 2010); Christina Corieri, "Everyone Deserves the Right to Try: Empowering the Terminally Ill to Take Control of Their Treatment," Goldwater Institute, 2014.

9. Remove regulatory barriers to medical innovation.

> Regulation hampers entrepreneurs and innovators seeking new ways to deliver health care that is more convenient, higher quality, and less expensive.

Entrepreneurs and innovators are developing new ways to deliver health care that are more convenient, higher quality, and less costly than currently available services. Unfortunately, public policies often stand in their way. Entrepreneurship in health care, as in other markets, requires that consumers are free to choose and producers are free to compete with one another. Policymakers should remove regulations that stifle innovation with red tape and price controls that do not allow reimbursement for new services.

Where to Find the Innovators

An excellent resource for policymakers and consumers searching for better ways to finance and deliver health care services is a website called The Wedge of Health Care Freedom at https://jointhewedge.com. The site, a project of the nonprofit Citizens' Council for Health Freedom, offers a directory of practices that follow eight "wedge principles": transparent, affordable pricing; freedom to choose; true patient privacy; no government reporting; no outside interference; cash-based pricing; protected patient-doctor relationship; and all patients welcome.

Twila Brase RN, PHN, president and cofounder of the Citizens' Council for Health Freedom, writes of the providers listed on her site: "All patients, insured or uninsured, are welcome. Payment is by cash, check or charge. Imagine a practice where your doctor, dentist or other health care practitioner really knows you. Imagine a practice that does not demand your insurance card and ID before the staff even say hello. Wedge Practices and their doctors are the way back to the future! A future where patients and doctors are free, prices are affordable and care is confidential—just between you and the doctor" (Brase 2017).

Another good place to find health care innovators is the website of the Free Market Medical Association at https://fmma.org. According to the site, the FMMA helps "identify patients willing to pay cash, doctors willing to list their prices, businesses attempting to provide affordable quality insurance, and providers/services/and patient advocates that are helping make everything work."

Three other resources reported earlier in this chapter, in Principle 7 on direct primary care, are Docs4PatientCare, DPC Frontier, and the Association of American Physicians and Surgeons. Their contact information appears in the directory at the end of this chapter.

Retail Health Clinics

Retail health clinics located in shopping malls or big-box retail outlets are increasingly popular because of their convenience, minimal waiting, low prices, and high quality of care. They typically are staffed by a nurse practitioner (NP) with a master's degree in nursing who focuses on diagnosing and treating relatively common and minor illnesses.

Prices are posted and cost per episode of care is generally less than in other health care settings (Martin 2007; Adamson 2010). In 2015, Americans visited retail clinics more than 10 million times (Japsen 2015). Global professional services company Accenture predicts retail health clinics will continue to grow rapidly, with 14 percent annual growth through 2017, a 46 percent increase over 2014 levels. In 2017, the number of retail clinics will exceed 2,800 (Accenture 2015).

Because they often are open on evenings and weekends, these clinics serve patients who might otherwise go to expensive emergency rooms (Parnell 2005a). These clinics can be hindered by legislation restricting the number of NPs a physician can supervise or limiting the scope of practice for NPs, or by preventing NPs from staffing clinics inside pharmacies (LoBuono 2006).

Specialty Hospitals

Specialty hospitals, typically owned at least in part by the doctors who practice in them, focus on a few areas of care, enabling them to increase efficiency and provide higher levels of care than general hospitals do (Parnell 2005b). Unfortunately, Obamacare prevents new physician-owned specialty hospitals from being established.

Critics of specialty hospitals, such as the American Hospital Association, cite concerns about physician self-referral and the loss by general hospitals of the most profitable medical procedures to these more efficient rivals. But specialization and competition lead to better quality and lower prices, and specialty hospitals have shown how innovations such as redesigned hospital layouts can reduce labor costs, decrease patient waiting times, and improve patient outcomes (Hogberg 2013).

Medical Tourism

Patients are increasingly traveling outside the United States for surgeries, often at prices one-fifth to one-third their cost in this country. Countries with highly advanced medical facilities specifically built or equipped for medical tourists include Belgium, Brazil, Costa Rica, Germany, India,

Malaysia, Mexico, Poland, Singapore, Spain, and Thailand (Herrick 2006b; VISA 2017).

Patients Beyond Borders, an organization founded in 2007 to connect patients with hospitals and specialty centers around the world, operates a website at https://patientsbeyondborders.com where visitors can search by treatment, region, country, or specialties. The choices provided on the site are vast, including specialties such as cardiology, cosmetic and reconstructive surgery, dentistry, fertility and reproductive health, oncology, ophthalmology, orthopedics, and weight loss surgery.

According to Patients Beyond Borders, spending on medical tourism in 2016, which includes people traveling to the United States from other countries for their medical care, was between $45.5 billion and $72 billion. Some 14 million cross-border patients worldwide generally spent between $3,800 and $6,000 per visit, including medically related costs, cross-border and local transport, inpatient stay, and accommodations.

Telemedicine

The internet and the spread of high-speed broadband services hold enormous potential for improving the quality and lowering the cost of health care. Patients can contact their doctors by email and get quick answers to questions, schedule meetings, and exchange test results. Doctors can monitor their patients' conditions remotely, store and access medical records more quickly, and minimize the amount of time spent on paperwork (Kleba 2007; Herrick 2006a).

Telemedicine can be held back by state laws requiring doctors be licensed in the state where the patient resides or is treated. Licensure reciprocity, discussed earlier (see Principle 3), is one way to remove that obstacle. Another obstacle is that Medicare and Medicaid may not reimburse doctors for time spent responding to emails or talking to patients by phone.

Concierge and Cash-Only

In concierge medicine, a patient pays an annual or monthly fee or retainer for all medical care provided by the physicians. Concierge physicians are often on call to patients 24/7 and are able to spend extra time with patients on matters such as preventive care. Concierge practices are growing in popularity (Parnell 2014).

Cash-only physicians refuse to take insurance and are willing to see patients who pay cash directly. Cash-only physicians are also able to spend more time with patients and often charge less than those who take insurance (Parnell 2013). Cash-only physicians do not have to spend precious time filling out insurance paperwork, and the savings result in lower prices and better quality for patients.

Health Care Sharing Ministries

Health care sharing ministries (HCSMs) are faith-based alternatives to conventional health insurance. Members pay monthly "shares" of approximately $200 per individual or $500 per family (Glans 2017b). As medical needs arise, members pay a portion of their expenses and forward their bills to their HCSM. The HCSM reimburses members for most of their expenses, with the "share" money contributed by other members. Approximately 625,000 people in the United States had memberships in HCSMs in 2016 (Sledge 2016).

HCSMs reimburse patients rather than pay doctors and other providers, a key difference that leads to lower spending. Members of the HCSMs are aware of how much is being spent on care by the group, and their monthly shares rise and fall based on it, further encouraging careful attention to costs. The ministries are nonprofit, which allows them to save some money on salaries and payouts to shareholders.

According to a 2015 report from the Charlotte Lozier Institute, "The savings will vary depending on the specific sharing ministry. Overall, the savings can range from 45 percent to 60 percent below the cost of health insurance sold in the individual market, depending on the ministry plan selected" (Daniels 2015).

Recommended Readings: Scott E. Daniels, *Health Care Sharing Ministries: An Uncommon Bond* (Washington, DC: Charlotte Lozier Institute, 2015); Sean Parnell, *The Self-Pay Patient* (website).

10. Reduce malpractice litigation expenses.

Malpractice insurance, litigation, and defensive medicine add to the unnecessarily high cost of health care in the United States.

Malpractice insurance, litigation, and defensive medicine add to the unnecessarily high cost of health care in the United States. Some of this expense is caused by over-reliance on third-party payers, which makes it difficult for patients to hold providers accountable for their mistakes without resorting to lawsuits.

The High Cost of Malpractice Litigation

In real terms, malpractice claims grew tenfold, and malpractice premiums tripled from the mid-1970s to 2005 (Frank and Grace 2006). Malpractice expenses grew 62.8 percent from 2005 to 2009, and although they have stabilized since 2009, the increase from 2002 to 2013 still equaled 81 percent (AMA 2013).

Even though doctors win an overwhelming majority of medical malpractice cases, these claims still impose huge costs on doctors and insurers. The average legal cost exceeds $46,000 in cases where the doctor successfully defends against a malpractice case—an increase of almost 63 percent since 2001—and is near $27,000 in cases where a claim is dismissed or dropped (AMA 2011).

Lawsuit abuse leads to "defensive medicine," the practice of physicians, hospital administrators, and other providers ordering tests and filing reports solely for the sake of reducing the possibility of litigation in the event a patient does not get well. One estimate puts the cost of defensive medicine at $480 billion annually (Oliver and Segal 2014).

Issues Regarding Award Caps

The plaintiff's bar and even some reform advocates say caps on awards discourage attorneys from taking on risky cases, deny appropriate compensation to victims of medical malpractice, and send a signal to hospitals and doctors that life-threatening mistakes are tolerable (Hyman and Silver 2006). Others are concerned federal legislation limiting awards or legal fees would usurp traditional state authority over matters of health care and tort law (Martin 2011).

Although these concerns are legitimate, caps may be a necessary part of an overall legal reform strategy because the plaintiff's bar opposes other reforms that would reduce their financial windfalls while ensuring victims receive fair and speedy compensation.

The Texas Experience

The experience in Texas since 2003 provides a model for state-level reform of malpractice litigation. In 2003, legislation was passed containing the following provisions (this summary is by Roger Stark, M.D. (2016)):

■ Juries should hear more evidence about who may really be at fault.

■ Only those individuals who cause harm should pay, and then only to the extent of their own fault.

■ Damages should be limited to the amount the injured patient paid or incurred or what someone, like an insurance company, paid or incurred on their behalf, thereby eliminating "phantom damages."

■ A medical report written by a physician in the same or similar field as the physician being sued should be submitted within 120 days of the filing of a lawsuit, clearly identifying the appropriate standard of care, how the standard of care was violated, and the damages that resulted from the violation of the standard of care.

■ Non-economic damages should be capped at $250,000 for any and all doctors sued with an additional cap of $250,000 for each of up to two medical care institutions.

■ Other procedural and substantive devices, such as forum shopping, used to tilt the scales of justice should be eliminated.

Malpractice insurance premiums in Texas dropped about 60 percent in the 10 years following passage of the legislation, and the number of licensed physicians in the state nearly doubled (Nixon and Texas Public Policy Foundation 2013). More recently, in 2016, Texas saw a malpractice insurance premium decrease of 0.5 percent (*Insurance Journal* 2016).

Dr. Stark concludes, "The experience of Texas shows that reasonable medical malpractice reform works. A meaningful legal cap on non-economic damages is the most effective element of successful lawsuit reform legislation. To a lesser extent, a statute of limitations on lawsuits and pre-trial screening are often effective in reducing the cost of specific medical malpractice lawsuits."

Other states that have passed legislation to reduce the cost of malpractice litigation include Alaska, California, Colorado, Florida, Maine, Michigan, Oklahoma, and Utah.

Reform Agenda

We recommend states follow the lead of Texas by adopting the policies summarized above.

Recommended Readings: Joseph Nixon and Texas Public Policy Foundation, "Ten Years of Tort Reform in Texas: A Review," *Backgrounder* No. 32830, The Heritage Foundation, 2013; Roger Stark, "The Cost of Medical Malpractice Lawsuits in Washington State— Lessons from Texas Reform," Washington Policy Center, April 2016.

References

AAPS (Association of American Physicians and Surgeons). 2017. *White Paper on Repeal/Replacement of the Affordable Care Act*. January 6.

Accenture. 2015. *US Retail Health Clinics Expected to Nearly Double by 2017 According to Accenture Analysis*.

Adamson, David M. 2010. "Health Care on Aisle 7: The Growing Phenomenon of Retail Clinics." *Research Highlights*. Rand Corporation.

Agrawal, Vishal, Tilman Ehrbeck, Kimberly O'Neill Packard, and Paul Mango. 2005. *Consumer-Directed Health Plan Report–Early Evidence Is Promising*. Pittsburgh, PA: McKinsey & Company.

AHIP (America's Health Insurance Plans). 2017. "2016 Census of Health Savings Account – High Deductible Health Plans." February.

Alonso-Zaldivar, Ricardo. 2016. "Obama Administration Announces Double-Digit Premium Hikes for Affordable Care Act." Associated Press. October 24.

AMA (American Medical Association). 2011. "New AMA Studies Show Cost Burden of the Medical Liability System." December 21.

———. 2013. *Advocacy Update*. Chicago, IL: American Medical Association.

American Funds. 2017. "Health Savings Accounts Are Growing at a Healthy Pace." March 20.

Asch, Steven M., Eve A. Kerr, Joan Keesey, John L. Adams, Claude M. Setodji, Shaista Malik, and Elizabeth A. McGlynn. 2006. "Who Is at Greatest Risk for Receiving Poor-Quality Health Care?" *New England Journal of Medicine* **354** (11): 1147–56. doi:10.1056/NEJMsa044464.

Associated Press. 2013. "Policy Notifications and Current Status, By State." *Yahoo! Finance* (website). December 26.

Azar, Alex M. II, *et al.* 2006. "Transparency in Health Care: What Consumers Need to Know." Speech delivered at The Heritage Foundation. October 3.

Baicker, Katherine, Sarah L. Taubman, Heidi L. Allen, Mira Bernstein, Jonathan H. Gruber, Joseph P. Newhouse, Eric C. Schneider, Bill J. Wright, Alan M. Zaslavsky, and Amy N. Finkelstein. 2013. "The Oregon Experiment—Effects of Medicaid on Clinical Outcomes." *New England Journal of Medicine* **368** (May): 1713–22. doi:10.1056/NEJMsa1212321.

Barnes, John. 2006. "Failure of Government Central Planning: Washington's Medical Certificate of Need Program." *Policy Brief*. Washington Policy Center.

Bast, Diane Carol. 2005. "Bill Would Allow Consumers to Purchase Health Insurance across State Lines." *Health Care News*. June.

Bast, Joseph L. 2004. "Destroying Insurance Markets: How Community Rating and Guaranteed Issue Have Destroyed the Individual Insurance Market in Eight States." *Health Care News*. February.

Bast, Joseph, Richard Rue, and Stuart Wesbury. 1993. *Why We Spend Too Much on Health Care*. Chicago, IL: The Heartland Institute.

Bisu, Rituparna. 2013. *The Broken State of American Health Insurance Prior to the Affordable Care Act: A Market Rife with Government Distortions*. Irvine, CA: Ayn Rand Institute.

Blue Cross and Blue Shield Association. 2005. "Blue Cross and Blue Shield Association Consumer Survey Shows High Rate of Satisfaction with HSAs, Cites Increased Reliance on Decision-Support Tools." September 29.

Brase, Twila. 2017. "About." *The Wedge of Health Freedom* (website).

Bryan, Darcy N., Jared Rhoads, and Robert Graboyes. 2016. "Occupational Regulation." Mercatus Center Healthcare Openness and Access Project. December 1.

Bunce, Victoria Craig. 2002. "Dirty Little Secrets about Clean Claims Laws." *Issues & Answers*. Council for Affordable Health Insurance. November.

———. 2013. *Health Insurance Mandates in the States, 2012*. Washington, DC: Council for Affordable Health Insurance.

CBO (Congressional Budget Office). 2014. "Labor Market Effects of the Affordable Care Act: Updated Estimated." Appendix C in *The Budget and Economic Outlook: 2014 to 2024*. Washington, DC: Congressional Budget Office.

CBS News. 2017. "What Happens When the Only Health Insurer Exits?" March 6.

Chen, Caroline. 2014. "Obamacare Insurer Wellpoint Sees Double-Digit Rate Rise." *Bloomberg News* (website). March 25.

Cigna. 2013. *Cigna Choice Fund Experience Study: Summary of Key Findings*. Bloomfield, CT: Cigna Health and Life Insurance Company.

Claxton, Gary, Matthew Rae, Nirmita Panchal, Anthony Damico, Nathan Bostick, Kevin Kenward, and Heidi Whitmore. 2013. *Employer Health Benefits: 2013 Annual Survey*. Menlo Park, CA: Henry J. Kaiser Family Foundation; Chicago, IL: Health Research & Educational Trust.

Clements, Nick. 2016. "Obamacare Premiums Increase 25%: Is the 'Death Spiral' Here?" *Forbes* (website). October 25.

CMS (Centers for Medicare and Medicaid Services). 2012. *National Health Expenditures; Aggregate and Per Capita Amounts, Annual Percent Change and Percent Distribution: Selected Calendar Years 1960–2012*.

Conover, Christopher. 2013. "No, David Axelrod, the 'Vast Majority of People in This Country' Are Not Keeping Their Plan." *Forbes* (website). October 30.

Conover, Christopher J., and Frank A. Sloan. 1998. "Does Removing Certificate-of-Need Regulations Lead to a Surge in Healthcare Spending?" *Journal of Health Politics, Policy and Law* 23 (3): 455–81.

Cordato, Roy. 2005. "Certificate-of-Need Laws: It's Time for Repeal." *Nathaniel Macon Research Series* No. 1. John Locke Foundation.

Corieri, Christina. 2014. "Everyone Deserves the Right to Try: Empowering the Terminally Ill to Take Control of their Treatment." Goldwater Institute.

Council for Affordable Health Insurance. 2007. *HSA State Implementation Report*.

Daniels, Scott E. 2015. *Health Care Sharing Ministries: An Uncommon Bond*. Washington, DC: Charlotte Lozier Institute.

deBrantes, Francois, and Suzanne Delbanco. 2016. *Report Card on State Price Transparency Laws*. Health Care Incentives Improvement Institute. July.

DeNavas-Walt, Carmen, Bernadette D. Proctor, and Jessica C. Smith. 2013. *Income, Poverty, and Health Insurance Coverage in the United States: 2012*. Washington, DC: U.S. Government Printing Office.

Dubay, Curtis. 2013. "After Repeal of Obamacare: Moving to Patient-Centered, Market-Based Health Care." The Heritage Foundation. October 31.

Emanuel, Jeff. 2008. "Health Savings Accounts." *Research & Commentary*. The Heartland Institute. May 15.

Employee Benefits Research Institute. 2015. "Satisfaction with Health Coverage and Care: Findings from the 2014 EBRI/Greenwald & Associates Consumer Engagement in Health Care Survey." *Notes* **36** (7).

Ferrara, Peter. 2010. *The Obamacare Disaster*. Chicago, IL: The Heartland Institute.

———. 2015. *Power to the People: The new road to freedom and prosperity for the poor, seniors, and those most in need of the world's best health care*. Arlington Heights, IL: The Heartland Institute.

Finkelstein, Amy. 2007. "The Aggregate Effects of Health Insurance: Evidence from the Introduction of Medicare." *Quarterly Journal of Economics* **122** (3): 1–37. doi:10.3386/w11619.

Flowers, Aricka T. 2007. "National Market Could Cure America's Health Care Crisis: Policy Analysts." *Health Care News*. January.

Frank, Ted, and Martin F. Grace. 2006. "Faulty Studies from Center for Justice & Democracy Are Stunting the Medical-Malpractice Debate." *Liability Outlook* No. 2. American Enterprise Institute.

Friedman, Milton. 2004. *Interview with Fox News*. May.

Gabel, Jon R., Ryan Lore, Roland D. McDevitt, Jeremy D. Pickreign, Heidi Whitmore, Michael Stover, and Ethan Levy-Forsythe. 2012. "More Than Half of Individual Health Plans Offer Coverage That Falls Short of What Can Be Sold through Exchanges as of 2014." *Health Affairs* **31** (6): 1339–48. doi:10.1377/hlthaff.2011.1082.

GAO (Government Accountability Office). 2011. *Health Care Price Transparency: Meaningful Price Information Is Difficult for Consumers to Obtain Prior to Receiving Care*. GAO–11–791. September.

———. 2017. "Progress on Many High-Risk Areas, While Substantial Efforts Needed on Others."

Garfield, Rachel, Anthony Damico, Cynthia Cox, Gary Claxton, and Larry Levitt. 2016. "Estimates of Eligibility for ACA Coverage among the Uninsured in 2016." Kaiser Family Foundation. October 18.

Giuliani Partners. 2005. *Examination and Assessment of Prescription Drug Importation from Foreign Sources to the United States*. Washington, DC: Pharmaceutical Research and Manufacturers of America.

Glans, Matthew. 2014a. "Experimental Drugs and the Right to Try." *Research & Commentary*. The Heartland Institute.

———. 2014b. "Certificate of Need Reform." *Research & Commentary*. The Heartland Institute. November 13.

————. 2016a. "Michigan Direct Primary Care Pilot Could Save Medicaid Millions." *Research & Commentary*. The Heartland Institute. May 31.

————. 2016b. "Are Maintenance of Certification Programs a Money Grab?" *Research & Commentary*. The Heartland Institute. April 22.

————. 2017a. "State High-Risk Pools for Health Insurance." *Research & Commentary*. The Heartland Institute. May 25.

————. 2017b. "Health Care Sharing Ministries a Good Alternative to ACA." *Research & Commentary*. The Heartland Institute. January 27.

————. 2017c. "Missouri Should Avoid Overregulating Dental Service Organizations." *Research & Commentary*. The Heartland Institute. June 21.

Gohmann, Stephan F., and Myra J. McCrickard. 2009. "The Effect of State Mandates on Health Insurance Premiums." *Journal of Private Enterprise* **24** (2): 59–73.

Goodman, John C. 2005a. "Drug Reimportation: The Free Trade Solution." *Brief Analyses* No. 503. National Center for Policy Analysis.

————. 2005b. "Making HSAs Better." *Brief Analyses* No. 518. National Center for Policy Analysis.

————. 2009. "Does Lack of Insurance Cause Premature Death?" *Health Affairs Blog*. September 21.

————. 2012. *Priceless: Curing the Health Care Crisis*. Oakland, CA: Independent Institute.

Goodman, John C., and Dorman E. Cordell. 1998. "The Nightmare in Our Future: Elderly Entitlements." *Policy Report* No. 212. National Center for Policy Analysis.

Goodman, John C., and Gerald L. Musgrave. 1992. *Patient Power: Solving America's Health Care Crisis*. Washington, DC: Cato Institute.

Gorman, Linda. 2008 "Dying for (Media) Coverage." *Health Policy Blog*. May 2.

Gottlieb, Scott. 2011. "Medicaid Is Worse Than No Coverage at All." *The Wall Street Journal*. March 10.

Graham, John R. 2008. *From Heart Transplants to Hairpieces: The Questionable Benefits of State Benefit Mandates for Health Insurance*. San Francisco, CA: Pacific Research Institute.

Hamilton, Michael. 2016a. "More States Consider Outlawing Forced Maintenance of Certification." June 7.

Hamilton, Michael. 2016b. "Policy Diagnosis: Direct Primary Care Helps Patients, Doctors, and the Health Care System." Interview with Hal Scherz, M.D., founder of Docs4PatientCare. *Health Care News*. April 6.

Hamilton, Michael, Bette Grande, and John Davidson, 2016. "The Case for Licensing Dental Therapists in North Dakota." *Policy Brief*. The Heartland Institute.

Herrick, Devon M. 2006a. "Telemedicine Provides Benefits, but Security and Privacy Risks Abound." *Health Care News*. June.

————. 2006b. "Medical Tourism Prompts Price Discussions." *Health Care News*. October.

————. 2006c. "Shopping for Drugs: 2007." *Policy Report* No. 293. National Center for Policy Analysis.

Herrick, Devon M. and John C. Goodman. 2007. "The Market for Medical Care: Why You Don't Know the Price; Why You Don't Know about Quality; And What Can Be Done about It." *Policy Report* No. 296. National Center for Policy Analysis. March 12.

HHS (Department of Health and Human Services). 2017. "HHS Report: Average Health Insurance Premiums Doubled Since 2013."

Hogberg, David. 2013. "Congress Should Repeal Limits on New Doctor-Owned Hospitals." *Washington Examiner*. March 6.

———. 2014a. "Obamacare's Little Noticed Victims." *American Spectator*. February 20.

HSA for America. 2017. "States Following Federal HSA Tax Treatment."

Hyman, D.A. and Silver, C. 2006. "Medical Malpractice Litigation and Tort Reform: It's the Incentives, Stupid." *Vanderbilt Law Review* **59** (4): 1085.

Insurance Journal. 2016. "Medical Malpractice Liability Premiums Remain Flat: Survey." October 10.

Jacobs, Chris. 2017. "Summary of Repeal and Replace Amendments." *Chris Jacobs on Health Care*. May 4.

Japsen, Bruce. 2015. "Retail Clinics Hit 10 Million Annual Visits But Just 2% Of Primary Care Market." *Forbes* (website). April 23.

KFF (Kaiser Family Foundation). 2015. "Distribution of the Nonelderly Uninsured by Federal Poverty Level (FPL)."

Kleba, Heather. 2007. "A Health Link Hits Home." *Governing*. March.

Kullgren, Jeffrey T., Katia A. Duey, and Rachel M. Werner. 2013. "A Census of State Health Care Price Transparency Websites." *Journal of the American Medical Association*. June 19.

Levy, Helen, and David Meltzer. 2008. "The Impact of Health Insurance on Health." *Annual Review of Public Health* **29**: 399–409.

Lichtenberg, Frank R. 2007. "Benefits and Costs of Newer Drugs: An Update." *Managerial and Decision Economics* **28** (4–5): 485–90. doi:10.1002/mde.1355.

LoBuono, Charlotte. 2006. "Cost Comparison Web Sites Enhance Choice for Prescription Drug Buyers." *Health Care News*. November.

Madden, Bartley J., and Gregory Conko. 2010. *Free to Choose Medicine: Better Drugs Sooner at Lower Cost.* Chicago, IL: The Heartland Institute.

Makla, Nathan, and Matthew Glans. 2016. "Direct Primary Care Saves Union County, North Carolina $1 Million." *Research & Commentary*. The Heartland Institute. March 21.

Martin, Maureen. 2011. "Heartland Institute Legal Expert Can Talk About New HEALTH Act, Tort Reform." May 12.

Martin, Trevor. 2007. "Retail Health Clinics." *Research & Commentary*. The Heartland Institute.

McCorry, Daniel. 2014. "Direct Primary Care: An Innovative Alternative to Conventional Health Insurance." August 6. The Heritage Foundation.

McKeown, Karen D. 2011. "Empowering Patients as Key Decision Makers in the Face of Rising Health Care Costs." *Backgrounder* No. 2635. The Heritage Foundation. December.

Medicare Board of Trustees. 2007. *2007 Annual Report of the Boards of Trustees of the Federal Hospital Insurance and Federal Supplementary Medical Insurance Trust Funds*. Washington, DC: Centers for Medicare and Medicaid Services.

———. 2013. *2013 Annual Report of the Boards of Trustees of the Federal Hospital Insurance and Federal Supplementary Medical Insurance Trust Funds*. Washington, DC: Centers for Medicare and Medicaid Services.

Meier, Conrad F. 1999. "Extending Affordable Health Insurance to the Uninsurable." *Policy Study*. The Heartland Institute. August 27.

Meier, Conrad F. 2005a. *Destroying Insurance Markets: How Guaranteed Issue and Community Rating Destroyed the Individual Health Insurance Market in Eight States*. Washington, DC: Council for Affordable Health Insurance and Chicago, IL: The Heartland Institute.

———. 2005b. "Campaign for Drug Importation Falters." *Health Care News*. February.

Moses, Stephen A. 2017. "How to Fix Long-Term Care Financing." Center for Long-Term Care Reform and the Foundation for Government Accountability. July 26.

NAHU (National Association of Health Underwriters). 2005. "Analysis of State-Level Health Insurance Market Reforms."

Neuman, Patricia, Michelle Kitchman Strollo, Stuart Guterman, William H. Rogers, Angela Li, Angie Mae C. Rodday, and Dana Gelb Safran. 2007. "Medicare Prescription Drug Benefit Progress Report: Findings from a 2006 National Survey of Seniors." *Health Affairs* **26** (5): w630–43. doi:10.1377/hlthaff.26.5.w630.

Nixon, Joseph, and Texas Public Policy Foundation. 2013. "Ten Years of Tort Reform in Texas: A Review." *Backgrounder* No. 32830. The Heritage Foundation.

OFR (Office of the Federal Register). 2010. "Interim Final Rules for Group Health Plans and Health Insurance Coverage Relating to Status as a Grandfathered Health Plan under the Patient Protection and Affordable Care Act." *Federal Register* **75** (116).

Oliver, Wayne, and Jeffrey Segal. 2014. "Do not Reform The Malpractice System To Reduce Healthcare Cost—Eliminate It." *Forbes* (website). November 5.

Ollove, Michael. 2017. "ACA Repeal Could Mean Return to 'High-Risk Pools.'" Pew Charitable Trust. February 16.

Palmieri Heck, Mia. 2017. "Overregulation Threatens Market-Driven Solutions in Dentistry." *The State Factor*. American Legislative Exchange Council.

Parnell, Sean. 2005a. "Nurse Practitioners Offer Effective, Low-Cost Care." *Health Care News*. October.

———. 2005b. "Specialty Hospitals Offer Savings, Improved Care in Future." *Health Care News*. January.

———. 2013. "Direct Primary Care Practices—Why Are They So Much Less Expensive?" *The Self-Pay Patient* (website). December 17.

———. 2014. "Wisconsin Direct Primary Care Practice Closing, But More Opening Nationally." *The Self-Pay Patient* (website). January 2.

Pioneer Institute, 2016. "National Survey Finds Limited Access To Price Estimates For Routine Hospital Procedure." February 21.

Pitts, Peter J. 2006. "Pharmaceutical Fakery is Health Care Terrorism." *Baltimore Sun*. August 15.

Restrepo, Katherine. 2016. "Union County Saves Big With Direct Primary Care." *Carolina Journal*. March 15.

Shatto, John D., and Kent Clemens. 2010. *Projected Medicare Expenditures under an Illustrative Scenario with Alternative Payment Updates to Medicare Providers*. Office of the Actuary, Centers for Medicare and Medicaid Services. August 5.

Sledge, Hayley. 2016. "Despite Increases, Health Care Ministry 'Shares' Stay Cheaper Than Insurance Premiums." *Health Care News*. November 29.

Stark, Roger. 2016. "The Cost of Medical Malpractice Lawsuits in Washington State— Lessons from Texas Reform." Washington Policy Center. April 11.

Stuart, Bruce C., Jalpa A. Doshi, and Joseph V. Terza. 2009. "Assessing the Impact of Drug Use on Hospital Costs." *Health Services Research* **44** (1): 128–44. doi:10.1111/j.14756773.2008.00897.x.

Thorpe, Kenneth E., and John C. Goodman. 2005. *Reforming the Health Care System*. Muncie, IN: Ball State University and Chicago, IL: The Heartland Institute.

Turner, Grace-Marie, and Conrad F. Meier. 2004. "Prescription Drug Importation: Just the Facts." *Health Care News*. June 1.

Ungar, Rick. 2013 "The Great American Hospital Pricing Scam Exposed—We Now Know Why Healthcare Costs Are So Artificially High." *Forbes* (website). May 8.

Vinton, Emma. 2017. "Virginia Lawmakers Approve Direct Primary Care Bills—Again." *Health Care News*. February 28.

VISA. 2017. "Mapping the Future of Global Travel and Tourism."

Wieske, J.P. 2007. *State Legislators' Guide to Health Insurance Solutions*. Washington, DC: Council for Affordable Health Insurance.

Wieske, J.P., and Merrill Matthews. 2007. *Understanding the Uninsured and What to Do About Them*. Washington, DC: Council for Affordable Health Insurance.

Additional Resources

Additional information about health care policy is available from The Heartland Institute:

- PolicyBot, The Heartland Institute's free online clearinghouse for the work of other free-market think tanks, contains thousands of documents on health policy issues. It is on Heartland's website at https://www.heartland.org/policybot/.

- https://www.heartland.org/Center-Health-Care/ is the website of Consumers for Health Care Choices, devoted to the latest research, news, and commentary about health care policy issues. Read headlines, watch videos, or browse the thousands of documents on health care policy issues available from PolicyBot.

■ From July 2001 until September 2017, Heartland produced *Health Care News*, a monthly newspaper devoted to health policy issues. It also produced *Consumer Power Report*, a weekly e-newsletter devoted to health policy, between August 2009 and September 2017. Back issues of both publications are available online at https://www.heartland.org/publications-resources/newsletters, and new issues will be posted there if the publications resume.

Directory

The following national organizations provide valuable information about health care financing and policy.

Alliance of Health Care Sharing Ministries, http://www.healthcaresharing.org/

Association of American Physicians and Surgeons, http://aapsonline.org/

Cato Institute, https://www.cato.org/

Center for Long-Term Care Reform, http://www.centerltc.com/

Charlotte Lozier Institute, https://lozierinstitute.org/

Citizens Council for Health Freedom, http://www.cchfreedom.org/

Docs4Patient Care Foundation, https://d4pcfoundation.org/

DPC Frontier, http://www.dpcfrontier.com/

Employee Benefit Research Institute, https://www.ebri.org/

Free to Choose Medicine, http://www.freetochoosemedicine.com/

Galen Institute, http://galen.org/

Goldwater Institute, http://goldwaterinstitute.org/en/

Goodman Institute for Public Policy Research, http://www.goodmaninstitute.org/

Heartland Institute, https://www.heartland.org/

Heritage Foundation, http://www.heritage.org/

HSA for America, http://www.hsaforamerica.com/

Kaiser Family Foundation, http://www.kff.org/

The Self-Pay Patient, http://theselfpaypatient.com/

The Wedge of Health Freedom, https://jointhewedge.com/about/

Chapter 2
Energy and Environment

Isaac Orr and James M. Taylor

---

10 Principles of Energy and Environment Policy

1. Global warming is not a crisis.
2. End the war on fossil fuels.
3. Hydraulic fracturing ("fracking") is safe and beneficial.
4. National security requires affordable energy.
5. Energy self-sufficiency is achievable.
6. Air pollution is a fading challenge.
7. End subsidies to alternative energy producers.
8. Biofuels cannot replace oil.
9. Corporate Average Fuel Economy standards sacrifice lives for oil.
10. Replace the Environmental Protection Agency.

Introduction

The United States has a competitive advantage over every other nation in energy abundance. It has more coal, oil, and natural gas resources than any other nation. Only one country, Russia, has even half as much of these energy resources as the United States (EIA 2016b). It is solely due to poor political choices that the United States behaves and suffers like an energy-poor nation despite its natural advantages.

The large-scale use of oil and gas need not cause environmental harm. Modern technologies have reduced emissions of the six principal pollutants tracked by the Environmental Protection Agency (EPA) more than 60 percent since 1980 (EPA 2016b). Today, virtually anything visible coming from the smokestacks of factories or electric generating stations is water vapor—steam—and poses no threat to human health or to the environment. The same is true of cars and trucks.

Despite these facts, many people live in fear that the world is getting dirtier and less safe with every passing year. Many people fear invisible poisons in the air, water, and the food they eat. They fear global warming will destroy the planet, if not in their lifetime then perhaps in their children's or grandchildren's. This fear is fanned by environmental groups, which use it to raise money and stay relevant in an increasingly clean and safe world, and by the media, which use it to sell newspapers and attract audiences to their broadcasts.

This chapter aims to correct these misconceptions. It presents 10 principles of energy and environmental policy: facts and policy recommendations we believe are essential to a fair and balanced understanding of the topic. Recommended readings appear at the end of each principle, and all sources cited in the body of the chapter appear in a bibliography at the end of the chapter.

1. Global warming is not a crisis.

Public policy should not be based on the exaggerated threat of man-made global warming.

Perhaps the biggest and most consequential environmental controversy of our age is "global warming," or more specifically, fear of man-made catastrophic climate change. Billions of dollars have been spent on scientific research trying to find a human impact on climate, and trillions of dollars have already been spent attempting to influence the weather. An agency of the United Nations, the Intergovernmental Panel on Climate Change (IPCC), claims to speak for all climate scientists when it pronounces on the subject, but it is politicized and unreliable. The elementary truth is that global warming is not a crisis.

Global warming fears arising first in the 1980s led to taxes, regulations, and subsidies aimed at reducing human emissions of carbon dioxide and other greenhouse gases. While climate is always changing and there is some evidence of a small human impact on regional weather, real-world observations and the best available scientific evidence do not support claims of an impending global warming crisis.

No Consensus

Rather than debate their numerous critics, global warming alarmists often appeal to a mythical scientific consensus. A frequent assertion is 97 percent of scientists agree humans are causing a global warming crisis. No survey of scientists has ever reached such a conclusion (Bast and Spencer 2014). The 97 percent figure is derived from just a few surveys with poor methodologies asking the wrong questions of the wrong people (Idso *et al.* 2016).

More meaningful surveys show only a minority of scientists believe humans are causing a global warming crisis. Two surveys of more than 500 climatologists and scientists reveal less than half are very concerned about global warming and believe the science justifies immediate political action (Bast 2010). In a more recent survey, fewer than 50 percent of climatologists and scientists working in related fields thought the potential was great or somewhat great for "catastrophe in the next 50 years resulting from climate change for the country in which you live" (Bray and von Storch 2016).

Two additional surveys of American Meteorological Society meteorologists reveal only a slim majority believe humans are primarily responsible for recent warming and only a small minority are very concerned about it (Taylor 2012). Finally, more than 31,000 scientists have signed a summary of the science explaining humans are not causing a global warming crisis (Global Warming Petition Project, n.d.).

Another frequent assertion is that every scientific association in the world has issued a statement saying humans are causing a global warming crisis. None of those societies surveyed its members, meaning these resolutions express the interests and opinions of the organizations' leaders and not actual scientists. Most of these societies didn't conduct their own scientific investigations, but instead say they endorse the findings of the United Nations' IPCC. But their own presidents are aware of the deep flaws in that organization's procedures. The InterAcademy Council, an organization composed of the presidents of the world's leading national science academies, published a stinging critique of the IPCC's studies pointing out violations of peer-review standards, use of gray sources, and political interference (IAC 2010).

Finally, many scientific associations have remained silent on the topic, and some have explicitly rejected the notion of a global warming crisis or a scientific consensus on the topic. The latter include the American Physical Society, Chinese Academy of Sciences, Danish National Space Center, Polish Academy of Sciences, and Russian Academy of Sciences.

What the Science Says

The Nongovernmental International Panel on Climate Change (NIPCC) is a more objective and reliable guide to climate science than the highly politicized IPCC. It has published five volumes in its *Climate Change Reconsidered* (CCR) series conclusively showing humans are not causing a global warming crisis (Idso *et al.* 2009, 2011, 2013, 2016; Idso *et al.* 2014). *CCR* constitutes thousands of pages of scientific summaries and thousands of citations of objective data and peer-reviewed scientific literature.

According to NIPCC, estimates of climate sensitivity to greenhouse gases appearing in the scientific literature since 2009 have fallen steadily below the estimates used by IPCC (Idso *et al.* 2016). Extensive peer-reviewed research shows recent changes in temperatures, sea level rise, and the frequency of extreme weather events are far from unusual in the historic and geophysical record (Pielke Jr. 2014; Hao *et al.* 2014; Zycher 2014).

The climate models relied upon by IPCC, EPA, and other sources of climate alarmism forecast twice as much warming as has been reported by satellites and weather balloons, meaning they have been invalidated (Christy 2016; Monckton *et al.* 2015). The climate models are programmed to assume human carbon dioxide emissions will set in motion a chain reaction that will cause a dramatic warming of Earth. They assume but cannot prove a causal connection between human carbon dioxide emissions and temperature rise (Green and Armstrong 2007).

According to the climate models, carbon dioxide emissions should be causing an uninterrupted increase in global temperatures at a pace of 0.2 to 0.3 degrees Celsius per decade (IPCC 2007). However, global temperatures fell from the 1940s through the 1970s, even though carbon dioxide emissions rose dramatically during this period (IPCC 1990). Also, global temperatures have remained essentially flat since late in the twentieth century, even though carbon dioxide emissions have risen faster than projected by the United Nations (Remote Sensing Systems 2015). The clear lesson is this: Carbon dioxide emissions have much less impact on global temperatures than computer models assume.

Costs and Benefits

Evidence shows the benefits of a modestly warming world outweigh the few observed harms in most parts of the world during the coming century or even longer. Bolstered by longer growing seasons, greater soil moisture, and enhanced atmospheric carbon dioxide, crop yields in the United States and around the world are setting records on an almost yearly basis (Idso *et al.* 2014; Taylor 2013a).

Tornadoes, hurricanes, droughts, wildfires, and other extreme weather events are becoming less frequent and less severe as our planet modestly warms, even assuming modest spurts of warming by some observations (Taylor 2013b). Deserts are receding, forests are expanding, and NASA satellites have documented a dramatic greening of the Earth (CSIRO Australia 2013).

Even if the costs of global warming exceeded the benefits, there still would be no case for trying to restrict carbon dioxide emissions because the human contribution to atmospheric carbon dioxide levels is so small. Dramatic reductions in our emissions, imposed at enormous cost, would have almost no impact on climate and temperature (Michaels and Knappenberger 2013).

Integrated assessment models based on IPCC's own (flawed) science suggest the benefits of global warming will exceed the costs for the next century, and only then begin to turn negative if warming exceeds 2°C. With improved models suggesting warming may never reach 2°C, this suggests only good will come from some modest warming. Economists look at this scenario and conclude, given the time value of money, that the best plan of action today and for decades to come is to do nothing at all (Kreutzer *et al.* 2016).

Policy Agenda

The action items that follow from the preceding discussion include the following:

■ Create a President's Council on Climate Change charged with cutting through the politics and bias that infected climate science and policymaking during the Obama administration and advising the president on what policies to repeal and what policies to pursue.

■ Build on the country's withdrawal from the Paris Climate Accord by withdrawing from the Framework Convention on Climate Change and ceasing funding for the United Nations' Intergovernmental Panel on Climate Change (IPCC) and Green Climate Fund.

■ Withdraw and suspend implementation of the Endangerment Finding for Greenhouse Gases and the Clean Power Plan.

■ Support legislation removing the fictitious "social cost of carbon" from federal rulemaking and regulatory consideration.

■ End the climate profiteering in America's energy sector by ceasing billions of dollars a year in direct and indirect subsidies to wind and solar companies.

■   Dramatically reduce government funding of climate change research.
    When funding such research, require that equal amounts go to
    studying natural and man-made climate change.

Recommended Readings: Roy W. Spencer, *The Great Global Warming
Blunder: How Mother Nature Fooled the World's Top Climate Scientists*
(New York, NY: Encounter Books, 2010); Craig D. Idso, Robert M.
Carter, and S. Fred Singer, *Why Scientists Disagree About Global
Warming* (Arlington Heights, IL: The Heartland Institute, 2016).

2. End the war on fossil fuels.

Elected officials and agency regulators at the national,
state, and local levels should repeal subsidies, taxes, and
regulations aimed at reducing the use of fossil fuels.

Abundant and affordable energy promotes human health, happiness, and
prosperity. When energy is abundant, falling energy prices work like an
across-the-board tax cut, goods and services become less expensive to
produce and transport, and lower prices result in greater consumer
purchasing power. People are able to buy more goods and services such
as education, health care, nutritious foods, quality housing, and durable
consumer goods, making lives healthier and more enjoyable.

When energy prices rise, as happens when government policies make
energy less plentiful or reliable, almost all goods and services become
more expensive to produce and transport. The resulting higher prices
make consumer products less affordable, destroy jobs, and lower living
standards.

The War on Fossil Fuels

During his campaign for president in 2008, Barack Obama famously told
the editorial board of a newspaper, "if somebody wants to build a coal-
powered plant, they can. It's just that it will bankrupt them because they
are going to be charged a huge sum for all the greenhouse gases that they
emitted" (Obama 2008). This was the first shot in what would be an
eight-year war on fossil fuels led by President Obama.

Between 2008 and 2014, the Obama administration reduced the
number of acres leased for oil and natural gas production on federal lands
by more than 25 percent, from 47 million acres to 35 million acres

(Bureau of Land Management 2014). The Obama administration further limited domestic energy production in late 2016 by removing 115 million acres in the Arctic and Atlantic Oceans from oil and gas development (Ware 2016). These policies have caused oil and natural gas production on federal lands to fall by 6 percent and 28 percent, respectively, and the average time to process an application to drill on federal lands increased 41 percent between 2006 and 2011.

These policies restrict supply and make production more expensive (Humphries 2014). The dramatic increase in U.S. oil and natural gas production since 2008 occurred *in spite of* federal government policies, primarily due to increases in production on private and state-owned lands.

According to environmental activists, stabilizing the global climate would require reducing carbon dioxide emissions 80 percent or even more by the middle of the century. Achieving this would require banning the use of fossil fuels—coal, oil, and natural gas—and relying instead on renewable fuels such as wind and solar. This is an impossible dream; wind and solar are intermittent and unreliable sources of energy that cannot be scaled up to meet current levels of demand for energy, much less the higher levels of demand that are expected to prevail decades from now (Clack 2017; Dears 2015).

Renewable energy typically costs two to three times as much as energy produced from fossil fuels. This enormous cost difference means access to energy in the Left's fantasy world would have to be rationed. Choices of housing and occupations and cars, among other goods and services, would be severely limited. Trucks and SUVs would be banned. Living more than five or 10 miles away from a workplace would be prohibited. Traveling by plane would be strictly limited, perhaps to one trip every decade or two. Population would have to be severely limited through policies even more severe than those used by China and other unfree countries.

Higher energy costs lead to slower economic growth, as affordable energy is the key to productivity growth and production of virtually all goods and services. The forced conversion away from fossil fuels already underway in Europe and other parts of the world has destroyed millions of jobs and trillions of dollars in wealth. The anti-fossil-fuel policies of the Obama administration caused serious harm to the U.S. economy, helping make the economic recovery since 2008 the slowest in the past 60 years.

If imposed on developing countries, anti-fossil-fuel policies would cause the premature death of millions of people (Driessen 2003). This doesn't worry the Left, because global population control is one of their highest objectives. But it should be of great concern to everyone with a sense of decency and concern for one's fellow man.

The Futility of Reducing Emissions

Despite the enormous costs, national and state-specific carbon dioxide restrictions have no discernible effect on global temperatures. IPCC data show completely eliminating *all* U.S. carbon dioxide emissions would alleviate only 0.13 degrees Celsius of warming by the year 2100 (Michaels 2013). Expensive carbon dioxide reduction mandates, like those contained in the Obama administration's now-halted Clean Power Plan, would reduce carbon dioxide emissions by only a small fraction of that already-tiny amount. Of course, completely eliminating all U.S. carbon dioxide emissions, or even a majority of them, is impossible (Dears 2017).

U.S. carbon dioxide emissions are not the reason global emissions continue to rise. U.S. emissions have fallen nearly 10 percent since the start of this century (EIA 2015a), yet global emissions have risen approximately 33 percent during that time (EIA 2015b). Emissions from China have more than doubled in this century (*Ibid.*). China emits more carbon dioxide than the combined total of every nation in the Western Hemisphere. Even if Argentina, Brazil, Canada, Mexico, the United States, and all other nations in the Western Hemisphere completely stopped using fossil fuels and eliminated all other sources of carbon dioxide emissions, new emissions from China would replace all those emissions in less than a decade.

Even more pointless are the actions of American city, county, and state officials who announce that even though the Trump administration is abandoning the Paris Climate Accord, they will adhere to it in their jurisdictions. Their actions will have no impact whatsoever on the alleged global warming problem but *will* harm their own economies and citizens. The so-called "We're Still In" movement might appear to be harmless "virtue signaling" by politicians and activists who want to be seen as standing for some supposedly noble cause, but the consequences of their efforts are higher energy costs and more restrictions on the economic liberty of enterprises and individuals.

Nations such as China and India produce much more of their electricity from carbon dioxide-intensive coal than does the United States. In an ultimate irony, high U.S. energy prices caused by regulations backed by environmentalists are chasing businesses and industries to these nations, *increasing* global carbon dioxide emissions. China and India do not require coal plants to employ basic technologies that reduce sulfur dioxide, soot, and other pollutants, resulting in higher emissions of real pollutants.

Why Reducing Emissions Is So Costly

Global expenditures to "stop global warming" exceeded $1.5 trillion a year in 2015, or approximately $4 billion a day (Hinderaker 2014). Expenditures in the United States to comply with existing climate change regulations and mandates are approximately $500 billion a year, or $4,275 per household.

Power generation, transportation fuels, and agricultural activity are the most significant sources of human greenhouse gas emissions. Restrictions on transportation emissions are especially problematic because there are currently few feasible alternatives to gasoline and the internal combustion engine. Those alternatives that do exist, such as ethanol and electric vehicles, emit as much or more carbon dioxide as gasoline and diesel when full energy use is taken into account. The lack of feasible alternatives to gasoline for transportation is one reason global warming restrictions, such as the Obama administration's Clean Power Plan, tend to target carbon dioxide emissions from power plants rather than transportation.

The principal mechanism for reducing power plant carbon dioxide emissions is inducing or mandating a transition from inexpensive coal power to more expensive low- or zero-carbon alternatives. Hydropower would provide an emissions-free source that is cost-competitive with coal, but environmental activist groups have strong-armed new hydropower facilities out of the political equation by persuading politicians that such facilities do unjustifiable harm to ecosystems.

Natural gas emits about half as much carbon dioxide as coal when burned and is, in some cases, less expensive than coal. However, environmental activist groups oppose natural gas production, and they convinced the Obama administration to reduce drilling permits on federal land and persuade many state and local governments to ban or restrict the use of hydraulic fracturing drilling technology. Trump is attempting to reverse these policies.

Nuclear power is the next least expensive available power source, has the best safety record of any form of electricity generation in the world, and is emissions-free. However, many environmental activist groups oppose nuclear power and have convinced states to enact nuclear power moratoria and persuaded the Obama administration to block approval of a permanent storage site for spent nuclear fuel in Yucca Mountain, Nevada. Trump has said he will open Yucca Mountain, but as of this chapter's writing that had not yet happened.

This leaves the most expensive energy sources of all, wind and solar power, as global warming activists' preferred means of producing energy without carbon dioxide emissions. Given their intermittency and scaling properties, it is simply impossible for today's electric grid to operate in an all-wind and -solar scenario (Dears 2017). A 2014 study published by the Brookings Institution found replacing conventional power with wind power would double electricity costs and using solar power would triple the costs (Frank 2014). The U.S. Energy Information Administration (EIA 2010) confirmed these higher costs and projected the price premiums for wind and solar power would continue for at least the next few decades.

Germany's attempt to move away from fossil fuels and nuclear power is an object lesson for America in what not to do. Germany already has the highest electricity prices in Europe. Germans also must cover the €20 billion costs of generating €3 billion worth of electricity via solar, wind, and biogas plants. And factories have been asked at times to shut down when the electricity supply didn't correspond properly with use (Spiegel 2013).

Policy Agenda

American consumers and workers would benefit if governments would encourage rather than discourage energy production. The following policies should be adopted to end the war on fossil fuels:

- Oppose cap-and-trade and carbon tax proposals based on the fictitious notion of a "social cost of carbon."

- Repeal mandates at the national level that the Department of Defense and other agencies use biofuels and other alternative energies, and mandates at the state level requiring utilities to source energy from renewables.

- Oppose the premature closure of coal-fired electric generation plants around the country.

- Remove barriers to exploration and development of fossil fuels offshore and on public lands.

- Approve Keystone XL and other pipelines blocked by President Barack Obama.

Recommended Readings: Alex Epstein, *The Moral Case for Fossil Fuels* (New York, NY: Penguin Publishing Group, 2014); Kathleen Hartnett White and Stephen Moore, *Fueling Freedom: Exposing the Mad War on Energy* (New York, NY: Regnery Publishing, 2016).

3. Hydraulic fracturing ("fracking") is safe and beneficial.

Hydraulic fracturing ("fracking") is environmentally safe, is helping America become energy self-sufficient ,and should not be discouraged by policymakers.

Cheap and reliable energy is more plentiful today than ever before thanks to a technological revolution in oil and natural gas production. Technological advances in hydraulic fracturing (or "fracking") and directional drilling have made it economically feasible to tap into oil and natural gas trapped in shale rock formations. Environmentalists are attacking fracking on spurious grounds. The Trump administration is removing regulatory obstacles to this safe and beneficial technology.

The Fracking Revolution

Hydraulic fracturing, or fracking, is a technique used by oil and natural gas drillers for decades to increase recovery from their wells. It consists of pumping a fluid composed of 99.51 percent water and sand, and .49 percent chemical additives, to open and hold pores in shale deposits, allowing oil and natural gas to collect in the pores and then to be pulled out by the well. The chemical additives in fracking fluid are mostly soaps and ingredients found in household products to prevent corrosion in the well, reduce surface tension in liquids, stabilize clay particles, adjust pH, and eliminate bacteria (Smith 2014b).

The "fracking revolution" occurred when fracking was paired with new horizontal drilling and computer-assisted underground monitoring to make more economical the process of extracting oil and natural gas from vast reserves (Orr 2013). Between 2012 and 2014, the shale oil industry generated 1.6 million new jobs in the oil industry and another 3.0 million throughout the economy (Gilje *et al.* 2016).

Due almost entirely to the fracking revolution, U.S. oil production has almost entirely recovered from a 40-year decline. In 2014, U.S. crude oil production reached 3.2 billion barrels, just 10 percent below its 1970 peak (EIA 2015d). In 2015, the United States produced approximately 9.4 million barrels of crude oil per day, the most since 1972 (EIA 2017a). Fracking has made the United States the top producer of oil and natural gas in the world, increasing oil production on non-federal lands by 61 percent and natural gas production on non-federal lands by 33 percent between 2009 and 2014 (Humphries 2014).

Natural gas is an increasingly important source of electrical power generation, so changes in natural gas availability and pricing have a substantial impact on the U.S. economy. Without the dramatic decline in oil and natural gas prices since mid-2008, the United States might still be wallowing in economic stagnation rather than experiencing a modest recovery from the Great Recession of 2008–09. According to a report by the U.S. Chamber of Commerce (2016), without fracking "by 2022, 14.8 million jobs could be lost, gasoline prices and electricity prices could almost double, and each American family could see their cost of living increase by almost $4,000."

Fracking also has a positive economic impact on local communities that allow the practice. A study conducted by researchers at the University of Chicago, Princeton University, and the Massachusetts Institute of Technology determined hydraulic fracturing activity brings $1,300 to $1,900 in annual benefits to local households, including "a 7 percent increase in average income, driven by rises in wages and royalty payments, a 10 percent increase in employment, and a 6 percent increase in housing prices" (Bartik et al. 2016).

Safety Concerns

Environmentalists claim methane (the main hydrocarbon in natural gas) and fracking fluid chemicals will contaminate groundwater aquifers and compromise drinking water supplies. An anti-fracking propaganda film titled "Gasland" featured someone lighting on fire the water running from the faucet of his Colorado home, allegedly due to nearby fracking. Like so much of the anti-fracking literature, "Gasland" is more fiction than fact. The Colorado Oil and Gas Conservation Commission (COGCC) determined the methane found in the well featured in the film was naturally occurring and unrelated to fracking (COGCC n.d.). The well did not test positive for chemicals used in the fracking process.

A study conducted by Duke University analyzed 68 water wells in the Marcellus Shale and found 85 percent of wells contained methane regardless of whether they were near gas industry operations. Here too, no evidence of fracking fluid was found in water samples (King et al. 2012).

Since 2010, at least 18 studies have been produced on the possible impact of fracking on drinking water. All found no impact (Benson 2017a). This finding was confirmed by a $29 million, six-year study by EPA of fracking's impact on groundwater sources, which failed to find any systemic impact caused by the 110,000 oil and natural gas wells that have been in use across the country since 2011 (EPA 2016a).

A 2017 peer-reviewed study of 112 drinking-water wells in Tyler and Hall Counties in northwestern West Virginia, led by researchers at Duke University and partially funded by the anti-fracking Natural

Resources Defense Council (NRDC), "found no indication of groundwater contamination over the three-year course of our study" (Harkness *et al.* 2017).

The large volumes of water required by fracking, typically between two million and four million gallons per well, also raises concerns. This sounds like a huge amount, but it is comparable on a gallons-per-btu basis to the amount of water used in coal mining and biofuel production, and it is small relative to household and agricultural use (Orr 2013). Hydraulic fracturing accounts for only about .3 percent of the total water consumed in the United States, compared to the .5 percent used to irrigate golf courses annually (*Ibid.*).

Another fear is that fracking causes earthquakes. A study of nearly 200 instances of manmade earthquakes found fracking was responsible for only three earthquakes large enough to be felt on the surface (Benson 2017b). Other human activities that triggered much larger earthquakes included building dams, filling reservoirs, and using explosives for mining. Injection wells used to dispose of wastewater from fracked wells can lubricate existing faults and cause small tremors. Reasonable regulation of injection wells, rather than restrictions on fracking, is the solution to this concern.

Policy Agenda

Environmental activist groups have called for state and local governments to impose aggressive regulation, moratoria, and even outright bans on fracking. New York implemented a fracking ban in 2014, and Maryland did so in April 2017 (Henry 2017). These policies are unnecessary and misguided. We recommend instead the following policy agenda:

■ Repeal existing state bans and moratoria on fracking.

■ Roll back unnecessary regulations on fracking offshore and on federal lands.

■ Impose reasonable regulation on injection wells to reduce the risk of tremors.

Recommended Readings: Tim Benson, "Peer-Reviewed Study Says Hydraulic Fracturing Not Responsible for Groundwater Contamination in West Virginia," *Research & Commentary*, The Heartland Institute, May 15, 2017; Isaac Orr, "Bill McKibben's Terrifying Disregard for Fracking Facts," *Heartland Policy Brief,* The Heartland Institute, August 19, 2016.

4. National security requires affordable energy.

Our military and national security are put at risk by public policies that discourage the production of affordable, reliable energy.

During the Obama administration, every department of the national government was weaponized in the war against fossil fuels. The Department of Defense was told to "get on board" by classifying climate change as a "threat multiplier" and to write contingency plans in case coastal military bases were flooded. Hundreds of millions of dollars that could have been devoted to providing better body armor and support for American troops went instead to experiments using algae-based biofuels to power airplanes and ships.

Trump issued an executive order bringing some of the Obama-era nonsense to an end, but more needs to be done. Global warming is not, in fact, a genuine threat to U.S. security. As documented earlier (in Principle 1 on global warming), more rapid sea level rise and severe weather are unlikely to occur in a warmer world. Warmer temperatures historically have coincided with periods of relative peace and prosperity, not war. The best way to ensure U.S. military superiority is to guarantee an ample and reliable supply of fossil fuels.

Climate and War

The empirical literature examining the causes of conflict offers little support for the notion that climate change will increase the likelihood of armed confrontations. A recent review of the literature concluded, "Taken together, extant studies provide mostly inconclusive insights, with contradictory or weak demonstrated effects of climate variability and change on armed conflict" (Theisen *et al.* 2013, p. 613). Another survey found "… the climate-conflict literature suffers from a lack of theoretical connections between its main driver (climate) and its possible consequence (conflict)" (Raleigh and Kniveton 2012).

Slettebak (2012) looked at whether natural disasters offer an explanation for civil wars since 1950. His analysis encompassed a range of impacts frequently associated with rising temperatures in the climate-conflict argument, notably storms, droughts, floods, landslides, wildfires, and extreme temperatures. He tests six models incorporating a host of variables and reaches a startling conclusion:

I set out to test whether natural disasters can add explanatory power to an established model of civil conflict. The results indicate that they can, but that their effect on conflict is the opposite of popular perception. To the extent that climate-related natural disasters affect the risk of conflict, they contribute to reducing it. This holds for measures of climate-related natural disasters in general as well as drought in particular (p. 174).

Another approach contends that as climate change produces more powerful and more frequent storms, floods, and other disasters, economic growth will slow and economic hardship will lead to civil conflict as individuals lack opportunities and are subject to repression by other groups, and as states lose the ability to maintain order. Bergholt and Lujala (2012) tested the climatic disaster-economic growth-conflict relationship over the period 1980–2007 covering 171 countries and more than 4,000 country-year observations. While natural disasters certainly slow economic growth, Bergholt and Lujala conclude, "climate-related natural disasters do not have any direct effect on conflict onset" (p. 148). They found no evidence that "economic shocks caused by climate-related disasters have an effect on conflict onset" (*Ibid.*).

Climate can affect economic growth in ways other than the onset of a natural disaster or storm. Koubi *et al.* (2012) tested how deviations in precipitation and temperature trends from their long-run averages relate to economic growth rates and civil conflict. Examining the 1980–2004 period, they found "climate variability … does not affect violent intrastate conflict through economic growth."

Two studies examined the long-run relationship between temperature and precipitation and violent conflict in China and Europe. Both reach conclusions that contradict the basic premise of the climate conflict argument. Zhang *et al.* (2007) determined conflict was more common during cold periods, with food scarcity being the likely reason. Tol and Wagner (2008) use climate data for Europe to replicate the Zhang work, concluding there is some evidence for the increased incidence of European conflict in cold periods, but not warm. Both studies suggest the rise of conflict in cold periods is associated with famine.

Tol and Wagner also found the relationship between temperature and conflict is declining over time. One could speculate that the introduction of modern agriculture and more responsive state structures mitigate the effect of temperature and climate over time. Famine remains a problem, but largely not in the developed world where modern agriculture provides stronger crops and food storage and management systems preserve food supplies more effectively.

To summarize the literature broadly, where climate has been a factor in war and peace, it has been cooling rather than warming that appears to have triggered wars. A warmer world is apt to be a more peaceful and socially stable world.

Energy Policy and National Security

The Obama administration proclaimed climate change to be a present and future threat to the security of the United States. Two National Security Strategies articulate the case for environmental forces creating security challenges domestically and around the world, and two successive Quadrennial Defense Reviews show the U.S. military is shifting its strategic thinking as well as resource allocations to accommodate these new threats. Together, they demonstrate the institutionalization of environmentally induced conflict as a U.S. security concern (Roadmap 2017).

According the U.S. Department of Defense, "the impacts of climate change may increase the frequency, scale, and complexity of future missions, including defense support to civil authorities, while at the same time undermining the capacity of our domestic installations to support training activities. Our actions to increase energy and water security, including investments in energy efficiency, new technologies, and renewable energy sources, will increase the resiliency of our installations and help mitigate these effects" (DoD 2014, p. iv).

Not everyone agrees with the Obama administration's fear-mongering on the alleged relationship between climate change and national security. As Kueter (2012) wrote,

> In summary, efforts to link climate change to the deterioration of U.S. national security rely on improbable scenarios, imprecise and speculative methods, and scant empirical support. Accepting the connection can lead to the dangerous expansion of U.S. security concerns, inappropriately applied resources, and diversion of attention from more effective responses to known environmental challenges. The danger of this approach is that it offers a sense of urgency which may not be warranted, given the gaps in the current state of knowledge about climate, the known flaws in the methods used to construct the scenarios on which these security scenarios are based, and confusion over the underlying causes of those security concerns (p. 5).

The historical record says global warming tends to promote social stability, as evidenced in the peer-reviewed papers discussed above. The predicted changes in temperature, sea level rise, extreme weather, and other adverse effects of climate change have failed to materialize, and the computer models that predict them have been invalidated and never were intended to be used to make forecasts. All this means U.S. military policy and strategies should not be determined by ungrounded fear of future climate change.

Real threats to U.S. security are restrictions on domestic exploration and drilling along with subsidies to renewable energies, enabling them to compete with and sometimes put out of business conventional fossil fuel producers, reducing our military's access to affordable energy. Forcing the U.S. military to utilize expensive alternative energy also reduces the funding available for personnel, weapons, and ammunition.

During the Obama administration, the U.S. Navy outfitted F/A-18 Super Hornet jet fighters to run on a mix of conventional jet fuel and biofuel from the camelina ("false flax") plant, costing $67.50 per gallon (Biello 2009). When the U.S. military is required to squander its budget on prohibitively expensive fuels, less is available for genuine needs.

A strong economy helps to ensure national security by providing the funding and public support needed to sustain military spending. Lower energy prices sustain a vibrant economy, whereas higher energy prices stifle economic output (Bezdek 2016). Cheap domestic energy production also eliminates some reasons for our government to become involved in foreign clashes in oil-producing regions. By contrast, government policies that favor expensive energy sources and impede domestic oil, natural gas, and coal production put our military and our national security at unnecessary risk.

The U.S. military is the strongest in the world because of the United States' economic strength: China and India dwarf the United States in population, and Russia dwarfs the United States in land area. The United States produces 24.5 percent of the world's gross domestic product. China is second at 15 percent (Knoema 2016). Empowered by this economic dominance, the United States spends more money on defense than all other nations in the world combined.

The 2014–15 Ukraine conflict is a reminder of what can happen when countries are dependent on expensive or foreign energy sources. European nations largely depend on Russia for the natural gas that powers much of their electricity, and natural gas and electricity prices are typically three to five times higher there than in the United States. European political leaders were restrained in responding to Russian aggression in the Ukraine because the European Union feared Russia would cut back on natural gas deliveries (Anishchuk 2014).

Thanks to the fracking revolution and prodigious energy resources, the United States can pursue its foreign policy objectives with fewer concerns about other nations limiting its access to energy—provided the government does not significantly restrict domestic production.

Policy Agenda

- Stop basing military planning and strategies on the predictions of flawed climate models.

- Support legislation repealing Obama's Executive Order 13693, which requires the Department of Defense to create a number of climate change programs and policies.

- Expand U.S. exports of coal, liquefied natural gas, and oil as a way to reduce the reliance of allies and other countries on energy imports from Russia and other bad actors in the international community.

Recommended Readings: Thomas B. Hayward, Edward S. Briggs, and Donald K. Forbes, *Climate Change, Energy Policy, and National Power* (Chicago, IL: The Heartland Institute, 2014); Commission on Energy and Geopolitics, *Oil Security 2025: US National Security Policy in an Era of Domestic Oil Abundance* (Washington, DC: Securing America's Future Energy, 2014).

5. Energy self-sufficiency is achievable.

While we should not seek energy independence, energy self-sufficiency produces many benefits and is within reach.

Some nations, thanks to natural endowments, the right civil institutions and laws, and political leadership can become energy self-sufficient by producing domestically at least as much energy as they use. Donald Trump appears to be the first U.S. president to recognize the economic power of achieving what he calls "energy dominance."

Abundant and affordable energy gives U.S. manufacturers an advantage over competitors in other countries, lowers the cost of living (especially for the poor and people in rural areas), and gives America more leverage in foreign affairs. Trump's "America First Energy Plan" is designed to achieve "energy dominance" and harvest these advantages.

Abundant Natural Resources

The United States has more combined oil, natural gas, and coal resources than any other nation and twice as much as any other nation except Russia (Behrens *et al.* 2011). However, despite recent gains in energy production made possible by the fracking revolution, the United States still depends on energy imports, primarily in the transportation sector. In 2015, foreign oil accounted for approximately 24 percent of net oil consumption in the United States (EIA 2016c).

The United States is not dependent on imported fossil fuels for electricity generation. All electricity in the United States is produced from domestic energy sources. Domestic coal and natural gas account for the majority of U.S. electricity generation. Nuclear power and hydropower are also domestically sourced. The United States has already attained energy self-sufficiency in electricity production.

The United States is well-positioned to be an exporter of natural resources for electricity production. It possesses the world's largest coal reserves, with 257 billion short tons of recoverable coal reserves from a demonstrated reserve base of 481 billion tons, enough to power the nation for 256 years based on 2014 levels of production (EIA 2016b).

Coal can be and increasingly is burned cleanly, as evidenced by dramatically declining power plant emissions during recent decades. According to the U.S. Environmental Protection Agency (EPA 2015a), emissions of the six principal pollutants tracked by EPA declined by more than 60 percent since 1980.

In 2014, the United States briefly became the world's largest producer of oil, surpassing Saudi Arabia. U.S. oil production now ranks third, behind Russia and Saudi Arabia, respectively (Carpenter 2017). As noted in Principle 3 above, hydraulic fracturing and horizontal drilling have made previously uneconomic oil and natural gas deposits accessible for extraction. The United States has approximately 78 billion barrels of technically recoverable crude oil in shale formations (EIA 2015c).

Federal lands have an estimated 635 trillion cubic feet of recoverable natural gas, but production is severely restricted by federal government policies. For example, roughly 47 percent of the natural gas reserves in five energy-rich Rocky Mountain states—Arizona, Colorado, New Mexico, Utah, and Wyoming—are off-limits to development, and 87 percent of offshore acreage is closed to oil and gas exploration and extraction (Bentsen 2016).

Nuclear and hydropower provide additional sources of electricity production, each being less expensive and more reliable than wind and solar power. Nuclear and hydropower are emissions-free sources of power, fulfilling the most frequently asserted justification for wind and solar power.

Why "Energy Independence" Is Undesirable

Energy self-sufficiency is different from what often is called "energy independence." Complete energy independence implies no energy imports at all, regardless of price differences or comparative advantages. It would require energy *isolationism* behind barriers to free trade with other countries.

Energy isolationism would slow economic growth, invite retaliation by trading partners, and raise prices. Free trade, not isolationism, is the way to enhance energy security and world peace. Although recent natural resource discoveries and technological advances allow the United States to become energy self-sufficient and even a net energy exporter, it makes economic sense for U.S. consumers to continue to purchase less-expensive oil produced in other nations when available.

Energy self-sufficiency means removing barriers to domestic oil and natural gas production and exports, enabling the United States to produce more oil and natural gas than it consumes. As a result, rising global energy prices would benefit the United States, as higher energy prices would mean more money from other nations pouring into the United States to purchase our surplus energy resources. Free trade makes that possible.

Policy Agenda

The Trump administration's America First Energy Plan offers a broad-strokes blueprint for achieving energy self-sufficiency. Some recommendations consistent with that plan include the following:

■ Rein in the Environmental Protection Agency (EPA), a rogue agency that routinely defies congressional oversight, abuses science, and imposes regulations whose costs vastly exceed their benefits.

■ Repeal global warming regulations, subsidies, and taxes aimed at reducing carbon dioxide emissions. Give the American people an annual global warming "peace dividend" worth hundreds of billions of dollars.

■ End climate profiteering by ethanol producers and wind and solar companies who have fleeced consumers and taxpayers out of billions of dollars while undermining our energy independence.

■ Lift legislative obstacles to energy production and development on public as well as private land. Don't "leave it in the ground." Tap the wealth that is under our feet.

■ Repeal the Corporate Average Fuel Economy (CAFE) program and allow consumers to choose the cars and trucks they want to own.

Recommended Readings: Donald Trump, "An America First Energy Plan," 2017, https://www.whitehouse.gov/america-first-energy; Joseph Bast, "Pro-Environment, Pro-Energy, and Pro-Jobs," The Heartland Institute, August 10, 2016; Mark Green, "Unlock US Energy Potential: Offshore Oil and Gas," The Energy Collective, 2013.

6. Air pollution is a fading challenge.

> Air quality in the United States has become so good that new regulations or tighter standards are unnecessary.

Concern over urban air pollution provides much of the impetus for the modern environmental movement. Few people realize how dramatically improved air quality is today … and a combination of environmental activists, government bureaucrats, and yellow journalists are hard at work to make sure they don't realize it, otherwise they might all lose their jobs.

America's improving air quality is one of the great success stories of the twentieth century. Rather than waste billions of dollars chasing the last molecule of a possible pollutant, we ought to allow laws already on the books to gradually improve air quality even further and welcome back to the country the manufacturers who were forced to close or outsource their jobs to China and other developing countries.

The Clean Air Success Story

Air quality is better today in all parts of the United States than at any time since measurements began. Data cited by Steven Hayward (2011), Indur Goklany (2007, 2012), and Moore and Simon (2000), much of it derived from EPA and other government sources, document a dramatic improvement in environmental protection, and consequently a reduction in possible threats to human health.

According to EPA, emissions of the six "criteria" air pollutants have fallen by more than 60 percent since 1980 even while GDP increased 147 percent, vehicle miles traveled increased 97 percent, and energy consumption increased 26 percent (EPA 2015). Lead emissions have fallen by 99 percent since 1980. Sulfur dioxide emissions fell 81 percent.

Carbon monoxide emissions fell 69 percent. Particulate matter (PM_{10}) emissions fell 58 percent. Nitrogen oxides fell 55 percent. Volatile organic compounds fell 53 percent.

The best available empirical research demonstrates current ambient levels of ozone and low levels of $PM_{2.5}$, a smaller form of particulate matter, have no adverse health effects. An important reanalysis of data from the American Cancer Society Cancer Prevention Study (CPS II) published in 2017 found no significant relationship between exposure and mortality in California or in the rest of the country (Enstrom 2017).

Similarly, Young *et al.* (2017) conducted a 12-year study of all major populations in California to determine death effects from small particle and ozone air pollution. The study looked at 2 million deaths, 37,000 exposure days, and multiple variables, including different lag times and a cloud program of data analysis that involved more than 70,000 data set ups and evaluations to assure reliability. The study concluded there was no small particle or ozone death effect in the eight most populous air basins studied in California.

A long-term government study that followed thousands of children in California found higher ozone levels were associated with a *lower* risk of developing asthma (Schwartz 2006). EPA's own technical analyses show reducing ozone levels in cities with the dirtiest air to levels necessary to meet the then-new federal eight-hour ozone standard would at best reduce respiratory-related hospital admissions and emergency room visits by only a few tenths of a percent (Hubbell *et al.* 2005).

Claims that ambient concentrations of $PM_{2.5}$ and other air pollutants cause fatalities are based on studies showing only very small statistical correlations between daily pollution levels and daily deaths. Such correlations fall well short of proving causation.

EPA's War on Science

Even though it can (and does) take credit for improving air quality in the United States, EPA has become the biggest single source of *misinformation* about air quality. Many EPA claims about the toxicity, lethality, and carcinogenicity of criteria air pollutants at ambient levels are simply false, intended mainly to advance the environmental movement's ideological campaign against fossil fuels (Chase 1995).

For example, EPA has claimed the Obama administration's Clean Power Plan will lead to climate and health benefits worth an estimated $55 billion to $93 billion in 2030, including avoiding 2,700 to 6,600 premature deaths and 140,000 to 150,000 asthma attacks in children (EPA 2015b). Then-EPA Administrator Lisa Jackson even claimed in 2011, "If we could reduce particulate matter to levels that are healthy we would have an identical impact to finding a cure for cancer" (quoted in Harris and Broun, 2011, p. 2). Cancer kills approximately 570,000 people in the U.S. annually, making this an astounding claim.

How does EPA justify its claim that air pollution is still a serious threat to human health when so much evidence points in the opposite direction? EPA relies on the "linear no-threshold assumption" that exposure to tiny amounts of substances that are toxic at higher doses produces adverse effects and even fatalities. This theory has been contradicted and rejected by many leading medical researchers (Tubiana *et al.* 2009; Calabrese 2015).

Failing to prove in toxicological studies that ambient levels of pollution pose a threat to human health, EPA relies on epidemiologic studies—studies that look for associations between exposure and health effects in large populations. But these studies, too, are very controversial (Kabat 2016). EPA has been shown to cherry-pick studies that support its point of view, sometimes overlooking scores or even hundreds of studies that have larger sample sizes and better methodologies and find no evidence of risk (Milloy 2016).

EPA combines these flawed epidemiologic studies with the equally flawed linear no-threshold assumption to claim hundreds of thousands of people die from air pollution every year, in flagrant violation of the Bradford Hill Criteria (Hill 1965) and guidelines set by the Federal Judicial Center (FJC), an education and research agency of the United States federal courts (FJC 2011).

There is no research properly evaluated that shows ambient air pollution caused by fossil fuels kills anyone, anytime in the United States. Even high levels of ambient air pollution that may be found in some areas of the world cannot be established by good toxicological studies to be acutely lethal. Air pollution death events are invariably extraordinary events caused by low-level inversions that trap very high levels of toxins, usually sulfur dioxide or heavy carbonaceous black soot—not the ambient small particulate air pollution targeted by EPA.

Policy Agenda

Air pollution is a rapidly falling health risk in the United States. Unnecessary regulations that impose huge costs on businesses and consumers pose a much bigger threat to our safety and prosperity. We recommend the following policy reforms:

■ Dramatically reduce government funding of environmental advocacy groups that use misinformation to frighten the public, including funds delivered to such groups through the "sue and settle" scam.

■ End the use of "secret science" by EPA and other regulatory agencies by requiring disclosure of databases used to justify excessive regulation.

- Formally end the use of the "linear no-threshold assumption" in determining safe levels of exposure to pollutants.

- End conflicts of interest on scientific review boards, whereby EPA grant recipients sit in judgment over their own work and block independent review.

- Delay or withdraw EPA's planned reduction in allowable ground-level ozone levels from 75 parts per billion to 70 parts per billion.

- Enforce the Data Quality Act with respect to the junk science promoted and funded by EPA on air pollution and toxicology.

Recommended Readings: Indur Goklany, *The Improving State of the World: Why We're Living Longer, Healthier, More Comfortable Lives on a Cleaner Planet* (Washington, DC: Cato Institute, 2007); Steve Milloy, *Scare Pollution: Why and How to Fix the EPA* (Washington, DC: Bench Press, 2016).

7. End subsidies to alternative energy producers.

Policymakers should end subsidies to alternative energy producers and mandates on government agencies and utilities to use alternative energy sources.

Environmental activist groups often tout alternative energy sources such as wind and solar power as capable of protecting human health, protecting the environment, and creating jobs. Perhaps someday, as entrepreneurs improve these sources of energy, they will provide such benefits. But today, subsidizing or mandating the use of alternative energy sources raises energy prices, kills jobs, and create environmental damages on par with those of the fossil fuels environmentalists say they want to replace.

Problems with Alternative Energy
Sunshine and wind may be "free," but they are not efficient sources of energy for human use. Energy and capital must be expended to create the

solar and wind "farms" needed to collect the energy, and more is then required to transport the energy to where it is needed. Consequently, the fuel and total production costs of coal, oil, and natural gas power are much lower than the costs of converting "free" wind and sunlight into usable power.

Just as importantly, coal, oil, and natural gas can be converted into usable power on demand, 24 hours a day and seven days a week, whereas wind and solar power rely on the vagaries of unpredictable breezes and clouds. This intermittency is a critical shortcoming of alternative energy since electrical grids need a constant flow of energy to operate (Clack *et al.* 2017; Dears 2015). Fossil fuels store relatively large amounts of energy in a small area, allowing them to be stored and transported safely and inexpensively. Wind and solar, in contrast, need expensive battery technology to store energy during the day and on windy days in order to provide energy at night and when the wind doesn't blow.

Another problem with alternative energy sources is the relatively small number of locations suitable for their use. Whereas conventional power plants can be built almost anywhere, wind and solar power are severely limited by geography. The wind blows most frequently and usefully along mountaintop ridges, offshore coastal regions, and the open Upper Plains—places where there are few large urban centers. Solar energy is most abundant in remote desert areas that are unattractive places for most businesses and residents. Bringing alternative power to urban population centers is expensive, inefficient, and disruptive to ecosystems between the facilities and the urban population centers.

Environmental Impacts of Alternative Energy

If environmental activists weren't so focused on the mythical threat of global warming, they would likely oppose wind and solar power due to the unacceptable environmental damages they cause. Up to 40 square miles of solar power equipment is necessary to replace a single conventional power plant (Hayden 2000). Such extensive land development can adversely affect desert habitats crucial to endangered species. Large solar projects such as the Ivanpah project in the Mojave Desert incinerate thousands of birds each year in mid-flight (Knickmeyer and Locher 2014).

Solar thermal power facilities use two to four times more water than conventional power plants (Glennon 2009), and water is already in short supply in the arid regions where solar power is most economically produced. Desert tortoises and other protected species are disproportionately harmed by new solar facilities.

Up to 600 square miles of wind turbines are required to replace a single conventional power plant, requiring extensive development of previously undisturbed lands (Hayden 2000). The most effective locations for wind power generation tend to be undisturbed landscapes and regions much loved by environmentalists as well as others: mountaintop ridges, coastal shorelines, and open plains. Those areas are often habitat or migration corridors for endangered bird species.

A 2013 peer-reviewed study found wind turbines kill 1.4 million birds and bats each year while generating just 3 percent of our nation's electricity (Smallwood 2013). Ramping up wind power production would greatly increase this death toll. Why do environmentalists, of all people, support commercial wind farms? Is it really about protecting the environment?

Renewable Power Mandates Drive up Energy Costs

Renewable power mandates (RPMs), which set aside a specified percentage of the electricity market for expensive, politically favored alternative power sources, are responsible for much of the growth in alternative energy production in the United States in recent years. These laws hide the higher cost of alternative energies in people's utility bills, making it less likely the public will object to their expense.

RPMs have caused electricity prices to increase dramatically in states that have enacted them. Data from the U.S. Energy Information Administration show nine of the 11 states utilizing the most wind power have electricity prices rising at a rate more than four times the national average (Taylor 2014b). A 2014 study by the Brookings Institution found replacing conventional power with wind power doubles the price of electricity (Frank 2014). The same study found replacing conventional power with solar power triples the price of electricity. Since 2008, electricity prices in states with RPMs have risen twice as fast as the national average (Burnett 2015).

According to a careful analysis by economist Timothy Considine (2016), RPS programs in 12 states in 2016 required expenditures of $7.5 billion and generated savings of approximately $1.7 billion, for total net costs of $5.7 billion. Considine projected annual net costs in just these 12 states to rise to $8.7 billion in 2025 and $8.9 billion in 2040. He concludes, "These findings suggest Renewable Portfolio Standards for the twelve states examined in this study are a costly and inefficient means to reduce greenhouse gas emissions and they reduce economic growth and employment" (p. 6).

Kansas enacted RPMs in 2009, and the state's electricity prices rose eight times faster than the national average between 2009 and 2013. Had electricity prices in Kansas merely risen at the national average rate during that period, the state's electricity consumers would have saved $557 million in electricity costs in 2013 alone. Between 2009 and 2013, the average Kansas household paid an extra $506 in electricity costs, or nearly $130 per household per year (Taylor 2014a). Faced with such rising electricity prices, the Kansas legislature in 2015 repealed the state's renewable power mandates, with many legislators who had previously championed the mandates leading the effort to repeal them.

Nuclear and Hydro Alternatives

Nuclear and hydroelectric power are far more economical and environmentally sound choices for persons seeking alternatives to fossil fuels. Curiously, both are opposed by environmentalists.

Nuclear power is moderately more expensive than coal, natural gas, and hydro power but significantly less expensive and more reliable than wind and solar power. Nuclear power also has an impressive environmental safety record. Contrary to popular opinion, the 2011 earthquake and tsunami at Fukushima, Japan are a testimony to how *safe* nuclear power has become.

In March 2011, the magnitude 9.0 earthquake 130 kilometers off the coast of Japan triggered a 50-foot tsunami that killed 16,000 people and resulted in severe damage to three of the six reactors at the Fukushima power plant. Safeguards typical of nuclear power plants limited the general public's exposure to radiation, prompting the United Nations Scientific Committee on the Effects of Atomic Radiation to conclude, "No discernible increased incidence of radiation-related health effects are expected among exposed members of the public or their descendants" (World Nuclear News 2014). Not a single person was killed or made seriously ill by the nuclear power plant damage.

Nuclear power plants produce no air pollution. Storage of spent nuclear fuel is the only significant environmental issue. Over the past four decades, the entire industry has produced 71,780 metric tons of used nuclear fuel, all of which has been safely stored at facilities across the nation (Nuclear Energy Institute 2014).

Permanent storage of spent fuel at Yucca Mountain, Nevada has been under consideration since the 1980s (Nuclear Energy Institute 2015) and would be safe (Cravens 2007), but the Obama administration terminated the licensing proceedings in 2010. Used nuclear fuel is currently stored in more than 100 aboveground facilities in 39 states. One centralized, underground, specially designed storage area would be inherently safer than having many inferior storage facilities near 39 population centers. Trump wants to revive the plan to use Yucca Mountain as a waste storage site.

Today's reactors utilize only 3 percent of the energy stored in uranium fuel pellets. Reprocessing spent fuel can recover up to 95 percent of the remaining energy. If the United States joined Britain, France, and Japan in recycling used fuel, existing and future spent fuel rods would provide a long-term supply of nuclear fuel while eliminating most of the used fuel that poses storage challenges.

Hydroelectric power, typically produced by dams, is less expensive than nuclear power and substantially less expensive than wind and solar (EIA 2010). Like nuclear power it produces no air pollution. Unlike nuclear power and fossil fuel plants, there are a limited number of good sites for locating dams, and most of the best locations are already being used.

The most frequently heard objection to increasing hydroelectric power is that hydroelectric dams change the natural flow of rivers and impede fish migration. However, even the largest of lakes created by hydroelectric dams pale in comparison to how wind turbines transform the landscape. The Arizona Power Authority (2012) reports the Hoover Dam has the capacity to produce more than 2,000 megawatts of energy and a yearly average generation of 4.5 billion kilowatt hours to serve the annual electrical needs of nearly eight million people in Arizona, southern California, and southern Nevada. The environmental footprint of the Hoover Dam is Lake Mead, which is 247 square miles. The lake is home to fish and other animals, is used for recreation, and itself is an environmental asset.

By comparison, up to 600 square miles of wind turbines would be needed to replace a single conventional power plant. Moreover, the transformation of a stretch of river into a lake environment brings environmental benefits as well as challenges, whereas the effect of covering hundreds of square miles of virgin landscape with wind turbines that kill birds and bats by the millions is almost entirely negative.

For these reasons, Connecticut recently joined a number of states in including large-scale hydroelectric power in its renewable power mandates (American Council on Renewable Energy 2014).

Policy Agenda

Alternatives to fossil fuels exist and successfully compete for customers without subsidies or mandates. This diversity and competition are good for consumers and should be encouraged. Current state and national policies, however, go well beyond encouragement and impose huge costs on consumers, often without their knowledge, without producing any clear benefits. We recommend the following policies:

- Repeal state Renewable Power Mandates (RPMs) where they exist and oppose their adoption in states that don't currently have them.

- End national and state tax exemptions, tax credits, and subsidies for alternative energy producers.

- Hold solar and wind power producers to the same environmental protection standards as are applied to coal and natural gas power generators.

■ Remove regulatory obstacles to the expansion of nuclear power and open the nuclear waste storage facility at Yucca Mountain.

Recommended Readings: Taylor Smith, "The Limitations on Solar Power," *Research & Commentary*, The Heartland Institute, 2014; Nuclear Energy Institute, "On-Site Storage of Nuclear Waste," 2014; Gwyneth Cravens, *Power to Save the World: The Truth about Nuclear Energy* (New York, NY: Alfred A. Knopf, 2007).

8. Biofuels cannot replace oil.

Policymakers should not subsidize or mandate the use of ethanol, biodiesel, or methanol fuels.

Biofuels are liquid or gaseous fuels—ethanol, biodiesel, and methanol—made from organic matter such as corn, switchgrass, and sugar cane. Environmentalists and some parts of the agricultural industry lobby for subsidies, tax breaks, and mandates to replace petroleum fuels with biofuels. Their case does not stand up to scrutiny.

The Ethanol Boondoggle

In 2007, Congress mandated that ethanol be blended into gasoline supplies through a program called the Renewable Fuels Standard (RFS). The program will require 15 billion gallons of ethanol to be mixed into the fuel supply during the 2018 calendar year. The Trump administration maintained the level required by the Obama administration in its last year in office, ending what had been a trend of increasing the amount each year.

Federal and state subsidies for ethanol totaled $6 billion in 2011, and an estimated $58 billion in tax credits were given to ethanol producers from 1980 through 2012 (Stevens 2016). Additionally, in 2012 biodiesel subsidies of one dollar per gallon, totaling more than $2 billion, were approved through 2013 in congressional trading for votes to pass legislation designed to avoid the "fiscal cliff."

Until 2012, Congress protected domestic ethanol producers by imposing a 2.5 percent tariff and 54 cents per gallon duty on imports.

Ethanol plants with annual production capacity of up to 60 million gallons were eligible for production incentives of 10 cents per gallon on the first 15 million gallons of ethanol produced each year. In addition to direct federal and state payments and protective tariffs, ethanol producers received a federal tax subsidy of 45 cents per gallon for blends (mixtures of gasoline and ethanol), amounting to tens of billions of dollars (Anderson 2012).

Although the subsidies and protective tariffs on ethanol expired in 2012, the industry still benefits from government intervention in the marketplace in the form of blending mandates. The Energy Independence and Security Act of 2007 mandated 15 billion gallons of corn-based ethanol and 21 billion gallons of non-corn biofuels in the nation's fuel supply by 2022.

Why Mandate Biofuels?

The ethanol industry has variously promoted its product as a means to reduce air pollution, greenhouse gas emissions, and energy costs; enhance national security (by replacing imported gasoline); and spur rural economic development. All these justifications come up short.

Studies show ethanol increases various forms of air pollutants and may have a net negative impact on air quality and carbon dioxide emissions. Using ethanol rather than gasoline reduces carbon monoxide emissions, but those are no longer a public health concern (Bryce 2016). Ethanol increases ozone production, which is still a problem in some cities at some times of the year. In addition, the lower gas mileage of ethanol means it requires greater use of fuel, thus increasing the amount of pollution in the air. Some environmental activist groups, including the Sierra Club, now oppose the use of ethanol (Cellarius 2015).

Research published in the peer-reviewed journal *Science* finds the production and use of a gallon of ethanol produces more carbon dioxide than does a gallon of gasoline (Fargione *et al.* 2008; Searchinger *et al.* 2008). A study published in the peer-reviewed journal *Nature Climate Change* found cellulosic ethanol increases carbon dioxide emissions by 7 percent over gasoline (Liska *et al.* 2014).

Algae biofuels are just as problematic as ethanol. Algae biofuels cost roughly $240 to $332 per barrel, approximately seven times the cost of oil in 2015 (Environmental News Network 2012). Algae biofuels are also environmentally destructive. A 2012 study by the National Research Council Sciences reports, "The scale-up of algal biofuel production sufficient to meet at least 5 percent of U.S. demand for transportation fuels would place unsustainable demands on energy, water, and nutrients with current technologies and knowledge" (National Research Council 2012).

Proponents of biofuels say greater production will increase the supply of transportation fuels and therefore lead to lower prices. But after initially reducing the price of gasoline by about 5 cents per gallon, a 30 percent jump in ethanol prices drove up prices at the pump by about 10 cents per gallon. Researchers at Rice University found in order to replace 2 percent of the nation's gasoline with biofuels in 2008, taxpayers spent $4 billion, the equivalent of $1.95 per gallon for biofuels replacing gasoline (Loris 2013).

If gasoline costs $1.59 before state and federal taxes are added and a gallon of ethanol costs $1.49, some consumers may think ethanol is more cost effective. However, because drivers get 33 percent fewer miles per gallon with ethanol than gasoline, their costs are actually higher, the equivalent of $1.98 per gallon compared to $1.59 per gallon for gasoline ($1.49 x 0.33= $.49. $1.49 + $.49=$1.98) (Grunwald 2008).

Even if ethanol helped to keep the price of a tank of gasoline lower than it would otherwise be, those savings are likely to be offset by an increase in the price of food caused by the RFS. Most ethanol is created from corn, which otherwise would have found its way to consumers as food. The result is a higher weekly grocery bill (Kreutzer 2012).

Biofuels are unlikely to contribute much to national security since they can replace only a trivial percentage of gasoline used in the United States and worldwide. Approximately 19.4 million barrels of oil per day are consumed in the United States (EIA 2016a). Globally, 96 million barrels of oil are consumed daily, or about 35 billion barrels per year.

When one considers there are 42 gallons in every barrel, the record-setting 14.7 billion gallons of ethanol produced in 2015 amounts to only 350 million barrels of ethanol (Urbanchuk 2016). This is the equivalent of about 18 days' worth, or approximately 5 percent, of oil-based fuel consumption in the United States, or 1 percent of annual world oil consumption.

In theory, biofuels may eventually be able to extend the life of domestic energy reserves, but we are at little risk of running out of fossil fuels, globally or in the United States, for centuries (Carroll 2006; Huber and Mills 2005). Fear of running out of cheap oil hundreds of years into the future is no reason to subsidize or mandate the use of expensive biofuels now.

Policy Agenda

In 2016, The Heritage Foundation's Nicolas Loris wrote: "Congress should not tinker around the edges with attempts to reform the RFS. Policymakers should recognize the mandate is a failure and the government has no legitimate place propping up one energy source or technology over another. Congress should eliminate the RFS entirely and empower free enterprise to drive fuel competition and choice" (Loris 2016). We can hardly improve on that recommendation.

Recommended Readings: Nicolas Loris, "Examining the Renewable Fuel Standard," The Heritage Foundation, March 17, 2016; Michael Grunwald, "The Clean Energy Scam," *Time*, March 27, 2008; David Kreutzer, "Renewable Fuel Standard, Ethanol Use, and Corn Prices," The Heritage Foundation, 2012.

9. Corporate Average Fuel Economy standards sacrifice lives for oil.

CAFE standards increase highway fatalities and are not an effective way to lower transportation fuel consumption.

Environmental activist groups call for ever-stricter Corporate Average Fuel Economy (CAFE) standards to force Americans to purchase and drive cars and trucks with better fuel economy. But there are more cost-effective ways to save fuel, and CAFE standards have a terrible unintended consequence: needless highway deaths.

Understanding CAFE

CAFE standards, created by the 1975 Energy Policy Conservation Act, require car and truck manufacturers to achieve minimum targets for the average fuel economy of their fleets, expressed in miles per gallon (mpg), based on a vehicle's size. CAFE standards currently mandate an average fuel economy of 35.5 mpg for passenger cars and 28.4 mpg for light trucks.

The Obama administration set mileage requirements at 54.5 mpg by 2025, nearly double the 27.5 mpg required in 2011. However, in early 2017 Trump announced EPA would reconsider that target with an eye to reducing it. There are currently no known technologies to meet the 2025 requirement, other than forcing American consumers to purchase more expensive electric or hybrid vehicles.

What CAFE Doesn't Achieve

The idea that consumers can be made better off by restricting their freedom of choice—the presumption that lies at the bottom of CAFE standards—is false. Consumers are better positioned than regulators to choose the size, fuel economy, and other features of the cars and trucks they buy to meet their safety and pocketbook needs. Fuel economy information is plainly posted on the price stickers of new cars, and the price of gasoline is advertised at gas stations.

Even EPA admitted in 2009 that CAFE standards don't benefit consumers, estimating their cost equals whatever benefits they could produce (Hennessy 2009). The National Auto Dealers Association calculated the new CAFE standards would increase the cost of the Chevy Aveo, the least-expensive car studied, by 24 percent, from $12,700 to $15,700. The average price for a new car would increase by $3,000, pricing an estimated 6.8 million would-be car owners out of the market for new vehicles. Under the new mandate, the Energy Information Administration warns, new cars under $15,000 may simply be no longer available in the United States (Wagner *et al.* 2012).

Estimates of lifetime fuel savings, which are used to justify higher sticker prices, are based on strikingly pessimistic projections of future gasoline prices and the unrealistic assumption that most vehicle owners will keep their vehicle for 30 years (for cars) and 37 years (for light-duty trucks). The claims of consumer benefits from higher CAFE standards rest on implausible assumptions.

Another thing CAFE standards don't do is reduce reliance on foreign sources of oil. In fact, CAFE standards could do just the opposite. Reduced demand for gasoline caused by higher CAFE standards would cause gasoline prices in the United States to be lower than they would be otherwise. Lower gasoline prices, in turn, increase our reliance on imported oil, measured as a percentage of total oil consumption, because domestically produced oil is more expensive than imported oil.

Although the Obama administration claimed global warming concerns were a significant factor in its adoption of the new CAFE standards, it is unlikely any greenhouse gas reductions realized by more-stringent CAFE standards would have a significant impact on the climate. Car and light truck emissions in the United States account for only 1.5 percent of all human-caused greenhouse gas emissions, a fraction that will become even smaller as emissions from developing countries rise.

Higher CAFE standards could actually increase emissions of pollutants and greenhouse gases by encouraging more driving (called the "rebound effect"). CAFE standards discourage ride-sharing and divert investment and innovation from genuine breakthrough technologies into compliance with regulations that have little to do with real-world environmental effects (Kleit 2002).

Trading Lives for Oil

One thing CAFE standards do achieve is unintended: more highway fatalities. The best way to achieve better fuel economy is to build lighter cars made of aluminum instead of steel. Lighter cars do not protect passengers nearly as well as heavier vehicles during traffic accidents.

An analysis by the Brookings Institution found a 500-pound

reduction in weight of the average car increased highway fatalities by 2,200 to 3,900 and serious injuries by 11,000 to 19,500 per year (Murdock 2012). A *USA Today* investigation estimated 7,700 deaths occurred for every mile-per-gallon increase in average fuel economy (*Ibid.*).

The National Academy of Sciences reports CAFE standards have caused an average of between 1,300 and 2,600 additional traffic deaths per year since they were established in 1975 (National Academy of Sciences 2001). A study by the National Highway Transportation and Safety Administration (NHTSA) calculated higher CAFE standards resulted in additional traffic deaths of 13,608 people in light cars, 10,884 people in heavier cars, and 14,705 people in light trucks between 1996 and 1999 (Murphy 2011).

Anti-war activists, many of them also environmental activists, sometimes accused the Bush administrations of "trading lives for oil" by deploying troops in the Middle East. CAFE standards, in an attempt to save a little oil, kill far more Americans each year than were dying in Iraq and Afghanistan.

Policy Agenda
The Corporate Average Fuel Economy (CAFE) program, like the Renewable Fuels Standard (RFS) addressed in the previous principle in this chapter, is a poorly designed and executed national program that serves no public purpose. Rather than allow regulators to tell consumers what their next car or truck should look like, Congress and the president should repeal the program entirely.

Recommended Readings: Tim Benson *et al.*, "Heartland Institute Experts React to New EPA Fuel Standards," The Heartland Institute, January 13, 2017; Robert P. Murphy, "Will Fuel Economy Mandates Increase Car Company Profits?" Institute for Energy Research, 2011.

10. Replace the Environmental Protection Agency.

State environmental protection agencies working together in a Committee of the Whole can more effectively address environment concerns than the federal government.

The U.S. Environmental Protection Agency (EPA) was created in December 1970 by an executive order issued by then-President Richard Nixon. Today, EPA regulations imposed on the U.S. economy are estimated to cost more than $330 billion every year (Crain 2014). A recent analysis from the Mercatus Center at George Mason University estimates there are at least 88,852 environmental regulations on the books, and depending on court interpretations, that figure could go as high as 154,350 (Young 2012).

EPA was originally designed to handle problems associated with major sources of pollution, such as billowing smokestacks, polluted water, and toxic waste sites. Since then, EPA has become less about advancing environmental protections based on sound science and more about promoting increasingly burdensome regulations on job creators and individuals.

Unintended EPA

EPA was originally put in charge of enforcing laws passed by Congress, such as the Clean Air Act and Clean Water Act. But as executive branch power has grown relative to congressional power, presidents have increasingly used EPA to enforce their agendas without congressional approval, in ways that would have shocked even the most vocal environmentalists in the 1970s.

For example, after President Barack Obama was unable to enact cap-and-trade legislation to combat the alleged global warming problem, despite having filibuster-proof Democratic majorities in both houses of Congress, he famously claimed, "Cap and trade was just one way of skinning the cat; it was not the only way." He then used federal agencies, especially EPA, to impose costly regulations and restrictions on U.S. consumers and businesses.

The Obama administration's Clean Power Plan to reduce carbon dioxide emissions by 30 percent by 2030, now on hold due to legal challenges and the Trump administration's pledge to withdraw it, would have cost between $8.4 billion and $50 billion per year, and hundreds of thousands of people would have lost their jobs because of it (Federal

Register 2015). According to EPA's own climate models, the regulations would have provided no significant climate benefits (Michaels 2015).

Bad Explanations for Expensive Regulations

As explained in Principle 6 on air quality, EPA has a long and sordid tradition of misusing science to justify unnecessary regulation. EPA defended the Obama administration's war on fossil fuels even when the science made it clear there were no health benefits. EPA administrators have exaggerated the public health threats of air pollution, pesticides, and "global warming" even as the scientific community has increasingly reached consensus that these are not legitimate threats after all.

EPA relies on the linear no-threshold assumption because it lends legitimacy to regulations that are popular with advocacy groups and politicians. The agency uses flawed epidemiologic studies whenever they can be portrayed as supporting its agenda.

Before it may implement a proposed rule, EPA must show the societal benefits of the rule will outweigh its costs. The process of creating this cost-benefit analysis, formally known as Regulatory Impact Analysis (RIA), is regulated by various statutes, executive orders, and Office of Management and Budget (OMB) guidance requirements designed to ensure the quality of the findings. RIAs are designed to provide affected entities, agencies, Congress, and the public with important information about the potential effects of new regulations (GAO 2014).

A recent investigation into EPA cost-benefit analyses shows the agency has routinely failed to follow OMB rules. The Government Accountability Office (GAO) reports EPA's cost-benefit analyses are of questionable value for creating policy and EPA did not "adhere to guidance requiring it to communicate information supporting regulatory decisions and enable a third party to understand how the agency arrives at its conclusions" (GAO 2014). Without complete and accurate RIAs, it is impossible to determine whether the cost-benefit conclusions drawn by EPA are valid.

A prime example of EPA data manipulation is the agency's analysis of the so-called "social cost of carbon" (SCC), where regulators used one set of assumptions to calculate the benefits of regulating carbon and a different set of assumptions to calculate the costs, resulting in numbers supporting EPA's intent to regulate carbon dioxide emissions (GAO 2014). GAO's findings support other studies that have concluded SCC estimates are so unstable in response to changes in assumptions as to make the SCC calculation entirely unsuitable for regulatory policy (Dayaratna and Kreutzer 2014). On March 28, 2017, Trump issued an executive order prohibiting the use of Obama's SCC calculations in rulemaking (White House 2017).

EPA ignores regulatory best practices in order to justify its attempts to concentrate more power within the agency and implement economically damaging regulations not supported by sound science. The good news is the nation's environmental problems have largely been solved in the years since EPA's formation. Further, Trump is in the process of addressing the practices that make EPA a greater threat to public health than is the pollution the agency allegedly is fighting.

Policy Agenda

Past efforts to reform EPA have failed because the incentives for the agency to pursue an impossible "zero risk" goal are simply too strong. A huge and permanent bureaucracy is largely ideologically committed to that goal and resists efforts by Congress and even presidents to change.

Rather than reform EPA, we recommend *replacing it* with a "committee of the whole" representing environmental agencies of the 50 states tasked with a limited agenda of fostering cooperation among the states and resolving interstate disputes. A plan to do this was worked out by Jay Lehr, a distinguished scientist who helped write the Clean Air Act and Clean Water Act (Lehr 2014). It's an ambitious plan, to be sure, but we fear nothing less will work to rein in EPA.

Recommended Readings: Jay Lehr, *Replacing the Environmental Protection Agency*, The Heartland Institute, 2014; Government Accountability Office, *Environmental Regulation: EPA Should Improve Adherence to Guidance for Selected Elements of Regulatory Impact Analysis* (Washington, DC: U.S. Government Accountability Office, 2014).

References

American Council on Renewable Energy. 2014. "Renewable Energy in Connecticut." *Renewable Energy in the 50 States*. June.

Anderson, Soren T. 2012. "The Demand for Ethanol as a Gasoline Substitute." *Journal Environmental Economics and Management* **63** (2): 151–68. doi:10.1016/j.jeem.2011.08.002.

Anishchuk, Alexei. 2014. "Russia Warns Europe of Gas Supply Cuts Over Ukraine Debt." *Reuters*. April 10.

Arizona Power Authority. 2012. "Hoover Dam (website)." Accessed August 21, 2017.

Bartik, Alexander W. *et al.* 2016. "The Local Economic and Welfare Consequences of Hydraulic Fracturing." National Bureau of Economic Research. December 22.

Bast, Joseph. 2010. "Analysis: New International Survey of Climate Scientists." The Heartland Institute.

———. 2016. "Pro-Environment, Pro-Energy, and Pro-Jobs." *Policy Tip Sheet*. The Heartland Institute. August 10.

Bast, Joseph, and Roy Spencer. 2014. "The Myth of the Climate Change '97%'." *The Wall Street Journal*. May 26.

Behrens, Carl E., Michael Ratner, and Carol Glover. 2011. *U.S. Fossil Fuel Resources: Terminology, Reporting, and Summary*. Washington, DC: Congressional Research Service.

Benson, Tim. 2017a. "Peer-Reviewed Study Says Hydraulic Fracturing Not Responsible for Groundwater Contamination in West Virginia." *Research & Commentary*. The Heartland Institute. May 15.

———. 2017b. "Thanks to Mitigation Measures, Induced Seismicity Risks Dropping Quickly." *Research & Commentary*. The Heartland Institute. April 5. https://www.heartland.org/publications-resources/publications/research--commentary-thanks-to-mitigation-measures-induced-seismicity-risks-dropping-quickly.

Benson, Tim, *et al*. 2017. "Heartland Institute Experts React to New EPA Fuel Standards." The Heartland Institute. January 13.

Bentsen, Lloyd. 2016. "Available and Off-Limits Offshore U.S. Oil and Natural Gas Resources." National Center for Policy Analysis. March 30.

Bergholt, D., and P. Lujala. 2012. "Climate-Related Natural Disasters, Economic Growth and Armed Conflict." *Journal of Peace Research* **49** (1): 147–62.

Bezdek, Roger. 2016. "Essential Role of Fossil Fuels in Future Economic Growth." *Public Utilities Fortnightly*. September.

Biello, David. 2009. "Navy Green: Military Investigates Biofuels to Power Its Ships and Planes." *Scientific American*. September 14.

Bray, Dennis, and Hans von Storch. 2016. *The Bray and von Storch 5th International Survey of Climate Scientists 2015/2016*.

Bryce, Robert. 2016. "Cheating VW's Are Cleaner Than Ethanol." *Bloomberg*. January 20.

Bureau of Land Management. 2014. "Table 3. Total Number of Acres Under Lease As of the Last Day of the Fiscal Year (website)." Accessed August 21, 2017.

Burnett, H. Sterling. 2015. "Pulling the Plug on Renewable Energy." *Freedom Pub* (blog). April 1.

Calabrese, E.J. 2015. "On The Origins Of The Linear No-Threshold (LNT) Dogma By Means Of Untruths, Artful Dodges And Blind Faith." *Environmental Research* **142** (October): 432–42.

Carpenter, Claudia. 2017. "Russia Overtakes Saudi Arabia as World's Top Crude Oil Producer." February 20.

Carroll, Joe. 2006. "Global Oil Output Won't Peak Until 2030, Yergin Says." *Bloomberg*.

Cellarius, Doris. 2015. "Sierra Club Guidance on Biofuels." Sierra Club Grassroots Network.

Chase, Alston. 1995. *In a Dark Wood: The Fight Over Forests and the Rising Tyranny of Ecology*. Boston, MA: Houghton Mifflin Company.

Christy, John. 2016. Testimony to U.S. House Committee on Science, Space & Technology. February.

Clack, Christopher T.M., *et al.* 2017. "Evaluation Of A Proposal For Reliable Low-Cost Grid Power With 100% Wind, Water, And Solar." *PNAS* **114** (26).

Commission on Energy and Geopolitics. 2014. *Oil Security 2025: US National Security Policy in an Era of Domestic Oil Abundance*. Washington, DC: Securing America's Future Energy.

Considine, Timothy J. 2016. "Evaluating the Costs and Benefits of Renewable Portfolio Standards." National Resource Economics, Inc.

COGCC (Colorado Oil and Gas Conservation Commission). n.d. *COGCC Gasland Correction Document*. Accessed August 21, 2017.

Crain, Mark. 2014. "The Cost of Federal Regulation to the U.S. Economy, Manufacturing and Small Business." National Association of Manufacturers. September 10.

Cravens, Gwyneth. 2007. *Power to Save the World: The Truth about Nuclear Energy*. New York, NY: Alfred A. Knopf.

CSIRO Australia. 2013. "Deserts 'Greening' from Rising Carbon Dioxide: Global Foliage Boosted across the World's Arid Regions." *Science Daily*.

Dayaratna, Kevin D., and David W. Kreutzer. 2014. "Unfounded FUND Yet Another EPA Model Not Ready for the Big Game." The Heritage Foundation.

Dears, Donn. 2015. *Nothing to Fear: A Bright Future for Fossil Fuels*. The Villages, FL: Critical Thinking Press.

————. 2017. *Clexit for a Brighter Future: The Case for Withdrawing from United Nations' Climate Treaties*. The Villages, FL: Critical Thinking Press.

DoD (Department of Defense). 2013. *Fiscal Year 2012 Operational Energy Annual Report*. Washington, DC: U.S. Department of Defense.

Driessen, Paul. 2003. *Eco-imperialism: Green Power, Black Death*. Bellevue, WA: Merril Press.

————. 2014. *Quadrennial Defense Review*. March 4.

EIA (U.S. Energy Information Administration). n.d. "How Much Carbon Dioxide Is Produced Per Kilowatt Hour When Generating Electricity With Fossil Fuels? (website)." Accessed July 12, 2017.

————. 2010. "Levelized Cost of New Generation Resources in the Annual Energy Outlook (website)." Accessed July 12, 2017.

————. 2015a. "U.S. Energy-Related Carbon Dioxide Emissions, 2014 (website)." Accessed July 12, 2017.

————. 2015b. "International Energy Statistics (website)." Accessed August 21, 2017.

————. 2015c. "World Shale Resource Assessments (website)." Accessed July 12, 2017.

————. 2015d. "U.S. Field Production of Crude Oil (website)." Accessed August 21, 2017.

———.2016a. "How Much Oil Is Consumed in the United States? (website)." March 17. Accessed July 12, 2017.

———.2016b. "How Much Coal Is Left? (website)." June 17. Accessed July 12, 2017.

———.2016c. "How Much Oil Consumed by the United States Comes from Foreign Countries? (website)." October 13. Accessed July 12, 2017.

———. 2017. "Petroleum & Other Liquids Data (website)." Accessed February 27, 2017.

Enstrom, James. 2017. "Fine Particulate Matter and Total Mortality in Cancer Prevention Study Cohort Reanalysis." *Dose-Response: An International Journal* **15** (1): 1–12. doi: 10.1177/1559325817693345.

Environmental News Network. 2012. "Why Are We Not Drowning in Algae Biofuel?" *Oil Price.*

EPA (Environmental Protection Agency). 2015b. "Fact Sheet: Clean Power Plan Overview, Cutting Carbon Pollution From Power Plants (website)." Accessed October 30, 2015.

———. 2015a. "Air Quality Trends (website)." Accessed November 23, 2016.

———. 2016a. "Hydraulic Fracturing for Oil and Gas: Impacts from the Hydraulic Fracturing Water Cycle on Drinking Water Resources in the United States (Final Report)."

———. 2016b. "National Air Quality: Status and Trends of Key Air Pollutants (website)." Accessed July 12, 2017.

Epstein, Alex. 2014. *The Moral Case for Fossil Fuels.* New York, NY: Penguin Publishing Group.

Fargione, Joseph, Jason Hill, David Tilman, Stephen Polasky, and Peter Hawthorne. 2008. "Land Clearing and the Biofuel Carbon Debt." *Science* **319** (5867): 1235–8. doi:10.1126/science.1152747.

FJC (Federal Judicial Center. 2011. *Reference Manual on Scientific Evidence. Third Edition.* Federal Judicial Center and National Research Council of the National Academies. Washington, DC: National Academies Press.

Federal Register. 2015. "Carbon Pollution Emission Guidelines for Existing Stationary Sources: Electric Utility Generating Units." October 23.

Frank, Charles. 2014. "Why the Best Path to a Low-Carbon Future is Not Wind or Solar Power." Brookings Institution. May 20.

GAO (Government Accountability Office). 2014. *Environmental Regulation: EPA Should Improve Adherence to Guidance for Selected Elements of Regulatory Impact Analysis.* Washington, DC: U.S. Government Accountability Office.

Gilje, Erik, Robert Ready, and Nikolai Roussanov. 2016. "Fracking, Drilling, And Asset Pricing: Estimating The Economic Benefits Of The Shale Revolution." *Working Paper* 22914. National Bureau of Economic Research. December.

Glennon, Robert. 2009. "The Unintended Consequences of Solar Power." *Washington Post.* June 7.

Global Warming Petition Project. n.d. Website accessed July 17, 2017.

Goklany, Indur M. 2012. "Humanity Unbound: How Fossil Fuels Saved Humanity From Nature And Nature From Humanity." *Cato Policy Analysis* #715. Cato Institute.

Goklany, Indur M. 2007. *The Improving State of the World: Why We're Living Longer, Healthier, More Comfortable Lives on a Cleaner Planet.* Washington, DC: Cato Institute.

Green, Kesten and J. Scott Armstrong. 2007. "Global Warming: Forecasts By Scientists Versus Scientific Forecasts." *Energy and Environment* **18**: 997–1021.

Green, Mark. 2013. "Unlock US Energy Potential: Offshore Oil and Gas." *The Energy Collective* (website). Accessed August 21, 2017.

Grunwald, Michael. 2008. "The Clean Energy Scam." *Time.* March 27.

Hao, Z., *et al.* 2014. "Global Integrated Drought Monitoring And Prediction System." *Scientific Data* **1**:140001. doi: 10.1038/sdata.2014.1.

Harkness, Jennifer S., *et al.* 2017. "The Geochemistry Of Naturally Occurring Methane And Saline Groundwater In An Area Of Unconventional Shale Gas Development." *Geochimica et Cosmochimica Acta* **208** (1): 302–34.

Harris, Andy, and Paul Broun. 2011. "Letter to The Honorable Cass R. Sunstein." U.S. House of Representatives Committee on Science, Space, and Technology. November 15.

Harrison Jr., David, Albert L. Nichols, James Johndrow, Mark LeBel, and Bernard Reddy. 2008. *Evaluation of NHTSA's Benefit-Cost Analysis of 2011-2015 CAFE Standards.* New York, NY: NERA Economic Consulting.

Hartnett White, Kathleen, and Stephen Moore. 2016. *Fueling Freedom: Exposing the Mad War on Energy.* New York, NY: Regnery Publishing.

Hayden, Howard. 2000. "Wind Turbines & Power Density." *The Energy Advocate* (website). Accessed August 21, 2017.

Hayward, S. 2011. *Almanac of Environmental Trends.* San Francisco, CA: Pacific Institute for Public Policy Research.

Hayward, Thomas B., Edward S. Briggs, and Donald K. Forbes. 2014. *Climate Change, Energy Policy, and National Power.* Chicago, IL: The Heartland Institute.

Hennessy, Keith. 2009. "Understanding the President's CAFE Announcement." May 19.

Henry, Devin. 2017. "Maryland Governor Signs Fracking Ban into Law." *The Hill.* April 4.

Hill, A.B. 1965. "The Environment and Disease: Association or Causation?" *Proceedings of the Royal Society of Medicine* **58** (5): 295–300.

Hinderaker, John. 2015. "Global Warming: A $1.5 Trillion Industry." *Powerline* (website). August 9.

Hubbell, Bryan J., Aaron Hallberg, Donald R. McCubbin, and Ellen Post. 2005. "Health-Related Benefits of Attaining the 8-Hr Ozone Standard." *Environmental Health Perspectives* **113** (1): 73–82. doi:10.1289/ehp.7186.

Huber, Peter W., and Mark P. Mills. 2005. *The Bottomless Well.* New York, NY: Basic Books.

Humphries, Marc. 2014. *U.S. Crude Oil and Natural Gas Production in Federal and Non-Federal Areas.* Washington, DC: Congressional Research Service. April 10.

IAC (InterAcademy Council). 2010. *Climate Change Assessments: Review of the Processes & Procedures of IPCC*. Committee to Review the Intergovernmental Panel on Climate Change. October.

Idso, Craig D., Robert M. Carter, and S. Fred Singer. 2009. *Climate Change Reconsidered: Report of the Nongovernmental International Panel on Climate Change NIPCC)*. Chicago, IL: The Heartland Institute.

———. 2011. *Climate Change Reconsidered: 2011 Interim Report*. Chicago, IL: The Heartland Institute.

———. 2013. *Climate Change Reconsidered II: Physical Science*. Chicago, IL: The Heartland Institute.

———. 2016. *Why Scientists Disagree About Global Warming: The NIPCC Report on Scientific Consensus* second edition. Arlington Heights, IL: The Heartland Institute.

Idso, Craig D., Sherwood B. Idso, Robert M. Carter, and S. Fred Singer. 2014. *Climate Change Reconsidered II: Biological Impacts*. Chicago, IL: The Heartland Institute.

IPCC (Intergovernmental Panel on Climate Change). 1990. "Observed Climate Variations and Change." In *Climate Change: The IPCC Scientific Assessment*. Cambridge, United Kingdom: Cambridge University Press.

———. 2007. "Projections of Future Changes in Climate." In *Working Group I Report The Physical Science Basis*. Cambridge, United Kingdom: Cambridge University Press..

Kabat, Geoffrey C. 2016. *Getting Risk Right: Understanding the Science of Elusive Health Risks*. New York, NY: Columbia University Press.

King, Jeffrey C., Jamie Lavergne Bryan, and Meredith Clark. 2012. "Factual Causation: The Missing Link in Hydraulic Fracture—Groundwater Contamination Litigation." *Duke Environmental Law & Policy Forum* **22** (Spring): 341–60.

Kleit, Andrew N. 2002. "CAFE Changes, by the Numbers." *Regulation*. Fall.

Knickmeyer, Ellen, and John Locher. 2014. "Emerging Solar Plants Scorch Birds in Mid-Air." Associated Press.

Knoema. 2016. "World GDP Ranking 2016 | Data and Charts | Forecast (website)." Accessed July 12, 2017.

Koubi, V., T. Bernauer, A. Kalbhenn, and G. Spilker. 2012. "Climate Variability, Economic Growth, and Civil Conflict." *Journal of Peace Research* **49** (1): 113–27.

Kreutzer, David. 2012. "Renewable Fuel Standard, Ethanol Use, and Corn Prices." *Backgrounder*. The Heritage Foundation. September 17.

Kreutzer, David, Nicolas D. Loris, Katie Tubb, and Kevin Dayaratna. 2016. "The State of Climate Science: No Justification for Extreme Policies." *Backgrounder*. The Heritage Foundation. April 26.

Kueter, Jeff. 2012. *Climate and National Security: Exploring the Connection*. George C. Marshall Institute.

Lehr, Jay. 2014. *Replacing the Environmental Protection Agency*. Chicago, IL: The Heartland Institute.

Liska, Adam J., Haishun Yang, Maribeth Milner, Steve Goddard, Humberto Blanco-Canqui, Matthew P. Pelton, Xiao X. Fang, Haitao Zhu, and Andrew E. Suyker. 2014. "Biofuels from Crop Residue Can Reduce Soil Carbon and Increase CO_2 Emissions." *Nature Climate Change* **4**: 398–401. doi:10.1038/nclimate2187.

Loris, Nicolas. 2013. "The Ethanol Mandate: Don't Mend It, End It." The Heritage Foundation.

———. 2016. "Examining the Renewable Fuel Standard." The Heritage Foundation. March 17.

Michaels, Patrick. 2013. "Reduce U.S. Carbon Dioxide Emissions To Zero, And the Temperature Decrease By 2100 Will Be Undetectable." *Forbes* (website).

———. 2015. "Spin Cycle: EPA's Clean Power Plan." *Cato at Liberty* (blog). August 5.

Michaels, Patrick, and Chip Knappenberger. 2013. "We Calculate, You Decide: A Handy-Dandy Carbon Tax Temperature Savings Calculator." *Cato at Liberty* (blog). July 23.

Milloy, Steve. 2016. *Scare Pollution: Why and How to Fix the EPA.* Washington, DC: Bench Press.

Monckton, C., W. W.-H Soon, D.R. Legates, and W.M. Briggs. 2015. "Keeping It Simple: The Value Of An Irreducibly Simple Climate Model." *Science Bulletin* **60** (15): 1378–90.

Moore, S. and J. Simon. 2000. *It's Getting Better All the Time: 100 Greatest Trends of the Last 100 Years.* Washington, DC: Cato Institute.

Murdock, Deroy. 2012. "CAFE Standards Kill." *National Review Online.* April 26.

Murphy, Robert P. 2011. "Will Fuel Economy Mandates Increase Car Company Profits?" Institute for Energy Research.

National Academy of Sciences. 2001. *Report of the National Academy of Sciences on the Effectiveness and Impact of Corporate Average Fuel Economy (CAFE) Standards.* August 2.

National Research Council. 2012. *Sustainable Development of Algal Biofuels in the United States.* Washington, DC: The National Academies Press. doi:10.17226/13437.

Nuclear Energy Institute. 2014. "On-Site Storage of Nuclear Waste (website)." Accessed August 21, 2017.

———. 2015. "Top 10 Facts About Yucca Mountain (website)." Accessed August 21, 2017.

Obama, Barack. 2008. Interview with the Editorial Board of the *San Francisco Chronicle* (video). January 17. Accessed August 21, 2017.

Orr, Isaac. 2013. "Hydraulic Fracturing a Game-Changer for U.S. Energy and Economies." *Policy Study.* The Heartland Institute. November.

———. 2016. "Bill McKibben's Terrifying Disregard for Fracking Facts." *Policy Brief.* The Heartland Institute. August 19.

Pielke Jr., Roger. 2014. *The Rightful Place of Science: Disasters and Climate Change.* Tempe, AZ: Arizona State University Consortium for Science Policy and Outcomes.

Raleigh, C., and D. Kniveton. 2012. "Come Rain or Shine: An Analysis of Conflict and Climate Variability in East Africa." *Journal of Peace Research* **49** (1): 51–64.

Roadmap. 2017. "National Defense." *Roadmap for the 21st Century.* National Tax-Limitation Committee and The Heartland Institute. February.

Remote Sensing Systems. 2015. "Global and Regional Time Series (website)." Accessed August 21, 2017.

Schwartz, Joel. 2006. "Health Risks of Ozone Are Exaggerated." *Environment & Climate News*. April.

Searchinger, Timothy, Ralph Heimlich, R.A. Houghton, Fengxia Dong, Amani Elobeid, Jacinto Fabiosa, Simla Tokgoz, Dermot Hayes, and Tun-Hsiang Yu. 2008. "Use of U.S. Croplands for Biofuels Increases Greenhouse Gases Through Emissions from Land-Use Change." *Science* **319** (5867): 1238–40. doi:10.1126/science.1151861.

Slettebak, R. 2012. "Don't Blame the Weather! Climate-Related Natural Disasters and Civil Conflict." *Journal of Peace Research* **49** (1): 163–76.

Smallwood, K. Shawn. 2013. "Comparing Bird and Bat Fatality-Rate Estimates among North American Wind-Energy Projects." *Wildlife Society Bulletin* **37** (1): 19–33. doi:10.1002/wsb.260.

Smith, Taylor. 2014a. "The Limitations on Solar Power." *Research & Commentary*. The Heartland Institute.

———. "Hydraulic Fracturing." *Policy Tip Sheet*. The Heartland Institute. January 13.

Spencer, Roy W. 2010. *The Great Global Warming Blunder: How Mother Nature Fooled the World's Top Climate Scientists*. New York, NY: Encounter Books.

Spiegel. 2013. "How Electricity Became a Luxury Good." September 7.

Stevens, Landon. 2016. *Ethanol and Renewable Fuel Standard*. Institute of Political Economy at Utah State University. February.

Taylor, James. 2012. "Shock Poll: Meteorologists Are Global Warming Skeptics." *Forbes* (website).

———. 2013a. "Fortified By Global Warming, Crop Production Keeps Breaking Records." *Forbes* (website).

———. 2013b. "Thank Global Warming for Softening the Blow of Hurricane Sandy." *Forbes* (website).

———. 2014a. "Kansas Renewable Power Mandates Causing Skyrocketing Electricity Prices." *Environment & Climate News*. January 24.

———. 2014b. "Wind Industry Study: Electricity Prices Skyrocketing In Largest Wind Power States." *Forbes* (website)..

———. 2014c. "Ethanol from Corn Residue Increases CO2 Emissions." *Environment & Climate News*. May.

Theisen, O.M., N.P. Gleditsch, and H. Buhaug. 2013. "Is Climate Change a Driver of Armed Conflict?" *Climatic Change* **117**: 613–25.

Tol, R., and S. Wagner. 2010. "Climate Change and Violent Conflict in Europe Over the Last Millennium." *Climatic Change* **99** (1–2): 65–79.

Trump, Donald. 2017. "An America First Energy Plan (website)." Accessed August 21, 2017.

Tubiana, Maurice, *et al*. 2009. "The Linear No-Threshold Relationship Is Inconsistent with Radiation Biologic and Experimental Data." *Radiology* **251** (1): 13–22.

Urbanchuk, John. 2016. "Contribution of the Ethanol Industry to the Economy of the United States in 2015." Renewable Fuels Association. February 5.

United States Chamber of Commerce. 2016. "What If Hydraulic Fracturing Was Banned?" Institute for 21st Century Energy. November 4.

Wagner, David, Paulina Nusinovich, and Esteban Plaza-Jennings. 2012. *The Effect of Proposed MY 2017–2025 Corporate Average Fuel Economy (CAFE) Standards on the New Vehicle Market Population.* Tysons, VA: National Automobile Dealers Association.

Ware, Doug. 2016. "Obama Bans Offshore Drilling in 115M More Acres in Atlantic, Arctic." United Press International. December 21.

White House. 2017. "Presidential Executive Order on Promoting Energy Independence and Economic Growth." March 28.

World Nuclear News. 2014. "UN Reports on Fukushima Radiation." April 2.

Young, Ryan. 2012. "Regulatory Report Card: Environmental Protection Agency." Competitive Enterprise Institute. December 19.

Young, S., R. Smith, and K. Lopiano. 2017. "Air Quality and Acute Deaths in California, 2000–2012." *Regulatory Toxicology and Pharmacology* **88**: 173–84.

Zhang, D., P. Brecke, H. Lee, Y.-Q. He, and J. Zhang. 2007. "Global Climate Change, War, and Population Decline in Recent Human History." *PNAS* **104** (49): 19214–19.

Zycher, Benjamin, 2014. "Five questions for Mr. Tom Steyer." *National Review* (website). April 22. Accessed August 21, 2017.

Additional Resources

Additional information about energy and environment issues is available from The Heartland Institute:

- PolicyBot, The Heartland Institute's free online clearinghouse for the work of other free-market think tanks, contains thousands of documents on environment and climate issues. It is on Heartland's website at https://www.heartland.org/policybot/.

- https://www.heartland.org/Center-Climate-Environment is the website of the Arthur B. Robinson Center on Climate and Environmental Policy, devoted to the latest research, news, and commentary about environment and climate issues. Read headlines, watch videos, or browse the thousands of documents on energy and environment issues available from *PolicyBot*.

- *Environment & Climate News* is The Heartland Institute's monthly newspaper devoted to this topic. Subscriptions with digital delivery are free, print subscriptions are $36/year for 10 issues.

■ http://climateconferences.heartland.org/ is the home page for The Heartland Institute's International Conferences on Climate Change, 12 of which have been held since March 2008. Video of hundreds of presentations on the causes, consequences, and economics of climate change are available here.

■ http://climatechangereconsidered.org/ is the home page for the series of *Climate Change Reconsidered* books published by the Nongovernmental International Panel on Climate Change (NIPCC). The entire text of all volumes is available here for free download.

Directory

The following organizations produce reliable information on energy and environment topics.

1000Frolley, https://www.youtube.com/user/1000frolly

Bishop Hill, http://www.bishop-hill.net/

Biweekly Updates from the Cooler Heads Coalition, http://www.globalwarming.org/category/blog/

C3 Headlines, http://www.c3headlines.com/

Center for Energy and Environment, Competitive Enterprise Institute, http://cei.org/issues/energy-and-environment

Climate Audit, https://climateaudit.org/

Climate Policy, The Heritage Foundation, http://www.heritage.org/issues/energy-and-environment

Climate Depot by Marc Morano, http://www.climatedepot.com/

Climate Etc., https://judithcurry.com/

Climate in Review, by C. Jeffery Small, http://go-galt.org/climategate.html

Climate Exam, http://www.climatexam.com/

CO2 Coalition, co2coalition.org

CO2 Science, http://www.co2science.org/

Committee for a Constructive Tomorrow, http://www.cfact.org

Cooler Heads Digest, http://www.globalwarming.org/2012/01/22/cooler-heads-digest

Cornwall Alliance for the Stewardship of Creation, http://www.cornwallalliance.org/

Dr. Roy Spencer, http://www.drroyspencer.com/

Gelbspan Files, http://www.gelbspanfiles.com

Global Science Report, http://www.cato.org/blog/tags/global-science-report

Global Warming, Cato Institute, http://www.cato.org/global-warming

GlobalWarming.org, http://www.Globalwarming.Org

Heartland Institute, https://www.heartland.org/

ICECAP by Joseph D'Aleo, http://www.icecap.us

International Conferences on Climate Change, http://climateconference.heartland.org

International Climate Science Coalition, http://climatescienceinternational.org/

JoNova, hosted by Joanne Nova, http://joannenova.com.au/

Junk Science by Steve Milloy, http://junkscience.com/

Master Resource, http://www.masterresource.org/

No Tricks Zone, http://notrickszone.com/

Power for USA, http://dddusmma.wordpress.com/

Real Science, https://realclimatescience.com

Science and Public Policy Institute, http://scienceandpublicpolicy.org/

Science and Environmental Policy Project (SEPP), http://sepp.org/

The Climate Bet, http://www.theclimatebet.com/

Watts Up With That? by Anthony Watts, http://wattsupwiththat.com

WiseEnergy, http://wiseenergy.org/

World Climate Report by Dr. Patrick Michaels, http://www.worldclimatereport.com/

Chapter 3
Elementary and Secondary Education

Joseph L. Bast and Vicki Alger

---

10 Principles of School Reform

1. The rising tide of mediocrity.
2. Common Core was not the answer.
3. Allow parents to choose.
4. School choice programs work.
5. Avoid new regulations.
6. School choice benefits teachers.
7. Design guidelines for voucher programs.
8. Design guidelines for ESAs.
9. Design guidelines for charter schools.
10. Digital learning: The future of education?

Introduction

Education has been a high priority for Americans since the first settlers arrived here. The Founding Fathers thought a free society would be impossible without an educated population. Thomas Jefferson, our third president, said, "If a nation expects to be ignorant and free, in a state of civilization, it expects what never was and never will be" (Padover 1939).

During America's first century, most schooling was done at home or in small schools run by institutions of civil society such as churches and private societies. Early in the Progressive Era, state governments gradually took over responsibility for financing and then providing elementary and secondary schooling. While private schools continue to operate today, about nine of every 10 students in the U.S. attend schools that are owned, operated, and staffed by government employees. About 70 percent of the teachers in those schools belong to unions, working under workplace rules that frustrate the best and brightest while protecting the incompetent and even dangerous teachers.

Why do public schools fail to satisfy so many parents? Why do U.S. students perform poorly compared with their peers in other developed countries? What kinds of reforms work best, and why? The 10 principles presented in this chapter attempt to answer these questions.

1. The rising tide of mediocrity.

> Government schools are failing to provide the quality education students, parents, and taxpayers deserve.

Defenders of government-run elementary and secondary schools in America typically claim they are doing just fine, given the broken homes and hostile-to-learning popular culture they must cope with. There is nothing wrong with the school system, they say, that more money could not fix. That narrative is completely wrong.

Government schools in America today are failing to perform their essential duty of passing along to the next generation the core of knowledge that makes civilization possible. Nearly 35 years ago, the National Commission on Excellence in Education warned "the educational foundations of our society are presently being eroded by a rising tide of mediocrity that threatens our very future as a Nation and a people" (NCEE 1983). The tide continues to rise.

Since 1983, many reforms were instituted and hundreds of billions of dollars in taxpayer money have been devoted *every year* to fixing the government schools, and yet in 2003 the Hoover Institution's Koret Task Force on K–12 Education concluded those reforms "have not improved school performance or student achievement" (Peterson 2003). In the intervening 20 years, about 80 million first graders "have walked into schools where they have scant chance of learning much more than the youngsters whose plight troubled the Excellence Commission in 1983."

Today, 14 years after the Koret Task Force report, evidence of inadequate public school performance continues to emerge:

■ Just 37 percent of public high school seniors nationwide scored proficient or better on the 2015 National Assessment of Educational Progress (NAEP) reading assessment and only 25 percent in math. Racial achievement gaps in both subjects persist (NCES 2016a, 2013b–d).

■ Proportionally fewer American students perform as well as students in other economically advanced nations. From 2009 to 2015 American students' math and science performance rankings dropped to 40th and 25th, respectively (Hanushek *et al.* 2014; OECD 2016a, 2013; Duncan 2013).

■ The national high school graduation rate for 2011–12 was 83.2 percent, indicating nearly one in five students drop out before graduating (NCES 2016c).

The problem is not a lack of spending. Between 1979–80 and 2013–14, per-pupil expenditures increased 75 percent in constant dollars (NCES 2015, table 236.65). Research by dozens of scholars has found no consistent relationship between higher spending and improvement in academic achievement (Hanushek *et al.* 2012; Pullmann 2012).

Declining Productivity

One way to measure the decline of American education is to measure its productivity, the ratio of outputs to inputs. This is a key measure of quality and success in all enterprises, whether public or private. Like achievement scores, productivity measures reveal a national school system in crisis (Hanushek *et al.* 2013; Walberg and Bast 2014a).

Then-Harvard economist Caroline Hoxby found between 1970–71 and 1998–99 American school productivity fell by between 55 and 73 percent. Writing in 2001, Hoxby reported that if schools then were as productive as they were in 1970–71, the average 17-year-old would perform at levels fewer than 5 percent of students actually achieved in 2001 (Hoxby 2001).

The decline in school productivity also stunts economic growth (Lynch 2015; Shultz and Hanushek 2012; Walberg 2014). Raising American 15-year-olds' Program for International Student Assessment (PISA) scores to match the scores of students in Poland would add an estimated $41 trillion to U.S. GDP within the coming generation and more than $100 trillion if they reached top-performing Finland

(Hanushek and Woessmann 2010, figures 1 and 2).

The falling productivity of government schools can be traced to three developments (Hanushek 1996; Vedder 1996). The first is the growth of non-teaching personnel (Scafidi 2012, 2013). Government schools in the United States spend more on non-teaching staff than any other developed Organisation for Economic Co-operation and Development (OECD) country, and teachers comprised just 50.3 percent of all American public elementary and secondary school staff in 2013 (OECD 2016b, indicator B6, table B6.2; NCES 2015, table 213.40).

The second trend is the fall in average class size. The number of teachers rose significantly faster than school enrollment after 1970, although not as rapidly as non-teaching personnel. Consequently, the average public school student/teacher ratio fell from 17.6 in 1987 to 16.1 in 2013, a decrease of 8.52 percent (NCES 2015, table 208.40).

The third reason for low productivity is a dropout rate that has not fallen despite large increases in spending and personnel. Students who drop out before graduating increase the cost per graduated student.

Lack of Competition and Choice

What explains the declining productivity of America's government schools? At the top of the list must be the lack of competition among schools for students and funding.

When protected from competition, even talented and well-intentioned public officials are motivated to act in ways intended to increase their income, authority, prestige, or leisure (Borcherding 1977). The usual bureaucratic approach is to minimize choices for people who need services and to routinize procedures as much as possible, usually in the name of fairness and efficiency but often simply to reduce the bureaucrats' workload. The result in public education has been large and impersonal schools, assignment of students to schools based on their zip codes rather than their specific needs, and school rules and collective bargaining agreements that stifle creativity and encourage mediocrity (Merrifield and Salisbury 2005).

The absence of competition and choice in public schooling has allowed teacher unions, representing the employees, to dominate school administrators (Lieberman 2007). Union leaders influence political decisions affecting school budgets and restrict access to information needed to implement regulations. The interests of union leaders are often different from and therefore compete with those of the students. For example, students might benefit from the dismissal of incompetent or even dangerous teachers, but union rules often protect such teachers.

Conflicts of Interest

Public schools are heavily regulated because their employees operate in an institutional setting rife with conflicts of interest. For example, superintendents influence standards, make policy, and propose budgets, as well as deliver services: hiring and managing teachers, choosing and maintaining facilities, and so on. They face powerful incentives to set low academic standards that are more attainable and, thus, when reached will seem to show them as highly effective educators. They have incentives to raise the budget to avoid difficult negotiations with teacher unions, and to defer facilities maintenance, since this will be little noticed in the short term or during their tenure.

Managers of private enterprises have incentives to keep the quality of their goods and services high and their prices reasonable lest they lose their customers. Government schools and the politicians who funnel taxpayer money to them can simply gloss over failures and demand more tax dollars be directed to schools "for the children," never mind that they are rewarding themselves for their own failures.

The plight of district superintendents is made worse by teacher unions (Moe 2011, 2014). A union steward who is dissatisfied can leak information to the school board that contradicts the superintendent's reports, leading to embarrassment and conflict with the board. Faced with having to discipline an incompetent teacher, the superintendent is torn between doing the right thing and appeasing union representatives (Antonucci 2015; Brimelow 2003). Surveys show the flexibility to fire bad teachers is the most popular reform among school leaders—even more important than increased funding (Loeb *et al.* 2007).

Policy Agenda

While the rest of this chapter will describe specific policy reforms that can improve schools, here are some key observations and objectives that should guide the search for solutions:

- Having governments own and operate schools is only one way to deliver K–12 schooling. Experience is teaching us it may not be the best way.

- America's government schools are simply not good enough. They are poor compared to schools in the past, compared to schools in other developed countries, and compared to the schools we should want and expect.

■ Government schools in America are well funded. The problem is that the funding is going to support staff and bureaucracy, and schools are unable to attract and retain the best teachers.

■ The biggest problems facing K–12 education in America today are institutional: They are inside the schools and not in our communities or legislatures. They are perverse incentives caused by a system that rewards the wrong behavior and discourages excellence.

Recommended Reading: Herbert J. Walberg, "Expanding Options," in Charles E. Finn Jr. and Richard Sousa, editors, *What Lies Ahead for America's Children and Their Schools* (Stanford, CA: Hoover Institution Press, 2014), pp. 71–86.

2. Common Core was not the answer.

Common Core State Standards give the federal government too much control over education, which should be controlled by parents, students, and teachers.

The failure of government schools caught the attention of former Microsoft CEO Bill Gates. With the leverage of hundreds of millions of dollars in grants from his foundation to teacher unions and liberal and even some conservative advocacy groups, he created something called Common Core State Standards (CCSS) (Alger 2015b; Layton 2014).

Why National Standards?
CCSS was a well-intended effort to address one of the conflicts of interest described in Principle 1, the tendency of teachers and administrators to lower standards in order to make their jobs easier and to avoid being held responsible for falling student achievement. What was needed, CCSS's proponents said, was a national curriculum that teachers, principals, and state legislatures couldn't dumb down, a curriculum that would make student achievement and teacher performance objectively measurable.

Thanks to its enthusiastic support by President Barack Obama, accompanied by billions of dollars in federal grants via the stimulus-funded "Race to the Top" program, CCSS was adopted in 2010 with little public debate by every state except Alaska, Nebraska, Texas, and Virginia.

Regrettably, CCSS was a step in the wrong direction, an expensive and divisive detour from the road of what actually needs to be done to improve America's government schools. There are several reasons for the failure, some of them described below, but the biggest one is that government-defined standards *simply don't work.* They haven't worked in other countries or in the United States at the state level.

There is no correlation between student scores on international achievement tests and whether or not a country has a national curriculum. According to Joy Pullmann, "On the TIMSS [Trends in International Mathematics and Science Study] tests in 2007, nine of the 10 lowest scoring countries in math, and eight of the lowest-scoring countries in science have centralized education standards. The same is true for eight of the 10 highest-scoring countries" (Pullmann 2014).

According to Stanford University economist Eric Hanushek, "There is no relationship between learning standards of the states and student performance" (Hanushek 2012). According to a report from the liberal Brookings Institution, "every state already has standards placing all districts and schools within its borders under a common regime. And despite that, every state has tremendous within-state variation in achievement" (Loveless 2012).

Advocates of national standards overlooked federal laws prohibiting the national government from setting standards. They also overlooked the fact that the country already has national *competing* testing programs in the form of SAT, ACT, and Iowa Basic tests as well as the National Assessment of Educational Progress, or NAEP (Anderson 2014). These tests already offer valid and well-respected measuring sticks comparing schools' progress across state lines.

Low Quality Standards

Despite claims that it is "rigorous," "high-quality," and "internationally benchmarked," CCSS is none of those (Moore 2013). In fact, several states had more rigorous standards in place *before* they adopted CCSS.

Evaluations by independent scholars and even by organizations with financial reasons to favor Common Core conclude it will at best prepare students for a two-year community college (Anderson 2014). Former U.S. Department of Education official and mathematician Ze'ev Wurman has said CCSS math standards would graduate students "below the admission requirement of most four-year state colleges" (Wurman and Wilson 2012). He points out CCSS pushes algebra back to grade 9, "contrary to the practice of the highest-achieving nations," which begin algebra in grade 8.

University of Arkansas professor and reading expert Sandra Stotsky, who served on CCSS's validation committee but, along with four other committee members, refused to sign it, has said the standards writers refused to provide evidence that research supports CCSS or claims that it is benchmarked to international tests (Stotsky 2012).

The standards set under CCSS may have seemed high and aspirational compared to those of some states, but this is only because No Child Left Behind, the previous national program that tried and failed to raise the academic achievements of U.S. students, created incentives for states to set their standards low, so they could report progress toward the unachievable goal of every child being "proficient" in every subject. This is another case of doubling down on bad policy.

Other Problems with the Core

As educators, parents, and policymakers across the country got a closer look at Common Core State Standards and related testing mandates, many did not like what they saw. Arizona, Missouri, South Carolina, and Tennessee have withdrawn from CCSS and are writing their own standards, and nine other states are reviewing the standards to decide how to proceed. Eighteen of the original 26 partnering states have dropped out of the Partnership for Assessment of Readiness for College and Careers (PARCC) consortium for Common Core aligned testing. In 2017, 12 states have bills to repeal and replace CCSS, with 22 state legislatures working on strong data privacy.

Parents and educators have raised concerns about the apparent politicization of the curriculum, with readings and quizzes featuring "identity politics" while basic historical facts and themes from American history are conspicuously missing (Moore 2013). Critics also raised concerns about student privacy, effects on higher education, and costs associated with implementation and testing (Lombard 2014).

CCSS's proponents have said they expect CCSS to change how teachers are trained and evaluated, making it far more than only a set of tests. Textbook publishers are taking their guidance from CCSS (and played no small role in developing the standards), giving rise to concerns about their undue influence over classrooms.

Policy Agenda

Pullmann (2013b) recommended "states should replace Common Core with higher-quality, state-controlled academic standards and tests not funded by the federal government. They should secure student data privacy and ensure national testing mandates do not affect instruction in private and home schools."

Pullmann and Bast (2016) described four ways states can repeal and replace CCSS, each accompanied by pros and cons:

■ Return to pre-existing state standards and tests.

■ Create new state standards and tests that do not largely rephrase or simply imitate CCSS.

■ Adopt the standards or tests of other states, such as Indiana, Massachusetts, and New York, which were highly regarded before they adopted CCSS.

■ Allow schools to choose the tests they administer, including among their options ACT, SAT, and pre-existing state tests.

Recommended Readings: Kirstin Lombard, editor, *Common Ground on Common Core* (DeForest, WI: Resounding Books, 2014); Joy Pullmann, *The Common Core: A Poor Choice for States*, The Heartland Institute, 2013.

3. Allow parents to choose.

Parents have the legal right to direct the education of their children and should be allowed to choose the schools their children attend.

Far better than simply spending more money on failing public schools or fighting over their curriculum is allowing parents to choose the schools, public or private, their children attend. This simple change in public policy would transform K–12 education by changing the incentives of teachers, principals, parents, and students.

John Chubb and Terry Moe wrote in 1990, "reformers would do well to entertain the notion that choice is a panacea. ... It has the capacity all by itself to bring about the kind of transformation that, for years, reformers have been seeking to engineer in myriad other ways" (Chubb and Moe 1990, p. 217).

Parents Have the Legal Right to Choose

Parents in the United States can properly assert the right, recognized by tradition and law, to direct the education of their children (Arons 1997; McCarthy *et al.* 1981; Skillen 1993). The U.S. Supreme Court ruled in *Pierce* v. *Society of Sisters* (268 U.S. 510 (1925)) that "the fundamental theory of liberty upon which all governments in this Union repose excludes any general power of the state to standardize its children by forcing them to accept instruction from public teachers only. The child is not the mere creature of the state; those who nurture him and direct his destiny have the right, coupled with the high duty, to recognize and prepare him for additional obligations."

In *Zelman* v. *Simmons-Harris* (536 U.S. 639 (2002)), the U.S. Supreme Court upheld the constitutionality of Cleveland's voucher program, with the majority writing, "In keeping with an unbroken line of decisions rejecting challenges to similar programs, we hold that the program does not offend the Establishment Clause."

Again in *Arizona Christian School Tuition Organization* v. *Winn* (131 S. Ct. 1436 (2011)), the Supreme Court affirmed that tax-credit scholarship programs comply with the Establishment Clause because "like contributions that lead to charitable tax deductions, contributions yielding tax credits are not owed to the State and, in fact, pass directly from taxpayers to private organizations."

Allowing parents to act as consumers, using public funds, often their own tax dollars, in the form of vouchers for special purposes or in recognitions of special circumstances, is not a radical idea. Existing voucher programs include food stamps, low-income housing vouchers, the G.I. Bill, Pell Grants for college students, federal day-care grants, and Social Security (Savas 2000). Social Security, for example, distributes about $725 billion annually to millions of seniors to spend as they wish (SSA 2012). The seniors spend their Social Security dollars on the goods and services of their choice, including donating some to charities, churches, temples, and mosques.

School Choice Is Spreading

Voucher programs—which allow public funds to be used to pay for tuition at private schools—currently operate in 14 states and Washington, DC. Tax-credit scholarship programs—which offer tax breaks to donors who contribute to scholarship-granting entities— operate in 17 states. An additional eight states—Alabama, Illinois, Indiana, Iowa, Louisiana, Minnesota (which has two programs), South Carolina, and Wisconsin—have tax credit or deduction laws that allow taxpayers to get back from their state governments some part of the amount they spend on private school tuition (EdChoice 2017a). Education savings account programs have been adopted by six states (Benson 2017).

School voucher, tax-credit scholarship, and education savings account programs served approximately 446,000 children during the 2016–17 school year. Participation in the Milwaukee Parental Choice Program has grown from 337 students in the 1990–91 school year to more than 28,000 in 2016–17. Indiana's Choice Scholarship Program, launched in 2011, enrolled 34,299 students in 2016–17 (EdChoice 2017a).

Public support for expanding school choice is strong: A recent survey found 60 percent support expanding tax-credit scholarships, 54 percent public charter schools, and 50 percent vouchers (Henderson *et al.* 2015). A different survey found close to two-thirds of Americans support education savings accounts, a way to finance school choice described in greater detail below (Carpenter 2014; DiPerna 2014). With just two exceptions, more than 40 credible public opinion analyses conducted between 2000 and 2013 found higher parental and public support for private schools than for government schools (Alger 2013).

Parents Can Be Trusted

Parents who participate in school choice programs tend to choose higher quality schools as measured by test scores, graduation rates, and other conventional measures of school success (Bast and Walberg 2004). Most parents who choose independent schools also do so on the basis of academic quality (Scafidi and Kelly 2013; Witte 2000; Zeehandelaar and Northern 2013) or adherence to parental values (Catt and Rhinesmith 2016).

The current system of school finance is based on the notion that government knows better than parents do when it comes to selecting schools, but this is patently untrue. Bureaucrats and so-called experts may have information that parents do not, but parents are more likely to know their children's individual needs and concerns, and they have much stronger incentives to choose the right schools for their children than bureaucrats do. Parents can acquire the information from experts in order to make informed choices; bureaucrats and experts can't possibly know or care about each child's special needs and interests the way their parents do (Coons and Sugarman 1978).

In recent years, parents have organized successfully to support school reforms against powerful vested education interests (Kelly 2014). The American Federation for Children, EdChoice (formerly the Friedman Foundation for Educational Choice), Black Alliance for Educational Options, and other national organizations work closely with thousands of local groups of parents and educators to promote and defend school choice programs. A group called National School Choice Week coordinates thousands of events across the country every year celebrating all types of school choice.

Policy Agenda

Public policies ought to reflect the right of parents to exercise control over the education of their children as well as evidence that parents choose wisely when given the freedom to do so. Specifically:

- The right of parents to control their children's education should always be paramount in discussions of school finance, curriculum, and other policies.

- Current policies penalize parents who choose private schools for their children by denying them access to tax dollars collected for the purpose of educating their children. That's just plain wrong.

- Patriots who want to get K–12 education in the United States back on track should be on the front lines of efforts to create or expand school choice programs.

- Such programs—whether vouchers, tax-credits, charter schools, or education savings accounts—promise to bring about the transformation needed to end the tide of mediocrity.

Recommended Readings: Greg Forster and C. Bradley Thompson, editors, *Freedom and School Choice in American Education* (New York, NY: Palgrave MacMillan, 2011); Milton Friedman and Rose Friedman, *Free to Choose* (New York, NY: Harcourt Brace Jovanovich, 1980).

4. School choice programs work.

Putting parents in charge of choosing the schools their children attend results in superior academic achievement, higher graduation rates, and higher parental satisfaction.

Peter Brimelow once called America's government schools "in essence a socialized business, the American equivalent of the Soviet Union's collectivized farms" (Brimelow 2003). It was a harsh comparison, but it spoke to the central truth about America's educational crisis. If they ever are to improve, America's government schools must compete with one another for students and tuition.

Competition Brings Out the Best in People

Many people's first reaction to the idea that schools should compete is negative. Teachers should choose their profession and stay in it because they love children and teaching. Principals should rise up through the ranks of teachers and become school leaders because they are respected by their colleagues. In such a system, we hope people are motivated by love and idealism to cooperate and collaborate for the common good.

This sentiment is right, but the conclusion is wrong. There is need for lots of love and compassion in schools. Teachers must have these attributes in abundance. We hope they do, and we hope they keep returning to the classroom year after year at least in part out of sheer love of teaching. But teachers need, enjoy, and benefit from friendly competition with one another and rewards for good work just as all people do.

Competition brings out the best in people, enterprises, and organizations—not because it appeals to greed or selfishness, but because the desire to innovate, earn the esteem of others, and be best in one's field is deeply and widely instilled (Walberg and Bast 2014b). Competitors provide benchmarks against which to measure individual efforts and also invaluable lessons in what to do and not to do. Rewards for high achievement are common in all fields, from athletics to music and medicine to science.

Requiring schools to compete should not be controversial. Competition is relied upon to provide food, clothing, shelter, transportation, smart phones, entertainment, and countless other essential goods and services. Competition among providers of pre-school and after-school services and higher education is allowed and encouraged. Yet constructive competition among primary and secondary schools is suppressed by assigning students to unchosen public schools and withholding public funds from private schools. Why?

Schools Improve When They Compete

A review of more than 200 analyses from 35 studies of the effect of competition on public schools found "a sizable majority of these studies report beneficial effects of competition across all outcomes" (Belfield and Levin 2001, p. 2). Another review found 31 of 33 empirical studies determined competition improved outcomes at public schools (Forster 2016).

Competition from both public and private school choice strengthens academic standards and improves student achievement in core subjects (Egalite 2014; Hoxby 2003a; Gray et al. 2014). A recent meta-analysis of 200 studies published from 1990 through 2013 also found that approximately two-thirds of them documented positive effects of competition from public and private school competition on student achievement, and none found negative effects of competition (Hood and Stoops 2014).

These findings wouldn't surprise us if they were about businesses competing to sell us food, clothing, or shelter. They surprise us because they looked at schools, which usually are nonprofit or government-run institutions. We think schools offer their goods for free because we often don't pay for them ourselves, or pay for only a small fraction of their true cost. But schools, at least the good ones, actually do compete ... for our tax dollars, tuition, charitable contributions, and with one another for the best staffs, best locations, and best deals on the services and goods they buy.

Schools improve when they compete. We need to keep this in mind whenever school finance and oversight is debated because too many people imagine competition isn't appropriate, isn't occurring, or shouldn't be necessary to make people do the right things.

Students Benefit from School Choice

Students attending private schools, which compete with each other and with "free" government schools for students and tuition, outperform public school students on most measures of academic achievement. According to the U.S. Department of Education, "For the past 30 years, NAEP has reported that students in private schools outperform students in public schools" (Perie *et al.* 2005, p. 2).

On average, the costs of private schools are about half that of public schools, and their graduates have higher college attendance and completion rates (Chingos and Peterson 2015). Most large-scale studies and surveys find beneficial effects of school choice on the achievement of students who participate by enrolling in private schools as well as the students who remain in the local public schools (Holley *et al.* 2013).

A recent meta-analysis reviewed more than 50 scientific studies and found that compared to district public schools, charter schools had higher achievement gains in math in most grades, as well as sizeable positive impacts on high school graduation, college enrollment, and student behavior (Betts and Tang 2014). Twelve of the 16 random assignment studies to date have documented academic benefits of voucher programs for all or some participating students, such as improved student achievement, higher high school graduation, college attendance, and college-degree completion rates (EdChoice 2017b; ERA New Orleans 2017; Friedman Foundation 2015).

Two studies of Louisiana's statewide voucher program found negative impacts in math and reading achievement during students' first year; however, during their second year in the program those negative impacts dissipated in reading and diminished in math. A third study of the Louisiana program found after three years the math and reading performance of participating students was similar to their peers who did not participate in the program. The sole study finding no significant impacts was subsequently discredited for its unscientific methodology. When Harvard University researchers repeated the analysis using scientifically credible methodologies, they found statistically significant positive results.

Research also shows that parents of voucher students reported less fighting, truancy, tardiness, and cheating in their children's private schools than in their children's previous public schools. Voucher parents further reported the private schools kept them much better informed about their children's behavior and academic progress (Forster and Carr 2007; Peterson 2006).

Parents and non-parents alike view charter and private schools more favorably than traditional public schools. Since 1993, parental satisfaction levels with private schools have remained at or above 80 percent; chosen public schools (e.g., charter schools) have satisfaction levels that have remained around 60 percent. In contrast, assigned public schools have parental satisfaction levels stuck at around 50 percent (Alger 2013). Yet policies limiting student participation in choice programs have resulted in students being turned away, with more than 1 million children on charter-school waiting lists nationwide (Kern and Gebru 2014; Walberg 2007).

The Fate of Failing Schools

If schools are made to compete with one another for students and tuition, failing schools would have to close their doors so new schools can open that can do a better job satisfying parents. This is not a bad thing. Schools and the systems that finance and operate them exist for the benefit of children, not for the adults they employ. This simple truth is often forgotten when the survival of "neighborhood schools" or the well-being of current teachers and administrators is put before the interests of children.

In a system of expanded school choice, the number of children needing to be educated would remain the same, so educators will be as much in demand after the plan takes effect as before. Good teachers and skilled administrators may face the inconvenience of taking new positions at different schools, but otherwise they should not fear a competitive marketplace.

One early voucher proposal provided guaranteed loans and similar assistance to community groups that founded voucher schools (Coons and Sugarman 1971). A revolving loan fund for such a purpose could be established with the funds earned from the sale or lease of public school space. Economics professor Richard Vedder (2000) proposed profit-sharing and an employee stock ownership plan that would enable public school teachers to own their schools.

"Parent Trigger" laws empower parents to demand that a public school be closed or converted into a charter school, or to receive vouchers to enroll their children in nearby private schools (Bast and Pullmann 2012; Bast *et al.* 2010). Failing schools in this case could become charter schools or be leased to teachers or entrepreneurs to become voucher schools.

Policy Agenda

Public policies should reflect the fact that competition and choice are appropriate and necessary in an education system, just as they ensure the efficient delivery of virtually all the other goods and services we need. Policymakers should acknowledge the following truths:

- Competition is not foreign or inappropriate in education. Just as it does in other arenas, competition among schools brings out the best in people.

- Empirical research overwhelmingly confirms that schools improve when they have to compete for students and tuition.

- Students benefit when schools compete for enrollment and tuition, as documented by higher test scores, graduation rates, and other conventional measures of success.

- The fact that not all schools will succeed in a competitive marketplace is no reason to avoid competition and choice. Failure is necessary if success is to be rewarded.

Recommended Readings: Herbert J. Walberg, *School Choice: The Findings* (Washington, DC: Cato Institute, 2007); Herbert J. Walberg and Joseph L. Bast, *Education and Capitalism* (Stanford, CA: Hoover Institution Press, 2003).

5. Avoid new regulations.

School choice programs should lead to less, not more, regulation of private schools.

Some advocates of school reform oppose school choice programs out of fear they will lead to more regulation of private schools or homeschoolers. This could happen if the school choice program is poorly designed and if parents and school administrators are not diligent, but properly designed programs should lead to less, not more, regulation.

Politics Makes Regulation Necessary

Regulations are the price we pay for choosing to rely on political systems instead of markets to detect and prevent inefficient or corrupt behavior. Every government layer of bureaucracy attempts to restrict the range of discretionary decision-making in the layer below it by imposing rules, requiring reports, and naming oversight committees. The more complex the service, the more costly, complicated, and detailed its rules and the less responsive it is in meeting the needs and desires of beneficiaries (Bast *et al.* 2014).

Federal and state officials, for example, annually direct spending of billions of dollars to "categorical" or "compensatory" educational programs. In theory, these funds go to special classes and services for children categorized as poor, migrant, bilingual, racially segregated, or psychologically impeded. School superintendents might otherwise be tempted to neglect these children because they represent few voters or are unlikely to complain about poor service. In practice, the programs have created huge bureaucracies counterproductive to learning.

Many public schools fail because they are overregulated. Regulations grew over time because school administrators faced conflicts of interest that led them, in the absence of competition, to act against the interests of students (Pullmann 2013a; Shuls 2013). Allowing parents to choose and requiring schools to compete would restore a proper incentive system, making deregulation possible (Walberg 2014).

Private school systems have less need for bureaucracy and regulations because success is *automatically* rewarded as more students enroll, generating more tuition income, while failure is penalized with fewer students and less income. When an incentive structure is right, it rewards activities and investments that actually benefit students and satisfy parents while penalizing and defunding decisions that serve only to reward staff or bureaucrats outside the classroom.

School Choice Empowers School Leaders

Education choice frees school leaders from excessive regulation by replacing politics with markets. Accountability comes "from the bottom up," parents making informed choices for their children, rather than "from the top down," bureaucrats and other officials imposing strict rules (Hill 2013; Moe and Hill 2012).

School choice ends the superintendents' conflict of interest between pleasing unions and serving students. As Savas (2000) explained, "The distinction between providing or arranging a service and producing it is profound. ... It puts the role of government in perspective" (p. 65). School choice means school boards and superintendents would be responsible only for funding schools chosen by parents that met certain standards of financial and academic accountability, civil rights, and safety. Responsibility for actually *producing* schooling would rest in the hands of the leaders of individual schools competing for students and public funds.

Private Schools Are Exempt from Many Rules

Secular and religiously affiliated private schools enjoy greater autonomy from government regulation than do government schools partly in recognition of the fact that markets hold them accountable to parents and others in the community. (Another reason for the light regulation is because parents organize to oppose heavier regulation.) This light regulation is typically a privilege rather than a right: Regulating schools is one of the powers left to the states by the U.S. Constitution, and most state constitutions do not guarantee freedom from excessive regulation.

For the most part, vouchers, tax-credit scholarships, tuition tax credits, and education savings accounts do not open any doors for government regulators that are not already open to them (Catt 2014). Religiously affiliated schools are protected by the First Amendment against federal or state regulations that interfere with freedom of religion, regardless of whether they participate in a school choice program.

School choice legislation should be written to ensure private schools retain their authority over curriculum and textbook selection, as well as student admissions, retention, and discipline. Private schools should continue to be exempt from statutes that guarantee teacher tenure and contract renewal and that restrict transfers and demotions. Private school employees should continue to keep their labor freedoms: For example, they should be free to determine for themselves whether they will belong to a union or professional association (Lieberman 1986; Valente 1985).

Some Concessions Can Be Made

Parental choice advocates should consider making some concessions to the public's concerns over the accountability of private schools that accept public dollars. The accountability goal can be accomplished using existing state and federal statutes.

Cleveland's voucher program, for example, expressly bars participating private schools from fostering unlawful behavior or teaching hatred (Ohio Rev. Code §§ 3313.974–79, see § 3313.976). Even private schools that do not accept federal funds are already prohibited from discriminating with respect to race, color, and national origin (42 U.S.C. § 1981). Schools that accept federal funds must comply with additional prohibitions against racial and disability discrimination (42 U.S.C. § 2000d; 29 U.S.C. § 794).

Education choice proponents may also agree to require participating schools to administer norm-referenced standardized achievement tests of each school's choosing and make aggregate test results publicly available. Because most private schools already administer such tests, this is unlikely to be a burdensome regulation. In a competitive marketplace, good schools would have sufficient motivation to publish and even advertise performance-based information.

Recent research findings, however, indicate regulations intended to ensure the quality of private schools participating in school choice programs are actually having the opposite effect (DeAngelis 2017; Sude *et al.* 2017; Bedrick 2016). Voucher programs in the District of Columbia and Louisiana stand out for being the most regulated programs in the country, with strict mandates dictating admissions, tuition, and testing policies for private schools. In response, many higher-performing private schools refuse to participate in the voucher programs, leaving families with fewer quality school options for their children.

Policy Agenda

Four strategies are available to legislators seeking to reduce the risk of an education choice program increasing regulations on private schools. They are:

- Adopt legislation establishing that the autonomy of private schools is in the public interest and thus will not be subject to any new regulations.

- Give opponents of increased regulation the legal standing and tax funding they need to protect school autonomy. This ensures private schools can retain quality legal representation when needed.

- Require any government body with regulatory powers over schools participating in a choice program to have a membership equally balanced between government and private school interests.

■ Combine with the choice plan an initiative to deregulate public schools. This could put public and private school leaders and teachers on the same side of the issue, so they could work together to resist new decrees.

Recommended Readings: Andrew D. Catt, *Public Rules on Private Schools: Measuring the Regulatory Impact of State Statutes and School Choice Programs* (Indianapolis, IN: Friedman Foundation for Educational Choice, 2014); Joseph Bast, "Why Conservatives and Libertarians Should Support School Vouchers," *Independent Review,* Fall/Winter 2002.

6. School choice benefits teachers.

Teachers, too, are empowered by a system of education choice and would see the same respect and rewards afforded other professionals.

Teacher unions are the main source of opposition to expanding school choice (Moe 2011; Lieberman 2000). In many cities and some states, they are the only source of organized opposition to school choice, yet their sheer size and political power make them formidable foes of reform. However, the unions have a major vulnerability: Their members benefit when school choice is expanded.

An Unfree Occupation
Compared to professionals in other fields, public school teachers are surprisingly unfree (Alger 2014; Hess 2010). To attain government certification to teach, they must attend teachers colleges and take courses that are often condemned as useless or even counterproductive in the classroom. They must join unions and have hefty dues withheld from their paychecks, largely for political campaigns without their consent. Merit pay is largely off-limits in public schools.

The lack of competition among schools within districts takes negotiating power away from teachers and puts it in the hands of public school administrators. Districts can hire the best teachers for less and offer few choices of teaching subjects, workloads, and working conditions, without worrying about these good teachers seeking better terms at other schools. Teachers are especially vulnerable to this kind of treatment because (1) they often are their household's second wage earners, so they are not free to move to another city or state, and (2) their skills do not qualify them for better-paying employment in other fields (Weisberg *et al.* 2009; Hoxby and Leigh 2005).

Public school teachers lost the rights that other professionals take for granted because the market forces that protect and reward professionals do not operate within the public school system. Bureaucracy rewards centralized authority, resulting in school districts and schools that are too large offering a single curriculum that is unlikely to be best for most students.

Centralized school systems cannot function with multiple and constantly changing curricula, as there can be no certainty about what students should have mastered in earlier grades, making it difficult for school boards, superintendents, and principals to accurately assess the performance of individual teachers (McShane 2014).

Teacher Unions Protect Teachers but at a High Price

Absent objective, professional competence measures and accountability to the parents who, through their tax dollars, foot the bills, teachers rightly fear favoritism and other kinds of managerial abuse. Powerful teacher unions offer insurance and collective bargaining protections that severely limit principals' managerial prerogatives. Consequently, incompetent teachers are almost never fired, and even the most troubled schools are seldom closed. This state of affairs has badly damaged the teaching profession and hurt generations of children.

Until recently, New York City was notorious for its "rubber rooms" (Brill 2009). Teachers unsuited for teaching but protected by union rules would simply be assigned, with full salaries, to large rooms with tables and chairs in which they could sit all day and read, sleep, surf the web, or whatever, all because it is too difficult and costly for administrators to fire them. Needless to say, good teachers resent this damage to the reputation of all teachers, to say nothing of the use of money on bad teachers that should go into the paychecks of the good ones.

Teaching is often disrespected as a profession. "New students [entering teachers colleges] are drawn disproportionately from the bottom third of American college students," as measured by their scores on high school achievement tests (Hoxby 2003b, p. 93). This situation corresponds with the advent of widespread collective bargaining, which imposed a rigid salary schedule and made the teaching profession unattractive to talented individuals who preferred to earn competitive salaries based on performance (Hoxby and Leigh 2005).

School Choice Offers a Better Route for Teachers

School choice allows public school teachers to recover their lost freedoms while boosting the productivity of K–12 schools. Private schools offer a glimpse of how school choice benefits teachers.

The 2011–12 "Schools and Staffing Survey," a national survey of teachers and principals conducted by the U.S. Department of Education, found public school teachers are twice as likely as private school teachers to say the stress and disappointments they experience at their schools are so great that teaching there isn't really worth it. Also, public school teachers are far more likely than private school teachers to say they would leave teaching if they could find a higher paying job. Moreover, in spite of the proliferation of administrative staff, nearly seven of 10 public school teachers report that routine duties and paperwork interfere with their teaching—compared to just four of 10 private school teachers (NCES 2013a, table 210.20).

If parents were allowed to choose schools for their children and if public funds followed them, superintendents would have little incentive to mislead parents or voters. Accurate consumer reports containing school-level information about student achievement and professional competence would become widely available, similar to those now available for automobiles, hospitals, consumer electronics, and other goods and services.

School choice would allow a variety of curricula to be applied consistently based on the needs of students and preferences of parents. This would allow more accurate evaluation of each teacher's contribution to a student's learning. Schools that retain unqualified employees would quickly lose students to those with merit-based employment policies.

Most teachers would benefit from a more competitive education industry. The teaching profession has as much to gain from increased choice and competition as students do (Hanushek 2011; Walberg and Bast 2014b). That is probably why the Association of American Educators, the nation's largest non-union teacher organization, supports school choice (Beckner 2011).

Policy Agenda

Teachers, along with students, parents, and even taxpayers, benefit when school choice is expanded. Policymakers should keep in mind the following facts about union opposition to school choice:

- Teacher unions are practically the only organized voice against expanding school choice in most cities and states.

- Teacher unions oppose school choice because schools that must compete for students and tuition are more difficult to organize, since they cannot afford the waste and inefficiency union policies produce.

■ Teachers benefit from expanding school choice because it gives them more choices of employers, opportunities for career advancement, and higher incomes.

■ Teachers working at private schools report much higher levels of satisfaction than those teaching in public schools.

Recommended Readings: Chester E. Finn Jr. and Richard Sousa, editors, *What Lies Ahead for America's Children and Their Schools* (Stanford, CA: Hoover Institution Press, 2014); Terry M. Moe, *Special Interest: Teachers Unions and America's Public Schools* (Washington, DC: Brookings Institution Press, 2011).

7. Design guidelines for voucher programs.

Voucher programs give parents a portion of the tax dollars raised for their children's education to use to pay tuition at the private schools of their choice.

Voucher programs give parents a portion of the tax dollars raised for their children's education to use to pay tuition at the private schools of their choice. There is no one best way to design a school voucher program. Programs can differ in which students are eligible, which schools may participate, the value of the voucher, and much more. Here are some insights into "best practices" for voucher programs.

Eligibility Standards
Most voucher programs operating today limit participation to students with disabilities or members of low-income households. Programs also typically exclude students already attending private schools and limit the number of vouchers to be granted or total spending on the program.

Limiting participation to low-income households addresses concerns that voucher programs will be used to fuel "white flight" from urban school districts or to favor wealthy families that can afford to pay private school tuition. Political opposition is thought to be less if only a small number of "truly needy" students are allowed to participate. Budget impacts on public schools are less if enrollment is kept small and students already in private schools are not allowed to participate.

Milton Friedman warned that government programs designed only for poor people will be poor programs, since they will lack a popular political base and end up being run for the benefit of bureaucrats and interest groups. Unfortunately, the history of the school voucher movement supports his prediction. Many voucher programs today are too small and heavily regulated to prove school choice works or to build a political constituency for more choice (Merrifield 2001).

Limiting participation to only public school students ignores the tremendous savings private and homeschooling parents provide by paying both out-of-pocket tuition and taxes for the schools their children do not attend (Alger 2013). Budgetary concerns are misguided: Rigorous analyses find state departments of education save between $1.50 and $2.50 or more for every dollar spent on voucher and tax-credit scholarship programs (Spalding 2014; Alger 2013).

Setting the Value of the Voucher

Milton Friedman, one of the earliest proponents of vouchers, originally called for them to be set at levels equal to the current per-pupil spending of public schools. He later recommended a lower voucher value reflecting the ability of the private sector to produce goods and services at approximately half the total cost the public sector can (Friedman and Friedman 1980).

Voucher and tax-credit scholarships currently average between $1,000 and $10,000 for regular education students, and up to $20,000 or more for special education students. Those amounts are around half or less than average public school per-pupil expenditures (Friedman Foundation 2015a; Lieberman and Haar 2003).

Allow Parents to "Top Off" Tuition

The lower the dollar value of the voucher, the fewer choices parents will have and the less competition there will be among schools. One way to offset a lower voucher value is to allow schools to charge more than the amount of the voucher, allowing parents to "top off" the choice funding.

Such "tuition add-ons" increase the number of schools willing to participate in a school choice program and, by requiring they have "skin in the game," coaxing parents to become more closely involved in their children's education (Merrifield and Salisbury 2005). But some school choice opponents and even proponents object to allowing parents to "top off" their choice funding, fearing that would worsen socioeconomic stratification and racial segregation in education (Witte 2000; Coons and Sugarman 1978).

Experience has shown such fears to be misplaced. Most private schools across the country are not ethnically or socially segregated; many already educate large numbers of low-income and minority students (Alt and Peter 2003). Moreover, nine of 10 recent empirical studies examining racial segregation in private schools that participate in school choice programs found school choice moves students from more segregated public schools into less segregated schools. One study found no net school choice effect on segregation (Forster 2016).

Preventing Tuition Inflation

If voucher levels were set at current government school spending levels, private schools that currently spend less could raise their tuition prices to match the scholarship or tuition tax-credit amount. Parents insulated from the true cost of their children's schooling would not be price-conscious shoppers, and schools would not be encouraged to become more cost-efficient.

To avoid this problem, voucher and tuition tax-credit proposals have long provided for education savings accounts (ESAs) in each qualified student's name into which parents can deposit the difference between the scholarship or tuition tax-credit value and the actual tuition charged (Bast 2002a; Ladner and Dranias 2011). If a voucher were worth $7,000, for example, and a parent chose a school charging $6,000 for tuition, the $1,000 difference would be deposited in the student's ESA.

Withdrawals from the ESA would be permitted only to pay for future tuition, tutoring, or other educational expenses for the student. When a student reaches a certain age (19, 21, and 23 are often suggested), anything left in the account would revert to taxpayers. Alternatively, funds remaining in the account upon a student's graduation from high school could be converted into a higher-education savings account, which would incentivize ongoing savings and minimize reliance on federal lending and student borrowing.

Indiana's Voucher Program

In 2011, Indiana adopted the Indiana School Scholarship Program (ISSP), a voucher program for families in Indiana with incomes up to 150 percent of the amount required for the family's children to qualify for the federal free or reduced-price school lunch program (Bast 2011). A family of four earning up to $61,000 per year would be eligible to participate in the program. Participation was limited to 7,500 students in the first year and 15,000 in the second, with no cap on enrollment after the second year.

Low-income families qualify for scholarships equal to private school tuition or 90 percent of the state's current share of per-pupil public school spending, whichever is less. Students from households with incomes between that mark and 150 percent of that mark qualify for scholarships equal to tuition or 50 percent of state per-pupil spending, whichever is less. Scholarships for students in grades 1–8 are capped at $4,500, but scholarships for high school students are not capped.

In 2012–13, more than 9,000 Indiana students received scholarships and nearly 300 schools participated in ISSP. In 2013 the law was expanded to include children attending failing public schools and special-needs students regardless of family income. The expansion also attached special-education funds of up to $8,350 to the scholarships received by children with special needs such as blindness and learning disabilities. Today, more than 34,000 students are enrolled.

The law features a fair and non-bureaucratic form of accountability by providing for suspension of scholarship payments for new students if a school fails to rise above either of the lowest two categories of public school performance currently set forth in the school code. Parents are allowed to use their own resources to add to the scholarship if tuition exceeds the value of the voucher, a laudable policy that encourages more parents and schools to participate. ISSP allows schools to retain control over admissions requirements and requires lotteries only if the number of applicants exceeds the number of vacancies.

An especially strong feature of ISSP is that it erects barriers to increased regulation of participating schools. The legislation memorializes the legislature's intent to preserve the autonomy of private schools, saying "the department or any other state agency may not in any way regulate the educational program of a nonpublic eligible school that accepts a choice scholarship under this chapter," and "the creation of the choice scholarship program does not expand the regulatory authority of the state, the state's officers, or a school corporation to impose additional regulation of nonpublic schools beyond those necessary to enforce the requirements of the school scholarship program in place on July 1, 2011."

ISSP isn't perfect legislation. The cap on the value of scholarships for grades K–8 is too low and not indexed for inflation or state per-pupil spending. By limiting participation to low-income families, ISSP requires parents to share their tax returns and other personal information with schools and government agencies to determine their eligibility for grants of different sizes, an invasion of privacy that will reduce participation. And ISSP limits participation to accredited schools, which Indiana currently over-regulates.

Despite these and other flaws, the Indiana School Scholarship Program serves as a good model for legislators considering drafting legislation for voucher programs in their states. As the program expands it could benefit millions of children in Indiana and prompt other states to follow Indiana's lead.

Policy Agenda

The focus in this chapter has been to use vouchers to transform public education, which means changing the way K–12 schooling is provided for all children. With that goal in mind, here are important best practices.

■ Allow all parents to choose. This may require phasing in the program over several years, perhaps by grade level or starting with poor families and then moving to universal eligibility.

■ Allow all schools to compete. Don't limit participation to only nonprofit, secular, or even accredited schools. Regulate primarily for safety and transparency and not for policies unrelated to student achievement such as class size or seat time.

■ Set the value of a scholarship at between half and three-quarters of current public per-pupil spending and allow schools to charge more than that amount, with parents making up the difference.

■ No new regulations should be imposed on schools that choose to participate in the scholarship program. Indiana's School Scholarship Program offers a good model in this regard.

■ If the scholarship program requires students be tested, then schools and parents should be allowed to choose among different norm-referenced tests rather than be required to take a single state-administered test.

■ Place administration of the program in the hands of a neutral oversight authority independent of the public school establishment, including the state school board.

Recommended Readings: Milton Friedman, *Public Schools: Make Them Private* (Washington, DC: Cato Institute, 1995); Herbert J. Walberg and Joseph L. Bast, *Rewards: How to Use Rewards to Help Children Learn – and Why Teachers Don't Use Them Well* (Chicago, IL: The Heartland Institute, 2014).

8. Design guidelines for education savings account programs.

Education savings account (ESA) programs act like vouchers but can be used to pay for a wider range of educational services.

Education savings account (ESA) programs act like vouchers, but tax dollars are deposited into government-authorized savings accounts, which parents can then use to pay for a wider range of educational services. President Ronald Reagan in 1983 proposed ESAs (he called them independent education accounts) and school choice activists have been proposing them at least since the early 1990s.

In recent years, ESAs are beginning to see legislative success (Benson 2017). ESA programs have been enacted in six states. Arizona was first in 2011, followed by Florida in 2014. Mississippi, Tennessee, and Nevada passed ESA laws in 2015, and North Carolina did so in 2017.

How ESAs Work

As vouchers move from theory to practice in cities and states across the country, greater attention is being focused on program design. One design feature mentioned previously (in Principle 7) is education savings accounts, or ESAs.

ESAs are tax-sheltered savings accounts similar to individual retirement accounts (IRAs) and the newer health savings accounts (HSAs). In the case of IRAs and HSAs, employers and individuals make deposits into the accounts and spending is limited or not allowed until the individual reaches a certain age for IRAs, and only for health care expenses for HSAs. An ESA operates similarly but with spending limited to education expenses and with governments depositing into the ESA each year the money collected from taxes that would otherwise go to public schools.

Parents and legal guardians are allowed to draw on their children's ESAs to pay for tuition at the public or private schools of their choice, or pay for tutoring and other educational expenses for their child. At the end of a student's K–12 career, anything left in the account could be applied to college tuition or technical training. When the student reaches a certain age (19, 21, or 23 are often suggested), anything left in the account would revert to taxpayers.

ESAs are not a new idea (Bast 2005). They were the central feature of a proposal made in 1992 by The Heartland Institute to the New American Schools Development Corporation as part of a national competition for "breakthrough" ideas for school reform. (The proposal placed in the top 4 percent of 686 competitors but did not receive funding.) A year later, ESAs were part of the first modern school choice initiative to appear on a ballot: the 1993 California Parental Choice in Education Initiative. Three years later, the California Educational Freedom Amendment contained similar language. Both initiatives were defeated. ESAs have been proposed by several researchers, including the authors of this chapter, in the years since then.

Why ESAs?

Supporters of ESAs recognize learning increasingly takes place outside brick-and-mortar buildings. Learning environments can be designed to accommodate the needs of individual students, meaning tuition may not be the only or even the largest expense confronting a highly engaged parent. Allowing parents to keep money left in the accounts at the end of each year for use later gives parents a financial incentive to find efficient ways to accelerate learning and for providers to compete on the basis of price rather than only promises of high quality.

ESAs could make school choice more popular among suburban parents who tend to think their government schools are high performing but impose too great a tax burden. Per-student spending for suburban high schools often exceeds $16,000, more than even relatively expensive private schools typically charge for tuition. With a universal ESA program in place, some of those parents would be tempted to enroll their children in a private school charging, say, $12,000 a year in tuition, and to place the remaining $4,000 in the student's ESA.

ESAs, finally, could protect parents and schools from increased government regulation, which is always a threat under charter school and voucher programs. An ESA would stand between governments and schools, with tax dollars first deposited into the student's account and then tuition or fees paid by check or debit card by the parent or guardian. Schools would not receive payment directly from government agencies.

Arizona's ESA Program

In 2011, Arizona became the first state to adopt education savings accounts into law. Called "Empowerment Scholarship Accounts," the program was first offered only to children with special needs who were previously enrolled in public schools. Parents use debit cards to pay expenses and send receipts to the Department of Education each quarter for approval.

Grants originally were set at 90 percent of what the school would have received from the state minus another 3 percent for administration costs, approximately $3,000. Parents agree to enroll their child in private or online schools or to homeschool their children. Instruction must cover reading, grammar, mathematics, social studies, and science. Participating students are not required to take tests.

In 2013, children in failing schools, children in military families, and adopted and foster children became eligible for the program. The amount of the annual grant was changed to 90 percent of state per-pupil charter school funding, approximately $6,000, plus whatever additional funds are allocated for special-needs children. Annual ESA deposits made to date have ranged from $1,500 to $27,500 and average about $11,500. In 2016–17, 3,547 students were enrolled in the program.

In 2017, Arizona lawmakers expanded the program to allow all 1.1 million K–12 students in the state to apply, but only about 5,500 students will be eligible each year and enrollment is capped at about 30,000 students by 2022 (Wingett Sanchez and O'Dell 2017). Research finds parents are using funds to pay for tuition at a variety of private schools, and more than one-quarter of parents (28 percent) also used their children's ESAs to customize learning options, including paying for private tutoring, therapy, specialized materials, and online courses (Butcher and Burke 2016).

No doubt Arizona's ESA program could be improved: true universal eligibility would dramatically boost participation. But the program has the admirable features of minimal rules, regulations, and bureaucracy. The program also has withstood the usual legal challenges from teacher unions and other entities opposed to change.

Policy Agenda

Education savings accounts (ESAs) are too new and existing programs too small to produce many lessons for reformers. Many of the best practices set forth above for voucher programs, however, apply equally to ESAs. Other issues and possible concerns include:

■ Misuse of funds is likely to be a bigger problem with ESAs than with voucher programs because a much larger universe of vendors will be qualified to receive payments from the accounts.

■ The state will require sophisticated data processing and auditing systems built around debit cards, a competence private-sector companies have but the government in a given state may not.

- ESAs require more from parents than traditional public schools or even scholarship programs. The state, in partnership with public and private schools and the emerging digital learning industry, must be prepared to field a team of advisors or coaches to lend their assistance.

- As parents use ESAs to take their children's education further and further away from the traditional K–12 school model, difficult issues of grade advancement, graduation, and remediation will need to be addressed.

Recommended Readings: Joseph L. Bast, "A Short History of Education Savings Accounts, *Policy Brief,* The Heartland Institute, 2005; Matthew Ladner and Nick Dranias, "Education Savings Accounts: Giving Parents Control of Their Children's Education," Goldwater Institute, 2011.

9. Design guidelines for charter schools.

Charter schools are public schools run by private entities that must compete with other schools for students and funding.

Charter schools are public schools run by private entities that must compete with other schools for students and funding. The schools' charters say the schools will receive a certain amount of funding per student only as long as they achieve specific outputs and comply with operating standards set forth in the agreement.

Allowing charter schools was among the first efforts to improve government schools by encouraging competition and choice. Measured by enrollment, the number of schools, and test scores, charter schools have been very successful. Some choice advocates, however, worry the charter school movement has become an obstacle to further reform.

The Charter School Success Story

Forty-four states and the District of Columbia have enacted charter school laws. Approximately 7 percent of all public schools were charter schools in 2014–15 (NCES 2017). Some 6,900 charter schools now enroll approximately 3.1 million students (NAPCS 2017a). In 2015, 14 school districts reported 30 percent or more of their students attended charter schools, and 160 districts reported 10 percent or more charter school enrollment (NAPCS 2015). Many of the students come from low-income homes, including some 80 percent of students in the 10 school districts with the highest charter school enrollment share. Nearly 90 percent of those students are minorities.

Charter school enrollment is growing rapidly, indicating the powerful demand from parents for more educational options. A 2015 study from the National Alliance for Public Charter Schools (NAPCS) reported, "Charter schools are the fastest-growing choice option in U.S. public education. Over the past five years, student enrollment in charter public schools has grown by 62 percent" (NAPCS 2015). Over the past 10 years, charter school enrollment has nearly tripled from 1.2 million students to around 3.1 million students (NAPCS 2017a). The share of students in Washington, DC, attending charter schools, for example, nearly doubled between 2005–06 and 2015–16, rising from 18,000 students to 39,000 students, meaning nearly half of all DC students now attend charter schools (Tuths 2016). Nearly 90 percent of students in New Orleans attend charter schools.

Yet the growth of new charter schools has slowed in recent years, coming to a virtual halt in 2016 according to the Center for Education Reform (CER 2017a). Meanwhile, the number of students on charter school waiting lists is growing, and now exceeds 1 million students nationwide (Kern and Gebru 2014; NAPCS 2014).

Because charter schools are heavily concentrated in low-income neighborhoods and big cities, determining their success relative to traditional public schools can be difficult and controversial. However, the best research on the subject—by Caroline M. Hoxby (2004), Bryan C. Hassel (2005), and Hoxby and Jonah E. Rockoff (2004)—shows convincing evidence of superior performance by charter schools. Importantly, randomized assignment studies—the "gold standard" for social science research—show charter schools have a positive effect on achievement, though these studies tend to be small-scale. (See Walberg 2007, Chapter 3, for a detailed survey of the literature.)

KIPP Charter Schools

Among the most successful charter school networks is the Knowledge Is Power Program (KIPP), a nationwide collection of open-enrollment middle schools commonly located in urban and poor communities. KIPP was founded in Houston, Texas in 1994 and has grown to 209 schools serving more than 88,000 students. Ninety-five percent of students enrolled in KIPP schools are minorities and more than 80 percent qualify for the federal free and reduced-price meals program for children from families in poverty.

KIPP schools identify five "operating principles" that distinguish their approach from other schools: clearly defined and measurable high expectations for academic achievement and conduct; parents and the faculty choose to be part of a KIPP school ("no one is assigned or forced to attend a KIPP school"); an extended school day, week, and year; principals who are empowered to lead their schools by having control over their school budget and personnel; and a tight focus on high student performance on standardized tests and other objective measures.

All five of these principles track what research shows to be the strategies of high-performing schools. Without the flexibility that charter school status provides, KIPP schools would not be able to adopt these policies, and without the public funding that follows low-income students to KIPP schools, the schools would be unable to compete with free public schools or serve disadvantaged communities. Public schools in districts where KIPP operates obviously could model some of their schools on the KIPP approach but, significantly, they have not done so. Thus, without KIPP, KIPP students would still be sitting in schools that are stubbornly unresponsive to their educational needs.

In 2013, the Mathematica Policy Research group published a multi-year study of KIPP schools and found that after three years in the program the students were 11 months ahead of their public school peers in math, eight months ahead in reading, and 14 months ahead in science. According to KIPP, by the end of eighth grade 62 percent of its students outperform their national peers in math, and 57 percent do so in reading. On state tests, by the end of eighth grade, 94 percent of KIPP classes outperform their local districts in reading; 96 percent do so in math.

KIPP is not the only network of successful charter schools, but KIPP schools illustrate how the charter mechanism can be used to reward students, parents, teachers, and school administrators who set high standards, work together, and use research-proven methods to accelerate learning.

Are Charters Enough?

Early in the history of the school choice movement, its leading advocates faced a difficult decision. Should they endorse charter schools as a modest first step toward the competitive marketplace for K–12 schooling they sought? Or was it too small a step, at best, or at worst a detour that might divert resources away from strategies, such as vouchers and tax-credit scholarships, that could more completely transform government schooling in America? With only a few exceptions, they endorsed charter schools.

The growth in charter school enrollment, studies of their academic achievements, evidence of public support and demand for more charter school capacity, and case studies of successful charter school chains such as KIPP make clear the tremendous amount of good they have achieved.

The lives of millions of students have been improved by this innovation. But nagging doubts about the strategy remain.

Charter schools are still *public* schools. Does this make it more likely they will be co-opted by the government school systems through increased regulation? There is evidence this is taking place (Allen 2016; Allen 2017). More than half of all charter school states—23 states and DC—cap the number of schools that can open, which means demand will continue to outpace supply (NAPCS 2017b). In recent years state agencies have increasingly regulated independent charter school authorizers, limiting charter schools' ability to innovate and offer parents options that meaningfully differ from district public schools (Allen 2017; CER 2017a; CER 2017b).

The Obama administration's Common Core standards have further homogenized public school curricula, teaching, and testing, so charter schools have less independence to distinguish themselves from their district counterparts (Frezza 2014; Walberg and Bast 2014; Butcher 2013). Charter schools are also increasingly under attack in cities like New York, Washington, DC, and even New Orleans. The president of the National Education Association, Lily Eskelsen Garcia, called privately managed charter schools "a failed and damaging experiment" (*Wall Street Journal* 2017).

Another concern is that much of the growth of charter schools has occurred at the expense of private schools, especially inner-city Catholic schools (Meyer 2007; Cavanaugh 2012). Additionally, philanthropists and taxpayers have spent billions of dollars building new charter schools or converting existing schools into charter schools. Had even a small fraction of that sum been devoted to political campaigns or referenda for voucher programs or tax-credit scholarships, either pilot programs like the one that operated for many years in Milwaukee (and more recently has become statewide) or statewide like the newer one in Indiana, many more students would be benefiting from school choice than are today. National surveys continue to show a majority of Americans favor private school choice (AFC 2017; Beck Research 2017). Research also suggests that in states such as Arizona and Florida, which treat public and private school options equally, both types of schools succeed, including Catholic schools (Smith 2017).

Harder to measure but perhaps even more troubling, how many of the parents of the 3.1 million students currently attending charter schools—and the tens of millions whose children attended charter schools in the past—would have been leaders in the effort for more *private* school choice, were it not for the charter school movement acting like the release valve on a pressure cooker, giving them a way to rescue their own children without transforming the government school system? Common Core may be changing this dynamic. It is probably no accident that education savings account legislation was introduced in at least 16 states in 2017 alone (Benson 2017).

Policy Agenda

Charter schools have been around for 25 years, and states vary in policies concerning their funding and accountability. A large body of research exists on best practices. Some of the more important insights include:

■ Do not limit or arbitrarily cap the number of charter schools or the number of students who can attend charter schools.

■ Do not attempt to overly specify what charter schools must look like by, for example, specifying student-teacher ratios, seat time, curriculum, or facilities.

■ Exempt charter schools from most school district laws and regulations, retaining only laws most necessary to safety, civil rights, financial stability, and accountability to parents. Follow North Carolina's lead and exempt charter schools from teacher certification requirements.

■ Fund charter schools at a level close to the amount the public schools receive in order to ensure real competition and choice.

■ Establish alternative authorizers. Allowing only a local school district to authorize a charter school often leads to too few schools to meet the demand.

■ Close charter schools that are failing to meet minimum performance thresholds.

Recommended Readings: National Alliance for Public Charter Schools (NAPCS), *A Growing Movement: America's Largest Charter School Communities, Tenth Annual Edition,* November 2015; Jeanne Allen, "A Movement at Risk: A Manifesto," Center for Education Reform, 2016.

10. Digital learning: The future of education?

Children today are much more comfortable using information technology than those of previous generations. Many grow up playing video games offering strong visual and audio stimulation, instant feedback on decisions, and nonfinancial rewards for achievement such as winning competitions, accumulating points, or being able to move to the next level of a game. The popularity of such games confirms what parents and good teachers know instinctively: Children can acquire knowledge and learn new skills at seemingly phenomenal speeds when they are fully engaged in the learning experience.

Technology applied to learning, also known as digital learning or online adaptive instruction, has vast potential to transform schooling. Terry Moe and John Chubb (2009) and Clayton Christensen and coauthors (2008) have made a strong case that technology will cause the "creative destruction" of America's K–12 school system. Either by itself or "blended" with traditional classroom teaching, digital learning is building a record of results substantially superior to traditional teaching and potentially far cheaper when used on a large scale.

Why Digital Learning?

Digital learning adds great value to the classroom because it enables teachers to adapt to the capacity and speed of individual learners, provide minute-by-minute feedback on learning progress, and provide rewards suitable for individual learners. It is similar to an imaginary inexhaustible, highly skilled tutor. Even the impressive results documented below are likely to be quickly surpassed since designers of digital courses can use billions of student responses not only to provide exemplary tutoring tailored to individual students' needs but also to continuously improve each step in the lessons.

Digital learning during childhood has the additional advantage of leading to mastery of skills, technological and other, that are necessary for further learning in subsequent grades, in college, and on the job. A survey of 300 professionals, for example, showed they spend 40 percent of their time in online communities interacting with others, and some 80 percent participate in online groups sharing information, ideas, and experiences (Valsiner and van der Veer 2000).

Online adaptive *testing* becomes a part of online adaptive *instruction* when computer programs and technology measure a student's progress while also selecting the next educational steps and lessons—sometimes called the student's "playlist"—that meet the student's specific instructional needs. Instead of passively listening to other students responding to questions asked by a teacher, each student actively responds at each step in a lesson. If the student is correct, the lesson immediately proceeds to the next step much like a tutor; if incorrect, the technology quickly remediates, making sure the student does not have to struggle with more advanced steps and lessons that rely on a piece of information or skill not yet acquired or, even worse, repeat and even practice mistakes. In these ways, technology resembles a skilled tutor but at a vastly lower per-pupil cost (Walberg 2011).

Online adaptive instruction can be "blended" with classroom instruction to create "hybrid" schools in which students spend part of the school day in front of computers and the rest of the day interacting with teachers and other students (Horn and Staker 2011). Data management systems can continuously update students' records on multiple devices enabling students, parents, and teachers to view a "dashboard" presenting data in ways best suited to their needs. Students spending time in a computer lab can be supervised by older students or teacher aides, freeing teachers to spend time in smaller seminar-style meetings or one-on-one sessions with students. The result is a boost in teacher productivity as well as in student learning.

A meta-analysis of 20 years of research showed adaptive online education programs on average provide better results than traditionally taught classes (Shachar and Neumann 2010). Most studies across various time periods showed superior results for the online programs. While 70 percent of all studies found online classes to be superior, 84 percent of studies published after 2002 found online superiority, suggesting (as we would expect) that online performance is improving over time. Studies after 2002 showed not only superiority but a very large average additional effect of +0.403, corresponding roughly to what is learned in four-tenths of a school year, which means the typical online education student exceeds 66 percent of traditionally taught students.

Rocketship Education

Rocketship Education charter schools provide an example of the use of online adaptive learning that appears to be economical, works for students from all backgrounds, and can be adopted on a large scale (see Spencer 2015; Schorr and McGriff 2011; DeGrow 2010).

Founded in San Jose, California in 2006, Rocketship Education charter schools offer "hybrid" learning to their K–5 students, some 90 percent of whom are poor and minority. Rocketship opened its first school, Mateo Sheedy Elementary, in 2007. It has since opened six additional K–5 elementary schools serving low-income and minority students in San Jose. An eighth Rocketship school, Rocketship Southside

Community Prep, opened in Milwaukee, Wisconsin in August 2013. According to Rocketship's website, its founders aspire "to ultimately open regional [school] clusters in 50 cities, effectively changing the lives of over 1 million students."

Rocketship students spend two hours a day in the Learning Lab, a computer lab where they work on software that teaches basic math and literacy skills. Computerized instruction focuses on repetitive and drill-intensive tasks such as arithmetic and spelling and gives teachers up-to-the-minute assessments of each student, which they then use to guide one-on-one and small group sessions with students during the rest of the school day. Rocketship says the time its students spend in the computer lab allows the company to hire between five and six fewer teachers in a school, about 25 percent of the total teaching staff, generating an annual savings of about $500,000.

Some of the savings is used for higher pay for teachers and to pay for the aides who act as coaches in the computer labs, but more importantly the savings make the model financially sustainable and scalable since charter schools typically receive per-pupil stipends that are less than what traditional public schools spend. In 2013, Rocketship Education announced plans to modify its system by placing teachers in addition to aides in the Learning Labs, with one teacher for each group of 90 students (Vanderkam 2013).

Data from the California Department of Education confirm the success of the Rocketship model. In 2012, Rocketship Mateo Sheedy Elementary, the first of the Rocketship schools to open, scored 924 on California's Academic Performance Index (API), well above the state average of 815. The five Rocketship schools enrolling students at the time the state tests were administered achieved an overall performance of 855, despite the lower socioeconomic status of their students.

In 2011, SRI International, a nonprofit research and development organization, conducted a 16-week study of Rocketship's use of DreamBox Learning, an online math tool. Students in kindergarten and first grade used the program. The study found, "Rocketship students who received additional online math instruction through the DreamBox Learning program scored substantially higher on an independent mathematics test than similar students who did not receive the additional online instruction time. For the average student, these gains would be equivalent to progressing 5.5 points in percentile ranking (e.g. from 50 percent to 55.5 percent) in just 16 weeks" (SRI International 2011). If that performance enhancement were continued over the course of a student's entire K–12 career, the difference in academic standing at graduation would be huge.

While many charter schools now incorporate adaptive instruction into the school day, Rocketship has concentrated on creating a business model that will enable it to produce hundreds of schools each generating superior results at a lower per-pupil cost than public schools. This requires designing schools that do not rely on charity or exceptional leaders or teachers willing to work 70 hours a week or longer and do everything from raising funds and recruiting and managing staff to providing after-school counseling to students.

Policy Agenda

Digital learning promises to truly transform K–12 education in America, creating opportunities to move beyond the "bricks and mortar" model and assumptions of conventional public schooling. Guidelines for incorporating digital learning into the school reform agenda include the following:

- All students, regardless of their background and socioeconomic background, can be digital learners and therefore all students should be eligible.

- Student progress should be based on demonstrated competency, not seat time.

- Students, schools, and parents should have access to multiple high-quality digital providers, not only a few approved by regulators.
- Public funding should encourage continued innovation in this field by empowering parents to choose schools that use digital learning—including "blended schools" and virtual schools—or to contract with alternative digital learning providers.

- Digital learning provides huge opportunities for homeschooling, making this a realistic option for millions of families.

Recommended Readings: Terry M. Moe and John E. Chubb, *Liberating Learning: Technology, Politics, and the Future of American Education* (San Francisco, CA: Jossey-Bass, Wiley, 2009); Clayton Christensen, Curtis W. Johnson, and Michael B. Horn. *Disrupting Class: How Disruptive Innovation Will Change the Way the World Learns* (New York, NY: McGraw-Hill, 2008).

References

AFC (American Federation for Children). 2017. "AFC Releases 2017 National Poll." Press release. January 12.

Alger (Murray), Vicki E. 2013. *Faith-Based Schools: Their Contributions to American Education, Society, and the Economy*. Scottsdale, AZ: Vicki Murray & Associates.

———. 2014. *Teacher Incentive Pay That Works: A Global Survey of Programs That Improve Student Achievement*. Vancouver, British Columbia: Fraser Institute.

———. 2015a. "Personalizing Learning Through Education Savings Accounts." Independent Women's Forum.

_____. 2015b. "Common Core: State Led or Gates Led?" Independent Women's Forum. January 1.

Allen, Jeanne. 2016. "A Movement at Risk: A Manifesto." Center for Education Reform.

_____. 2017. Quoted in "The Center for Education Reform Releases the 17th Edition of its National Charter School Law Rankings & Scorecard." Cision PR Newswire.

Anderson, David V. 2014. *Replacing Common Core with Proven Standards of Excellence*. Chicago, IL: The Heartland Institute.

Antonucci, Mike. 2015. "Teachers Unions and the War Within." *Education Next* **15** (1): 28–35.

Arons, Stephen. 1997. *Short Route to Chaos*. Amherst, MA: University of Massachusetts Press.

Bast, Joseph L. 2002a. *The Heartland Plan for Illinois: Model School Voucher Legislation*. Chicago, IL: The Heartland Institute.

_____. 2002b. "Why Conservatives and Libertarians Should Support School Vouchers." *Independent Review* **VII** (2): 265–76.

———. 2005. "A Short History of Education Savings Accounts." *Policy Brief.* The Heartland Institute.

_____. 2011. "The Indiana School Scholarship Act (House Bill 1003): Commentary and Analysis." *Policy Brief.* The Heartland Institute. June 7.

Bast, Joseph L., Bruno Behrend, Ben Boychuk, and Mark Oestreich. 2010. "The Parent Trigger: A Model for Transforming Education." *Policy Study.* The Heartland Institute.

Bast, Joseph L., Lindsey M. Burke, Andrew J. Coulson, Robert Enlow, Kara Kerwin, and Herbert J. Walberg. 2014. "Choosing to Earn." *National Review Online* (website).

Bast, Joseph L., and Joy Pullmann. 2012. "The Parent Trigger: Justification and Design Guidelines." *Policy Brief.* The Heartland Institute.

Bast, Joseph L., and Herbert J. Walberg. 2004. "Can Parents Choose the Best Schools for Their Children?" *Economics of Education Review* **23** (4): 431–40.

Beck Research LLC. 2017. "School Choice Survey Research Results." Memorandum to the American Federation for Children. January 10.

Beckner, Gary. 2011. "AAE is In for School Choice in 2011." Association of American Educators.

Bedrick, Jason. 2016. "The Folly of Overregulating School Choice." *Education Next* (website) January 5.

Belfield, Clive R., and Henry M. Levin. 2001. *The Effects of Competition on Educational Outcomes: A Review of U.S. Evidence.* New York, NY: National Center for the Study of Privatization in Education.

Benson, Tim. 2017. "Education Savings Accounts: The Future of School Choice Has Arrived." *Policy Brief.* The Heartland Institute, June 20.

Betts, Julian R., and Y. Emily Tang. 2014. *A Meta-Analysis of the Literature on the Effect of Charter Schools on Student Achievement.* Seattle, WA: Center for Reinventing Public Education.

Borcherding, Thomas E. 1977. *Budgets and Bureaucrats: The Sources of Government Growth.* Durham, NC: Duke University Press.

Brill, Steven. 2009. "The Rubber Room." *The New Yorker.* August 31.

Brimelow, Peter. 2003. *The Worm in the Apple: How the Teacher Unions Are Destroying American Education.* New York, NY: Harper Collins.

Butcher, Jonathan. 2013. "Common Core vs. Charter School Independence." *Real Clear Policy* (website). November 19.

Butcher, Jonathan, and Lindsey M. Burke. 2016. *The Education Debit Card II: What Arizona Parents Purchase with Education Savings Accounts.* Indianapolis, IN: EdChoice.

Carpenter, Dick M. 2014. *School Choice Signals: Research Review and Survey Experiments.* Indianapolis, IN: Friedman Foundation for Educational Choice.

Catt, Andrew D. 2014. *Public Rules on Private Schools: Measuring the Regulatory Impact of State Statutes and School Choice Programs.* Indianapolis, IN: Friedman Foundation for Educational Choice.

Catt, Andrew D., and Evan Rhinesmith. 2016. *Why Parents Choose: A Survey of Private School and School Choice Parents in Indiana.* Indianapolis, IN. EdChoice.

Cavanaugh, Sean. 2012. "Catholic Schools Feeling Squeeze From Charters." *Education Week* (website). August 28.

CER (Center for Education Reform). 2017a. "National Charter School Law Ranking and Scorecard." Press release. March 22.

_____. 2017b. *National Charter School Law Ranking and Scorecard 2017.*

Chingos, Matthew M., and Paul E. Peterson. 2015. "Experimentally Estimated Impacts of School Vouchers on College Enrollment and Degree Attainment." *Journal of Public Economics* **122** (February): 1–12. doi:10.1016/j.jpubeco.2014.11.013.

Christensen, Clayton, Curtis W. Johnson, and Michael B. Horn. 2008. *Disrupting Class: How Disruptive Innovation Will Change the Way the World Learns.* New York, NY: McGraw-Hill.

Chubb, John, and Terry Moe. 1990. *Politics, Markets, and America's Schools.* Washington, DC: Brookings Institution Press.

Coons, John E., and Stephen D. Sugarman. 1971. "Family Choice in Education: A Model State System for Vouchers." *California Law Review* **59** (2): 321–438. doi:10.15779/Z38PR23.

———. 1978. "Amid Perplexity, Who Should Decide?" Chapter 4 in *Education by Choice: The Case for Family Control*, 45–70. Troy, NY: Educator's International Press.

DeAngelis, Corey A. 2017. "Unintended Impacts of Regulations on the Quality of Schooling Options." *Education Next* (website). July 19.

DeGrow, Ben. 2010. "California Charter 'Rockets' to Hybrid Learning Success." *School Reform News*. March 24.

DiPerna, Paul. 2014. *Schooling in America Survey: Perspectives on School Choice, Common Core, and Standardized Testing*. Indianapolis, IN: Friedman Foundation for Educational Choice.

Duncan, Arne. 2013. "The Threat of Educational Stagnation and Complacency." U.S. Department of Education.

EdChoice. 2017a. *The ABCs of School Choice, 2017 Edition*. Indianapolis, IN: EdChoice.

———. 2017b. "Gold Standard Studies: Evaluating School Choice Programs (website)." Last modified March 23.

Egalite, Anna Jacob. 2014. *Competitive Impacts of Means-Tested Vouchers on Public School Performance: Evidence from Louisiana and Indiana*. Cambridge, MA: Harvard Kennedy School.

ERA New Orleans. 2017. "New Policy Brief Released: 'How Has the Louisiana Scholarship Program Affected Students? A Comprehensive Summary of Effects after Three Years.'" Press release. Education Research Alliance for New Orleans. June 26.

Finn Jr., Chester E., and Richard Sousa (editors). 2014. *What Lies Ahead for America's Children and Their Schools*. Stanford, CA: Hoover Institution Press.

Forster, Greg. 2016. *A Win-Win Solution: The Empirical Evidence on School Choice*. 4th edition. Indianapolis, IN: EdChoice.

Forster, Greg, and Matthew Carr. 2007. *Disruptive Behavior: An Empirical Evaluation of School Misconduct and Market Accountability*. Indianapolis, IN: Friedman Foundation for Educational Choice.

Forster, Greg, and C. Bradley Thompson (editors). 2011. *Freedom and School Choice in American Education*. New York, NY: Palgrave MacMillan.

Frezza, Bill. 2014. "Common Core Razes Charter School Standards." *Forbes* (website). April 18.

Friedman Foundation for Educational Choice. 2015a. *The ABCs of School Choice, 2015 Edition*. Indianapolis, IN: Friedman Foundation for Educational Choice.

———. 2015b. "Gold Standard Studies: Evaluating School Choice Programs (website)."

———. 2015b. "Does School Choice Have a Positive Academic Impact on Participating Students? (website)" Last modified February 26.

Friedman, Milton. 1995. *Public Schools: Make Them Private*. Washington, DC: Cato Institute.

Friedman, Milton, and Rose Friedman. 1980. *Free to Choose*. New York, NY: Harcourt Brace Jovanovich.

Gray, Nathan L., John D. Merrifield, and Kerry A. Adzima. 2014. "A Private Universal Voucher Program's Effects on Traditional Public Schools." *Journal of Economics and Finance* **40** (2): 319–44.

Hanushek, Eric A. 1996. *The Productivity Collapse in Schools*. Rochester, NY: W. Allen Wallis Institute of Political Economy, University of Rochester.

———. 2011. "Valuing Teachers." *Education Next* **11** (3): 41–5.

———. 2012. "Is the Common Core Just a Distraction?" *Education Next* (blog).

Hanushek, Eric A., Paul E. Peterson, and Ludger Woessmann. 2012. *Achievement Growth: International and U.S. State Trends in Student Performance*. Cambridge, MA: Harvard University's Program on Education Policy and Governance & Education Next.

———. 2013. *Endangering Prosperity: A Global View of the American School*. Washington, DC: Brookings Institution Press.

———. 2014. "U.S. Students from Educated Families Lag in International Tests." *Education Next* **14** (4): 9–18.

Hanushek, Eric A., and Ludger Woessmann. 2010. *The High Cost of Low Educational Performance: The Long-Run Economic Impact of Improving PISA Outcomes*. Paris: Organisation for Economic Co-operation and Development.

Hassel, Bryan C. 2005. *Charter School Achievement: What We Know*. Chapel Hill, NC: Public Impact.

Henderson, Michael B., Paul E. Peterson, and Martin R. West. 2015. "No Opinion on the Common Core: Also Teacher Grades, School Choices, and Other Findings from the 2014 EdNext Poll." *Education Next* **15** (1): 9–19.

Hess, Frederick M. 2010. "Teachers and Teaching." In *The Same Thing Over and Over: How Reformers Get Stuck in Yesterday's Ideas*. Cambridge, MA: Harvard University Press. pp. 131–62.

Hill, Paul T. 2013. "Picturing a Different Governance Structure for Public Education." In *Education Governance for the Twenty-First Century: Overcoming the Structural Barriers to School Reform*, edited by Patrick McGuinn and Paul Manna, 329–52. Washington, DC: Brookings Institution Press.

Holley, Marc J., Anna Jacob Egalite, and Martin F. Lueken. 2013. "Competition with Charters Motivates Districts." *Education Next* **13** (4): 28–35.

Hood, John, and Terry Stoops. 2014. *Educational Freedom Works: Scholarly Research Shows Gains from School Choice and Competition*. Raleigh, NC: John Locke Foundation.

Horn, Michael B., and Heather Staker. *The Rise of K–12 Blended Learning*. Innosight Institute. January 2011.

Hoxby, Caroline M. 2001. "School Choice and School Productivity, or Could School Choice Be a Tide That Lifts All Boats?" In *Economics of School Choice*, edited by Caroline Minter Hoxby. Chicago, IL: University of Chicago Press. pp. 287–341.

———. 2003a. "School Choice and Competition: Evidence from the United States." *Swedish Economic Policy Review* **10** (2): 9–66.

———. 2003b. "What Has Changed and What Has Not." In *Our Schools and Our Future: Are We Still at Risk?* Stanford, CA: Hoover Institution Press. pp. 73–110.

Hoxby, Caroline M., and Andrew Leigh. 2005. "Wage Distortion." *Education Next* **4** (2): 51–6.

Hoxby, Caroline M., and Jonah E. Rockoff. 2004. "The Impact of Charter Schools on Student Achievement."

Kelly, Andrew P. 2014. *Turning Lightning into Electricity: Organizing Parents for Education Reform*. Washington, DC: American Enterprise Institute.

Kern, Nora, and Wentana Gebru. 2014. *Waiting Lists to Attend Charter Schools Top 1 Million Names*. Washington, DC: National Alliance for Public Charter Schools.

Ladner, Matthew, and Nick Dranias. 2011. *Education Savings Accounts: Giving Parents Control of Their Children's Education*. Phoenix, AZ: Goldwater Institute.

Layton, Lindsey. 2014. "How Bill Gates Pulled Off the Swift Common Core Revolution." *Washington Post*. June 7.

Lieberman, Myron. 1986. "The Due Process Fiasco." Chapter 4 in *Beyond Public Education*. New York, NY: Praeger Publishers.

_____. 2000. *The Teacher Unions: How They Sabotage Educational Reform and Why*. New York, NY: Encounter Books.

———. 2007. *The Educational Morass: Overcoming the Stalemate in American Education*. Lanham, MD: Rowman & Littlefield Publishers.

Lieberman, Myron, and Charlene K. Haar. 2003. *Public Education as a Business: Real Costs and Accountability*. Lanham, MD: Scarecrow Press.

Loeb, Susanna, Anthony Byrk, and Eric Hanushek. 2007. *Getting Down to Facts: School Finance and Governance in California*. Stanford, CA: Stanford University.

Lombard, Kirsten (editor). 2014. *Common Ground on Common Core*. DeForest, WI: Resounding Books.

Loveless, Tom. 2012. *2012 Brown Center Report on American Education: How Well Are American Students Learning?* Washington, DC: Brookings Institution.

Lynch, Robert. 2015. "The Economic and Fiscal Consequences of Improving U.S. Educational Outcomes." Washington Center for Equitable Growth.

McCarthy, Rockne, Donald Oppewal, Walfred Peterson, and Gordon Spykman. 1981. *Society, State and Schools: A Case for Structural and Confessional Pluralism*. Grand Rapids, MI: William B. Eerdmans.

McShane, Michael Q. 2014. "Back to Bad Schools." *Washington Examiner*. September 8.

Merrifield, John D. 2001. *The School Choice Wars*. Lanham, MD: Roman & Littlefield Publishers.

Merrifield, John D., and David Salisbury. 2005. "The Competitive Education Industry Concept and Why It Deserves More Scrutiny." *Cato Journal* **25** (2): 181–95.

Meyer, Peter. 2007. "Can Catholic Schools Be Saved?" *Education Next* **7** (2): 12–20.

Moe, Terry M. 2011. *Special Interest: Teachers Unions and America's Public Schools*. Washington, DC: Brookings Institution Press.

————. 2014. "Facing the Union Challenge." In *What Lies Ahead for America's Children and Their Schools*. Charles E. Finn Jr. and Richard Sousa (editors). Stanford, CA: Hoover Institution Press. pp. 37–50.

Moe, Terry M., and John E. Chubb. 2009. *Liberating Learning: Technology, Politics, and the Future of American Education*. San Francisco, CA: Jossey-Bass, Wiley.

Moe, Terry M., and Paul T. Hill. 2012. "Moving to a Mixed Model: Without an Appropriate Role for the Market, the Education Sector Will Stagnate." In *The Futures of School Reform*. Jal Mehta, Robert B. Schwartz, and Frederick M. Hess (editors). Cambridge, MA: Harvard Education Press.

Moore, Terrence O. 2013. *The Story-Killers: A Common-Sense Case Against the Common Core*. CreateSpace Independent Publishing Platform. October 30.

NAPCS (National Association of Public Charter Schools). 2014. "Students Names on Charter Schools Waiting Lists Top 1 Million for the First Time." Press release. May 5.

————. 2015. *A Growing Movement: America's Largest Charter School Communities, Tenth Annual Edition*. November.

————. 2017a. "Estimated Charter Public School Enrollment, 2016–17." February 1.

————. 2017b. *Measuring Up to the Model: A Ranking of State Charter School Laws, Eighth Edition*. March.

NCEE (National Commission on Excellence in Education). 1983. *A Nation at Risk: The Imperative of Educational Reform*. Washington, DC: U.S. Department of Education.

NCES (National Center for Education Statistics). 2013a. *Digest of Education Statistics 2013*. Washington, DC: Institute of Education Sciences.

————. 2013b. *The Nation's Report Card: Trends in Academic Progress 2012*. Washington, DC: Institute of Education Sciences.

————. 2013c. *NAEP Mathematics 2013 State Snapshot Reports: Illinois*. Washington, DC: Institute of Education Sciences.

————. 2013d. *NAEP Reading 2013 State Snapshot Readings: Illinois*. Washington, DC: Institute of Education Sciences.

————. 2015. *Digest of Education Statistics 2015*. Washington, DC: Institute of Education Sciences.

————. 2016a. *The Nation's Report Card: 2015 Mathematics and Reading Grade 12 Assessments*. Washington, DC: Institute of Education Sciences.

————. 2016b. *Public high school 4-year adjusted cohort graduation rate (ACGR), by race/ethnicity and selected demographics for the United States, the 50 states, and the District of Columbia: School year 2014–15*.

————. 2016c. *Digest of Education Statistics, 2016*. Washington, DC: Institute of Education Sciences.

————. 2017. "Charter Schools" (website.)

OECD (Organisation for Economic Co-operation and Development). 2016a. *PISA 2015 Results in Focus*. Paris: OECD Publishing.

————. 2016b. *Education at a Glance 2016: OECD Indicators*. Paris: OECD Publishing. doi: 10.1787/eag-2016-21-en

Padover, Saul K. 1939. *Thomas Jefferson on Democracy*. New York, NY: Appleton-Century Company, Inc.

Perie, Marianne, Alan Vanneman, and Arnold Goldstein. 2005. *Student Achievement in Private Schools: Results from NAEP 2000–2005*. Washington, DC: National Center for Education Statistics.

Peterson, Paul E. 2003. *Our Schools and Our Future ... Are We Still at Risk?* Stanford, CA: Hoover Institution Press.

———. 2006. "Thorough and Efficient Private and Public Schools." In *Courting Failure: How Schools Finance Lawsuits Exploit Judges' Good Intentions and Harm Our Children*. Eric A. Hanushek (editor). Stanford, CA: Education Next Books of Hoover Institution Press. pp. 195–234.

Pullmann, Joy. 2012. "Education Spending and Student Achievement." *Research & Commentary*. The Heartland Institute.

———. 2013a. *Common Core: A Poor Choice for States*. Chicago, IL: The Heartland Institute.

———. 2013b. "Common Core Standards." *Policy Tip Sheet*. The Heartland Institute.

———. 2014. "Testimony on House Bill 597 to Repeal and Replace Common Core to the Ohio House Rules and Reference Committee." The Heartland Institute.

Savas, Emanuel S. 2000. *Privatization and Public Private Partnerships*. New York, NY: Chatham House Publishers.

Scafidi, Benjamin. 2012. *The School Staffing Surge: Decades of Employment Growth in America's Public Schools*. Indianapolis, IN: Friedman Foundation for Educational Choice.

———. 2013. *The School Staffing Surge: Decades of Employment Growth in America's Public Schools: Part II*. Indianapolis, IN: Friedman Foundation for Educational Choice.

Scafidi, Benjamin, and James P. Kelly. 2013. *More Than Scores: An Analysis of Why and How Parents Choose Private Schools*. Indianapolis, IN: Friedman Foundation for Educational Choice.

Schorr, Jonathan and Debora McGriff. 2011. "Future Schools." *Education Next* **11** (3): 10–7.

Shachar, Mickey, and Yoram Neumann. 2010. "Twenty Years of Research on the Academic Performance Differences Between Traditional and Distance Learning: Summative Meta-Analysis and Trend Examination." *MERLOT Journal of Online Learning and Teaching* **6** (2): 318–34.

Shuls, James V. 2013. "Why We Need School Choice." *Education News*.

Shultz, George P., and Eric A. Hanushek. 2012. "Education is the Key to a Healthy Economy." *The Wall Street Journal*. May 1.

Skillen, James W. (editor). 1993. *The School-Choice Controversy: What Is Constitutional?* Grand Rapids, MI: Baker Publishing Group.

Spalding, Jeff. 2014. *The School Voucher Audit: Do Publicly Funded Private School Choice Programs Save Money?* Indianapolis, IN: Friedman Foundation for Educational Choice.

Smith, Nicholas Wolfram. 2017. "Will Catholic Schools Be Left Behind by School Choice?" *National Catholic Register*. May 18.

Spencer, Kyle. 2015. "Rocketship Education, California's Tech-heavy Charter Network, Is Growing, Some Say Too Fast." *The Hechinger Report* (website). July 5.

SRI International. 2011. "SRI Study: Rocketship Students Experience Stronger Math Gains with More Online Instruction." August 2.

SSA (U.S. Social Security Administration). 2012. *Annual Statistical Supplement, 2011*. Washington, DC: U.S. Social Security Administration.

Stotsky, Sandra. 2012. "Invited Testimony on the Low Quality of the Common Core Standards." Colorado State Board of Education. December 6.

Sude, Yujie, Corey A. DeAngelis, and Patrick J. Wolf. 2017. "Supplying Choice: An Analysis of School Participation Decisions in Voucher Programs in DC, Indiana, and Louisiana." *Louisiana Scholarship Program Evaluation Report* #9. School Choice Demonstration Project, University of Arkansas, Fayetteville, Arkansas, and the Education Research Alliance for New Orleans, Tulane University, New Orleans, Louisiana. Last updated July.

Tuths, Peter. 2016. "A Changing Landscape: Examining How Public Charter School Enrollment Is Growing in DC." DC Fiscal Policy Institute. April 28.

Valente, William D. 1985. *Education Law: Public and Private*. St. Paul, MN: West.

Valsiner, Jaan, and René van der Veer, 2000. *The Social Mind*. New York, NY: Cambridge University Press.

Vanderkam, Laura. 2013. *Blended Learning: A Wise Giver's Guide to Supporting Tech-assisted Teaching*. Washington, DC: Philanthropy Roundtable.

Vedder, Richard K. 1996. *The Three "Ps" of American Education: Performance, Productivity, and Privatization*. St. Louis, MO: Center for the Study of American Business.

———. 2000. *Can Teachers Own Their Own Schools?* Oakland, CA: Independent Institute.

Walberg, Herbert J. 2007. *School Choice: The Findings*. Washington, DC: Cato Institute.

———. 2011. *Tests, Testing, and Genuine School Reform*. Stanford, CA: Hoover Institution Press.

———. 2014. "Expanding Options." In *What Lies Ahead for America's Children and Their Schools*. Charles E. Finn Jr. and Richard Sousa (editors). Stanford, CA: Hoover Institution Press. pp. 71–86.

Walberg, Herbert J., and Joseph L. Bast. 2003. *Education and Capitalism*. Stanford, CA: Hoover Institution Press.

———. 2014a. "Why Academic Achievement Matters." *Human Events*.

———. 2014b. *Rewards: How to use rewards to help children learn – and why teachers don't use them well*. Chicago, IL: The Heartland Institute.

Wall Street Journal. 2017. "State of the Teachers Union." July 5.

Weisberg, Daniel, Susan Sexton, Jennifer Mulhern, and David Keeling. 2009. *The Widget Effect: Our National Failure to Acknowledge and Act on Differences in Teacher Effectiveness*. New York, NY: The New Teacher Project.

Wingett Sanchez, Yvonne, and Rob O'Dell. 2017. "Arizona is Expanding Its School-voucher Program. What Does It Mean for Parents?" *Azcentral* (website).

Witte, John F. 2000. *The Market Approach to Education: An Analysis of America's First Voucher Program*. Princeton, NJ: Princeton University Press.

Wolf, Patrick J., Brian Kisida, Babette Gutmann, Michael Puma, Nada Eissa, and Lou Rizzo. 2013. "School Vouchers and Student Outcomes: Experimental Evidence from Washington, DC." *Journal of Policy Analysis and Management* **32** (1): 246–70. doi:10.1002/pam.21691.

Wurman, Ze'ev and W. Stephen Wilson. 2012. "The Common Core Math Standards." *Education Next* **12** (3): 44–50.

Zeehandelaar, Dara, and Amber Northern (editors). 2013. *What Parents Want: Education Preferences and Trade-Offs; A National Survey of K–12 Parents*. Washington, DC: Thomas B. Fordham Institute.

Additional Resources

Additional information about elementary and secondary education policy is available from The Heartland Institute:

- PolicyBot, The Heartland Institute's free online clearinghouse for the work of other free-market think tanks, contains thousands of documents on education issues. It is on Heartland's website at https://www.heartland.org/policybot/.

- https://www.heartland.org/Center-Education/ is the website of Heartland's Center for Transforming Education, devoted to the latest research, news, and commentary about K–12 education issues. Read headlines, watch videos, or browse the thousands of documents on education issues available from PolicyBot.

- *School Reform News* is The Heartland Institute's monthly newspaper devoted to education issues. Subscriptions with digital delivery are free, print subscriptions are $36/year for 10 issues. Subscribe at www.heartland.org/subscribe.

Directory

The following national organizations provide valuable information about K–12 education policies.

American Federation for Children, https://www.federationforchildren.org/

Association of American Educators, https://www.aaeteachers.org/

Black Alliance for Educational Options, http://www.baeo.org

Cato Institute, https://www.cato.org/

Center for Education Reform, https://www.edreform.com/

Center on Reinventing Public Education, http://www.crpe.org/

EdChoice (formerly Friedman Foundation for Educational Choice), https://www.edchoice.org/

Education Next, http://educationnext.org/

Heartland Institute, https://www.heartland.org/

Home School Legal Defense Association, https://hslda.org/

KIPP Charter Schools, http://www.kipp.org/

Koret Task Force of Hoover Institution, http://www.hoover.org/research-teams/k-12-task-force

National Alliance for Public Charter Schools, http://www.publiccharters.org/

National Center for Education Statistics, http://nces.ed.gov

National Center for the Study of Privatization in Education at Teachers College – Columbia University, http://ncspe.tc.columbia.edu/

National School Choice Week, https://schoolchoiceweek.com

Program on Education Policy and Governance at Harvard University, https://sites.hks.harvard.edu/pepg/

Reason Foundation, http://reason.org/

RedefinEd, https://www.redefinedonline.org/

University of Arkansas, Department of Education Reform, http://www.uaedreform.org

Chapter 4
Higher Education

Richard Vedder, Joshua Distel, and Justin Strehle

---

10 Principles of Higher Education Policy

1. Higher education in the United States isn't working.
2. Make students foot a larger share of the bill.
3. Promote free expression of ideas.
4. Increase transparency of costs and results.
5. Promote alternatives to college.
6. Emphasize instruction and raise academic standards.
7. Restructure university ownership and governance.
8. Revamp or eliminate federal student financial aid.
9. End destructive government regulation.
10. Reform or eliminate accreditation.

Introduction

A national survey released by the Pew Research Center in 2017 found only 55 percent of Americans said higher education had a positive impact on the nation (Pew 2017). This is hardly a ringing endorsement of an institution that spends $500 billion a year, much of it given involuntarily by taxpayers. Even more telling, only 36 percent of Republicans and Republican-leaning independents said colleges and universities have a positive effect on the country, and a stunning 58 percent said higher education has a negative effect.

Republicans, and more generally conservatives, used to support higher education. In just two years, according to Pew, their support plummeted from 54 percent 36 percent. Anyone paying attention can guess why this has happened.

The political left's conquest of higher education has been documented and lamented for many years (e.g., Bloom 1987; Bok 2006). Eight years of President Barack Obama emboldened many liberal activists who happen to be college professors to lecture the country on the correctness of progressive causes (Fish 2012) … and most recently, the terrible evil of candidate and now President Donald Trump.

With their professors' implicit or explicit approval, students on some campuses are shouting down conservative speakers, demanding enforcement of bans on politically incorrect speech, and even wearing masks and carrying bats on campuses to threaten those who don't agree with their extremist political views (*Modern Age* 2017; Kabbany 2017).

The failure of higher education in the United States is on the front pages of our newspapers and on the evening news on television. Past methods of governance and finance simply aren't working anymore. This chapter documents the problem and offers a policy agenda to fix it.

Recommended Readings: Alan Bloom, *The Closing of the American Mind* (New York, NY: Simon and Schuster, 1987); Derek Bok, *Our Underachieving Colleges: A Candid Look at How Much Students Learn and Why They Should Be Learning More* (Princeton, NJ: Princeton University Press, 2006).

1. Higher education isn't working.

> Higher education in the United States costs too much, often produces a low-quality educational experience, and is resistant to reform.

The United States spends about $500 billion per year on various forms of postsecondary education—the equivalent of 3 percent of the nation's total economic output—triple the proportion of a half-century ago (NCES 2014a). Higher education costs per student are greater in the United States than in any other large country (IPEDS 2014). Increasing evidence suggests much of this spending is wasted:

- "[C]olleges and universities have done a poor job of ensuring the civic literacy on which our nation depends. Too many institutions fail to require courses that ensure civic knowledge and often allow community service projects, well-intentioned as they are, to substitute for deep learning about our nation's institutions of government and their history" (ACTA 2016a).

■ A 2015 survey of employers found "just 23 percent of employers say that recent college graduates are well prepared when it comes to having the ability to apply knowledge and skills in real world settings, and 44 percent rate them as not that or not at all prepared" (Hart Research Associates 2015).

■ Although difficult to quantify, by any reasonable measure productivity in higher education is at best stagnant and probably falling (Vedder 2004).

■ Falling teaching loads have led to a proliferation of articles published in obscure academic journals that few people read (Bauerlein *et al.* 2010).

■ Forty percent of students enrolling in bachelor's degree programs full-time fail to earn a degree within six years (NCES 2009b).

■ Although college graduates have a higher level of reading comprehension than their counterparts of a decade ago, they still have fallen from the comprehension levels of 1993 (PIAAC 2012).

■ Students are burdened with excessive debt from college, sometimes larger than can be sustained on their modest post-college incomes (Leef 2016b).

■ The cost of obtaining a four-year degree has more than doubled since 1975 in inflation-adjusted dollars (NCES 2009a).

■ The typical college student of today spends about 25 percent less time on academic pursuits than his or her counterpart of a half-century ago, as grade inflation makes it easier to perform well with less work (Babcock and Marks 2010; NSSE 2015).

■ Universities devote more of their budgets than previously to non-instructional pursuits, such as swollen and highly paid bureaucracies, country club-like recreational facilities, and research with low value outside the academic community (Martin 2009; Fried 2011).

■ Upwards of one-half of college graduates are "underemployed," taking jobs requiring far fewer skills than are usually associated with people of their educational level (Vedder *et al.* 2013).

Policy Agenda

Higher education in America isn't working for students, their parents, or for taxpayers. Public policies ought to reflect this reality:

■ We spend hundreds of billions of dollars on colleges and universities every year. Making more efficient use of those resources should be a high national goal.

■ Many colleges and universities are failing to deliver the quality of educational experience that would justify their high spending levels.

■ Colleges and universities are failing to prepare their graduates for the marketplace, resulting in excessive levels of underemployment for college graduates.

■ At a time when national and state government deficits are increasingly viewed as unsustainable, higher education deserves to be on a short list of candidates for spending reductions.

Recommended Readings: Richard Vedder, *Going Broke by Degree: Why College Costs Too Much* (Washington, DC: AEI Press, 2004); Charles Murray, *Real Education: Four Simple Truths for Bringing America's Schools Back to Reality* (Washington, DC: Crown Forum, 2008).

2. Make students foot more of the bill.

Government and private subsidies to higher education have caused spending to soar and disempowered students, who should be the real consumers.

Higher education has become politicized, bloated, and unproductive because students are paying too small a share of the cost of the services provided. When someone other than the customer is paying the bills, producers have little incentive to cut costs or make the customer happy.

Are Public Subsidies Justified?

Government and private subsidies to colleges are often justified on two grounds. First, it is argued that higher education is a "public good" that confers benefits not just on the individual educated but on the broader society as well. However, the empirical evidence relating to these positive spillover effects is murky at best, and some of it even suggesting government subsidies have a negative spillover effect: lower rates of economic growth (Vedder 2004; Alchian 1968).

Second, subsidy proponents contend higher education is a means to achieve the American Dream: to ensure anyone, no matter what their economic or family circumstances, can succeed in the United States. Yet here too the evidence that third-party payments have brought about educational equality is scant. Among all college students earning bachelor's degrees, the proportion of those from families in the bottom quartile of income has actually decreased over 45 years, despite large increases in federal student aid in the form of Pell Grants and college loans (Mortenson 2009). The number of bottom-quartile degree-earners has grown by only 3 percent, while the other three quartiles averaged almost 20 percent growth (Sherman 2015).

College graduates benefit from having their degrees, with the earnings differential between college graduates and high school graduates averaging well over 60 percent since 1980 (O'Keefe and Vedder 2008). Given that higher education is a good investment for many, why not let students pay the costs just as we do with other personal investments?

An Opportunity to Save Taxpayers' Money

Reducing public funding of higher education by both national and state governments would result in students—the real consumers of higher education—footing a larger share of the bill. This would make colleges and universities more accountable to students and their parents. Since the economic benefits of higher education are largely captured by the college graduate, not by the rest of society, students can rightly be asked to foot the bill themselves.

Some students from low-income families benefit from government and private support of higher education, and some or all of that aid could continue, but most federal aid goes to students and families who are well-off and could afford to pay tuition without public assistance. As former Education Secretary Bill Bennett (1987) hypothesized and others have demonstrated empirically (Lucca et al. 2015; Gordon and Hedlund 2016), federal student aid has contributed to tuition price inflation, so much federal support indirectly goes to the providers in the form of higher salaries and more administrative bloat.

As state government budgets are squeezed by rising costs of Medicaid, corrections, and other functions, many are starting to resist new higher education spending. State appropriations fell in the aftermath of the 2008 financial crisis and have not fully recovered in many states— 15 states spent less on higher education in 2016 than in 2011 (Palmer 2016).

Perhaps the time has come to begin to privatize some public universities. Institutions such as the universities of Colorado, Michigan, and Virginia now get 10 percent or less of their budgets from state appropriations (IPEDS 2014). Why not phase out the state subsidies and related bureaucracy altogether?

Another big subsidy is the tax breaks for those who give money to a college or university, even if the money goes to fund non-educational facilities, such as stadium renovations or luxury dormitories. Perhaps allowing deductions only for donations to activities, facilities and equipment—laboratories, computers—would be a better approach. Such a move might also dampen down rising costs of the "academic arms race" of schools spending ever-larger amounts of money to entice good students to attend with nonacademic inducements.

As paradoxical as it may seem, the best thing taxpayers can do for higher education is to stop funding it. A system that relied more on tuition and profits, and less on government subsidies and tax-advantaged charity, would be more efficient and more responsive to the needs of its customers.

If despite the arguments above, governmental student aid is continued, put limits on support in five ways. First, limit assistance to genuinely lower income students who likely otherwise would not attend college. Second, put some time limits on receipt of aid—to four or at most five years for a full-time student pursuing a bachelor's degree. Third, insist on some minimal academic standards as is common with private scholarship grants. Fourth, severely restrict aid for graduate or professional school education, which tends to be exceedingly expensive and primarily benefits recipients financially. Why should the federal government fund middle class students seeking MBAs that lead to high paying jobs? Fifth, pass legislation supporting privately funded Income Share Agreements (ISAs) rather than federal grants and loans. Under ISAs, students give up a percentage of postgraduate earnings to a private investor who finances part of undergraduate college costs.

Policy Agenda

Over-reliance on third-party payers for college tuition is at the root of many of the problems facing higher education. The following reforms would directly address that problem:

■ Reduce federal and state aid to higher education while allowing public institutions to raise tuition or cut spending as necessary to balance their budgets.

■ Focus aid on students from lower-income families who genuinely need financial support to achieve the American Dream.

■ End state funding altogether of public universities that already get the lion's share of their income from sources other than state funding.

■ Restrict tax deductions for private contributions to universities that are earmarked for non-educational facilities such as stadium renovations and athletic programs.

Additionally, aid, in the form of vouchers should be:

■ Targeted to undergraduates, who often are overlooked and shortchanged by today's universities.

■ Limited to four years, encouraging students to finish their degrees on schedule.

■ Awarded in amounts reflecting both financial need and academic success.

■ Available to alternatives to traditional state-supported colleges and universities.

Also, private forms of financing, such as Income Share Agreements (ISAs) should be encouraged.

Recommended Readings: Milton Friedman, "The Role of Government in Education," Chapter 6 in *Capitalism and Freedom* (Chicago, IL: University of Chicago Press, 1962); Richard Vedder, *Over Invested and Over Priced* (Washington, DC: Center for College Affordability and Productivity, 2007); Andrew Gillen, *Financial Aid in Theory and Practice: Why It Is Ineffective and What Can Be Done About It* (Washington, DC: Center for College Affordability and Productivity, 2009).

3. Promote free expression of ideas.

Universities receiving government aid should face adverse consequences for condoning restrictions on peaceful expression of opinions.

Colleges should be sanctuaries where individuals can utter unpopular, often heretical thoughts without fear of intimidation. Campuses thrive on the give-and-take of debate and ardent but peaceful discussion.

Yet on numerous campuses that vital debate has come under assault. Invited guest speakers are being "disinvited" or physically prevented from speaking, protestors shout them down, etc. Jane Shaw reported on one such episode for *School Reform News*:

> A group of people protesting an event featuring a conservative speaker at the University of California-Berkeley committed numerous acts of assault and vandalism and succeeded in having the event canceled.
>
> Masked and dressed in black, approximately 150 rioters streamed into the area around the student union of the university on the night of February 1. The rioters threw rocks and fireworks at police, set fires, broke windows, and threw Molotov cocktails, causing $100,000 in damage and minor injuries.
>
> The rioters' stated goal was to disrupt a speech scheduled for that evening by a controversial editor of *Breitbart News*, Milo Yiannopoulos. They succeeded; the university canceled the speech (Shaw 2017).

University administrations often tacitly or even explicitly support these efforts at suppressing First Amendment rights. That must stop at schools receiving substantial state or federal support.

To be sure, campus independence from the political process is highly desirable, and care must be exercised so the cure to the problem is not worse than the disease. Yet it is not unreasonable to require schools receiving government aid to protect peaceful speakers from disruption, denying funds to schools failing to honor that commitment.

Policy Agenda
Colleges and universities can be incentivized to promote free expression of ideas by adopting the following policies:

■ Reduce significantly federal and state aid to schools and their students for verified violations of the principle of free expression for students, faculty, and campus speakers;

■ Encourage colleges to approve as official institutional policy a statement similar to that elucidated in the Chicago Principles adopted by the University of Chicago, Princeton, Purdue and several other major universities.

Recommended Reading: Harvey A. Silverglate, David French, and Greg Lukianoff, *FIRE's Guide to Free Speech on Campus*, Foundation for Individual Rights in Education, 2012.

4. Increase transparency of cost and results.

Students and their parents need better information to make informed decisions about their higher education plans.

Making informed decisions about what college or university to attend and what degree to pursue without good information on costs and performance is impossible. Did Harvard have a good year in 2015? Who knows? Do its seniors know more than its freshmen do? Is the research of its humanities faculty read by many people? Has it materially improved our understanding of the human condition?

Do students graduating from Harvard get good jobs, and does that vary greatly by major? Does it cost more to educate a historian than a sociologist? How much time do students spend studying, as opposed to partying or pursuing other nonacademic activities?

How much of the university's resources are used for Ph.D. training relative to undergraduate learning? How does its performance compare with five years ago or with competing institutions, such as Yale and Princeton? By and large, the answers to these questions are unknown.

One effort to increase transparency in higher education is *What Will They Learn?*, an annual survey produced by the American Council of Trustees and Alumni (ACTA) of core requirements of more than 1,100 colleges and universities (ACTA 2016b). The latest survey found "two-thirds earn a 'C' or lower for their general education requirements, leaving large numbers of graduates with significant gaps in their knowledge and ill-prepared for their careers."

With only a few exceptions, all postsecondary institutions receive significant amounts of government or private philanthropic aid. Yet those subsidies are provided blindly, with taxpayers getting little information about how efficiently their hard-earned money is being used. Colleges often have valuable information from instruments such as the National Survey of Student Engagement and the Collegiate Learning Assessment about how students use their time or what level of critical thinking skills they have obtained. This information is rarely shared with the public.

The College Scorecard (DoE 2015) provides useful data about student debt loads and default rates and postgraduate earnings, but the earnings data are skewed by incomplete reporting. The Internal Revenue Service can and should provide earnings information on 100 percent of those completing college.

Likewise, there is a lack of precise information on faculty teaching loads, the salary and fringe benefits of key employees, and the allocation of resources among undergraduate and graduate teaching and nonteaching activities. Information on teaching loads in Oklahoma and Texas, obtained under public record laws, shows many faculty do scant teaching, receive hefty salaries, and seldom publish (Vedder and Hennen 2014).

Extremely costly nonacademic facilities receive little evaluation on cost-benefit grounds. NC State's $120 million Talley Student Union building has a 1,200-seat ballroom, fireplace lounges, and nine upgraded dining choices, not to mention installed pieces of art works (Robinson 2017). Princeton constructed Whitman College, a residential housing facility for about 400 undergraduates, for a cost of $136 million—at least $340,000 per student (Marks 2002). For that money, you could buy 400 houses!

Classroom space is wasted. According to a higher education consultant who specializes in facilities management, on average only 49 percent of classrooms are being used at any one time during a school week, Monday through Friday, 8:00 am to 10:00 pm (Cheston 2012).

States could readily obtain and publicly report performance and cost data about their institutions. Why shouldn't universities publish the teaching loads, salaries, and research grants received by their faculty, as the governments in Oklahoma and Texas compelled their state universities to do? Why not do the same for administrative staff? Perhaps this would shame universities into putting more emphasis on teaching and reveal excesses in compensation.

Given that they support public universities and community colleges, state governments have a responsibility to collect and report the data needed to hold higher education's leaders accountable for results. Simply supplying students and their parents with accurate outcomes information alone would force the state's colleges and universities to be more responsive to students.

If students and families were really in charge of their spending on higher education, they would demand this information. In addition, making institutions directly accountable to students would allow the state to reduce its oversight role, thus saving taxpayer dollars and reducing government intrusion.

Policy Agenda

Colleges and universities that receive public funding should be required to disclose the following information:

- student graduation rates, debt loads, default rates, and postgraduate earnings;

- teaching loads, salaries, fringe benefits, and research grants received by their entire faculty;

- job descriptions, salaries, and benefits of administrative staff; and

- allocation of resources among undergraduate and graduate teaching and nonteaching activities.

Recommended Reading: Derek Bok, *Higher Education in America* (Princeton, NJ: Princeton University Press, 2013); Richard Vedder and Anthony Hennen, *Dollars and Sense: Assessing Oklahoma's Public Universities* (Oklahoma City, OK: Oklahoma Council of Public Affairs, 2014).

5. Promote alternatives to college.

A college education is not for everyone, and public policy should not skew students toward choosing a college education if they don't need or want one.

President Barack Obama (2015) and many other federal and state elected officials promoted or still promote efforts to increase college enrollments, saying the percentage of young adults with college degrees is lower in the United States than in many other nations. But college education is not for everyone, and public policy should not skew students toward choosing a college education if they don't need or want one.

College Education Not Required

It is often argued that increases in college attendance will increase worker skills, "human capital," and economic growth. This attempt to increase college enrollment has at least three major drawbacks.

First, there are wide variations in human cognitive skills and motivations. Many of those who choose not to pursue college education do so for a perfectly rational reason: They consider it unlikely they will succeed. Even among those already going to college, more than half drop out or take longer to get a degree than anticipated (NCES 2009b). Expanding the pool of those entering college will increase the number of disappointed college dropouts.

Second, as greater numbers of less academically qualified people enter college, remedial education costs rise and the standards of rigor decline in order to maintain respectable graduation rates. Data already show low critical thinking skills and basic knowledge growth among U.S. college students (Arum and Roksa 2011; PIAAC 2012).

Third, Bureau of Labor Statistics job projections suggest most new jobs created over the next decade will *not* require skills of the type acquired in traditional college and university programs (Vedder *et al.* 2013; Employment Projections 2015). For example, the U.S. Department of Labor projects some 348,000 more home health aides, 331,000 more retail salespersons, and 180,100 more construction workers will be needed by 2024. Their skills are best learned mostly on the job or in specialized postsecondary career schools, not through a college degree program (Employment Projections 2015).

Wasted Degrees

The United States is beginning to accumulate large numbers of college-educated people who perform jobs for which they are overqualified. It was reported in 2012 that more than 13 percent of the nation's parking lot attendants and more than 14 percent of hotel clerks have at least a bachelor's degree (O'Shaughnessy 2012). "Credential inflation" has led many people to pursue degrees to try to stay ahead of other applicants, even though the jobs for which they're applying do not require such training (Vedder, Denhart, *et al.* 2010).

The use of postsecondary education vouchers would provide greater incentives for students to attend nontraditional institutions offering training in skills such as truck driving, plumbing, or welding. For many, a six-month course in learning how to drive large semi-trailer trucks is likely to have a bigger payoff than a four-year course resulting in a bachelor's degree in, say, sociology. Less debt is incurred, the probability of successfully completing the program is greater, and the postgraduate earnings are likely to compare favorably with the four-year college alternative.

Microsoft co-founder Bill Gates dropped out of Harvard. So did Facebook creator Mark Zuckerberg. Apple co-founder Steve Jobs spent less than a year at Reed College. All three revolutionized communications and information, became among the richest men in the world, and proved colleges degrees are not a prerequisite to success. Indeed, Paypal co-founder and venture capitalist Peter Thiel—Facebook was one of his investments!—argues not only against the dogma that college is for everyone but that we are in an "education bubble" that could pop, leaving those who invest too much in it at a big monetary and career loss (Thiel 2014; Vedder and Denhart 2014).

Alternatives to College

Public policy has provided more subsidies and recognition to the high-priced elite private institutions and flagship public research universities than to others (NCES 2014b). Accreditation has proven to be a major barrier of entry to for-profit firms and other less-expensive alternatives, and government regulations have attacked innovative for-profit providers primarily using online instruction (see Principles 9 and 10 below). Yet there is evidence that online education very often is better than traditional classroom instruction (DoE 2010).

Private online programs cost state governments nothing at all and would often cost relatively little under a voucher plan. The move toward including inexpensive online courses (such as massive open online courses, known as MOOCs) as part of low-cost degrees is an encouraging development.

Some of the proposals discussed above—in particular higher education vouchers—could help reduce the excessive public investment in very expensive schools. States giving vouchers might make them usable only at relatively lower-cost schools, such as community colleges and some proprietary institutions, for students whose academic profile suggests a high probability of academic failure at four-year schools. This would reduce the financial exposure of taxpayers in cases where students fail to take advantage of the academic resources provided to them. Students completing courses with a satisfactory academic record at, say, community colleges or for-profit private schools could then receive vouchers for an additional two years at a four-year university.

States moving to student-centered funding of higher education might consider funding higher education investment accounts for eligible students. For example, each K–12 student who performs satisfactorily could withdraw up to $25,000 over a lifetime, at a rate not to exceed

$5,000 a year, from his or her account. Those attending a community college that costs $4,000 in annual tuition for two years and then for two more years at a four-year school costing $8,000 annually would need a total of $24,000. The program could allow them to keep all or a portion of the amount below $25,000 after graduation, giving students an incentive to attend low-cost schools and finish their studies.

Students can demonstrate high school-level proficiency by passing the General Equivalency Diploma (GED) examination. Why not have a similar College Equivalence Examination, a several-hour test examining for critical reasoning capabilities (perhaps using the Critical Learning Assessment instrument) and the basic knowledge well-educated people should have? Students doing well on such an exam could be viewed as having capabilities equivalent to those of a bachelor's degree holder, allowing some to demonstrate competency to employers by using an alternative to a college diploma, at a much lower cost.

Policy Agenda

By focusing too much attention and too many resources on conventional colleges and universities, countless billions of dollars have been wasted on worthless degrees that leave graduates unprepared for the workforce. This can be changed with the following policy agenda:

■ Make higher education vouchers usable only at relatively lower-cost schools, such as community colleges and some proprietary institutions, for students whose academic profile suggests a high probability of academic failure at four-year schools.

■ Allow postsecondary education vouchers to be used to pay tuition at nontraditional institutions such as six-month training programs in welding, computer programming, and the like.

■ Remove accreditation barriers to for-profit firms and other less-expensive alternatives.

■ Remove government regulations that stand in the way of for-profit providers using online instruction such as massive open online courses (MOOCs).

■ Allow students to demonstrate college-level proficiency by passing a College Equivalence Examination, modeled after the General Equivalency Diploma (GED) examination for high school proficiency.

Recommended Readings: Richard Vedder, Christopher Denhart, and Jonathan Robe, *Why Are Recent College Graduates Underemployed?* (Washington, DC: Center for College Affordability and Productivity, 2013); Richard Vedder, Andrew Gillen, Daniel Bennett, *et al.*, *25 Ways to Reduce the Cost of College* (Washington, DC: Center for College Affordability and Productivity, 2010).

6. Emphasize instruction and raise academic standards.

Too many institutions of higher education have de-emphasized instruction and should refocus their attention on educating students.

The single most important mission of higher learning should be educating students, yet incentive systems within universities often downgrade instruction. Big salary increases go to those who write articles for obscure academic journals that often go unread and uncited.

Anything But Learning
Surveys show the critical thinking skills of graduating seniors are little better than those of entering freshmen (Arum and Roksa 2011). One reason is simply time on task: College students average fewer than 30 hours a week on academics, over a period of just 30 weeks a year—less time than eighth graders spend learning.

Grade inflation has reduced college work effort and almost certainly learning (Leef 2016a; Babcock and Marks 2010). Many universities and colleges must devote class time and resources to remedial education to make up for the failures of K–12 schools and popular pressure on mediocre and unmotivated students to attend college.

Political correctness is also reducing time spent on learning at many colleges and universities. Self-described Progressives increasingly stifle free expression and discussion of ideas, the very core of what higher education is all about. Speaker dis-invitations and attempts to marginalize some forms of speech undermine the quality and diversity of academic life and exemplify the loss of free inquiry and scholarly independence (Young 2017). Worse, individuals with conservative or perceived "non-progressive" views must also worry about violence directed at them by leftist thugs who, rather than being expelled, are often coddled by college administrators (Timpf 2016).

Most comprehensive universities, and even some liberal arts colleges, engage in many activities unrelated to the academic experience. They operate restaurant and lodging facilities, conference centers, hospitals, entertainment enterprises (notably intercollegiate athletics), and recreational facilities such as golf courses and weight/conditioning operations, etc. These ventures have little to do with the twin goals of any university: the dissemination (teaching) and production (research) of knowledge.

On average, universities are not as effective and efficient as private restaurant and lodging companies at food and housing services. To their credit, many schools have outsourced these activities, but they could, and usually should, outsource maintaining buildings, teaching remedial courses, running hospitals, and many other things they currently do that have little or nothing to do with college-level teaching (Vedder 2014).

Similarly, an explosion in university bureaucracies has increased costs and reduced emphasis on instruction. According to Benjamin Ginsberg, a professor of political science at Johns Hopkins University, in 1970 U.S. colleges employed more professors than administrators, but in 2011 teachers made up less than half of all college employees. Since 1970, "the number of full-time professors increased slightly more than 50 percent, while the number of administrators and administrative staffers increased 85 percent and 240 percent, respectively" (Ginsberg 2011).

Also according to Ginsberg, adjusted for inflation, from 1947 to 1995, overall university spending increased 148 percent, administrative spending by 235 percent, and instructional spending by only 128 percent. The average pay of heads of public universities, according to the *Chronicle of Higher Education* (Bauman 2017), was about $464,000 in 2016. However, if the numbers are limited to presidents who served the whole year (a differentiation that reveals the turmoil that can surround a president's job), the average president pulled in a little more than $521,000.

The Publications Racket

Teaching is often devalued on college and university campuses in the name of research. Many faculty members would rather devote time to their own research than teach in a classroom, and as a result, many classes at major universities are taught by graduate students and associate or adjunct professors rather than tenured faculty.

Much of the research done by faculty at higher education institutions is of dubious value. A significant decline in teaching loads has occurred over the decades to allow time for more research, and the number of academic journals has multiplied several-fold to accommodate the flood (Vedder 2004). Diminishing returns on research have set in: More than

35,000 articles have been written about William Shakespeare since 1950. Have the last 34,000 of those articles really added much to our understanding of either Shakespeare or the advance of Western civilization (Bauerlein 2009)? Weren't 1,000 articles enough?

"Publish or perish" is a bizarre racket in which professors obtain tenure or salary increases simply for turning out papers no one reads but which cite other scholars who, in turn, cite those professors so they can demonstrate their faux influence. There certainly is research that might appear useless to nonspecialists and nevertheless be influential and well-regarded in a small community of scholars. Still, research should be subject to cost-benefit scrutiny, which would lead to increases in teaching loads, allowing for a reduction in college costs (fewer faculty members would be needed to provide any given amount of instruction).

Having aid money follow the student instead of being given directly to institutions would help ensure research, when it takes place, is concentrated on areas that enhance learning and increase educational value to students instead of being a vehicle for professors' professional advancement.

Measures of Success

Having funding directed to students instead of institutions should increase the attention paid to actually educating students. Forcing universities to share payments for federal loan defaults would lead to more rigorous admission standards and more effective instruction.

Holding colleges accountable for maintaining high standards is difficult, largely because of the lack of transparency and failure to measure academic progress discussed earlier. For that reason, value-added measures of academic performance are needed, and third-party financial support should be made dependent on demonstration that colleges are positively adding to the learning, critical thinking skills, or other desired qualities expected in a college graduate. Policymakers could compare, for example, first- and fourth-year student performance on a well-accepted exam such as the Critical Learning Assessment.

A special issue is intercollegiate athletics. Some would argue it has contributed to the downplaying of academics, while others attribute to it whatever public support higher education still has. Huge scandals at highly regarded schools such as Penn State and the University of North Carolina hint at widespread corruption taking place unobserved at other universities. Other legitimate issues include the overpaying of coaches and the underpaying of student athletes.

It is time for a new, collective effort to contain exploding athletic costs, perhaps by ending the tax-deductibility of gifts earmarked for athletic programs, divesting commercial sports from university operations, and implementing multiuniversity agreements to contain costs and redirect commercial sports revenues to core academic activities. In any case, government budget and tax policies should be changed to stop encouraging the waste of resources on intercollegiate athletics.

Policy Agenda

Colleges and universities can be incentivized to focus on instruction by adopting the following policies:

- Track and report to parents and funders the average amount of time students spend on academics and make increasing that amount of time an institutional priority.

- Require faculty to teach and increase the teaching load of tenured faculty.

- Reduce the weight given to publication records in faculty hiring, compensation, and retention decisions.

- Critically review activities that divert attention and resources from the core mission, such as operation of restaurants and lodging facilities, conference centers, hospitals, and athletics.

Recommended Readings: Richard Arum and Josipa Roksa, *Academically Adrift: Limited Learning on College Campuses* (Chicago, IL: University of Chicago Press, 2011); Benjamin Ginsberg, *The Fall of the Faculty: The Rise of the All-Administrative University and Why It Matters* (Oxford: Oxford University Press, 2011).

7. Restructure university ownership and governance.

The way universities are currently structured—unclear ownership and "shared governance," for example—stifles innovation and increases costs.

Most American universities are organized on a management model, called "shared governance," originally developed in the Middle Ages and essentially unchanged over the past century. It is not clear at all who "owns" the university and has the right to govern it (Martin 2009). This vagueness leads to costly, often delayed, and timid decision-making (Vedder 2004). Bold innovations are stifled by interest groups and the politics associated with them.

It also leads to flamboyant spending in the name of education. One commentator says nonprofit colleges actually do make profits, but they "take their profits in the form of spending on some combination of research, graduate education, low-demand majors, low faculty teaching loads, excess compensation, and featherbedding" (Fried 2011).

Shared governance is much revered by faculty. Faculty members with lifetime appointments face little consequence from obstructing changes that might reduce their power or increase their teaching loads. Most university decisions are made by committees with various interest groups each given a limited veto power, forcing costly and illogical compromises; e.g., adding faculty in department A as a condition of approving new programs for department B.

Conflicted Role of the President
At a typical university, the president is pulled in several different directions. He raises funds to placate …

- faculty (high salaries, low teaching loads, good parking);

- students (decent housing, low academic expectations, plenty of free time, and easy access to recreational facilities);

- alumni (good football and basketball teams, a nice alumni/ conference center, and prestigious faculty superstars);

- senior administrators (high pay and perks such as international travel, a fancy office, and lots of assistants to do the heavy lifting); and

- trustees (nice perks, luxurious facilities for meetings, and travel).

The president may or may not be an entrepreneur, but instead of seeking to put resources to their highest and most productive use in order to satisfy customers, he spends his time coaxing funds from third parties to pay what economists call the "economic rents" (payments beyond what is necessary to provide the service) to all those who could create trouble. University trustees ought to be aware of this hazard and support presidents who buck the tide, but they typically are ignorant of campus practices and disengaged (Schmidt 2014; Martin 2009).

A Better Model

Competition from for-profit institutions has the potential to force traditional universities to at least partially abandon the inefficiencies of the current management model. Institutions such as Apollo Corp. (University of Phoenix), Kaplan Higher Education, Bridgepoint Education, and others have clearly defined ownership and management. Institutional priorities are concentrated on improving the bottom line (profits, perhaps stock price or market share), something traditional schools cannot do since they have no clearly defined bottom lines.

Successful institutions are organized in ways that reward decisions leading to cost-effective, high-quality goods and services sold to willing customers. Colleges and universities too often are organized in a nearly opposite way, as if cost-effectiveness doesn't matter or is to be avoided, quality cannot be or shall not be measured, and students and their parents are not to be viewed as customers, but only as inconveniences and distractions from achieving other objectives. For-profit colleges can teach by example, even if nonprofit and government-owned institutions can't necessarily adopt the same governance model.

Removing barriers to the spread of market-based education and letting that sector absorb future enrollment increases would reduce the ownership and governance problems. Fortunately, the Trump administration is acting to remove some of the rules and regulations adopted by the Obama administration that discriminate against for-profit schools.

Policy Agenda

College and university ownership and management need to change if higher education is ever going to be made to work again for students, their parents, and taxpayers. Some guidelines for this reform include the following:

- Communicate to all stakeholders the central goal of the institution—instruction—and the most important customers—students and their parents—and adopt policies and budgets that move resources to them and away from anything else.

- Move away from the doctrine of "shared governance" to more clearly place authority in the hands of an executive team.

- Limit the authority of department chairs and faculty to their own departments and refocus their goals on instruction.

■ Repeal regulations that discriminate against for-profit colleges and graduate schools.

Recommended Readings: Daniel L. Bennett, Adam R. Lucchesi, and Richard K. Vedder, *For-Profit Higher Education: Growth, Innovation and Regulation* (Washington, DC: Center for College Affordability and Productivity, 2010); Robert Zemsky, *Making Reform Work: The Case for Transforming American Higher Education* (New Brunswick, NJ: Rutgers University Press, 2009).

8. Revamp or eliminate federal student financial aid.

Federal student aid programs have mostly failed, contribute to the upward spiral in higher education costs, and should be revamped or ended.

The Pell Grant program, the largest of the federal student financial aid programs, has exploded in size in the past decade, going from $15 billion in 2005–06 to $30.3 billion in 2014–15. Originally designed to expand access to college for low-income Americans, it instead has caused tuition to spiral upward, increased dropout rates, and burdened millions of students with debts they will never be able to repay.

Evidence of Failure

Federal aid programs have dramatically contributed to the tuition price explosion (Lucca *et al.* 2015). In the several decades before 1978, when loan programs were either nonexistent or small, tuition price increases averaged roughly 1 percent per year, corrected for inflation. In the nearly four decades since, when loan programs were rapidly growing, tuition increases have roughly tripled (to more than 3 percent per year) in inflation-adjusted dollars (Vedder *et al.* 2014).

Due at least in part to unaffordable tuition levels, the proportion of recent college graduates from the bottom quartile of the income distribution is actually lower today than it was in 1970 (Mortenson 2009). The graduation rate among Pell Grant recipients is probably 20 to 25 percentage points lower than that of non-recipients. (The U.S. Department of Education does not provide comprehensive, reliable data on Pell Grant six-year recipient graduation rates, so this is only our best estimate.)

Total federal student loan indebtedness is approximately $1.3 trillion, larger than overall credit card debt. Although the mean student debt obligation is slightly less than $30,000, there are large numbers of students with debts of $50,000 or more (Vedder *et al.* 2014). The official delinquency and default rates on the federal student loan programs understate the problem, as it is comparatively easy to defer repayment of loans. Nonetheless, nearly 25 percent of these loans were "seriously delinquent" in early 2014, according to a New York Federal Reserve Bank assessment (Brown *et al.* 2014).

Reform Proposals

On various occasions, Obama and other lawmakers proposed easing terms on borrowers through lower interest rates, partial loan forgiveness, limiting repayment to a proportion of income, etc. These reforms simply double down on a failed approach to financing higher education. They leave in place the incentives for college and university administrators to raise tuition, for weak students to attend college, and for politicians to posture as advocates for the poor and disadvantaged when their policies actually are hurting those very people.

These proposals also create a huge "moral hazard" problem: If students think they can have loans partially forgiven or get better terms, they will simply not repay, aggravating an already serious problem and expanding the taxpayer liability for the loans. It's like pouring gasoline on a fire.

Policy Agenda

In a perfect world, federal student aid programs would be phased out over a short period of time, replaced by private lending as well as new approaches to financing, such as income share agreements where private investors finance college expenses in return for a share of the postgraduate income of those graduating (Chaparro 2017). Unfortunately, the magnitude of the loan programs and powerful constituencies favoring them may make it necessary in the short run to limit reforms to serious revisions rather than eliminating the programs altogether.

Effective reforms that can at least begin the process of revamping and eventually eliminating federal student financial aid include the following:

■ Introduce minimal credit and academic standards, such as limiting future loan borrowing for students with very poor academic success records.

- Put stricter time limits on borrowing.

- Make colleges absorb some of the taxpayer losses associated with unusually high loan delinquency or default ("skin in the game").

- Turn administration of loan programs over to private loan providers.

- Limit or eliminate government-subsidized loans for attendance at graduate and professional schools.

- End the Parent Loan for Undergraduate Students (PLUS) program.

- End tuition tax credits for higher education, which mainly benefit middle-income families.

Recommended Reading: Richard Vedder, Christopher Denhart, and Joseph Hartge, *Dollars, Cents, and Nonsense: The Harmful Effects of Federal Student Aid* (Washington, DC: Center for College Affordability and Productivity, 2014).

9. End destructive government regulation.

Government regulation of higher education, especially by the federal government, has increased dramatically and does more harm than good.

Government regulation of higher education has grown extensively over time, especially at the federal level. Much of it has been intrusive and has done little to improve educational outcomes, while raising costs.

A strong case can be made that higher education today is actually worse off on a variety of measures than before the U.S. Department of Education was created in the late 1970s (Vedder 2015). For example, the Department of Education's own Adult Literacy survey shows a decline in literacy among college graduates (NAAL 2006). Similarly, average verbal GRE (Graduate Record Examination) scores in 1979 were 476; by 2009 they had fallen to 456. (Data are unavailable for 2010, and in 2011 the scoring scale was modified, making comparisons of pre-2009 to post-2011 data difficult (NCES 2015, Table 327.10)).

Destructive Regulations

In 2015, a Task Force on Federal Regulation of Higher Education reported federal mandates amount to some 2,000 pages of rules and regulations. "As a result," it found, "colleges and universities find themselves enmeshed in a jungle of red tape, facing rules that are often confusing and difficult to comply with. They must allocate resources to compliance that would be better applied to student education, safety, and innovation in instructional delivery. Clearly, a better approach is needed" (Task Force 2015).

Two examples of extremely disruptive federal regulation make the point. Beginning in 2010, the Obama administration issued a variety of regulations specifically targeting for-profit institutions. The most destructive of these regulations is the so-called gainful employment rule relating to the postgraduate vocational success of students. This rule concerns the debt-to-income rates of graduates of vocational programs, primarily at for-profit schools.

Although it is reasonable to expect students borrowing taxpayer funds to have high rates of repayment, applying these rules to only one type of provider resulted in a playing field tilted against for-profit schools and damaging to students. Since for-profit colleges have been most successful in attracting low-income students into higher education, they necessarily face higher default rates and lower graduation rates than those of traditional four-year colleges. The Obama regulations failed to address the bigger problems routinely faced by students attending high-priced nonprofit colleges: high dropout rates and underemployment by their graduates, leaving them unable to pay off their government student loans.

A second area where the U.S. Department of Education has intervened in recent years involves how colleges and universities respond to sexual assault cases. The department's Office for Civil Rights decreed, without the formal public comment period required by law, that colleges must use a low "preponderance of evidence" standard, as opposed to the "beyond a reasonable doubt" or "clear and convincing evidence" standard used in court cases of alleged sexual assault. Higher education institutions are being forced to disregard due process, and in some cases these proceedings are ruining the careers of innocent students.

Eminent faculty at Harvard Law School have strongly protested, to no avail (Gersen 2016). In light of high-profile cases of false or completely unproven assault accusations, like the one in a now-retracted *Rolling Stone* article on a case at the University of Virginia, one would think governments would renew their insistence on strict due process.

Regulatory excess is also imposed at the state and local level. Under the federal Higher Education Act, states must authorize institutions to offer courses and programs, verify the institutions are legitimate enterprises, and provide a venue for students to lodge complaints. In many states, requirements for authorization duplicate or conflict with accreditation requirements, imposing considerable costs and barriers to entry. Some states require online colleges to comply with complex and expensive regulations before they can enroll students even if the schools are authorized in their home states (NGA 2013).

Replacing Regulation with Markets

The task force referenced above called for adopting a dozen "guiding principles to govern the development, implementation, and enforcement of regulations," many of them common-sense nostrums such as "regulations should be related to education, student safety, and stewardship of federal funds" and "regulations should be clear and comprehensible." Without dismissing the important work of the task force, we suggest a better way to curb abuses by colleges is to rely more on markets and less on regulators.

Regulation is always an attempt to overcome the perverse incentives created by relying on other people's money to pay for goods and services they use. Reducing reliance on third-party payers in higher education makes deregulation possible, just as doing so works in health care (see Chapter 1) and K–12 schooling (see Chapter 3). When college students and their parents have to pay the full cost of college tuition (or amounts closer to that cost than is now the case) they will insist on efficiency, demand transparency, and refuse to pay for bloated bureaucracies or gold-plated stadiums and arenas. Regulation isn't needed when consumers are empowered and motivated.

Policy Agenda

Some ways to use market discipline to make deregulation possible include the following:

- Outsource services of public institutions of higher education to competitive private companies.

- Introduce internal markets by, for example, renting space to departments, with prices set to encourage nonpeak use.

- Vary tuition charges by the costs of instruction and the popularity of course offerings. Courses taken in the evening or on weekends can be priced lower than those taken in prime-time from Monday through Thursday.

■ Return colleges to the professorial compensation model praised by Adam Smith in 1776, in which students directly pay professors, who in turn remit some of the funds to the university for administrative help, academic support, and facility services. In this way, instructor compensation increases with the number of students taught and the popularity of the instruction.

■ Contract with groups of professors operating private firms to provide, say, political science instructional services, instead of paying salaried professors individually.

Recommended Reading: Richard Vedder, Andrew Gillen, Daniel Bennett, *et al.*, *25 Ways to Reduce the Cost of College* (Washington, DC: Center for College Affordability and Productivity, 2010).

10. Reform or eliminate accreditation.

Higher education accreditation is expensive, unnecessary, and too focused on inputs rather than outputs.

Starting a college or university is not easy, especially given state and federal government obstacles to entry into the higher education business (Bishirjian 2017). Most importantly, students cannot get federal loans or grants to attend non-accredited schools. Also, it is virtually impossible for for-profit packagers of education services to "bundle" courses from several universities to create the equivalent of a degree. Why not? This option would increase competition and student choice.

Freezing Out New Schools

Current accreditation procedures tend to be based on inputs—spending money—instead of outputs, which are the demonstrated proof that students are actually receiving a beneficial education. The cost of meeting accreditation standards is often very high, measured in millions of dollars (Gillen *et al.* 2010). In addition to accreditation rules many states require schools to be licensed, requiring a separate and often duplicative series of applications and inspections. For online companies operating in all 50 states, these costs can amount to millions of dollars.

Small entrepreneurs are essentially frozen out of competition, which reduces incentives for efficiency in the system.

What is the point of accreditation? Accreditation hasn't boosted the reputation or quality of colleges and universities. Only 55 percent of Americans believe higher education produces more benefits than harms to the country (Pew 2017); surely plumbers and auto mechanics score higher than that, and they don't even field football teams. Accreditation has not prevented bad colleges, even "the worst school in America," from staying open and cheating students (Ronson 2014). In fact, by making it difficult for new schools to start and compete with failing traditional colleges, accreditation protects incompetence and failure rather than protecting consumers from them.

Accreditation organizations offer mainly a binary assessment: You are either accredited or not accredited, implicitly and incorrectly assuming all accredited organizations are qualitatively the same. Markets provide much more nuanced and useful information. Magazines or agencies such as *Consumer Reports* or J.D. Power and Associates help consumers assess the quality of products and services offered for sale in order to make their own decisions. It works: There is no huge problem with unscrupulous or unreliable auto manufacturers.

Yelp and major online companies like Amazon allow customers to rate goods and services. Higher education accreditation could do what *Consumer Reports* and magazine rankings such as those of *U.S. News & World Report* or *Forbes* do: give consumers useful information regarding the quality of institutions.

Accreditation also suffers from other defects, the most notable of which are the huge conflicts of interest involved in the process. An accrediting team visits and accredits Institution A today, and tomorrow faculty from Institution A serve on the same accrediting team, assessing positively the schools of other team members. Boards of regional accreditors are dominated by representatives of the schools being accredited. Instead of operating as an honest broker, the accrediting association resembles more of a cartel intent on excluding outsiders from entry.

Policy Agenda

A reliable, easy-to-use, and relatively uniform system of data on both the performance and financial conditions of undergraduate institutions could go a long way toward doing the job of accreditation and, in fact, could significantly improve the current system by providing more information. The following public policies would encourage movement in that direction:

■ New schools should be authorized to offer courses without formal accreditation by completing a much less complicated and expensive application process.

■ Accreditation should be earned or maintained by demonstrating positive student outcomes, such as the proportion of graduating students scoring well on the Graduate Record Exam, Critical Learning Assessment, or another relevant instrument.

■ If graduates' income and job prospects are made part of the accreditation process, these requirements must be applied equally to all types of colleges and universities, not applied selectively against for-profit or online schools.

Recommended Readings: Andrew Gillen, Daniel L. Bennett, and Richard Vedder, *The Inmates Running the Asylum? An Analysis of Higher Education Accreditation* (Washington, DC: Center for College Affordability and Productivity, 2010); George C. Leef and Roxana D. Burris, *Can College Accreditation Live Up to Its Promise?* (Washington, DC: American Council of Trustees and Alumni, 2002); Anne D. Neal, "Dis-Accreditation," *Academic Questions* **21** (4): 431–45.

References

ACTA (American Council of Trustees and Alumni). 2016a. *A Crisis in Civic Education.* January.

_____. 2016b. *What Will They Learn?* (website). September 29.

Alchian, Armen. 1968. "The Economic and Social Impact of Free Tuition." *New Individualist Review* **5** (1): 42–52.

Arum, Richard, and Josipa Roksa. 2011. *Academically Adrift: Limited Learning on College Campuses.* Chicago, IL: University of Chicago Press.

Babcock, Philip, and Mindy Marks. 2010. *Leisure College, USA: The Decline in Student Study Time.* Washington, DC: American Enterprise Institute.

Bauerlein, Mark. 2009. "Diminishing Returns in Humanities Research." *Chronicle of Higher Education* (website). July 20.

Bauerlein, Mark, Mohamed Gad-el-Hak, Wayne Grody, Bill McKelvey, and Stanley W. Trimble. 2010. "We Must Stop the Avalanche of Low-Quality Research." *Chronicle of Higher Education* (website). June 13.

Bauman, Dan. 2017. "Executive Compensation at Public Colleges Rises by 5%, With Texas Leading the Way." *Chronicle of Higher Education* (website). June 27.

Bennett, William J. 1987. "Our Greedy Colleges." *The New York Times* (website). February 18.

Bennett, Daniel L., Adam R. Lucchesi, and Richard K. Vedder. 2010. *For-Profit Higher Education: Growth, Innovation and Regulation.* Center for College Affordability and Productivity.

Bishirjian, Richard. 2017. *The Coming Death and Future Resurrection of American Higher Education.* South Bend, IN: Saint Augustine's Press.

Bloom, Alan. 1987. *The Closing of the American Mind.* New York, NY: Simon and Schuster.

Bok, Derek. 2006. *Our Underachieving Colleges: A Candid Look at How Much Students Learn and Why They Should Be Learning More.* Princeton, NJ: Princeton University Press.

_____. 2013. *Higher Education in America.* Princeton, NJ: Princeton University Press.

Brown, Meta, Andrew Haughwout, Donghoon Lee, Joelle Scally, and Wilbert van der Klaauw. 2014. "Measuring Student Debt and Its Performance." *Staff Report* No. 668. Federal Reserve Bank of New York. April.

Chaparro, Frank. 2017. "Investors Are Paying College Students' Tuition – But They Want A Share Of Future Income In Return." *Business Insider* (website). April 8.

Cheston, Duke. 2012. "Students in Space" (website). James G. Martin Center for Academic Renewal. October 30.

DoE (U.S. Department of Education). 2010. *Evaluation of Evidence-Based Practices in Online Learning: A Meta-Analysis and Review of Online Learning Studies.* Washington, DC: Office of Planning, Evaluation, and Policy Development.

_____. 2015. "College Scorecard" (website). U.S. Department of Education.

Employment Projections. 2015. "Fastest Growing Occupations" (website). U.S. Bureau of Labor Statistics.

Fish, Stanley. 2012. *Save the World on Your Own Time.* Oxford, United Kingdom: Oxford University Press.

Fried, Vance. 2011. "Federal Higher Education Policy and the Profitable Nonprofits." *Policy Analysis* No. 678. Cato Institute. June 15.

Friedman, Milton. 1962. "The Role of Government in Education." Chapter 6 in *Capitalism and Freedom.* Chicago, IL: University of Chicago Press.

Gersen, Jacob B. 2016. "How the Feds Use Title IX To Bully Universities." *The Wall Street Journal* (website). January 25.

Gillen, Andrew. 2009. *Financial Aid in Theory and Practice: Why It Is Ineffective and What Can Be Done About It.* Center for College Affordability and Productivity.

Gillen, Andrew, Daniel L Bennett, and Richard Vedder. 2010. *The Inmates Running the Asylum? An Analysis of Higher Education Accreditation.* Center for College Affordability and Productivity.

Ginsberg, Benjamin. 2011. *The Fall of the Faculty: The Rise of the All-Administrative University and Why It Matters.* Oxford, United Kingdom: Oxford University Press.

Gordon, Grey, and Aaron Hedlund. 2016. "Accounting for the Rise in College Tuition." *NBER Working Paper* No. 21967. National Bureau of Economic Research.

Hart Research Associates. 2015. *Falling Short? College Learning and Career Success*. January 20.

IPEDS (Integrated Postsecondary Education Data System). 2014. IPEDS Data Center (website). Last accessed July 31, 2017. National Center for Education Statistics.

Kabbany, Jennifer. 2017. "Evergreen Official Asks Student Vigilantes to Stop Patrolling Campus Armed with Bats, Batons." *The College Fix* (blog). June 5.

Leef, George C. 2016a. "Grades Just Keep on Inflating; Why Does It Matter?" (website). James G. Martin Center for Academic Renewal. April 20.

_____. 2016b. "Students Need Much Better Counseling Before Going Into Debt for College" (website). James G. Martin Center for Academic Renewal. November 23.

Leef, George C., and Roxana D. Burris. 2002. *Can College Accreditation Live Up to Its Promise?* American Council of Trustees and Alumni.

Lucca, David O., Taylor Nadauld, and Karen Shen. 2015. *Credit Supply and the Rise in College Tuition: Evidence from the Expansion in Federal Student Aid Programs*. Federal Reserve Bank of New York.

Marks, Marilyn. 2002. "Meg Whitman to Support New Residential College at Princeton" (website). Princeton University.

Martin, Robert E. 2009. *The Revenue-to-Cost Spiral in Higher Education*. James G. Martin Center for Academic Renewal. July.

Modern Age. 2017. "Assault on Higher Education: Reports from the Front." Essays by Roger Scruton, Benjamin Ginsberg, Zena Hitz, Thomas S. Hibbs, Mark Bauerlein, and John E. Seery. Summer.

Mortenson, Tom. 2009. "Higher Education Equity Indices for Students from Bottom Family Income Quartile, 1970 to 2007." Postsecondary Education Opportunity.

Murray, Charles. 2008. *Real Education: Four Simple Truths for Bringing America's Schools Back to Reality*. New York, NY: Crown Forum.

NAAL (National Assessment of Adult Literacy). 2006. *A First Look at the Literacy of America's Adults in the 21st Century*. National Center for Education Statistics. Page 14.

NCES (National Center for Education Statistics). 2009a. Table 334. In *Digest of Education Statistics: 2009*. National Center for Education Statistics.

_____. 2009b. Table 326.10. In *Digest of Education Statistics: 2009*. National Center for Education Statistics.

_____. 2014a. Table 106.10. In *Digest of Education Statistics: 2013*. National Center for Education Statistics.

_____. 2014b. Table 333.70. In *Digest of Education Statistics: 2013*. National Center for Education Statistics.

_____. 2015. Table 327.10. In *Digest of Education Statistics: 2014*. National Center for Education Statistics.

NGA (National Governors Association). 2013. "Regulating Online Postsecondary Education: State Issues and Options" (website). January.

NSSE (National Survey of Student Engagement). 2015. National Survey of Student Engagement (website). Indiana University School of Education.

Neal, Anne D. 2008. "Dis-Accreditation." *Academic Questions* **21** (4): 431–45.

Obama, Barack. 2015. *Making College More Affordable*. The White House.

O'Keefe, Bryan, and Richard Vedder. 2008. *Griggs v. Duke Power: Implications for College Credentialing*. John William Pope Center for Higher Education Policy.

O'Shaughnessy, Lynn. 2012. "Janitors, Clerks and Waiters with College Degrees." *CBS Moneywatch* (website).

Palmer, James. 2016. Grapevine Survey, Fiscal Year 2015–16. Illinois State University.

Pew Research Center. 2017. "Sharp Partisan Divisions in Views of National Institutions" (website). July 10.

PIAAC (Program for the International Assessment of Adult Competencies). 2012. "PIACC Results Portal" (website). National Center for Education Statistics.

Robinson, Jenna. 2017. "Bigger's Better? In Higher Ed's Amenities Arms Race, Bigger's Just Bigger!" James G. Martin Center for Academic Renewal. January 30.

Ronson, Jon. 2014. "Shimer College: The Worst School in America?" *The Guardian* (website). December 6.

Schmidt, Benno C. 2014. *Governance for a New Era: A Blueprint for Higher Education Trustees*. American Council of Trustees and Alumni.

Shaw, Jane S. 2017. "Rioters at California University Shut Down Lecture." *School Reform News* (website). The Heartland Institute. April.

Sherman, Erik. 2015. "Wealthy Kids 8 Times More Likely to Graduate College than Poor." *Forbes* (website).

Silverglate, Harvey A., David French, and Greg Lukianoff. 2012. *FIRE's Guide to Free Speech on Campus*. Foundation for Individual Rights in Education.

Smith, Adam. (1776) 1976. *An Inquiry into the Nature and Causes of the Wealth of Nations*. Oxford: Oxford University Press.

Task Force. 2015. *Recalibrating Regulation of Colleges and Universities*. Task Force on Federal Regulation of Higher Education. February 12.

Thiel, Peter. 2014. "Thinking Too Highly of Higher Ed." *The Washington Post* (website). November 21.

Timpf, Katherine. 2016. "16 Most Ridiculously PC Moments on College Campuses in 2016." *National Review* (website). December 30.

Vedder, Richard. 2004. *Going Broke by Degree: Why College Costs Too Much*. Washington, DC: AEI Press.

———. 2007. *Over Invested and Over Priced*. Center for College Affordability and Productivity.

———. 2014. *Thirty-Six Steps: The Path to Reforming American Education*. Center for College Affordability and Productivity.

———. 2015. "The U.S. Department of Education and Higher Education: An Assessment After 35 Years." Testimony before the Committee on Homeland Security and Government Affairs. October 1.

Vedder, Richard, and Christopher Denhart. 2014. "How the College Bubble Will Pop." *The Wall Street Journal* (website). January 8.

Vedder, Richard, Christopher Denhart, Matthew Denhart, Christopher Matgouranis, and Jonathan Robe. 2010. *From Wall Street to Wal-Mart: Why College Graduates Are Not Getting Good Jobs*. Center for College Affordability and Productivity.

Vedder, Richard, Christopher Denhart, and Joseph Hartge. 2014. *Dollars, Cents, and Nonsense: The Harmful Effects of Federal Student Aid*. Center for College Affordability and Productivity.

Vedder, Richard, Christopher Denhart, and Jonathan Robe. 2013. *Why Are Recent College Graduates Underemployed?* Center for College Affordability and Productivity.

Vedder, Richard, Andrew Gillen, and Daniel Bennett, *et al*. 2010. *25 Ways to Reduce the Cost of College*. Center for College Affordability and Productivity.

Vedder, Richard, and Anthony Hennen. 2014. *Dollars and Sense: Assessing Oklahoma's Public Universities*. Oklahoma Council of Public Affairs.

Young, J.T. 2017. "Why Colleges Lean Left." *Washington Times* (website). March 20.

Zemsky, Robert. 2009. *Making Reform Work: The Case for Transforming American Higher Education*. New Brunswick, NJ: Rutgers University Press.

Additional Resources

Additional information about higher education policy is available from The Heartland Institute:

- PolicyBot, The Heartland Institute's free online clearinghouse for the work of other free-market think tanks, contains thousands of documents on education issues. It is on Heartland's website at https://www.heartland.org/policybot/.

- https://www.heartland.org/Center-Education/ is the website of The Heartland Institute's Center for Transforming Education, devoted to the latest research, news, and commentary about higher education as well as K–12 education issues. Read headlines, watch videos, or browse the thousands of documents on education issues available from PolicyBot.

- *School Reform News*, a monthly publication from The Heartland Institute, is available for free online at the websites described above, or subscribe to the print edition for $36/year (10 issues).

Directory

The following national organizations provide valuable information about higher education policies.

American Council of Trustees and Alumni (ACTA),
https://www.goacta.org/

American Legislative Exchange Council, Center to Protect Free Speech,
https://www.alec.org/policy-center/center-to-protect-free-speech/

Center for College Affordability and Productivity,
http://www.centerforcollegeaffordability.org

Chronicle of Higher Education, http://chronicle.com

The College Fix, http://www.thecollegefix.com

Heartland Institute, https://www.heartland.org/

Integrated Post Secondary Education Data System,
http://nces.ed.gov/ipeds/datacenter/

James G. Martin Center for Academic Renewal (formerly the John W.
Pope Center for Higher Education Policy),
https://www.jamesgmartin.center/about/

National Association of Scholars, http://www.nas.org

National Center for Education Statistics, http://nces.ed.gov

National Survey of Student Engagement, http://nsse.iub.edu/

Chapter 5
Privatization

Leonard Gilroy, Adrian Moore, and Austill Stuart

---

10 Principles of Privatization

1. Identify privatization opportunities.
2. Prepare a business case evaluation.
3. Create a privatization center of excellence.
4. Choose contractors on best value, not lowest price.
5. Use performance-based contracting.
6. Provide effective monitoring and oversight.
7. Bundle services for better value.
8. Prepare a real property inventory.
9. Divest non-core assets.
10. Make the case to the public.

Introduction

Privatization means shifting some or all aspects of service delivery from government to private-sector providers. It is a strategy to lower the costs of government and to achieve higher performance and better outcomes for tax dollars spent.

Policymakers in many jurisdictions in the United States and around the world increasingly use privatization to better the lives of citizens by producing higher-quality services at lower costs, delivering greater choices, and ultimately providing more efficient and effective government. Thousands of national, state, and local government agencies in the United States have successfully privatized scores of services

(Gilroy 2016). Researchers have documented the successful privatization of airports (Poole 2016a), electric and telecommunications utilities (Newbery 2001), prisons (Krisai *et al.* 2016), schools (Koteskey and Smith 2016), transportation (Poole 2016b), and many other services.

Why Privatize?

States and local governments are still recovering from severe fiscal traumas during and in the aftermath of the Great Recession, and future pressures loom large. The National Association of State Budget Officers (NASBO) found in FY 2016, total state expenditures and revenues finally surpassed their pre-recession peaks seen in FY 2008, after adjusting for inflation. Nineteen states projected a combined $19.7 billion in budget deficits to close in FY 2017 (NASBO 2016).

Legislators, government officials, and concerned citizens can use privatization to achieve a number of goals:

- *Access to expertise:* Contracting gives governments access on an as-needed basis to expertise they do not have in-house. For example, it is often cheaper to retain architects, engineers, lawyers, and information technology specialists on an as-needed basis than to hire them as full-time employees.

- *Better quality:* Privatization can improve the quality of services in several ways. The process of competitive bidding encourages firms to offer the best possible combination of price and service quality to beat their rivals. Further, performance-based contracting can be used to hold contractors accountable for delivering a higher quality service than can be attained in the existing civil service, especially when the threat of penalties or even contract cancellation looms as potential consequences of underperformance.

- *Cost savings:* Privatization can produce cost savings in a variety of ways, including reduced labor costs, economies of scale, improved technologies, more efficient business practices, and other innovations. A landmark Reason Foundation review of more than 100 privatization studies found savings up to 50 percent, depending on the type of service (Hilke 1993).

- *Improved risk management:* Privatization can transfer key risks from government—and thus taxpayers—to a private partner. Contractors, rather than the government, can be held responsible for cost overruns, project delivery deadlines, regulatory compliance, strikes, delays, and other risks (Lehrer and Murray 2007).

■ *Innovation:* Competition to win and retain contracts spurs the discovery of new, cutting-edge solutions. Without competition, even top-notch employees may stop looking for ways to improve how they meet customers' needs.

■ *Meeting peak demand:* Demand for some public services fluctuates significantly over time, yet governments often incur higher than necessary costs by retaining permanent capital and staff at a level needed to satisfy peak-period demands. Examples include winter snowplowing services or handling the summer influx of visitors to national and state parks. Contracting allows governments to obtain additional help only when it is needed to provide services.

■ *Timeliness:* When time is of the essence, privatization contracts can be written to include penalties for delays. Contractors have more flexibility in recruiting additional workers or providing performance bonuses to meet or beat deadlines, options that often are unavailable to in-house staff.

Privatization is no magic wand or panacea. If badly executed, privatization can fail. For example, taxpayers are served poorly when privatization initiatives are not scoped properly, when private providers fail to perform, and when governments fail to properly administer contracts.

To avoid these pitfalls, we have the successful experiences of governments in the United States and around the world from which to learn. The following 10 principles of privatization capture best practices that have emerged from those experiences.

Recommended Readings: Leonard C. Gilroy, editor, *Annual Privatization Report 2016* (Los Angeles, CA: Reason Foundation, 2016); Chris Edwards, "Options for Federal Privatization and Reform Lessons from Abroad," *Policy Analysis* No. 794, Cato Institute, 2016; Lawrence L. Martin, "Making Sense Of Public-Private Partnerships (P3s)," *Journal Of Public Procurement* **16** (2): 191–207.

1. Identify privatization opportunities.

Privatization can be applied to most things government does without interfering with its legitimate obligations.

Former New York governor Mario Cuomo once said, "It is not a government's obligation to provide services, but to see that they are provided" (Tolchin 1985). Privatization can be applied to most things government does without interfering with its legitimate obligations. The following is a partial list of services that governments in the United States and around the world have privatized successfully:

accounting
airports and air traffic control
animal shelter operations and
    management
bridge repair and maintenance
building financing, operations,
    and maintenance
correctional facilities and
    services
daycare facilities
engineering
financial planning
golf course operations
graphic design and printing
health care administration and
    services
human resources administration
information technology
    infrastructure and network
    services
legal services
library services and operations

lottery operations
mental health facilities and
    services
park operations and maintenance
parking lots and parking meters
planning and permitting
public works
risk management (claims
    processing, loss prevention)
road maintenance
school construction, buses,
    cafeterias, and driver's
    education
social infrastructure assets (e.g.,
    courthouses, hospitals, public
    buildings, etc.)
stadium and convention center
    management
street cleaning and snow removal
toll roads
zoo and museum operations and
    maintenance

Privatization is also widely used by local governments. According to the International City/County Management Association (ICMA), local governments on average contract out 17 percent of all services to for-profit businesses and 16 percent to other government entities; for example, a town government contracting with a county government for trash services. Nonprofit organizations, such as community organizations, animal welfare groups, and churches deliver 5 percent of public services. Franchises, subsidies, and volunteers collectively account for less than 2 percent of service delivery (ICMA 2009).

How to Privatize

There are many ways to privatize public services. The four most common methods are listed below, from most to least, by how much responsibility government retains to oversee or subsidize the service:

- *Contracting out:* Governments contract with private for-profit firms or nonprofit organizations to deliver individual public services, typically on a fee-for-service basis or through shared user fees.

- *Franchises or concession agreements:* Governments award private firms exclusive rights to provide public services or operate public assets, usually in return for annual lease payments or a one-time, up-front payment and subject to meeting performance expectations outlined by the government agency. This is also sometimes called leasing or concessions.

- *Vouchers:* Governments give consumers vouchers or certificates that can be redeemed for a specific service provided by a participating private business or nonprofit organization. Vouchers are used in several states to expand school choice (Walberg 2010).

- *Service shedding or divestiture:* Governments shed responsibility for providing a service, activity, or asset entirely, often through outright sales. Governments routinely sell off aging or underutilized land, buildings, and equipment, returning them to private commerce where they may be more productively used.

The Yellow Pages Test

Government managers should regularly review all services and activities they engage in and classify them as either "governmental"—those that should be performed only by public employees—or "commercial"—those that can be obtained from private businesses or nonprofit organizations. Former Indianapolis mayor Stephen Goldsmith (1999) calls this the "Yellow Pages test" because if a service can be found in the Yellow Pages of a phone book, then government ought to buy it rather than produce it.

The Yellow Pages test helps government concentrate on delivering inherently governmental services, such as public safety and judicial systems, while contracting with businesses and nonprofit organizations to produce other services. This has the added benefits of ending taxpayer-subsidized competition with private businesses, freeing up resources for agencies to complete their missions, and saving taxpayers money.

The Yellow Pages test asks, "Is it really the best use of taxpayer dollars to hire and manage public employees to cut grass, change oil in cars and trucks, sweep the streets, and clean government buildings, when existing businesses already perform these tasks well and almost always less expensively than government?" When governments attempt to provide these services in-house, they are effectively competing unfairly against the private sector, undermining economic development and free enterprise.

This unfair competition can be quite extensive. One analysis in Virginia in 1999 identified 205 commercial activities being performed by more than 38,000 state employees, accounting for nearly half of all state workers (Commonwealth Competition Council 1998).

Government will always squander resources; it is not designed to turn a profit. Focusing resources on the services government alone can and should deliver helps it achieve its highest goals while creating opportunities for entrepreneurs and businesses to provide other services at lower cost to taxpayers.

Recommended Readings: Stephen Goldsmith, "The Yellow Pages Test: Let Your Fingers Do the Walking," *Nevada Journal*, 1999; E.S. Savas, *Privatization in the City: Successes, Failures, Lessons* (Washington, DC: CQ Press, 2005).

2. Prepare a business-case evaluation.

> While private business managers think carefully about the potential costs and benefits of major resource allocations, public-sector managers rarely do.

Robust competition in the marketplace forces business managers to think carefully about the potential costs and benefits of major resource allocations. This discipline leads companies to routinely prepare business-case evaluations—analyses of the goals, costs, benefits, and impacts associated with potential sourcing options—to help managers make informed choices.

Surprisingly, this type of common-sense analysis is rare in the public sector. Requiring business-case evaluations be written and frequently revisited gives agencies, policymakers, and citizen watchdogs an opportunity to ask questions that get to the heart of the matter: What public services are we seeking to deliver, and are they best delivered in-house or by private businesses? What does the in-house option really cost? Could we achieve better performance and improve services through privatization?

The business-case evaluation can serve as a roadmap for how a privatization project should be implemented and managed. It should be a living document that travels with the initiative through the development, procurement, and implementation processes and should be continuously updated to reflect new data or changing conditions.

Key elements of a business-case evaluation include:

■ *Assumptions and methodology:* List and describe any assumptions associated with policy, legislation, agency direction, and market conditions that are germane to the privatization decision. Explain the methodology used to make cost comparisons and quality evaluations.

■ *Benchmarking:* Document the capital and operating costs of the service as currently delivered by the government. Benchmark data can be used to evaluate privatization proposals and, if adopted, their success or failure over time. This is often difficult to do with precision given standard government accounting practices, so the limitations of the base case must be understood and accounted for.

■ *Rationale and justification:* State the reasons privatization is being considered. Why is the status quo undesirable? Is it because of excessive costs or poor service quality? Have needs and opportunities changed, making government delivery obsolete or unnecessary? What alternatives were considered? Why were they dismissed? Why can't the function be improved internally? Can the private sector deliver more value than the in-house option?

■ *Recommendation:* Present the privatization proposal in sufficient detail to allow comparison with the benchmark data. Identify fiscal impacts (e.g., savings, avoided costs, income from assets sold or leased, and new expenses); performance standards and outcomes; new management structures; implementation timelines and milestones; length of contracts; and term before re-competition or renewal.

■ *Success factors:* How will public administrators be able to distinguish success from failure? Success factors should be measurable, tangible, and include minimum performance metrics that should be incorporated in the final contract.

■ *Transition management:* Describe how the transition in service delivery will be managed. Will a new management structure need to be created? How will stakeholders be brought into the planning process and issues relating to customer awareness and employee transition and training be addressed? How would privatization of one service affect the delivery of related services?

At this point, the business-case evaluation could conclude the project should not be outsourced or privatized after all. Future managers and watchdogs should be able to review past business-case evaluations and decide if circumstances have changed or relevant information was overlooked and privatization should be reconsidered.

Private companies routinely perform business-case evaluations before embarking on new outsourcing. Governments should do the same thing, and citizen watchdogs can help. The business-case evaluation offers policymakers and administrators a powerful tool to conduct due diligence on privatization proposals.

Recommended Reading: Benjamin Herzberg and Andrew Wright, *The PPD Handbook: A Toolkit for Business Environment Reformers* (Washington, DC: World Bank, 2006).

3. Create a privatization center of excellence.

Global experience with privatization shows the value of having a single independent decision-making body to manage privatization initiatives.

Global experience with privatization shows the value of having a single independent decision-making body to manage privatization initiatives. Richard D. Young (2005) identified 14 such councils overseeing statewide privatization initiatives. While some have been temporary in nature—non-permanent, gubernatorial-appointed advisory commissions such as New Jersey's Privatization Task Force in 2010—at least two councils are currently active: Utah's Free Market Protection and Privatization Board and the Texas Council on Competitive Government.

Florida's former Council on Efficient Government—shut down amid deep state budget cuts in the wake of the Great Recession—still offers an excellent model for other states (Gilroy 2010). Developed in 2004, it was a key component of a strategy that realized more than $550 million in cost savings through more than 130 privatization and competition initiatives. In 2009 alone, the council evaluated 23 new business cases for potential agency outsourcing projects with a cumulative value of more than $225 million, identifying more than $31 million in projected savings to the state (Florida Council on Efficient Government 2010).

A privatization center of excellence should be given the responsibility and authority to:

- assist agencies in developing a business-case evaluation for any proposed privatization initiative, stating the rationale for the initiative such as cost savings, service quality improvements, and changing obsolete business practices;

- conduct an annual or biennial inventory of all functions and activities performed by government, distinguishing between inherently governmental and commercial activities;

- create a uniform cost accounting model to facilitate "apples-to-apples" cost comparisons between public- and private-sector service provision;

- develop a standardized, enterprise-wide process for identifying and implementing competitive sourcing;

- develop rules instituting performance-based contracting and business-case development as requirements for state procurement;

- disseminate lessons learned and best practices across government agencies; and

- review and take action on complaints regarding inappropriate government competition with the private sector.

A center of excellence along these lines can facilitate regular and comprehensive reviews of state government activities, with an eye toward right-sizing government through competition and privatization.

At the same time, successful privatization requires a high standard of due diligence in contracting, which in turn requires a staff of experts committed to the goal of greater value to taxpayers and power to make decisions.

Experience in Florida, Utah, and other states also suggests privatization centers of excellence increase the public's confidence in outsourcing and help reduce perceptions of impropriety, a common concern with privatization initiatives.

Recommended Readings: Henry Garrigo, "Look Before You Leap into Privatization: Florida's Council on Efficient Government Sets a New Standard in Transparency, Due Diligence in Privatization and Contracting Decisions," interview by Leonard Gilroy, Reason Foundation, 2010; Florida Council on Efficient Government, *2009 Annual Report for FY 2008–2009* (Tallahassee, FL: Florida Department of Management Services, 2010).

4. Choose contractors on best value, not lowest price.

> Best practices for government procurement and service contracting have evolved toward "best-value" techniques.

Government procurement processes in the United States tend to be oriented towards "low-bid" selections in which the contractor offering the lowest price automatically wins. While this approach may make sense when buying office supplies and other simple and inexpensive goods and services, it is often overly simplistic and inadequate for outsourcing more complex services. When asked how he felt as he awaited blast-off for his first mission in 1962, John Glenn, America's first man in orbit, is said to have quipped: "I felt exactly how you would feel if you were getting ready to launch and knew you were sitting on top of two million parts—all built by the lowest bidder on a government contract." Glenn was hoping low prices were paired with quality and reliability!

In some cases, a government agency may be attempting to privatize not to save money, but rather to hold spending constant while improving service quality.

Best practices for government procurement and service contracting have evolved toward "best-value" techniques. Rather than selecting a private partner based on low cost alone, governments should choose the best combination of cost, quality, and other considerations. Such criteria may include process reinvention, financing plans, total project life-cycle costs, risk transfer, technological innovation, expertise, and experience. The more complex the service, the more important it is that best-value selection criteria be used.

Successful best-value contracting requires three things:

- Early determination of key parameters such as completion date, security requirements, and mobilization.

- Development of evaluation criteria quantified either in dollars or by objective measures of technical excellence, management and financial capability, prior experience and performance, optional features offered, completion date, and risk to government.

- Translation of key project outcomes into performance and output measures.

Opening up the bid process to non-price considerations does not open the door to cronyism and other types of corruption so long as the policy is accompanied by measures ensuring accountability and transparency. Such measures can be set forth in the business-case evaluation (see Principle 2) and required or enforced by the privatization center of excellence (see Principle 3).

Some "best-value" procurement processes give preferential weight to local or in-state providers. Politicians may come under pressure from constituents and campaign donors to keep outsourced work local, but this is almost never a valid consideration. Keeping the price of a good or service low and its quality high should always trump who is producing the service or where they might be located. Bias against out-of-state or international providers limits competition, drives up costs, and precludes the true best-value option from being properly considered.

National and international firms are increasingly bidding to provide public services at the state and local levels, bringing valuable expertise, access to capital, and often economies of scale to the task at hand. Out-of-state and international firms tend to hire the bulk of their project-level staff locally, so regardless of who wins a competition, local workers often stand to benefit. Preferential treatment of local or in-state providers, therefore, should be avoided.

Recommended Readings: Edward Markus, "Low Bid Alternatives," *American City & County*, August 1, 1997; Adrian T. Moore and Geoffrey F. Segal, *Weighing the Watchmen: Evaluating the Costs and Benefits of Outsourcing Correctional Services – Part 1: Employing a Best Value Approach to Procurement* (Los Angeles, CA: Reason Public Policy Institute, 2002).

5. Use performance-based contracting.

> Performance-based contracting means focusing on outputs rather than inputs when choosing whether to privatize a service and which proposal to accept.

The use of best-value sourcing, as described in Principle 4, works hand-in-hand with performance-based contracting, which means focusing on outputs rather than inputs when choosing whether to privatize a service and which proposal to accept.

Government managers often think of their own programs in terms of the management and budget constraints they face: procedures, processes, wages to be paid, cost of materials and supplies, and the amount or type of equipment needed. When they think about outsourcing a service, they may frame the contract in those same terms, specifying how much manpower and equipment must be allocated to do the job. But forcing contractors to emulate in-house procedures contradicts many of the reasons to privatize.

Performance-based contracts specify outcomes and results rather than inputs. They typically have three key components:

- *Financial incentives and penalties:* Keeping employees accountable and productive requires close and effective personnel management. Outsourcing a service to a private contractor means the government sheds that management role and in its place uses incentives and penalties to ensure the contractor produces the required outcomes. The concession agreement in the Indiana Toll Road lease, for example, sets the conditions for the state to cancel the contract and resume operations of the road should the contractor fail to perform as required. Other contracts specify payments that correspond with reaching certain performance thresholds such as productivity, costs, and timeliness.

■ *Identify the real objectives:* The U.S. Air Force used to require a janitorial service to strip and re-wax floors once a week. Then it realized it didn't matter how often the floors were stripped and waxed so long as they are kept clean, free of scuff marks, and have a glossy finish. When the Air Force modified its statement of work in the contract, the contractor was able to achieve the real objective in a more cost-effective way, which led to a 50 percent savings for the Air Force (OMB 1998). Similarly, state departments of transportation in Florida, Texas, and Virginia switched to performance-based contracts for statewide highway maintenance and reported savings ranging from 6 percent to 20 percent (Segal and Montague 2004).

■ *Quantify the required outputs:* Once the objective is identified, it becomes possible for the manager to focus on how success or failure can be objectively measured. The 2006 Indiana Toll Road lease, for example, is governed by a detailed concession agreement designed to protect the public's interests (Gilroy and Aloyts 2013)—so much so that when the original concessionaire filed for bankruptcy in 2014, it was required to maintain full operations until a new concessionaire later stepped in to take over the remainder of the original lease. That lease agreement establishes an array of performance expectations, including the maximum amount of time the concessionaire has to respond to vehicle incidents and remove snow, roadkill, and graffiti, for example, and it even requires the concessionaire to expand the roadway at its own expense should traffic volumes reach certain thresholds. Many of the standards in the contract exceed the standards applied to roads under the control of the Indiana Department of Transportation.

Performance-based contracts often make payments and contract extension or renewal dependent on the contractor achieving certain performance targets. Pay for Success (PFS) contracts, for example, pay if the program delivers on its promised results. Although relatively new, there are now more than 50 PFS contracts underway or completed globally, with 11 in the United States (Coletti 2016). This shifts the risk of failure, delay, or price overruns from taxpayers to the provider.

Contracts should be written to hold providers accountable for failure as well as success, which means avoiding taxpayer bailouts or guarantees and applying real penalties for failure to meet performance goals. Using performance-based contracts can be challenging. Officials must choose services suitable to performance-based contracts and devise ways to tie payment to results the public expects of the agency.

Recommended Readings: Adrian T. Moore and Wade Hudson, "The Evolution of Privatization Practices and Strategies," in Robin Johnson and Norma Walzer (editors), *Local Government Innovation: Issues and Trends in Privatization and Managed Competition,* (Westport, CT: Quorum Books, 2000); Robert D. Behn and Peter A. Kant, "Strategies for Avoiding the Pitfalls of Performance Contracting," *Public Productivity and Management Review* **22** (4): 470–89.

6. Provide effective monitoring and oversight.

> Once a privatization proposal has been selected and put into effect, the role of the public sector shifts from planning to monitoring and oversight.

Once a privatization proposal has been selected and put into effect, the role of the public sector shifts from planning to monitoring and oversight. Except in cases involving the outright sale of an asset or shedding responsibility for delivering a service (see Principle 9), the public entity should never sign a contract and simply walk away.

Importance of Monitoring

Strong reporting, evaluation, and auditing components must be put in place to monitor the provider's performance. Effective monitoring pays for itself by improving quality, transparency, and accountability.

While monitoring and oversight systems are becoming more refined, governments still have a ways to go. According to New York University economics professor Jonas Prager, "Public sector decision makers have yet to learn from the private sector the significance of managing outsourcing. ... Efficient monitoring, though costly, pays for itself by preventing overcharges and poor quality performance in the first place, by recouping inappropriate outlays, and by disallowing payment for inadequate performance" (1994, p. 182).

Government managers should think about how they will monitor providers before they issue a request for proposal or sign the contract. "The design of the deal can make an enormous difference in the future success of monitoring the contractor," according to Tom Olsen, former director of enterprise development for the city of Indianapolis. "Strategic thinking on monitoring needs to begin at the time a deal is structured, not after" (quoted in Eggers 1997, p. 22).

A well-designed monitoring plan, sometimes called a quality assurance plan, defines precisely what a government must do to guarantee the contractor's performance meets the agreed-upon standards. The monitoring plan should include specific reporting requirements on quantified outputs, regular meetings with minutes, complaint procedures, and access to the contractor's records on request. The plan should focus on monitoring and evaluating the major outputs of the contract so monitors need not waste much time and resources on mundane tasks that aren't central to the contract.

The Right People
Effective privatization requires having the right people with the right training in positions to oversee the letting and execution of contracts. As contracting grows, the management of contracts becomes a more important part of how agencies accomplish their goals. One function of a privatization center of excellence (see Principle 3) would be to help agencies and departments develop and train their contract oversight staff.

Different services require different types and levels of monitoring. For highly visible services that directly affect citizens, such as snow removal and garbage pickup, poor service will be exposed through citizen complaints. For highly complex or technical services, it may make sense to hire a third party to monitor the contractor. Where the consequences of even minor problems are large—for example, aircraft maintenance—high-cost and high-control preventive monitoring techniques may be necessary.

Public Employee Transition
Privatization typically results in very few net employee layoffs. Instead, the contractor hires many public employees (at least on a provisional basis), the government re-assigns them to another public position, or they take early retirement. Regardless, it is important that management communicate early and often with employees and unions regarding privatization initiatives and develop a plan to manage public employee transitions.

Employee transition plans often focus on developing job placement policies for affected employees, such as requiring each affected employee be interviewed and considered for job placement within the vendor company, as well as provided with severance compensation and early retirement incentive packages. Officials also should consider developing re-employment and retraining assistance plans for employees not retained or employed by the contractor and offer critical employee retention salary increases to retain those individuals identified as critical to successful transitions.

Recommended Readings: William D. Eggers, "Performance Based Contracting: Designing State of the Art Contract Administration and Monitoring Systems," Reason Foundation, 1997; Jonas Prager, "Contracting Out Government Services: Lessons from the Private Sector," *Public Administration Review* **54** (2): 176–84.

7. Bundle services for better value.

Greater economies of scale, cost savings, and value for money may be had by bundling several services together for a single outsourcing initiative.

Public administrators may find greater economies of scale, cost savings, and value for money by bundling several, or even all, of the services delivered by a department or subdivision into a single outsourcing initiative, rather than treat individual services or functions separately.

Administrative Support

Because many governments and private companies outsource payroll, information technology, mail, risk management, and other support functions, there are robust and competitive markets of providers for these services. Service bundling across divisions and departments can drive down costs by eliminating redundancy and expanding the pool of potential providers.

Bundling can occur among cities and counties, among departments of state government, and even among states. In January 2009, Tim Pawlenty, a Republican, and Jim Doyle, a Democrat, at the time governors of Minnesota and Wisconsin, respectively, each signed executive orders calling for department heads to identify activities, programs, and services on which the two states could cooperate to lower costs (Pawlenty 2009).

Contract Cities

Since 2005, six cities have incorporated in metropolitan Atlanta as "contract cities," and most of them contract with private businesses to deliver the bulk of their non-safety-related public services, dramatically reducing costs and improving services (Gilroy and Moore 2013). California has 69 contract cities (CCCA n.d.).

Sandy Springs, Georgia was the first of the contract cities (Gilroy and Moore 2013). After residents voted to incorporate as an independent city, the new city leaders opted to contract out for nearly all government services (except police and fire services) instead of creating a new municipal bureaucracy.

The city's successful launch was facilitated by a $32 million contract with a private firm that oversaw and managed day-to-day municipal operations. The contract value was just above half what the city traditionally was charged in taxes by Fulton County. When it was time to rebid, city leaders ultimately decided to disaggregate some of the contracted services into a handful of contracts, but it still retained the contract city model. Sandy Springs maintains ownership of assets and budget control by setting priorities and service levels, while its contractors are responsible for staffing and all operations and services.

On a smaller scale, Centennial, Colorado privatized all of its public works functions in 2008 and negotiated a public works contract lasting through 2018. Similarly, Pembroke Pines, Florida privatized its entire building and planning department in June 2009.

Facility Maintenance in Georgia

Georgia's Department of Juvenile Justice began outsourcing facility maintenance at 30 of its 35 facilities in 2001, marking the first successful outsourcing of state correctional-system maintenance to a private firm (Gilroy et al. 2010). The partnership was structured to provide long-term, performance-based maintenance without increasing the budget.

For the first six months of the contract, corrective-maintenance work orders outnumbered preventive-maintenance work orders as long-standing maintenance needs were addressed. After two years, preventive-maintenance work orders were almost double the corrective work orders, but the cost of preventive maintenance remained at year-2000 labor costs (before maintenance was outsourced). Recognizing the success of this approach, Georgia officials initiated a similar large-scale outsourcing contract for the management and maintenance of numerous other secure-site facilities.

Recommended Readings: Oliver Porter, "Public-Private Partnerships for Local Governments: The Sandy Springs Model," interview by Leonard Gilroy, Reason Foundation, 2010; Leonard C. Gilroy, Adam B. Summers, Anthony Randazzo, and Harris Kenny, *Public-Private Partnerships for Corrections in California: Bridging the Gap Between Crisis and Reform* (Los Angeles, CA: Reason Foundation, 2010).

8. Prepare a real property inventory.

Many governments in the United States do not have property and asset inventories and do not productively manage their properties.

How much land and other property does your local or state government own? It is an important question taxpayers should ask, yet most do not. Many state and local governments in the United States, even the federal government, do not have the property and asset inventories needed to answer this question. And many of those that do are not putting the information to use by productively managing what they own.

How to Prepare an RPI

A real property inventory (RPI) is a written record of real property assets, which typically are immovable property such as office buildings, warehouses, heavy equipment, and bridges. Governments also can track additional property, such as vehicles, in a comprehensive inventory.

The cost of establishing an RPI is not trivial, but it reaps significant benefits. A government that knows what it owns, what it is worth, and what it is using is in a better position to get the most out of its assets and to stop wasting unused ones. A good RPI identifies the property and its location, condition, value, best use, and lease information, if any.

Geographic information systems (GIS) are increasingly used by governments to identify their land and asset holdings, map parcels, and build digital databases in order to create an RPI. In a GIS survey, aerial photography, property deeds, lists of property history, and historical information are collected to complete the inventory process.

Using an RPI and a GIS

After developing an inventory, officials can use computerized maintenance management system (CMMS) software to reallocate resources to their best possible use. This increases fiscal responsibility, as state agencies can determine, for example, if there are two or more offices in proximity to each other that could be combined. This financial management also helps the budgeting process by finding assets to sell, increasing the revenue stream, and potentially decreasing lease and maintenance costs through space consolidation.

The process of creating an RPI can suggest additional ways to save money. While using a GIS auditing process to map its real property in the late 1990s, for example, the state of Wyoming found approximately

250,000 parcels that were not listed on tax rolls. Similarly, the Cincinnati Metropolitan Sewer District used GIS to find parcels with sewer connections that were not being billed. The district generated thousands of dollars in missing revenue, more than enough to pay for its GIS unit.

Case Study: Georgia

In the early 2000s, a commission created by then-Georgia governor Sonny Perdue found the state's $10.5 billion portfolio of more than 11,000 facilities was losing value due to poor maintenance, emerging safety issues, and underutilization. This prompted Perdue to issue an executive order in 2005 to bring overlapping, multi-agency management of the state's real estate into one portfolio, with a central manager, and he ordered the creation of the state's first comprehensive, enterprise-wide asset inventory. As a result of the RPI and more efficient management, the state has sold or conveyed to other governments dozens of state-owned properties, renegotiated leases at lower rates, and adopted uniform construction guidelines (Gilroy 2012). The fiscal benefits Georgia attained did not come from passive management, but intentional pursuit of efficiency.

Recommended Readings: Local Government and School Accountability, "Conducting a Capital Assets Inventory," in *Capital Planning and Budgeting: A Tutorial for Local Government Officials* (Albany, NY: New York State Office of the State Comptroller, no date); Fernando Fernholz and Rosemary Morales Fernholz, *A Toolkit For Municipal Asset Management* (Research Triangle Park, NC: RTI International, 2007); Anthony Randazzo and John Palatiello, "Knowing What State and Local Governments Own," Reason Foundation, 2010.

9. Divest non-core government assets.

> Financially stressed firms often find it good practice to divest non-core, non-essential assets, and governments should do the same.

In the business world, financially stressed firms often find it good practice to divest non-core, non-essential assets. The same practices can be used by governments. Asset sales (outright sale of government land or assets) and asset leases (long-term leases of public assets to private-sector investor-operators) are no longer a new or radical proposition:

- Electric and gas utilities have been privatized in a number of countries. In the United States, nearly 70 percent of all electricity customers in the United States receive power generated by an investor-owned utility (IOU), according to the American Public Power Association, and government-owned utilities generate only about 10 percent of U.S. electric power (APPA 2016). Similarly, of the 7,591,218 trillion BTUs sold by the gas industry in 2015, IOUs provided 78 percent of the total, municipal utilities provided 8 percent, and pipeline entities provided 13 percent (AGA n.d.).

- More than 100 airports have been sold or privatized throughout the world, including ones in Buenos Aires, Frankfurt, Johannesburg, London, Madrid, Melbourne, Paris, and Rome.

- Several cities and public university systems are considering leasing their parking assets after seeing long-term (50+ year) leases of government-owned parking meters, garages, and lots in Chicago and Indianapolis and at Ohio State University.

- Toll roads and private highways have been built in dozens of Asian, European, and Latin American countries. Since 2005, government-run toll roads have been privatized in Colorado (Northwest Parkway), Illinois (Chicago Skyway), Indiana (Indiana Toll Road), and Virginia (Pocahontas Parkway).

- Water supply and distribution systems have been privatized in many countries, including Argentina, France, Great Britain, and, to a lesser extent, the United States. Private water companies in the United States serve about 75 million customers—about one-quarter of the population (NAWC n.d.).

State and local governments pursue asset divestiture for a variety of reasons. For example, Indiana officials entered a long-term lease of the Indiana Toll Road to generate revenue that could be redeployed to invest in new and modernized transportation infrastructure across the state. Similarly, Ohio State University entered into a long-term lease of its parking system in 2012 to generate hundreds of millions of dollars to deposit into its university endowment to generate revenue for scholarships and other programs that support its academic mission.

Fiscal distress can be another motivator. Orange County, California raised more than $300 million through asset sales and sale-leasebacks over 18 months to help recover from the county's collapse into bankruptcy in 1995. And under emergency manager control, Pontiac, Michigan has sold off a number of assets since 2011 to reduce debt and operating costs, including its Department of Public Works building, excess capacity in its city wastewater system, a city-owned golf course, a city-owned downtown theater, several shuttered community centers, and numerous vacant land parcels.

Looming fiscal challenges can also prompt asset divestiture. As it has worked to balance its budget in the wake of the Great Recession, Tulsa, Oklahoma has sold more than 40 parcels of land since 2009, including an old city hall building that had been vacant for years. Not only did the city shed tens of thousands of dollars in annual maintenance costs for a building it wasn't using, it also generated $1 million from the sale (Gilroy and Moore 2013).

In Allentown, Pennsylvania, city officials approved a 50-year lease of its water and wastewater systems to the nonprofit, quasi-public Lehigh County Authority in 2013, a move designed to generate more than $210 million in upfront revenue the city used to pay down $160 million in underfunded pension obligations, as well as pay down water system debt and shore up the city's rainy day fund (Gilroy 2015).

The initial windfall to government is generally the most dramatic financial impact of privatizing infrastructure, but these initiatives also can generate ongoing revenue streams. Most state and municipal enterprises are exempt from taxation, so converting an airport or highway or water system into an investor-owned business converts it also into a tax-paying business.

In the case of asset leases, public administrators realize the benefits of not only upfront payments but also professional asset management, greater operating efficiency, lower operating and maintenance costs, better customer service, less political patronage, access to equity markets for capital, and shareholders who will hold management accountable.

Agreements to sell or lease assets should make clear the government entity will not be liable for debts or liabilities if the new owner is unsuccessful. The promise, even implicit, that government will bail out the private company can undermine incentives to be efficient and thus the rationale for privatization.

Recommended Readings: Adrian T. Moore, Geoffrey F. Segal, and John McCormally, *Infrastructure Outsourcing: Leveraging Concrete, Steel, and Asphalt with Public-Private Partnerships* (Los Angeles, CA: Reason Foundation, 2000); E.S. Savas, *Privatization and Public-Private Partnerships* (New York, NY: Chatham House, 2000).

10. Make the case to the public.

> When launching a privatization initiative, policymakers should explain the rationale, pros, and cons to the public early on.

People rightly want to know how privatization might affect their everyday lives. Policymakers should explain the rationale, pros, and cons to the public early on to ensure a full debate, rally public support, and seek related input. Some key steps in making the case to the public include:

- being ready to compromise;

- committing to an open and transparent process;

- developing a comprehensive communications strategy that combines traditional and social media channels;

- involving as early as possible public employees and other interested parties who might be predisposed to oppose privatization;

- knowing who the possible private-sector partners are;

- comprehensively reaching out to the public using web resources, news media, public meetings, and direct contact with community groups, bloggers, taxpayer advocates, and others.

The introduction and initial discussions of privatization will set the tone and define the terms of debate for the rest of the process. Naming a blue-ribbon task force of citizens and public- and private-sector representatives to study the options and issue a report is often a good way to collect and present factual information and set possible timelines without politicizing the issue.

Meetings of the task force should be public, and potential critics should be invited to participate and treated well. Questions that ought to be anticipated include: Why can't the government provide the services as efficiently as the private sector? Why not a two-year contract instead of a 10-year deal? Will the government lose control over the services? Who will citizens call if the service is improperly provided?

A communications strategy should involve public meetings that have formal notices, agendas, and minutes; a schedule of meetings with stakeholders, editorial boards, bloggers, and civic and business leaders; presentations to government entities and local service organizations; preparation and submission of letters to the editor and editorials; participation in online discussions; and availability of spokespersons to reporters, bloggers, and talk radio show hosts.

All these elements must be organized and coordinated early in the process and should continue after a proposal has been accepted and implemented. The purpose for planning the campaign is not to "orchestrate public opinion" or "control the message" but to avoid simple mistakes that unintentionally offend key stakeholders or lead to erroneous claims or undeliverable promises being made.

It is sometimes necessary for proponents to modify elements of the proposal to gain the required votes. For example, a 20-year contract proposal could be pared back to a 10-year deal with a 10-year option for renewal. An initial contract proposal involving public employees moving to private employment can be scaled back to a management contract involving private management while the employees stay employed with the public entity. These strategies are best considered during the initial discussions.

Ultimately, a clear communications and public relations strategy is crucial to getting buy-in for a privatization initiative. Credible community leaders, the media, and active citizens need to understand the initiative and its expected outcomes. This helps avert failure by building support up-front and getting clarity on expectations. It also helps to tailor the privatization to things people really care about, making it more likely the outcome will align with what citizens want.

Recommended Readings: Daniele Calabrese, *Strategic Communication for Privatization, Public-Private Partnerships, and Private Participation in Infrastructure* (Washington, DC: World Bank, 2007); Robin A. Johnson, *How to Navigate the Politics of Privatization* (Los Angeles, CA: Reason Foundation, 2002); Cecilia Cabañero-Verzosa and Paul Mitchell, *Communicating Economic Reform* (Washington, DC: World Bank, 2002).

References

AGA (American Gas Association). n.d. "Table 6-10: Gas Industry Sales by Class of Service and Company Type, 2005–2015."

APPA (American Public Power Association). 2016. "U.S. Electric Utility Statistics." In *2015–2016 Annual Directory & Statistical Report*.

Behn, Robert D., and Peter A. Kant. 1999. "Strategies for Avoiding the Pitfalls of Performance Contracting." *Public Productivity and Management Review* **22** (4): 470–89.

Cabañero-Verzosa, Cecilia, and Paul Mitchell. 2002. *Communicating Economic Reform*. Washington, DC: World Bank.

Calabrese, Daniele. 2007. *Strategic Communication for Privatization, Public-Private Partnerships, and Private Participation in Infrastructure*. Washington, DC: World Bank.

CCCA (California Contract Cities Association). n.d. "Member Cities" (website).

Coletti, Joe. 2016. *Pay for Success Contracting: The Emerging Paradigm*. Reason Foundation.

Commonwealth Competition Council. 1998. *Annual Report of the Commonwealth Competition Council to the Governor, the General Assembly and the Small Business Commission*. Richmond, VA: Commonwealth Competition Council.

Edwards, Chris. 2016. "Options for Federal Privatization and Reform Lessons from Abroad." *Policy Analysis* No. 794. Cato Institute.

Eggers, William D. 1997. *Performance Based Contracting: Designing State of the Art Contract Administration and Monitoring Systems*. Reason Foundation.

Fernholz, Fernando, and Rosemary Morales Fernholz. 2007. *A Toolkit For Municipal Asset Management*. Research Triangle Park, NC: RTI International.

Florida Council on Efficient Government. 2010. *2009 Annual Report for FY 2008–2009*. Tallahassee, FL: Florida Department of Management Services.

Garrigo, Henry. 2010. "Look Before You Leap into Privatization: Florida's Council on Efficient Government Sets a New Standard in Transparency, Due Diligence in Privatization and Contracting Decisions." Interview by Leonard Gilroy. Reason Foundation.

Gilroy, Leonard C. 2010. "State Competitive Government Commission: A Tool for 'Right-Sizing' Kansas Government" (website). Reason Foundation.

———. 2012. "FLAIR Act Would Bring Efficiency, Accountability to Federal Land Management" (website). Reason Foundation.

———. 2015. *Paying Down Unfunded Pension Liabilities Through Asset Sales and Leases*. Reason Foundation. June.

———. 2016. *Annual Privatization Report 2016* (website). Reason Foundation.

Gilroy, Leonard C., and David Aloyts. 2013. "Leasing the Indiana Toll Road: Reviewing the First Six Years of Private Operation." *Policy Brief* No. 108. Reason Foundation. May.

Gilroy, Leonard C., and Adrian Moore. 2013. "Savings for Fresno: The Role for Privatization." *Policy Brief* No. 104. Reason Foundation. May.

Gilroy, Leonard C., Adam B. Summers, Anthony Randazzo, and Harris Kenny. 2010. *Public-Private Partnerships for Corrections in California: Bridging the Gap Between Crisis and Reform*. Reason Foundation.

Goldsmith, Stephen. 1999. "The Yellow Pages Test: Let Your Fingers Do the Walking." *Nevada Journal* (website).

Herzberg, Benjamin, and Andrew Wright. 2006. *The PPD Handbook: A Toolkit for Business Environment Reformers*. Washington, DC: World Bank.

Hilke, John. 1993. "Cost Savings from Privatization: A Compilation of Findings." *How-To Guide* No. 6. Reason Foundation. March.

ICMA. 2009. *Profile of Local Government Service Delivery Choices 2007*. Washington, DC: International City/County Management Association.

Johnson, Robin A. 2002. *How to Navigate the Politics of Privatization*. Reason Foundation.

Koteskey, Tyler, and Aaron Garth Smith. 2016. "School Choice, Funding Portability, and Trends." Reason Foundation.

Krisai, Lauren, Austill Stuart, and Leonard Gilroy. 2016. "Developments in Criminal Justice and Corrections." Reason Foundation.

Lehrer, Eli, and Iain Murray. 2007. "The Continuing Value of Privatization." *CEO OnPoint* No. 123. Competitive Enterprise Institute. October 26.

Local Government and School Accountability. n.d. "Conducting a Capital Assets Inventory." In *Capital Planning and Budgeting: A Tutorial for Local Government Officials*. Albany, NY: New York State Office of the State Comptroller.

Markus, Edward. 1997. "Low Bid Alternatives" (website). *American City & County*. August 1.

Martin, Lawrence L. 2016. "Making Sense Of Public-Private Partnerships (P3s)." *Journal of Public Procurement* **16** (2): 191–207.

Moore, Adrian T., and Geoffrey F. Segal. 2002. *Weighing the Watchmen: Evaluating the Costs and Benefits of Outsourcing Correctional Services – Part 1: Employing a Best Value Approach to Procurement*. Reason Public Policy Institute.

Moore, Adrian T., Geoffrey F. Segal, and John McCormally. 2000. *Infrastructure Outsourcing: Leveraging Concrete, Steel, and Asphalt with Public-Private Partnerships*. Reason Foundation.

Moore, Adrian T., and Wade Hudson. 2000. "The Evolution of Privatization Practices and Strategies." In *Local Government Innovation: Issues and Trends in Privatization and Managed Competition*. Robin Johnson and Norman Walzer (editors). Westport, CT: Quorum Books.

NASBO (National Association of State Budget Officers). 2016. *The Fiscal Survey of the States*. Spring 2016.

NAWC (National Association of Water Companies). n.d. "Private Water Solutions" (website). Accessed August 28, 2017.

Newbery, David M. 2001. *Privatization, Restructuring, and Regulation of Network Utilities*. Cambridge, MA: MIT Press.

OMB (Office of Management and Budget). 1998. *A Guide to Best Practices for Performance-Based Service Contracting*. Washington, DC: Office of Federal Procurement Policy.

Pawlenty, Tim. 2009. "Minnesota and Wisconsin Governors Sign Groundbreaking Executive Orders to Explore Shared State Services." News release. January 13.

Poole, Robert. 2016a. "Privatization of Airports, Air Traffic Control and Airport Security." Reason Foundation.

_____. 2016b. "Developments in Transportation Finance and Infrastructure Investment." Reason Foundation.

Porter, Oliver. 2010. "Public-Private Partnerships for Local Governments: The Sandy Springs Model." Interview by Leonard Gilroy. Reason Foundation.

Prager, Jonas. 1994. "Contracting Out Government Services: Lessons from the Private Sector." *Public Administration Review* **54** (2): 176–84. doi:10.2307/976527.

Randazzo, Anthony, and John Palatiello. 2010. "Knowing What State and Local Governments Own." Reason Foundation.

Savas, E.S. 2005. *Privatization in the City: Successes, Failures, Lessons*. Washington, DC: CQ Press.

_____. 2000. *Privatization and Public-Private Partnerships*. New York, NY: Chatham House.

Segal, Geoffrey F., and Eric Montague. 2004. *Competitive Contracting for Highway Maintenance: Lessons Learned from National Experience*. Washington Policy Center.

Tolchin, Martin. 1985. "More Cities Paying Industry to Provide Public Services." *New York Times* (website). May 28.

Walberg, Herbert. 2010. *Advancing Student Achievement*. Stanford, CA: Hoover Institution Press.

Young, Richard D. 2005. *On Privatization—Competitive Sourcing In State Government*. Columbia, SC: Institute for Public Service and Policy Research at the University of South Carolina.

Additional Resources

Additional information about privatization is available from The Heartland Institute:

- PolicyBot, The Heartland Institute's free online clearinghouse for the work of other free-market think tanks, contains thousands of documents on privatization and related issues. It is on Heartland's website at https://www.heartland.org/policybot/.

- https://www.heartland.org/topics/government-spending/ is a website devoted to the latest research, news, and commentary about government spending and ways to get it under control, including privatization. Read headlines, watch videos, or browse the thousands of documents on privatization and related topics available from PolicyBot.

■ *Budget & Tax News* is The Heartland Institute's monthly newspaper devoted to government regulation, spending, and tax issues. Subscriptions with digital delivery are free, print subscriptions are $36/year for 10 issues. Subscribe at www.heartland.org/subscribe.

Directory

The following national organizations provide valuable information about privatization.

American Legislative Exchange Council (ALEC),
 https://www.alec.org/tag/privatization/

Cato Institute, https://www.cato.org/research/privatization

Heartland Institute, https://www.heartland.org/

International City/County Management Association,
 http://legacy.icma.org/en/icma/knowledge_network/topics/kn/Topic/
 207/Privatization

Reason Foundation, http://www.reason.org

Texas Council on Competitive Government,
 https://comptroller.texas.gov/purchasing/programs/ccg/

Utah Free Market Protection and Privatization Board,
 https://gomb.utah.gov/operational-excellence/privatization-board/

Chapter 6
Firearms

Joseph L. Bast and Publius

---

10 Principles of Firearms Policy

1. Americans have an individual right to keep and bear arms.
2. Bans on "assault weapons" are incoherent and self-defeating.
3. An increase in the number of guns does not lead directly to more gun crime.
4. Firearms possession among law-abiding citizens deters crime.
5. Defensive gun use saves lives.
6. Right to carry laws do not increase crime and may generate social benefits.
7. "Stand Your Ground" laws have been the historical norm in the United States.
8. The risk of firearms accidents is small and falling.
9. Large-scale illegal gun-running is a myth.
10. International experience does not support gun control in the United States.

Introduction

Firearms policy debates often occur in a context of crisis, with emotion and simple intuition ruling the conversation. We see images of mass shootings of innocent people in movie theaters or other public places and the natural reaction of nearly everyone is: "This is unacceptable! What can we do to make sure this never happens again?" Often the gut reaction to such gut-wrenching incidents is "Let's ban guns!" But is that reaction any more doable, desirable, or constitutional than saying that to prevent 30,000 annual deaths in auto accidents, "Let's ban cars!"?

Even during periods of calm, discussions of firearms policy are often burdened by a variety of erroneous assumptions about the risks and benefits of firearms and basic mistakes about firearms technology.

The Second Amendment to the U.S. Constitution states, "A well regulated Militia, being necessary to the security of a free State, the right of the people to keep and bear Arms, shall not be infringed."

The 10 principles provided here, with references for further research and documentation if desired, provide a framework for understanding and promoting sound policies regarding firearms in America.

1. Americans have an individual right to keep and bear arms.

The Second Amendment to the U.S. Constitution affirms the right of individuals to carry arms for private self-defense.

In 2008, the U.S. Supreme Court in *District of Columbia* v. *Heller* (554 U.S. 570 (2008)) recognized the Second Amendment to the Constitution affirms a preexisting right to arms for private self-defense. The Second Amendment "was not intended to lay down a novel principle but rather codified a right 'inherited from our English ancestors.'... It was clearly an individual right having nothing whatever to do with a militia," the majority opinion stated.

Already a Right

The *Heller* decision explained that even if militia concerns animated the codification of the right to arms, a motive for codification does not define the preexisting right. In his dissenting opinion in *United States* v. *Verdugo-Urquidez* (494 U.S. 259 (1990)), Justice William Brennan provided a classic articulation of this principle, explaining constitutional rights were not granted by the new federal government but predate the Constitution:

> The Framers of the Bill of Rights did not purport to "create" rights. Rather, they designed the Bill of Rights to prohibit our Government from infringing rights and liberties presumed to be

pre-existing. See e.g., U.S. Const., Amdt. 9 ("The enumeration in the Constitution of certain rights, shall not be construed to deny or disparage others retained by the people").

Critics of gun rights today argue that because the Founders identified the need for militias in the Second Amendment, they meant to limit ownership of guns for individual needs. But the militia conversation in the founding era arose in the context of anti-Federalists' objections to federal as opposed to state authority over the militia. Anti-Federalists lost that argument, and federal control of the militia was memorialized in Article I, Section 8, of the Constitution. The Second Amendment was not a repeal of the federal militia power granted in Article I, Section 8. Instead, the aim was to make explicit the Federalists' assertions that the new government was one of limited, enumerated powers and would not infringe on pre-existing individual rights (Madison [1789] 1979).

Who Controls Militias?

Before *Heller*, some courts concluded the Second Amendment established only a state right. But if the "states' rights" view of the Second Amendment were sound, conflict between federal and state governments over militia control is the place where it should operate. In the long history of state litigation objecting to federal control of state militia forces, the conflicts did not reference the Second Amendment (Heath 2001; *Pepich* v. *Department of Defense* 496 U.S. 334 (1990); *Selected Draft Law Cases* 245 U.S. 366 (1918); *Martin* v. *Mott* 25 U.S. 19, 28–33 (1827); *Houston* v. *Moore* 18 U.S. 1 (1820)).

Evidence affirming the individual right to arms is expansive. The post-ratification commentary (including treatments by luminaries such as St. George Tucker, William Rawle, and Joseph Story) richly demonstrates the constitutional right to arms is an individual right. The early nineteenth century cases interpreting the Second Amendment "universally support an individual right to arms unconnected to militia service" (*District of Columbia* v. *Heller* 554 U.S. 570 (2008)).

Guns and Civil Rights

The debate leading to and surrounding passage of the Fourteenth Amendment, which affirms equal protection of the rights of all citizens and passed in the wake of the freeing of slaves, overwhelmingly affirms the individual right to arms. The Second Freedman's Bureau Act explicitly guaranteed to freed slaves "the constitutional right to bear arms" against explicitly racist gun prohibitions of the southern Black Codes. Newly formed black political organizations and state conventions filed numerous petitions with Congress pleading for protection of their right to arms for individual self-defense. Black newspapers widely distributed the orders of the occupying Union army affirming the freedmen's constitutional right to arms for self-defense.

These concerns coalesced in the adoption of the Fourteenth Amendment, which Sen. Jacob Howard introduced by explaining "the great object" of the amendment is "to restrain the power of the states and compel them in all times to respect these great fundamental guarantees" that are "secured by the first eight amendments of the Constitution; such as ... the right to keep and to bear arms" (Cong. Globe, 39th Cong., 1st Sess. 2764, 2765–2766 (1866)).

The overwhelming evidence from the post–Civil War era affirms the individual right to arms. In the words of the *Heller* court (554 U.S. 570 (2008)), "Every late 19th century legal scholar that we have read interpreted the Second Amendment to include an individual right unconnected with militia service."

"Arms in Common Use for Lawful Purposes"

The Supreme Court's most significant treatment of the Second Amendment before *Heller* was *United States* v. *Miller*. In *Miller* (307 U.S. 174 (1939)), the Court considered whether ownership of a sawed-off shotgun regulated as a "gangster weapon" under the National Firearms Act was protected by the Second Amendment. The *Miller* decision was often misinterpreted, but its meaning is illuminated by considering exactly the arguments presented to the Court.

The government made two arguments in *Miller*. The first argument was that the Second Amendment "gave sanction only to the arming of the people as a body to defend their rights against tyrannical and unprincipled rulers" and "did not permit the keeping of arms for purposes of private self-defense." The government argued the right was "only one which exists where the arms are borne in the militia or some other military organization provided for by law and intended for the protection of the state" (*Miller* 307 U.S. 174 (1939)). This is essentially the argument made by dissenters in *Heller*.

The second argument was that "The term 'arms' [in the Second Amendment] refers only to those weapons which are ordinarily used for military or public defense purposes and does not relate to those weapons which are commonly used by criminals" (*Miller* 307 U.S. 174 (1939)).

The *Miller* court embraced the government's second argument, focusing on the gun and concluding there was no evidence it was part of ordinary military equipment, offering this widely cited phrasing: "In the absence of any evidence tending to show that the possession or use of a [sawed-off shotgun] at this time has some reasonable relationship to the preservation or efficiency of a well-regulated militia, we cannot say the Second Amendment guarantees the right to keep and bear such an instrument" (307 U.S. 174 (1939)).

However, the Court described the militia in terms consistent with an individual right of the people to keep and bear arms. The militia, said the Court, is "all males physically capable of acting in concert for the common defense" who when called "were expected to appear bearing *arms supplied by themselves and of the common use at the time*" [emphasis added]. The *Heller* court carried forward the *Miller* "common use" test to determine the types of guns that are constitutionally protected, explaining, "*Miller*'s reference to ordinary military equipment must be read in tandem with what comes after. ... The traditional militia was formed from a pool of men bringing arms in common use for a lawful purpose like self-defense" (554 U.S. 570 (2008)). As a result, the Second Amendment does grant a right to shotguns but not bazookas, howitzers, or nuclear weapons.

States Recognize Gun Rights

Another powerful indicator of the nature of the American right to arms is the state constitutions, which broadly affirm the individual right to arms for self-defense. Forty-four of the 50 state constitutions affirm a right to arms. Over time, the trend has been in favor of right to arms provisions. Since 1875, 13 new states have joined the union. Twelve of them included right to arms provisions in their constitutions. Since 1978, 12 states have added or strengthened a guarantee to own and bear arms. Some state constitutions refer generally to the right to keep and bear arms, and 37 states explicitly guarantee a right to self-defense (Volokh 2006; Johnson 2005).

These state constitutional guarantees demonstrate the individual right to arms is no outdated vestige of another era. The most recent state arms guarantee was Wisconsin's 1998 constitutional amendment, in favor of which 74 percent of voters cast ballots.

The alternative policy of sweeping gun bans also has been tested by referenda in Massachusetts and California. On November 5, 1976, with 86 percent voter turnout, 69 percent of Massachusetts voters opposed banning private ownership of handguns. In 1983, California voters also considered a handgun ban initiative. Sixty-three percent of voters opposed the handgun ban (Bordua 1983).

Recommended Readings: John R. Lott, Jr., *The War on Guns: Arming Yourself Against Gun Control Lies* (Washington, DC: Regnery Publishing, 2016); Stephen P. Halbrook, *The Founders' Second Amendment: Origins of the Right to Bear Arms* (Oakland, CA: Independent Institute, 2012).

2. Bans on "assault weapons" are incoherent and self-defeating.

Politically contrived categories such as "assault weapon" and "civilian sniper rifle" are technically indefensible and should not be the basis for public policy.

Some people still confuse "assault weapons" with machine guns. Early proponents of the term were counting on that confusion, and the calculation was political. A 1988 memorandum of the Violence Policy Center lamented the public had lost interest in handgun control, and it counseled the anti-gun lobby to switch to the "assault weapon issue." According to the memorandum:

> The issue of handgun restriction consistently remains a non-issue with the vast majority of legislators, the press, and public. ... Assault weapons ... are a new topic. The weapons' menacing looks, coupled with the public's confusion over fully automatic machine guns versus semi-automatic assault weapons—anything that looks like a machine gun is assumed to be a machine gun— can only increase the chance of public support for restrictions on these weapons (Violence Policy Center 1988).

Law professors Bruce Kobayashi and Joseph Olson (1997) identified the assault weapon characterization as a salient example of technically inaccurate pejoratives used to label regulated activity: "Prior to 1989, the term 'assault weapon' did not exist in the lexicon of firearms. It is a political term, developed by anti-gun publicists to expand the category of 'assault rifles' so as to allow an attack on as many additional firearms as possible on the basis of undefined 'evil' appearance."

Assault Weapons vs. Assault Rifles

Some people confuse the manufactured political term "assault weapon" with "assault rifle," which has an actual technical meaning. After World War II, "assault rifle" became a standard military term to describe *a specific type of machine gun*. The U.S. Department of Defense manual on Communist small arms states:

> Assault rifles are short, compact, selective-fire weapons [i.e., machine guns] that fire a cartridge intermediate in power between submachine-gun and rifle cartridges. Assault rifles have

mild recoil characteristics and, because of this, are capable of delivering effective full-automatic fire at ranges up to 300 meters.

The usage became so accepted that the U.S. Supreme Court referred to the American Armed Forces M-16 selective-fire rifle as the "standard assault rifle" (Halbrook 2009).

In contrast, there are no boundaries on what may be called an "assault weapon." Under the defunct 1994 Assault Weapon Ban, "assault weapons" were principally *semiautomatic* firearms. They were described as having features like pistol grips, folding stocks, and bayonet lugs that feed ammunition through a detachable box magazine. The label is sometimes used to include other types of guns as well. True assault rifles (i.e., fully automatic rifles) are regulated under the stringent provisions of the National Firearms Act of 1934, and there are fewer than 200,000 of these guns in civilian hands (Johnson 2005).

For current political purposes, assault weapons are generally some subset of semiautomatic firearms. Distinctions among semiautomatic firearms border on incoherent. This was evident under the 1994 Assault Weapons Ban, which put some of the *same guns on both the banned and permitted lists of guns*, depending on whether they had accoutrements like pistol grips, folding stocks, and flash hiders.

In Common Use

Some have claimed assault weapons are a dangerous new type of firearm. This is false. Semiautomatic technology is at least a century old. For example, the Browning Auto-5 semiautomatic shotgun was introduced in 1902; the Colt 1911 .45-caliber semiautomatic pistol was adopted as the U.S. military sidearm in 1911; the Remington Model 8 semiautomatic rifle was patented in 1900; and the Winchester Model 7 rifle looks like a modern assault weapon (with its detachable box magazine protruding below the breech) but was introduced in the market in 1907. These guns and tens of millions of other semiautomatic rifles, pistols, and shotguns have circulated in the civilian inventory for generations.

Estimating the total number of semiautomatics in the private inventory is difficult. Many were sold before even nominal recordkeeping was required under federal law. Many others were sold by the U.S. government under the century-old Civilian Marksmanship Program. In the early debate over the 1994 assault weapons ban, researchers from the Harvard School of Public Health found 60 percent of gun owners reported owning some type of semiautomatic firearm (Hemenway and Richardson 1997).

Semiautomatics with such features as pistol grips and detachable box magazines have dominated firearms sales in recent years. For several years running, the AR-15 has been the best-selling rifle type in the United States. In 2011, the D.C. Circuit Court of Appeals acknowledged the AR-15 (with several million in circulation) was a gun in common use (*Heller* v. *District of Columbia* 670 F.3d 1244 (2011)).

A Specious Designation

"Assault weapon" is a specious designation made up to suggest some special danger from guns that often had simply cosmetic differences from arms that have long been legal and pose no special danger. All guns have legitimate uses and dangers from illicit use that vary by circumstance.

When gauged against objectively measurable characteristics, the use of the term "assault weapon" inaccurately describes the class and more accurately describes guns that assault weapon legislation generally classifies as less dangerous and permissible. This renders the assault weapon category incoherent and ultimately self-defeating.

The 1994 Assault Weapon Ban was illusory because it defined the prohibited class by functionally less significant characteristics that some people thought were scary or aggressive looking, such as pistol grips, bayonet lugs, and folding stocks. With these characteristics removed, operationally similar guns remained available. However, the ban did cause a scare in the market that accelerated demand for and increase ownership of functionally similar guns and other substitutes.

The assault weapon classification is the current rendition of the "bad gun" regulatory formula that claims to ban only limited categories of firearms, such as guns "criminals choose" or exceptionally dangerous ones. This regulatory formula has a long history, but it has no basis in real-world gun safety or constitutional law.

The *Heller* decision determined guns in common use are constitutionally protected. Politically contrived categories such as "assault weapon" and "civilian sniper rifle" are technically indefensible designations that defy the constitutional protection of common rifles, shotguns, and handguns. They are constitutionally unsustainable distractions from useful policymaking.

Recommended Readings: Stephen P. Halbrook, "Reality Check: The 'Assault Weapon' Fantasy & Second Amendment Jurisprudence," *Georgetown Journal of Law & Public Policy* **47** (2016); John R. Lott, Jr., "The Truth about Assault Weapons Bans and Background Checks," *Fox News*, February 28, 2013.

3. An increase in the number of guns does not lead directly to more gun crime.

Gun crime has declined as the number of privately owned guns has increased to record levels.

Some people assume increases in the number of guns in the general population will lead to roughly proportionate increases in gun crime. This basic assumption has fueled supply-control initiatives ranging from gun buy-backs to sweeping gun bans. But the simplistic intuition that more guns equal more gun crime is refuted by the simultaneous increase in the gun inventory to record levels and decline of gun crimes.

Widespread Ownership
Since 1948, the rate of gun ownership per 100,000 population has increased steadily. Firearms ownership in the United States is at an all-time high. Estimates put the gun stock at roughly 350 million firearms in private hands. A 2016 Pew Research Center poll found 44 percent of American adults had a gun in their home—a seven percentage point increase in the past two years—and another 5 percent won't reveal whether they own a gun (Pew 2016).

People are not always truthful with pollsters, so surveys may undercount gun owners. One sign gun ownership is probably rising more rapidly than surveys show is the number of concealed handgun permits, which rose from 2.7 million in 1999 to more than 14.5 million in 2016 (Lott 2016b). New gun purchases, measured by Bureau of Alcohol, Tobacco, Firearms, and Explosives (ATF) instant check data, have soared to record levels in the past decade The National Instant Criminal Background Check System (NICS) shows the number of firearms background checks initiated through NICS nearly tripled from 1999 to 2016 (NICS 2017).

Homicide Rates vs. Gun Ownership
The rate of gun homicides in the United States has oscillated in a pattern that shows no support for the theory that more guns should lead to proportionately more homicide. From 1948 to 2009, the U.S. per-capita number of firearms rose by 186 percent. At the same time, the homicide rate varied widely. At its peak in 1980, the homicide rate was 82 percent higher than in 1948. In 2009, the rate was 11 percent lower than in 1948 (CDC 2014; Kleck 1997; ATF 2013; FBI 2006–2016).

In 2010 an estimated 1,246,248 violent crimes occurred nationwide, 13.2 percent below the 2006 level and 13.4 percent below the 2001 level. In 2017, FBI reported the number of violent crimes in the country fell 5.4 percent from 2012 to 2013, fell 4.6 percent from 2013 to 2014, rose 1.7 percent from 2014 to 2015, and rose 5.3 percent from 2015 to 2016 (FBI 2017).

In 2016, Florida State University criminologist Gary Kleck and coauthors examined data on gun ownership, 19 types of gun control laws, and violent crime rates in every U.S. city with a population of 25,000 or more. They found "gun control laws generally show no evidence of effects on crime rates, possibly because gun [ownership] levels do not have a net positive effect on violence rates." They also observe, "requiring a license to possess a gun, and bans on purchases of guns by alcoholics appear to reduce rates of both homicide and robbery. Weaker evidence suggests that bans on gun purchases by criminals and on possession by mentally ill persons may reduce assault rates, and that bans on gun purchase by criminals may also reduce robbery rates" (Kleck et al. 2016).

In 2015, John R. Lott Jr. and coauthors found "between 2007 and 2014, murder rates have fallen from 5.6 to 4.2 (preliminary estimates) per 100,000. This represents a 25 percent drop in the murder rate at the same time that the percentage of the adult population with [concealed carry] permits soared by 156 percent. Overall violent crime also fell by 25 percent over that period of time. States with the largest increase in permits have seen the largest relative drops in murder rates" (Lott et al. 2015).

Most Killers Already Were Criminals

For criminal homicide in general, the killers are usually not law-abiding people, which suggests homicide rates are dependent on the overall incidence of criminality, not the number of guns in people's hands.

Kennedy and Braga's analysis of 1988 national data on homicide in 33 large cities showed 54 percent of killers had a prior adult criminal record; 2 percent had a juvenile record only; no information was available on 25 percent; and 20 percent did not have criminal records. They concluded, "Homicide offenders are likely to commit murders in the course of long criminal careers consisting primarily of nonviolent crimes but including larger than normal proportions of violent crimes" (Kennedy and Braga 1998).

Of Illinois murderers in 2001, 43 percent had an Illinois felony conviction within the previous 10 years and 72 percent had an Illinois arrest (Cook et al. 2005). City-level studies come to similar conclusions. A *New York Times* study of the murders in New York City in 2003–05 found "[m]ore than 90 percent of the killers had criminal records"

(McGinty 2006). In 1989, *The New York Times* reported that in Washington, DC, almost all the murderers and victims were "involved in the drug trade" (Berke 1989).

In Lowell, Massachusetts, "some 95 percent of homicide offenders" had been "arraigned at least once in Massachusetts courts," the average being nine prior arraignments (Braga *et al.* 2006). Baltimore police records show 92 percent of murder suspects in 2006 had criminal records (Sentementes 2007). The Kennedy and Braga (1998) study of Minneapolis homicide offenders found 73 percent had been arrested at least once by the Minneapolis Police Department, with an average number of 7.4 arrests.

A comprehensive review of the data concluded, "The vast majority of persons involved in life threatening violence have a long criminal record with many prior contacts with the justice system" (Elliott 1998).

Recommended Readings: Gary Kleck, Tomislav Victor Kovandzic, and Jon Bellows, "Does Gun Control Reduce Violent Crime?" June 21, 2016; Don Kates and Gary Mauser, "Would Banning Firearms Reduce Murder and Suicide? A Review of International and Some Domestic Evidence," *Harvard Journal of Law and Public Policy* **30** (2007): 649–94.

4. Firearms possession among law-abiding citizens deters crime.

Research shows criminal activity is discouraged by armed citizens.

Armed citizens are a disincentive to criminals. A famous study conducted for the National Institute of Justice interviewed felony prisoners in 11 state prisons in 10 states and found the following:

- Thirty-four percent of the felons reported personally having been "scared off, shot at, wounded or captured by an armed victim."

- Eight percent said the experience had occurred "many times."

- Sixty-nine percent reported the experience had happened to another criminal whom they knew personally.

■ Thirty-nine percent had personally decided not to commit a crime because they thought the victim might have a gun.

■ Fifty-six percent said a criminal would not attack a potential victim known to be armed.

■ Seventy-four percent agreed with the following statement: "One reason burglars avoid houses where people are at home is that they fear being shot" (Wright and Rossi 1986).

In these interviews, "the highest concern about confronting an armed victim was registered by felons from states with the greatest relative number of privately owned firearms" (Wright and Rossi 1986). Wright and Rossi concluded,

> The major effects of partial or total handgun bans would fall more on the shoulders of the ordinary gun-owning public than on the felonious gun abuser of the sort studied here. ... It is therefore also possible that one side consequence of such measures would be some loss of the crime-thwarting effects of civilian firearms ownership (*Ibid.*, p. 238).

These findings suggest many criminals are rational actors. They make choices about committing crimes in a way that maximizes expected benefits, minimizes the risks they run, or both. Thus, they prefer soft targets (such as unarmed victims) and avoid hard ones.

A national study of how frequently firearms are used to defend against burglaries was conducted by the Centers for Disease Control and Prevention (CDC) (Ikeda *et al.* 1997). Extrapolating the polling sample to the national population, the researchers estimated that in the previous 12 months there were approximately 1,896,842 incidents in which a householder retrieved a firearm but did not see an intruder. There were an estimated 503,481 incidents in which the armed householder *did* see the burglar, and in 497,646 (98.8 percent) of those incidents, the burglar was scared away by the presence of the firearm.

In the United States, a household member is present during 27 percent of home burglaries. In 26 percent of burglaries in which a household member is present, he or she will be the victim of a violent crime (Catalano 2010).

Criminologists attribute the prevalence of daytime burglary to burglars' fear of confronting an armed occupant. Burglars report they avoid late-night home invasions because "that's the way you get yourself shot" (Rengert and Wasilchick 2000; Conklin 1972). The most thorough study of burglary patterns was a St. Louis survey of 105 currently active burglars. The researchers observed, "One of the most serious risks faced by residential burglars is the possibility of being injured or killed by occupants of a target. Many of the offenders we spoke to reported that this was far and away their greatest fear" (Wright and Decker 1994).

An American burglar's risk of being shot while invading an occupied home is greater than his risk of going to prison. Presuming that the risk of prison deters some potential burglars, the risk of armed defenders may deter even more. Because burglars do not know *which* homes have a gun, people who do not own guns enjoy substantial free-rider benefits because of the deterrent effect from the known existence of many homes that do keep arms (Kopel 2001; Cook and Ludwig 1996; Kopel 2003).

Recommended Readings: David B. Kopel, "The Costs and Consequences of Gun Control," *Policy Analysis* No. 784, Cato Institute, December 1, 2015; H. Sterling Burnett, "Suing Gun Manufacturers: Hazardous to Our Health," *Texas Review of Law & Politics* **5** (2001): 433.

5. Defensive gun use saves lives.

Research shows armed citizens effectively use guns to defend themselves, even if only by showing the weapon to a would-be assailant.

There have been 14 major surveys inquiring into the frequency of defensive gun uses (DGUs) in the modern United States. The surveys range from a low of around 700,000 annually to a high of 3,000,000. The surveys asked respondents directly whether they had used a gun defensively.

One general survey did not ask this question directly and yielded far lower rates of defensive gun use. The data for this survey were derived from face-to-face interviews conducted in the subjects' homes by the Census Bureau in conjunction with the Department of Justice. The National Crime Victimization Survey (NCVS) counts only defensive gun uses volunteered by survey participants. The NCVS data for the years 1992–2005 suggests about 97,000 DGUs annually.

One of the most thorough surveys of defensive gun uses was conducted by Kleck and Gertz (1995), who found guns were used defensively approximately 2.5 million times per year. They also found

80 percent of defensive uses involved handguns and 76 percent of defensive uses did not involve firing the weapon, rather merely brandishing it to scare away an attacker. The Kleck/Gertz findings received an important endorsement from Marvin Wolfgang , president of the American Society of Criminology and an ardent supporter of gun prohibition. Reviewing the Kleck/Gertz findings, Wolfgang wrote he could find neither methodological flaw nor any other reason to doubt the correctness of their figure:

> I am as strong a gun-control advocate as can be found among the criminologists in this country. ... I would eliminate all guns from the civilian population and maybe even from the police. I hate guns. ... Nonetheless, the methodological soundness of the current Kleck and Gertz study is clear. ... The Kleck and Gertz study impresses me for the caution the authors exercise and the elaborate nuances they examine methodologically. I do not like their conclusions that having a gun can be useful, but I cannot fault their methodology. They have tried earnestly to meet all objections in advance and have done exceedingly well (Wolfgang 1995, p. 188).

Skeptics of the Kleck/Gertz DGU survey conducted their own survey for the Police Foundation and obtained similar results: an estimate of 1.46 million DGUs (Cook and Ludwig 1996).

Some of the resistance to crediting the DGU survey estimates is rooted in the difference between the total number of defensive gun uses (seemingly in the millions) and the very small number of justifiable homicides (by private parties and police), around 1,000 per year. This underscores the character of the typical defensive gun use. In most cases, no shots are fired, and where shots are fired, typically no one is hit.

The danger that someone using a gun for self-defense will have it taken away, or that resistance will enrage the criminal into a fatal attack, is very low. Victims' weapons are taken by attackers in no more than 1 percent of cases in which the victim uses a weapon. Data from the NCVS and other sources also show "there is no sound empirical evidence that resistance does provoke fatal attacks" (Kleck and Tark 2005). Resisting with a firearm does not increase the chance of victim injury. A study of data on robberies from 1979 to 1985 found resistance with a gun was in fact the most effective form of resistance. It was both the method most likely to thwart the crime and the method that most reduced the intended victim's likelihood of injury (Kleck and DeLone 1993; Kleck and Gertz 1995; Wells 2002).

"The use of a gun by the victim significantly reduces her chance of being injured" in situations when the robber is armed with a non-gun weapon (Southwick 2000). If the robber has a gun, or has no weapon, victim gun possession did not seem to affect injury rates. Southwick (2000) concluded if 10 percent more robbery victims had guns, the rate of serious victim injury from robbery would fall by 3 to 5 percent.

Recommended Readings: Gary Kleck and Jongyeon Tark, "Resisting Crime: The Effects of Victim Action on the Outcomes of Crimes," *Criminology* **42** (4): 861–909; William Wells, "The Nature and Circumstances of Defensive Gun Use: A Content Analysis of Interpersonal Conflict Situations Involving Criminal Offenders," *Justice Quarterly* **19** (2002): 127–57.

6. Concealed carry laws do not increase crime and may generate social benefits.

> Research suggests concealed carry laws deter criminals and generate billions of dollars of benefits per year in avoided costs of crime.

Seventy-three percent of violent victimizations take place away from the victim's home (BJS 2016), making the right to carry a firearm for self-defense an important and necessary application of the right to bear arms. Forty-four states have constitutional provisions protecting the right to keep and bear arms, but restrictions on the right to carry or conceal weapons vary from state to state. Of the six states that do not constitutionally protect firearms ownership—California, Iowa, Maryland, Minnesota, New Jersey, and New York—one, New York, protects gun ownership via statutory civil rights law.

Firearm owners are subject to the laws of the state they are in, not where they reside, so traveling with a gun in a state with restrictive regulations can result in unintentionally breaking state laws. Some states recognize others' permits in return for their permits being recognized by the other state, called reciprocity, but this is not always the case.

Concealed Carry Laws

"Concealed carry" laws protect the individual right to carry a weapon in public in a concealed manner, either on one's person or in close proximity. Such laws may not refer only to firearms: In Florida, for example, carrying a pepper spray device with more than two ounces of chemical requires a concealed carry permit.

All 50 states have passed laws allowing qualified individuals to carry certain concealed firearms in public, either without a permit or after obtaining a permit. In most states, concealed carry legislation is mostly under "shall-issue" rules: After a background check and, generally, completion of a training program, permits shall be issued without further restrictions or requirements. State laws are not uniform, but 42 states are explicitly or essentially shall-issue jurisdictions.

In 2015, gun expert John D. Lott, Jr. and coauthors reviewed new research on the extent of concealed carry laws and reported the following statistics (Lott *et al.* 2015):

- 5.2 percent of the total adult population of the United States has a concealed carry permit.

- In five states, more than 10 percent of the adult population has concealed handgun permits.

- In 10 states, a permit is no longer required to carry in all or virtually all of the state.

- Since 2007, the number of permits issued to women has increased by 270 percent and to men by 156 percent.

- Some evidence suggests permit-holding by minorities is increasing more than twice as fast as for whites.

- States with the largest increase in permits have seen the largest relative drops in murder rates.

- Concealed handgun permit holders are extremely law-abiding. In Florida and Texas, permit holders are convicted of misdemeanors or felonies at one-sixth the rate that police officers are convicted.

Social Benefits of Concealed Carry

Lott argues one of the most substantial drivers of crime reduction is the proliferation of shall-issue concealed-carry licenses to law-abiding people (Lott and Mustard 1997; Lott 1999, 2010). More guns in the hands of honest people in public spaces deter criminals and generate billions of dollars of benefits per year in avoided costs of crime.

The majority of researchers who have tested Lott's hypothesis have at least partially agreed with him (finding some reduction in crime), although a significant minority have found concealed-carry laws to have no statistically discernible effect on crime.

In 2005, the National Research Council, the research arm of the U.S. National Academy of Sciences, National Academy of Engineering, and National Academy of Medicine, published the results of its assessment of Lott's claims (NRC 2005). While a six-member majority of the NRC panel concluded the data were inadequate to conclude whether right-to-carry laws increased or decreased crime, one panelist, political scientist James Q. Wilson, filed a blistering dissent (Wilson 2005). Wilson, one of the most respected political scientists of recent decades, had supported gun control measures in the past (Wilson 1994).

Wilson found "some of [Lott's] results survive virtually every reanalysis done by the committee." Specifically, "Lott argued that murder rates decline after the adoption of [right-to-carry] laws even after allowing for the effect of other variables that affect crime rates. The committee has confirmed this." Also, Wilson stated studies by Lott's critics "do not show that the passage of RTC laws drives the crime rates up (as might be the case if one supposed that newly armed people went about looking for someone to shoot). The direct evidence that such shooting sprees occur is nonexistent. The indirect evidence ... is controversial."

Wilson concluded: "This suggests to me that for people interested in RTC laws, the best evidence we have is that they impose no costs but may confer benefits. That conclusion might be very useful to authorities who contemplate the enactment of RTC laws."

Recommended Readings: National Research Council (NRC), *Firearms and Violence: A Critical Review,* Committee to Improve Research Information and Data on Firearms (Washington, DC: The National Academies Press, 2005); John R. Lott, Jr., John E. Whitley, and Rebekah C. Riley, "Concealed Carry Permit Holders Across the United States," *Report from the Crime Prevention Research Center,* July 13, 2015.

7. "Stand Your Ground" laws have been the historical norm in the United States.

> "Stand your ground" laws— where a claim of self-defense does not require the individual prove he or she attempted to retreat—are not new in the United States.

"Stand Your Ground" (SYG) laws state a claim of self-defense does not require the individual prove he or she attempted to retreat from an assailant (Branca 2013). Similar "Castle Doctrine" laws apply to home invasion. These laws have come under heavy fire in recent years, with objections apparently rooted in a belief they represent some new and dangerous approach to resolving self-defense claims. That assessment is mistaken.

SYG laws are a codification of judicial rulings that have been part of American common law for more than a century. A recent detailed assessment counts 34 states as "no-retreat" states, where a claim of self-defense does not require the individual prove he or she attempted to retreat from an assailant (Branca 2013).

An American Tradition

In every U.S. jurisdiction, there are four basic things a defendant must show to make a successful claim of self-defense. In "retreat jurisdictions," a defendant must make one additional showing to sustain a self-defense claim. In both SYG and retreat jurisdictions, a successful self-defense claim requires the following:

1. *Innocence*—the individual was not a criminal aggressor;

2. *Imminence*— the person was in immediate danger;

3. *Proportionality*—the force used was proportionate to the threat, meaning deadly force can be used only against the threat of death or serious bodily harm; and

4. *Reasonableness*—the conduct was objectively and subjectively reasonable under the circumstances.

In jurisdictions that require retreat, a successful self-defense claim requires a *fifth* showing: The use of deadly force could not have been avoided by retreating. The retreat rule is and always has been the minority rule in the United States.

Two early U.S. Supreme Court cases demonstrate this in detail. The first case includes the famous assessment by Justice Oliver Wendell Holmes: "Detached reflection cannot be demanded in the presence of an uplifted knife." The fuller quotation below captures the Court's assessment of the American rule:

> Many respectable writers agree that, if a man reasonably believes that he is in immediate danger of death or grievous bodily harm from his assailant, *he may stand his ground,* and that, if he kills him, he has not succeeded the bounds of lawful self-defense. ... Therefore, in this Court at least, it is not a condition of immunity that one in that situation should pause to consider whether a reasonable man might not think it possible to fly with safety or to disable his assailant, rather than to kill him (*Brown* v. *United States* 256 U.S. 335 (1921)).

In *Beard* v. *United States* (158 U.S. 550 (1895)), the Court opinion authored by John Marshall Harlan, quoted in part below, shows modern SYG statutes are fully consistent with the century-old American rule:

> The application of the doctrine of "retreating to the wall" was carefully examined by the Supreme Court of Ohio in *Erwin* v. *State,* 29 Ohio St. 186, 193, 199. ... Upon a full review of the authorities and looking to the principles of the common law as expounded by writers and courts of high authority, the Supreme Court of Ohio held that the charge was erroneous, saying:

> "... The question, then, is simply this: does the law hold a man who is violently and feloniously assaulted responsible for having brought such necessity upon himself on the sole ground that he failed to fly from his assailant when he might safely have done so? ... [A] true man, who is without fault, is not obliged to fly from an assailant, who by violence or surprise maliciously seeks to take his life, or to do him enormous bodily harm."

The Court ruled a person was justified in killing an assailant without retreating:

> In our opinion, the court below erred in holding that the accused, while on his premises, outside of his dwelling house, was under a legal duty to get out of the way, if he could, of his assailant, who, according to one view of the evidence, had threatened to kill the defendant, in execution of that purpose had armed himself with a deadly weapon, with that weapon concealed upon

his person went to the defendant's premises, despite the warning of the latter to keep away, and by word and act indicated his purpose to attack the accused. The defendant was where he had the right to be … [and] he was not obliged to retreat nor to consider whether he could safely retreat, but was entitled to stand his ground and meet any attack made upon him with a deadly weapon in such way and with such force as, under all the circumstances, he at the moment, honestly believed, and had reasonable grounds to believe, were necessary to save his own life or to protect himself from great bodily injury (*Beard* v. *United States* 158 U.S. 550 (1895)).

In *Runyan* v. *State* (57 Ind. 80 (1877)), which was an indictment for murder and where the instructions of the trial court involved the present question, the Court said:

The weight of modern authority, in our judgment, establishes the doctrine that when a person, being without fault and in a place where he has a right to be, is violently assaulted, he may, without retreating, repel force by force, and if, in the reasonable exercise of his right of self-defense, his assailant is killed, he is justified.

Deep Roots in Common Law

Opposition to requiring the fifth showing in self-defense cases, that use of deadly force could have been avoided by retreating, predates the founding of the United States. In Sir Edward Hyde East's *A Treatise of Pleas of the Crown* (1803), the author, considering what sort of an attack was lawful and justifiable to resist even by the death of the assailant, wrote:

A man may repel force by force in defense of his person, habitation, or property against one who manifestly intends and endeavors, by violence or surprise, to commit a known felony, such as murder, rape, robbery, arson, burglary, and the like, upon either. *In these cases he is not obliged to retreat* [emphasis added], but may pursue his adversary until he has secured himself from all danger, and if he kill him in so doing, it is called justifiable self-defense.

Similarly, Sir Michael Foster wrote in *Crown Cases* (1792):

In the case of justifiable self-defense, the injured party may repel force with force in defense of his person, habitation, or property against one who manifestly intendeth and endeavoreth, with violence or surprise, to commit a known felony upon either. *In these cases he is not obliged to retreat* [emphasis added], but may pursue his adversary till he findeth himself out of danger, and if, in a conflict between them, he happeneth to kill, such killing is justifiable.

These early legal statements and later treatments by the U.S. Supreme Court confirm that very early on, consistent with modern SYG laws, U.S. common law did not require retreat. SYG laws reflect the longstanding common law assessment of the proper burden to place on a person who is fighting to defend his or her life. He or she must meet a rigorous four-part test that has long been demanded of those claiming self-defense.

SYG laws do not change traditional self-defense rules. They simply say people who have had to defend themselves against murderous assaults are not *also* forced to prove a negative: That in the middle of a deadly attack, they could not have safely run away.

The Current Debate

Concern over rising violent crime rates, especially in urban areas, has generated interest in passing or strengthening existing SYG laws. Early successes of this movement generated a tremendous backlash from anti-gun activists who accused advocates of SYG laws of being racists (e.g., ABA 2015) or responsible for rising homicide rates (e.g., Humphreys *et al.* 2017). Thankfully, these claims do not stand up to careful inspection.

In 2014, the American Bar Association released a preliminary version of a report it would eventually publish in 2015 purporting to show SYG laws had a disparate impact on African-Americans and other minorities, increased homicide rates, were unnecessary, and unnecessarily limited judicial discretion. The report got wall-to-wall uncritical coverage by the mainstream media, none of them reporting ABA's longstanding anti-gun bias. But surely that was relevant, since ABA is a lobbying organization for lawyers and not an independent research organization. The National Rifle Association—itself a lobbying organization but on the other side of this issue—couldn't resist pointing it out:

> The American Bar Association (ABA), which supports handgun registration and handgun owner licensing, supports a ban on general-purpose semi-automatic rifles like the AR-15, thinks the Consumer Products Safety Commission should dictate what kind of firearms are "safe" enough to manufacture, supports legislation to ban the manufacture of pistols that don't micro-stamp ammunition, thinks that anti-gun groups should be able to file frivolous lawsuits against the firearm industry, and opposes "shall

issue" carry permit laws and federal "Right-to-Carry" reciprocity legislation has come out against Stand Your Ground laws.

Who, pray tell, could have predicted it (NRA 2014)?

NRA goes on to describe how the ABA report relies on studies with small sample sizes, or that fail to distinguish between defensive homicides and murders, or that don't report whether a SYG law was invoked during defense proceedings. These are crippling defects for serious research, but it seems clear ABA never intended to conduct or even report serious research into the matter.

The idea that SYG laws discriminate against African-Americans is based on the assumption that blacks are more likely to commit violent crimes than whites, but the issue at stake in the SYG debate is the right of *victims* to fight back, and all empirical evidence suggests African-Americans are more likely than whites to be victims of violent attacks. John Lott wrote, "Who benefits from the law? Actually, since poor blacks who live in high-crime urban areas are the most likely victims of crime, they are also the ones who benefit the most from stand your ground laws. The laws make it easier for would-be victims to protect themselves when the police can't arrive fast enough. Therefore, rules that make self-defense more difficult disproportionately impact blacks" (Lott 2013b). Lott also pointed out African-Americans make up 16.6 percent of Florida's population but account for 31 percent of the defendants invoking the stand your ground defense (*Ibid.*).

In 2017, the *Journal of the American Medical Association* published a study purporting to show Florida's SYG had led to an increase in "murders" in the state (Humphreys *et al.* 2017). Attorney and legal self-defense expert Andrew Branca wrote a withering critique of the study (Branca 2016). The authors compared Florida's homicide rate to rates in four states they thought did not have SYGs, when in fact one of the four enforced statutes that were the equivalent of an SYG. Worse, the authors didn't distinguish between homicides and "murders," even though the first includes justifiable use of deadly force while the latter does not. Wrote Branca,

> By failing to distinguish between "murder" and "homicide," the JAMA paper conflates unlawful and lawful killings. Indeed, it is quite possible that fully 100 percent of the increase in Florida homicides, which the paper attributes to the Stand Your Ground law, were in fact lawful acts of self-defense, the alternative to which would have been the murder, maiming, and rape of innocent victims. If so, the effect of the Stand Your Ground law has been to reduce the murder, maiming, and rape

of innocent victims, arguably the very social good intended by its passage (Branca 2016).

Recommended Readings: Jorge Amselle, "Why We Need 'Stand Your Ground' Laws," *The Daily Caller,* March 11, 2014; Andrew Branca, "What to Make of the New Study of Florida's 'Stand Your Ground' Law," *National Review,* November 16, 2016.

8. The risk of firearms accidents is small and falling.

> The accidental death rate from firearms, including accidental deaths among children, has been falling for the past four decades.

The image of a child killed by a firearm provokes our deepest emotions. That emotion is sometimes exploited and exaggerated in the political process. For example, Washington state initiative 676, a failed gun-licensing scheme, was pitched as a child safety regulation (Johnson 2005). But the truth about firearms accidents is that the risk is low and falling.

Small and Falling Risk

A careful analysis conducted by the National Safety Council (NSC) released in 2011 found the following:

> How many children are killed by guns is a complicated question. If the age range is 0–19 years, and homicide, suicide, and unintentional injuries are included then the total firearms-related deaths for 2007 are 3,067. This is a figure commonly used by journalists. The 3,067 firearms-related deaths for age group 0–19 breaks down into 138 unintentional, 638 suicides, and 2,161 homicides, 60 of which the intent could not be determined, and 25 due to legal intervention. Viewed by age group, 85 of the total firearms related deaths were of children under 5 years old, 3,134 were children 5–14, and 2,669 were teens and young adults 15–19 years old (NSC 2011).

Gun ownership has increased greatly in the past few generations, yet this has not corresponded with an increase in fatal gun accidents. From 1948 to 2009, U.S. per-capita ownership of firearms rose by 186 percent, yet the per-capita death rate from firearms accidents fell by 88 percent. Over the same period (starting in 1950 when childhood accident data became available), the accidental gun death rate for children (ages 0 to 14) has fallen by 93 percent, from 1.10 per 100,000 population to 0.08. Thus, the fatal gun accident rate for all ages is today at an all-time low, while the per-capita gun supply is at an all-time high. The annual risk level for a fatal gun accident is around 0.18 per 100,000 in the population—less than the risk caused by taking two airplane trips a year or getting a whooping cough vaccination (Breyer 1993).

By way of comparison, swimming pools are involved in far more accidental child fatalities than are firearms (NSC 2007). In 2003, there were seven accidental firearms deaths for children under five, and 49 deaths for ages five to 14. For the same two combined age groups in that same year, there were 86 accidental deaths in bathtubs and 285 deaths in swimming pools. Swimming pool accidents cause more deaths of children under 10 years of age than *all* forms of death by firearm combined—accident, homicide, and suicide. For accidents, "the likelihood of death by pool (1 in 11,000) versus death by gun (1 in more than 1,000,000) isn't even close" (Levitt and Dubner 2006).

The one in-depth study on firearms accidents among adults found the adult victims to have high rates of "arrests, violence, alcohol abuse, highway crashes, and citations for moving traffic violations" (Waller and Whorton 1973). In addition, about half of all fatal gun accidents involve hunting. Starting with New York State in 1948, all states have adopted regulations requiring those applying for a hunting license to pass a hunting safety class. These classes have probably reduced hunting fatalities from all sorts of carelessness, such as carrying a loaded gun while climbing over a fence or sitting in a tree stand without a safety harness.

Child Access Prevention Laws

In 2016, 18 states mandated safe storage of firearms with so-called Child Access Prevention (CAP) laws (What Works for Health 2016). Empirical studies of CAP laws have come to conflicting conclusions. Some studies have found the laws may decrease the number of firearm suicides (Santaella-Tenorio et al. 2016) and reduce unintentional firearm deaths and injuries among youth (DeSimone et al. 2013), but other studies find no impact (Gius 2015; Lee et al. 2013).

In 2001, Lott and Whitley compared crime, accident, and suicide trends in states with CAP laws with trends in other states, while controlling for the effects of numerous sociological factors (Lott and

Whitley 2001). They found no statistically significant reduction in accidents involving children or teenagers. Teenage gun suicide decreased, but not the overall teenage suicide rate. There were also large, statistically significant *increases* in violent crime and homicide, suggesting perhaps the guns were less available to scare or fend off home invaders.

Lawmakers considering enacting restrictions to lower the firearms accident rate should understand the rate is already very low, and more restrictive firearms laws may have negative unintended consequences.

Recommended Readings: John R. Lott, Jr. and John E. Whitley, "Safe Storage Gun Laws: Accidental Deaths, Suicides, and Crime," *Journal of Law and Economics* **44** (October 2001): 659–89; Centers for Disease Control and Prevention, "Deaths: Final Data for 2014," *National Vital Statistics Reports* **65** (4).

9. Large-scale illegal gun-running is a myth.

Research shows sellers of illegal guns generally are not professionals, specialists, or part of criminal organizations devoted to gun trafficking.

The worry about guns purchased from retail outlets in one state being trafficked illegally to states with more stringent limits on retail sales has commanded much public attention and has led to proposals for limits on retail purchases, such as "one gun a month" laws. Andrew Cuomo, then attorney general of New York, exemplified the simplistic and politically motivated nature of claims about gun-running when he stated in 2006, "A wave of illegal guns has been breaking over New York for years. Incredibly, 1 percent of gun dealers account for the majority of illegal guns. We need to crack down on their illegal behavior and put them out of business" (Cuomo 2006).

This policy is based on the assumption that a significant share of guns is diverted into criminal hands by corrupt or negligent federal firearms licensees (FFLs) and unlicensed, criminal gun traffickers. Some social scientists claim this is a major source of guns used in crime. But claims of a pipeline of illicit high-volume gun trafficking are not sustained by direct evidence of arrests and convictions of large-scale gun traffickers. Instead, they are grounded primarily on proxies that researchers claim are indicators of gun trafficking. An example is labeling as "new trafficked crime guns" all guns with a time-to-crime of less than one year (a time of less than a year between purchase of the gun and a crime committed with it), and whose criminal possessor was not the original retail purchaser, even though some or even all of these guns may simply have been stolen from their lawful buyers within a year of purchase (Kleck and Wang 2009).

One of the most comprehensive and recent studies of how criminals acquire guns used in crime was conducted by prize-winning researchers Gary Kleck and Shun-Yung Kevin Wang. Kleck and Wang (2009) show how criminals obtain guns from a wide variety of largely interchangeable non-trafficker sources, such as (1) directly or indirectly as a by-product of thefts, primarily residential burglaries, not committed specifically for the purpose of obtaining guns; (2) buying guns one at a time from friends and relatives who neither regularly sell guns nor act as straw purchasers; or (3) if they have no criminal convictions, lawfully purchasing guns from licensed dealers, to whom they are indistinguishable from buyers who will not go on to commit crimes.

Kleck and Wang demonstrate high-volume or persistent traffickers are rare and, in the aggregate, are of little significance in the arming of criminals. Sellers of illegal guns generally are not professionals, specialists, or part of criminal organizations devoted to gun trafficking, and they do not sell guns persistently or in large numbers: "Illicit gun sellers are more likely to be thieves who sell a few guns (typically fewer than a half-dozen per year) along with other saleable property they steal, drug dealers who occasionally sell guns as a sideline to their drug business, or friends and relatives of the criminal recipient who do not regularly sell guns" (Kleck and Wang 2009, p. 1241).

City-level data on recovered crime guns show the actual number of verifiably trafficked guns is extremely small and gun theft explains most criminal access to firearms. Kleck and Wang wrote, "Even in ... exceptional urban areas with stringent gun controls, where traffickers are supposed to flourish, criminals pay *under* the retail price for handguns. Consequently, the notion that criminals could make significant profits by selling guns purchased at retail prices from FFLs is not plausible even in cities with unusually low gun ownership rates and unusually strict gun laws, such as New York, Washington, D.C. or Chicago" (*Ibid.*, p. 1251).

William J. Vizzard (2000), a political scientist and veteran ATF agent, summarized the empirical work on gun trafficking as follows:

Nothing in the available studies supports an assumption of a well-structured illicit market in firearms. Transactions appear to be casual and idiosyncratic. My own experience, and that of most other agents I have interviewed, supports an assumption that the majority of sources is very dispersed and casual, and regular traffickers in firearms to criminals are few (p. 31).

Vizzard (2000) concludes "regular traffickers in firearms" are rare because of the huge reservoir of guns in the United States, which allows criminals to draw easily on many different sources for guns. In surveys of incarcerated criminals, 46 to 70 percent reported they owned and used stolen handguns.

Using data from 1987 through 1992, the National Crime Victim Survey estimated an average of 340,700 guns were stolen each year (NRC 2005). Another study estimated an average of 500,000 guns is stolen each year (Cook *et al.* 1995). More recent estimates put the number of stolen guns even higher, at 1.2 million per year (Kleck and Wang 2009).

The large number of gun thefts reflects the huge number of guns in the nation, but the data do not show large gun-running organizations are operating in the country. Illegal gun dealers and straw purchasers should be vigorously prosecuted. However, claims about massive illegal gun-running are unsupported and should not drive public policy decisions.

Recommended Readings: Gary Kleck and Shun-Yung Kevin Wang, "The Myth of Big-Time Gun Trafficking and the Overinterpretation of Gun Tracing Data," *UCLA Law Review* **56** (2009): 1233–94; William Vizzard, *Shots in the Dark: The Policy, Politics, and Symbolism of Gun Control* (Lanham, MD: Rowman & Littlefield, 2000).

10. International experience does not support gun control in the United States.

Proposals that the United States adopt gun control policies in place in other countries ignore the large number of privately held guns in the United States.

Some anti-gun activists assert the United States should adopt gun control policies similar to those of other developed nations, including gun bans and confiscation of certain types of firearms. Such proposals, however, wrongly assume those policies are effective in reducing crime or accidental deaths in other countries and fail to take into account the fact that the United States has far more privately held guns than other countries.

Unregistered Guns Overseas

Data from international experiments with gun prohibition and registration illustrate a powerful and nearly universal individual impulse to defy those controls. With data from 77 countries, the International Small Arms Survey (Berman *et al.* 2007) reports massive illegal parallel holdings, yielding two illegal guns for every legal one. This average is pulled down by rare cases like Japan, which the report notes has "unregistered gun holdings ... one-quarter to one-half as large as registered holdings."

In England and Wales, where there were 1.7 million legally registered firearms in 2005, the number of illegal, unregistered guns was estimated as high as four million (Berman *et al.* 2007, p. 50). The Chinese reported 680,000 legal guns in 2005, with estimates of nearly 40 million illegal guns (*Ibid.*, pp. 47, 50). The German police union estimates Germany has "about 45 million civilian guns: about 10 million registered firearms; 20 million that should be registered, but apparently are not; and 15 million firearms such as antiques ... and black-powder weapons ... that do not have to be registered" (*Ibid.*, p. 51).

The German experience tells us something about the staying power of defiance. Registration was introduced in Germany in 1972, "when the nation's civilian holdings reportedly totaled 17–20 million firearms" (Berman *et al.* 2007). Only 3.2 million of these guns were registered. "In the thirty-five years since then, roughly 8 million additional firearms were legally acquired, accounting for the rest of the registered guns thought to exist today. ... Similar totals come from scaling up regional estimates. ... [Bavaria] has some 1.5 million legal and 3 million unregistered firearms," Berman and others (2007) note.

The International Small Arms Survey reports similar numbers for other nations. With close to seven million registered guns, Canada is estimated to have about 10 million unregistered guns. Brazil reports nearly seven million registered guns and estimates 15 million unregistered. India reports fewer than six million registered guns against an estimated 45 million illegal ones. France has fewer than three million guns registered and estimates nearly 20 million unregistered. Mexico reports fewer than five million registered versus about 15 million unregistered guns (Berman *et al.* 2007)

Although there are exceptions such as Japan, where unregistered guns are a fraction of those legally registered, nearly every country surveyed produced estimates of unregistered guns that are a multiple of registered guns.

Failed U.S. Bans

In recent years, several U.S. states and municipalities have passed laws mandating the registration (and subsequent prohibition) of assault rifles. These laws failed miserably, primarily due to owner resistance. In Boston and Cleveland, for example, the rate of compliance with the ban on assault rifles is estimated at 1 percent. In California, nearly 90 percent of the approximately 300,000 assault weapons owners did not register their weapons.

Of the 100,000 to 300,000 assault rifles estimated to be in private hands in New Jersey, only 947 were registered, an additional 888 were rendered inoperable, and four were turned over to the authorities (Jacobs and Potter 1995, p. 106). More recently, extensive noncompliance with the New York SAFE Act (banning certain semiautomatic rifles) has been reported. As of June 2015, fewer than 45,000 assault-style weapons had been registered in accordance with the 2013 law, of an estimated nearly one million such weapons in the state (Edelman 2015).

Extrapolating 90 to 99 percent defiance of state or municipal assault weapons bans to the nation as a whole may be too aggressive, but applying the international data conservatively indicates adopting aggressive supply controls like those of other developed nations would result in three or more people defying those restrictions for each one who complies.

Australia Is Not the United States

The Obama administration praised Australia's gun control efforts and suggested America emulate them (Obama 2015). After a mentally unstable man used a stolen semiautomatic rifle to kill 34 people in Tasmania in 1996, the government of Australia banned all semiautomatic rifles and all repeating shotguns (the equivalent of many tens of millions of guns in the United States). Owners of the roughly 700,000 existing guns were required to turn them in for destruction, and the confiscation was facilitated by a preexisting registration program that made it easier for the government to identify gun owners. The Australian government called this a "buyback," but gun owners were not given any legal choice but to cooperate.

This sort of confiscation cannot work in the United States. Our country has many more guns in private hands than other nations do (roughly 325 million, orders of magnitude more than any other country), tightly held by citizens steeped in a gun-rights culture with a constitutional guarantee of a right to bear arms. If a total ban were imposed, despite constitutional protections, and Americans defied it at just the average rate that has occurred internationally, 100 million guns or more would flood into the black market. That danger and the other discernible consequences of an American gun ban would leave us far worse off than we are now.

The American attachment to the gun is exceptional. We own close to half the world's private firearms and buy half the world's output of new civilian guns each year. This demand and cultural attachment present a unique obstacle to gun-control legislation in the United States. Whatever courts say about the Second Amendment, a significant majority of Americans believe they have a right to own a gun.

U.S. adoption of gun control policies similar to those of Australia would result in a seismic shift of guns into the gray and black markets. Proponents of such policies have the burden of showing why that would not make things worse.

Recommended Readings: David B. Kopel, *The Samurai, the Mountie and the Cowboy* (Amherst, NY: Prometheus Books, 1992); Nicholas James Johnson, "Imagining Gun Control in America: Understanding the Remainder Problem," *Wake Forest Law Review* **43** (2009): 837–91.

References

ABA (American Bar Association). 2015. *National Task Force on Stand Your Ground Laws, Final Report and Recommendations.*

Amselle, Jorge. 2014. "Why We Need 'Stand Your Ground' Laws." *The Daily Caller* (website). March 11.

ATF (U.S. Bureau of Alcohol, Tobacco, Firearms, and Explosives). 2013. *Annual Firearms Manufacturing and Export Report.*

Berke, Richard L. 1989. "Capital Offers a Ripe Market to Drug Dealers." *The New York Times* (website). March 28.

Berman, Eric G., Keith Krause, Emile LeBrun, and Glenn McDonald (editors). 2007. *Small Arms Survey 2007: Guns and the City.* Cambridge, United Kingdom: Cambridge University Press.

BJS (Bureau of Justice Statistics). 2016. "The National Crime Victimization Survey (NCVS)." Unnumbered table titled "Average Annual 2004–2008." Washington, DC: Bureau of Justice Statistics. Accessed July 29, 2017.

Bordua, David J. 1983. "Adversary Polling and the Construction of Social Meaning: Implications in Gun Control Elections in Massachusetts and California." *Law and Policy* **5** (3): 345–66.

Braga, Anthony, Jack McDevett, and Glenn L. Pierce. 2006. "Understanding and Preventing Gang Violence: Problem Analysis and Response Development in Lowell, Massachusetts." *Police Quarterly* **9** (1): 20–46.

Branca, Andrew F. 2013. *The Law of Self Defense: The Indispensable Guide for the Armed Citizen*. Maynard, MA: Law of Self Defense LLC.

_____. 2016. "What to Make of the New Study of Florida's 'Stand Your Ground' Law." *National Review* (website). November 16.

Breyer, Stephen. 1993. *Breaking the Vicious Circle: Toward Effective Risk Regulation*. Cambridge, MA: Harvard University Press.

Burnett, H. Sterling. 2001. "Suing Gun Manufacturers: Hazardous to Our Health." *Texas Review of Law & Politics* **5** (2): 433.

Catalano, Shannan. 2010. *Victimization during Household Burglary*. Washington, DC: Bureau of Justice Statistics. September.

CDC (Centers for Disease Control and Prevention). 2014. "Compressed Mortality File" (website).

_____. 2016. "Deaths: Final Data for 2014." *National Vital Statistics Reports* **65** (4).

Conklin, John E. 1972. *Robbery and the Criminal Justice System*. Philadelphia, PA: J.B. Lippincott.

Cook, Philip J., and Jens Ludwig. 1996. *Guns in America: Results of a Comprehensive National Survey of Firearms Ownership and Use*. Washington, DC: Police Foundation.

Cook, Philip J., Jens Ludwig, and Anthony A. Braga. 2005. "Criminal Records of Homicide Offenders." *Journal of the American Medical Association* **294** (5): 598–601.

Cook, Philip J., Stephanie Molliconi, and Thomas B. Cole. 1995. "Regulating Gun Markets." *Journal of Criminal Law and Criminology* **86** (1): 59–92.

Cuomo, Andrew. 2006. "Andrew Cuomo on the Role of the Attorney General." *New York Law Journal* (website). November 1.

DeSimone, J. *et al.* 2013. "Child Access Prevention Laws and Nonfatal Gun Injuries." *Southern Economic Journal* **80** (1): 5–25.

East, Edward Hyde. 1803. *A Treatise of the Pleas of the Crown*. London, England: A. Strahan.

Edelman, Adam. 2015. "Low Assault-Weapon Registration Stats Suggest Low Compliance with Gov. Cuomo's Landmark SAFE Act Gun Control Law." *New York Daily News* (website). June 23.

Elliott, Delbert S. 1998. "Life-Threatening Violence Is *Primarily* a Crime Problem: A Focus on Prevention." *University of Colorado Law Review* **69** (Fall): 1081.

FBI (Federal Bureau of Investigation). 2006–2016. *Uniform Crime Reports* (website).

_____ 2017. "2016 Crime in the United States, Preliminary Semiannual Uniform Crime Report" (website).

Foster, Sir Michael. 1792. *A Report of Some Proceedings on the Commission for the Trial of the Rebels in the Year 1746, in the County of Surry, and of other Crown Cases: To Which are Added Discourses upon a Few Branches of the Crown Law*. London, England: E. and R. Brooke.

Gius, M. 2015. "The Impact of Minimum Age and Child Access Prevention Laws on Firearm-related Youth Suicides and Unintentional Deaths." *The Social Science Journal* **52** (2):168–75.

Halbrook, Stephen P. 2009. *Firearms Law Deskbook*. Eagan, MN: Thomson Reuters.

_____. 2012. *The Founders' Second Amendment: Origins of the Right to Bear Arms.* Oakland, CA: Independent Institute.

_____. 2016. "Reality Check: The 'Assault Weapon' Fantasy & Second Amendment Jurisprudence." *Georgetown Journal of Law & Public Policy* **14** (1): 47–76.

Heath, J. Norman. 2001. "Exposing the Second Amendment: Federal Preemption of State Militia Legislation." *University of Detroit Mercy Law Review* **79**: 39–73.

Hemenway, David, and Erica Richardson. 1997. "Characteristics of Automatic or Semiautomatic Firearm Ownership in the United States." *American Journal of Public Health* **87** (2): 286–88.

Humphreys, D.K., A. Gasparrini, and D.J. Wiebe. 2017. "Evaluating the Impact of Florida's "Stand Your Ground" Self-defense Law on Homicide and Suicide by Firearm, An Interrupted Time Series Study." *Journal of the American Medical Association Internal Medicine* **177** (1): 44–50. doi:10.1001/jamainternmed.2016.6811.

Ikeda, Robert M., Linda L. Dahlberg, Jeffrey J. Sachs, James A. Mercy, and Kenneth E. Powell. 1997. "Estimating Intruder-Related Firearms Retrievals in U.S. Households, 1994." *Violence and Victims* **12** (4): 363–72.

Jacobs, James B., and Kimberly A. Potter. 1995. "Keeping Guns Out of the Wrong Hands: The Brady Law and the Limits of Regulation." *Journal of Law and Criminology* **86** (1): 93–120.

Johnson, Nicholas James. 2005. "A Second Amendment Moment: The Constitutional Politics of Gun Control." *Brooklyn Law Review* **71** (2): 715–96.

———. 2009. "Imagining Gun Control in America: Understanding the Remainder Problem." *Wake Forest Law Review* **43**: 837–91.

Kates, Don B., and Gary Mauser. 2007. "Would Banning Firearms Reduce Murder and Suicide? A Review of International and Some Domestic Evidence." *Harvard Journal of Law and Public Policy* **30** (2): 649–94.

Kennedy, David, and Anthony Braga. 1998. "Homicide in Minneapolis: Research for Problem Solving." *Homicide Studies* **2** (3): 263–90.

Kleck, Gary. 1997. *Targeting Guns: Firearms and Their Control.* Hawthorne, NY: Aldine de Gruyter.

Kleck, Gary, Tomislav Victor Kovandzic, and Jon Bellows. 2016. "Does Gun Control Reduce Violent Crime?" June 21.

Kleck, Gary, and Miriam DeLone. 1993. "Victim Resistance and Offender Weapon Effects in Robbery." *Journal of Quantitative Criminology* **9** (1): 73–7.

Kleck, Gary, and Marc Gertz. 1995. "Armed Resistance to Crime: The Prevalence and Nature of Self-Defense with a Gun." *Journal of Criminal Law and Criminology* **86** (1): 150–87.

Kleck, Gary, and Jongyeon Tark. 2005. "Resisting Crime: The Effects of Victim Action on the Outcomes of Crimes." *Criminology* **42** (4): 861–909.

Kleck, Gary, and Shun-Yung Kevin Wang. 2009. "The Myth of Big-Time Gun Trafficking and the Overinterpretation of Gun Tracing Data." *UCLA Law Review* **56** (5): 1233–94.

Kobayashi, Bruce H., and Joseph E. Olson. 1997. "In Re 101 California Street: A Legal and Economic Analysis of Strict Liability for the Manufacture and Sale of 'Assault Weapons.'" *Stanford Law and Policy Review* **8** (1): 41–52.

Kopel, David B. 1992. *The Samurai, the Mountie and the Cowboy*. Amherst, NY: Prometheus Books.

_____. 2001. "Lawyers, Guns, and Burglars." *Arizona Law Review* **43** (Summer): 345–67.

_____. 2003. "Comment on 'The Effects of Gun Prevalence on Burglary: Deterrence vs Inducement' by Philip J. Cook & Jens Ludwig." In Jens Ludwig and Philip J. Cook (editors). *Evaluating Gun Policy: Effects on Crime and Violence*. Washington, DC: Brookings Institution Press.

_____. 2015. "The Costs and Consequences of Gun Control." *Policy Analysis* No. 784. Cato Institute. December 1.

Lee, J.L., *et al*. 2013. "Value-based Insurance Design: Quality Improvement But No Cost Savings." *Health Affairs* **32** (7): 1251–7.

Levitt, Steven B., and Stephen J. Dubner. 2006. *Freakonomics*. New York, NY: William Morrow.

Lott Jr., J.R. 1999. "More Guns, Less Crime: A response to Ayres and Donohue." *Working Paper* No. 247. Program for Studies in Law, Economics and Public Policy, Yale Law School.

_____. 2010. *More Guns, Less Crime: Understanding Crime and Gun Control Laws*. 3rd ed. Chicago, IL: University of Chicago Press.

_____. 2013a. "The Truth about Assault Weapons Bans and Background Checks." *Fox News* (website). February 28.

_____. 2013b. "Perspective: In Defense of Stand Your Ground Laws." *Chicago Tribune* (website). October 28.

_____. 2016a. *The War on Guns: Arming Yourself Against Gun Control Lies*. Washington, DC: Regnery Publishing.

_____. 2016b. "Gun Ownership Is Up in America. So Why Isn't the Media Telling You About It?" *Fox News* (website). September 8.

Lott Jr., John R., and D.B. Mustard. 1997. "Crime, Deterrence, and Right-to-carry Concealed Handguns." *Journal of Legal Studies* **26** (1):1–68.

Lott Jr., John R., and John E. Whitley. 2001. "Safe Storage Gun Laws: Accidental Deaths, Suicides, and Crime." *Journal of Law and Economics* **44** (October): 659–89.

Lott Jr., John R., John E. Whitley, and Rebekah C. Riley. 2015. "Concealed Carry Permit Holders Across the United States." July 13.

Madison, James. (1789) 1979. "From James Madison to Edmund Randolph, 15 June 1789." In Charles F. Hobson and Robert A. Rutland (editors). *The Papers of James Madison*. Charlottesville, VA: University of Virginia Press.

McGinty, Jo Craven. 2006. "New York Killers, and Those Killed, by the Numbers." *The New York Times* (website). April 28.

NICS (National Instant Criminal Background Check System). 2017. "NICS Firearm Checks: Month/Year." Federal Bureau of Investigation.

NRA (National Rifle Association). 2014. "No Surprise Here: ABA Opposes Self-Defense and Stand Your Ground Laws (website)." August 15.

NRC (National Research Council). 2005. *Firearms and Violence: A Critical Review.* Committee to Improve Research Information and Data on Firearms. Washington, DC: The National Academies Press.

NSC (National Safety Council). 2007. *Injury Facts, 2007 Edition.* Itasca, IL: National Safety Council.

———. 2011. *Injury Facts, 2011 Edition.* Itasca, IL: National Safety Council.

Obama, Barack. 2015. "Statement by the President on the Shootings at Umpqua Community College, Roseburg, Oregon." October 21.

Pew Research Center. 2016. "Opinions on Gun Policy and the 2016 Campaign." August 26..

Rengert, George F., and John Wasilchick. 2000. *Suburban Burglary: A Tale of Two Suburbs.* Springfield, IL: Charles C. Thomas Pub.

Santaella-Tenorio, J., *et al.* 2016. "What Do We Know about the Association Between Firearm Legislation and Firearm-related Injuries?" *Epidemiologic Reviews* **38** (1):140–57.

Sentementes, Gus G. 2007. "Patterns Persist in City Killings: Victims, Suspects Usually Black Men with Long Criminal Histories." *Baltimore Sun.* January 1.

Southwick, Lawrence. 2000. "Self-Defense with Guns: The Consequences." *Journal of Criminal Justice* **28** (5): 351–70.

Violence Policy Center. 1988. *Assault Weapons and Accessories in America* (website). Washington, DC: Violence Policy Center.

Vizzard, William. 2000. *Shots in the Dark: The Policy, Politics, and Symbolism of Gun Control.* Lanham, MD: Rowman & Littlefield.

Volokh, Eugene. 2006. "State Constitutional Rights to Keep and Bear Arms." *Texas Review of Law and Politics* **11** (1): 192–217.

Waller, Julian A. and Elbert B. Whorton. 1973. "Unintentional Shootings, Highway Crashes, and Acts of Violence—A Behavior Paradigm." *Accident Analysis & Prevention* **5** (4): 351–6.

Wells, William. 2002. "The Nature and Circumstances of Defensive Gun Use: A Content Analysis of Interpersonal Conflict Situations Involving Criminal Offenders." *Justice Quarterly* **19** (1): 127–57.

What Works for Health. 2016. "Child Firearm Access Prevention Laws." University of Wisconsin Population Health Institute and School of Medicine and Public Health.

Wilson, James Q. 1994. "Just Take Away Their Guns." *New York Times Magazine.* March 20.

———. 2005. "Appendix A, Dissent." In *Firearms and Violence: A Critical Review.* National Research Council, Committee to Improve Research Information and Data on Firearms. Washington, DC: The National Academies Press.

Wolfgang, Marvin E. 1995. "A Tribute to a View I Have Opposed." *Journal of Criminal Law and Criminology* **86** (1): 188–92.

Wright, Richard T. and Scott H. Decker. 1994. *Burglars on the Job: Streetlife and Residential Break-Ins.* Boston, MA: Northeastern University Press.

Wright, James D. and Peter H. Rossi. 1986. *Armed and Considered Dangerous: A Survey of Felons and Their Firearms.* New York, NY: Aldine de Gruyter.

Additional Resources

Additional information about firearms policy is available from The Heartland Institute:

- PolicyBot, The Heartland Institute's free online clearinghouse for the work of other free-market think tanks, contains hundreds of documents on firearms policy. It is on Heartland's website at https://www.heartland.org/policybot/.

- The Heartland Institute's multimedia offerings—high-quality video and daily podcasts—address a wide range of topics, including Second Amendment issues and firearms policy. You can search by topic at https://www.heartland.org/multimedia/.

Directory

The following legal scholars and organizations offer valuable information about firearms policy.

Bureau of Alcohol, Tobacco, Firearms, and Explosives (ATF), https://www.atf.gov/

Firearms and Liberty, https://www.firearmsandliberty.com/

Guncite, http://www.guncite.com/

Gun Owners of America, https://www.gunowners.org/

Heartland Institute, https://www.heartland.org/

Nicholas James Johnson, professor of law, Fordham University School of Law, https://www.fordham.edu/info/23149/nicholas_johnson

Gary Kleck, David J. Bordua professor emeritus, Florida State University, http://criminology.fsu.edu/faculty-and-staff/college-faculty/gary-kleck/

David Kopel, research director, Independence Institute, http://www.davekopel.org/

Library of Congress: United States: Gun Ownership and the Supreme Court, https://www.loc.gov/law/help/second-amendment.php

Library of Law and Liberty, http://www.libertylawsite.org/

National Rifle Association, https://home.nra.org/

Uniform Crime Reporting (FBI), https://ucr.fbi.gov/

Chapter 7
Telecommunications

Steven Titch, Hance Haney, and George Gilder

---

10 Principles of Telecommunications Policy

1. Don't mandate net neutrality.
2. Eliminate rules left over from the monopoly era.
3. Avoid municipal broadband projects.
4. Reform carrier of last resort and build-out obligations.
5. Reform regulation of inter-carrier access charges and interconnection fees.
6. Repeal discriminatory taxes and fees on telecom services.
7. Prohibit the collection of sales taxes on online purchases that cross state lines.
8. Strengthen privacy and Fourth Amendment protections.
9. Prohibit government regulation of content.
10. Don't thwart expansion of Internet applications and e-commerce.

Introduction

Three decades of U.S. telecommunications policy was reversed on February 26, 2015, when the Federal Communications Commission (FCC), by a 3–2 vote, issued its Open Internet Order reclassifying broadband telecommunications as a public utility under Title II of the Communications Act of 1934. As this is written in 2017, a new FCC chairman says he will work to reverse that decision.

At the time of reclassification, then-FCC Chairman Thomas Wheeler said the agency would "forbear"—that is, put off for the time being—exercising the full scope of regulatory powers it now had. But by the time he stepped down in January 2017, Wheeler had opened Title II-based inquiries into the operation of set-top cable TV boxes and internet service provider (ISP) pricing plans.

The new FCC chairman, Ajit Pai, has said "These utility-style regulations ... were and are like the proverbial sledgehammer being wielded against the flea—except that here, there was no flea" (Goodman 2017). Pai is stepping back from the aggressive regulation sought by his predecessor. His approach marks a return to policies toward telecommunications and the internet that supported deregulation of voice services, light regulation of ISPs, and almost no regulation of internet content and applications.

Issues such as network neutrality, excessive telecom taxes, and municipal broadband have been matters of controversy for more than a decade. In recent years, widespread adoption of broadband and the general disruption caused by the digital economy have raised new policy issues. Governments at all levels are now debating privacy, internet hate speech, and "sharing economy" services such as Uber and Airbnb.

This chapter sets out 10 important principles for broadband and telecommunications policymaking today; explains why they are important; identifies the dangers of ignoring them; and documents ways federal, state, and local agencies have constructively applied them.

1. Don't mandate net neutrality.

> Reclassifying internet service providers (ISPs) as common carriers and imposing "network neutrality" mandates would hurt consumers.

"Network neutrality" (often referred to as "net neutrality") is the label given to four common-sense rules or guidelines followed by internet service providers (ISPs) since at least 2005. Proposals to give FCC authority to *mandate* that ISPs follow these rules plus a fifth rule, the so-called "nondiscrimination rule," are based on an anti-market ideology and ought to be opposed by patriots and policymakers (Lakely 2009). A much better and simpler policy guideline is for the government to "keep its hands off the internet."

FCC Tries to Regulate the Internet

The original four principles of network neutrality, as set forth by FCC in 2005, established that consumers are entitled to access the lawful internet content of their choice; run their preferred applications and services, subject to the needs of law enforcement; connect their choice of legal devices that do not harm the network; and see competition among network, content, application, and service providers. Violations were few. Since 2005, there have been only five neutrality violations, all by small service providers and all fairly contained. This argues for a reactive approach—penalizing violations when they occur—as opposed to acting preemptively against the entire industry.

Many net neutrality advocates want much more than the largely voluntary standards of 2005. Their proposals amount to regulating the internet like a utility, if not immediately then eventually, even though such regulation is sure to slow innovation and investment, empower government bureaucrats, and limit choices for consumers.

A principal reason FCC reclassified ISPs as Title II common carriers was to pursue the net neutrality agenda. Reclassification allows FCC to regulate ISPs the same way it regulates the dwindling number of U.S. landline telephone monopolies. The reclassification order specifically applied to ISPs Sections 201, 202, and 210 of the Telecommunications Act of 1996, all pertaining to pricing. In other areas, such as content, service bundling, and customer service, Wheeler said the commission would not regulate the internet, although reclassification gave it the authority to do so.

Even longtime network neutrality advocates such as the Electronic Frontier Foundation expressed concern reclassification went too far (McSherry 2015). As FCC was getting ready to vote on reclassification, an alliance of small ISPs and some 30 municipal broadband operators petitioned to be exempt from the new rules. The night before FCC voted, Google—a longtime net neutrality supporter now in the process of expanding its own facilities-based broadband operation, Google Fiber—lobbied the commission to make changes in the final order.

Barring Bargains for Customers

Despite his pledge of forbearance, in late 2016 Wheeler's FCC notified AT&T that the company's DirecTV Now pricing plan violated net neutrality because it does not apply streamed DirecTV programming against customers' data caps—that is to say, it offered customers real bargains.

The pricing strategy, known as zero-rating, has become popular, especially among wireless carriers that, with limited spectrum, face more network management challenges in delivering bandwidth-intensive services. For example, zero rating is touted in a T-Mobile ad for its "Binge On" pricing plan, in which a young driver must choose between streaming Ariana Grande and using her navigation app. With Binge On, the driver gets her music *and* her app without paying more. Wheeler openly questioned whether such pricing plans were net neutrality violations, despite their making broadband internet access more affordable. Giving customers what they wanted was not "neutral," and FCC vowed to stop it.

Pai seems poised to drop the inquiries launched by Wheeler. Even if he does not, FCC does not have the final word. Reclassification can be viewed as rewriting the law, the exclusive purview of Congress under the U.S. Constitution. Congress may yet amend the Communications Act to prohibit network neutrality regulation. Until it does so, the principled position is to urge FCC to concentrate on network neutrality principles and forebear regulation in other areas.

The Nondiscrimination Rule

In the Open Internet Order, FCC added a fifth rule to the original four largely voluntary net neutrality principles: the "nondiscrimination" rule. It prohibits ISPs from prioritizing or optimizing any application, voice, or data as they cross the networks, although it allows for "just and reasonable" network management.

The nondiscrimination rule is increasingly controversial as video content providers such as Netflix, YouTube, and Hulu consume ever-greater amounts of bandwidth. By late 2015, for example, Netflix and YouTube videos accounted for almost 55 percent of North American ISP traffic on any given evening. All together, streaming services account for more than 70 percent of peak traffic (Protalinski 2015).

ISPs such as Comcast, AT&T, and Verizon want to charge these video content providers for the network management and optimization required to deliver bandwidth-, time-, and error-sensitive programming. By contrast, content providers say ISPs should be obligated to provide the necessary "fast lanes" required for quality service and spread those costs over their entire user base. Content providers carried the day with FCC, and the nondiscrimination rule was adopted.

Mandating nondiscrimination raises four major problems. First, content providers already pay for specialized content delivery networks to prioritize and groom content until it reaches the last-mile provider. The anti-discrimination argument that all data be treated the same starts crumbling as soon as the latest episode of *Orange Is the New Black* leaves the server.

Second, content providers have huge investments in their own server infrastructure. Speaking in 2013, Microsoft's Steve Ballmer said his company had more than one million internet servers. He estimated Google had at least 900,000 servers as of 2009 and had likely eclipsed Microsoft at the time of his speech (Anthony 2013). With this many servers, content providers can place their services and applications in multiple locations, cutting time and latency. This is another way companies with major capital resources can improve quality of service. But this also means the internet is not neutral, and forcing one group of companies in the internet ecosystem to operate as if it were will be counterproductive.

Third, mandating nondiscrimination reduces investment. By regulating the prices ISPs can charge for network transmission or disallowing these fees altogether, FCC will prevent ISPs from maximizing returns on their broadband investment. Bans on prioritization, whether paid or not, essentially are a "taking" of property. It is similar to FCC's Unbundled Network Elements Platform (UNE-P) regulation in the 1990s and early 2000s, which required telephone companies to share network capacity with competitors at rates below capital cost. The courts rejected UNE-P regulations twice before FCC abandoned the policy. By then, according to one research report, UNE-P rules had reduced telecom investment by $5.4 billion to $12.7 billion a year (Eisenach and Lenard 2003). Network neutrality regulation will have the same suppressive effect.

Fourth, network neutrality regulation will make broadband more expensive. Under Title II, internet access is now a telecommunications service subject to all the taxes and fees federal, state, and local governments levy on phone service: excise taxes, universal service fees, regulatory cost recovery fees, and more. The Progressive Policy Institute estimates the average annual increase in state and local fees levied on U.S. wired and wireless broadband subscribers will be $67 and $72, respectively. The annual increase in federal fees per household will be roughly $17. In total, Title II reclassification may cost broadband consumers up to $11 billion (Litan and Singer 2014). In order to keep broadband affordable, state and local governments should resist the urge to burden consumers with even more telecom taxes and fees.

Opposing Net Regulation

FCC's decision to regulate the internet as a utility was a mistake and should be walked back by the agency or overruled by Congress. We should return to the bipartisan telecom policy that encouraged deregulation of voice services and last-mile internet connections and discouraged regulation of internet content, applications, and information services. Net neutrality, as it is being implemented via reclassification, places an unprecedented layer of regulation on ISPs that will hurt, not benefit, consumers.

Recommended Readings: Bob Zelnick and Eva Zelnick, *The Illusion of Net Neutrality: Political Alarmism, Regulatory Creep and the Real Threat to Internet Freedom* (Stanford, CA: Hoover Institution Press, 2013); Thomas W. Hazlett, *The Fallacy of Net Neutrality* (New York, NY: Encounter Books, 2011).

2. Eliminate rules left over from the monopoly era.

Cities and towns can reduce barriers to investment and signal they want the private sector to succeed by eliminating legacy utility regulations and fees.

Governments at all levels can encourage greater investment in telecom services by revising or eliminating regulations and fees that linger from the monopoly era. Effective reforms cut the time and cost involved in siting and building new facilities. Four areas where such reforms can occur are franchise fees, pole attachment rules, "dig once" rules, and tower-siting reviews.

Franchise Fees

Taxes and franchise fees should reflect the cost imposed on the common community infrastructure and not discriminate among market participants. Franchise fees have long been abused by local governments to extract funds from cable television providers. In exchange for an exclusive franchise, the cable company agrees to pay a portion of its revenues to the city, town, or village.

These arrangements could last only as long as cable companies held a monopoly. Satellite television providers, which did not pay franchise fees, turned these added costs into a competitive issue for cable providers. Franchise fees came under further pressure as telephone companies began to offer multichannel TV services. As municipalities were burdening telephone companies with a separate set of surcharges and fees, disparities were soon apparent in the fee structures city governments were charging to companies offering identical services.

Between 2005 and 2008, 19 states legislated franchise reform, essentially developing uniform franchise fee structures for cable and telephone companies to be used statewide. States that adopted reforms experienced higher investment, decreasing prices, and increasing internet use rates (Bagchi and Sivadasan 2015). An earlier study by Diane Katz showed a surge of deployment in California, Indiana, and Texas, which were among the first states to enact franchise reform (Katz 2006).

Pole Attachment Rules

Pole attachment rules are another holdover from the monopoly era. Traditionally, power companies built and maintained poles and leased space to telephone and cable companies. In some cases, pole attachment rates for telephone companies were four to five times higher than for cable companies. Critics have warned the disparity "could undermine the public's access to advanced services and broadband by distorting infrastructure investment decisions" (Huther and Magee 2013).

Several states have used different strategies to lower the cost and speed up the process of giving new internet providers access to poles. (St. John 2013; Hyman and Starr 2017). One strategy is to allow a process called "one-touch, make-ready," which allows new broadband competitors to hire utility-approved contractors to connect their lines to poles instead of relying on the staffs of legacy companies. FCC is planning to remove its own outdated regulations while also pushing cities and states to adopt one-touch, make-ready policies and take other steps to "make it easier, faster, and less costly" for attachers to access and use utility poles for the deployment of new broadband facilities and networks (FCC 2017). If states and cities continue to drag their feet, a federal solution might be necessary.

"Dig Once" Programs

Cities can better manage construction projects to allow conduit and cable to be placed inexpensively by using "dig once" programs that allow all service providers access to an open trench. Doing so lowers costs for service providers and provides incentives for new investment.

Independent studies have shown coordination of highway construction and broadband buildout can create immense savings and efficiencies (Lennett and Meinrath 2009). Construction costs for highways are generally at least $3 million per lane per mile. Installing conduit pipe for fiber-optic cable at the same time adds only $10,000 to $30,000 per mile—as little as 1 percent on average—to the overall cost.

Some cities take a public-private partnership approach, using public works projects as an opportunity to lay fiber with an eye toward leasing it to commercial service providers. In Arlington, Virginia, the Connect Arlington project included additional fiber-optic capacity when the city was laying fiber for traffic signals. When the City of Durango, Colorado adds fiber and conduit to connect government facilities during sidewalk replacement projects, waterline replacements, and upgrades to electric utility plants, it makes available additional capacity for leasing out to private providers (Hovis and Afflerbach 2014).

Timely Tower-Siting Reviews

With wireless broadband now popular with consumers, additional towers and antennas are often necessary to ensure optimal coverage and service. Unfortunately, towers and antennas can be intrusive. When communities learn of plans to place a tower in a neighborhood, there is often organized, vocal opposition.

Residents deserve to be heard, and it's good business for service providers to take aesthetic issues into account when planning tower placement. But to be viable competitors, wireless companies must be able to deliver high-quality, reliable voice and high-speed data connections that require more investment in towers and antennas.

The primary obstacle to wireless tower siting is not the permitting or public hearing process itself but, rather, the power that can be wielded by a small group of intransigent opponents or a recalcitrant neighborhood governing board to delay indefinitely any decision or resolution. One tactic opponents use is to file petition after petition for site review, environmental impact studies, and extended comment or review periods. Town boards and homeowners' associations have been known to sit on applications for months, only to return them as "incomplete" just prior to a hearing. In such cases, the hearing is likely to be postponed while the service provider is forced to resubmit the application and start the process over again.

Most reform efforts are aimed at eliminating these tactical bureaucratic delays. Georgia and Missouri provide models for states looking to balance community concerns with timely action. Georgia House Bill 176, enacted in July 2014, holds local governments to a 150-day deadline to approve or deny an application. The measure also requires local governments to return incomplete applications within 30 days and end the practice of imposing excessive permit-processing fees (Hill 2014). It also hastens approval of site modifications and does not require a rehearing if a proposed change would make no difference to the appearance, height, or design of a facility.

Missouri's bill, the Uniform Wireless Communications Infrastructure Deployment Act, which passed in July 2013, places even more limits on local government, requiring authorities to make decisions within 120 days for new wireless applications, 90 days for a "substantial" modification, and 45 days for a colocation application. The act also prohibits authorities from issuing moratoria of more than six months on the construction or approval of wireless facilities unless good cause is shown.

Recommended Readings: David C. St. John, "State and Local Government Role in Facilitating Access to Poles, Ducts, and Conduits in Public Rights-of-Way," Fiber to the Home Council, 2013; Steven Titch, "Alternatives to Government Broadband," *Policy Study* No. 27, R Street Institute, 2014.

3. Avoid municipal broadband projects.

Municipal broadband projects across the country are not providing high-quality service with cheaper rates, but they are generally losing money and face looming debt.

As part of its second-term agenda, the Obama administration promoted municipal-owned and -operated networks for broadband expansion and competition. For example, on February 26, 2015, the same day FCC approved Title II reclassification, the commission voted to preempt state laws preventing municipalities from funding, building, and operating competitive broadband networks.

Advocates of municipal broadband claim internet service providers are entrenched duopolies that overcharge, invest only in wealthy neighborhoods, and have dragged their feet on investing in new fiber-to-the-home broadband networks. But this wasn't true a decade ago, when the municipal broadband movement was especially popular (see Bast 2004), and it definitely isn't true today, when competition among ISPs using a variety of technologies is far greater. Government-financed, owned, and operated broadband networks are unnecessary, historically have produced low-quality services, and expose taxpayers to substantial financial risks.

Why Municipal Broadband Systems Fail

Municipal systems in operation, such as in Lafayette, Louisiana and Chattanooga, Tennessee, have not achieved their goals of providing ubiquitous fiber-to-the-home, higher-quality service with cheaper rates than incumbents. And although they may boast positive cash flow, they are still losing money, facing looming debt, and falling short of their revenue plans.

A recent study of 10 large municipal broadband projects by researchers with the New York Law School (Davidson and Santorelli 2014) found the following:

- Overly optimistic assumptions about costs and consumer demand ("take-rates") often doom networks before they are launched.

- Moderately successful municipal networks generally were developed under unique circumstances that would be difficult to replicate.

- Municipal networks, especially those deployed by municipal utilities, raise fundamental concerns regarding sustainability, fair competition, and consumer welfare.

- The substantial costs of building, maintaining, and operating municipal networks outweigh any real benefits.

- Their economic impact, especially in job creation, can be difficult to measure. Instead, the report notes, investments in municipal networks typically divert scarce public resources from more pressing local infrastructure priorities.

- Governments are not well-equipped to compete in dynamic markets. In general, municipal governments do not have a good record of keeping pace with technological advances.

An earlier report by The Heartland Institute (Bast 2004) identified four reasons why municipal broadband schemes usually fail:

- The cost of construction exceeds initial projections and burdens the utility with high debt retirement costs.

- Legal restrictions prevent cities from subsidizing their municipal broadband networks directly with tax dollars or by raising rates for other utilities.

■ Optimistic projections of the number of customers delivered by contract-seeking consultants have misled many city officials.

■ The failure to find content consumers will pay for limits the appeal of municipal networks.

If FCC's reclassification of internet service as a Title II utility holds up, municipal broadband companies, like their private-sector counterparts, may come under rate regulation or be required to collect FCC-mandated funds, such as a universal service fee. This is why some 43 municipal broadband operations, including the Cedar Falls operation touted by Obama, cosigned an American Cable Association letter to FCC asking to be exempted from the Title II rulemaking.

Meanwhile in the marketplace, the rise of streaming video networks—an area first staked out by Netflix and Hulu and since joined by Showtime, CBS, Amazon, ESPN, and others—that bypass cable TV systems stand to make cable "cord-cutting" even more attractive than it is. Nearly 25 million U.S. households—20.4 percent of all U.S. households—were cable-free at the end of 2015. That figure was projected to rise to 26.7 million households, or 21.9 percent of all U.S. households, by the end of 2016 (Pressman 2016).

Nearly one-fifth of U.S. residents who have Netflix or Hulu Plus accounts don't subscribe to a cable or satellite TV service, according to research from Experian Marketing Services (Experian 2014). These consumers may be using internet service only, or fourth-generation wireless service. To municipal broadband operations that banked on bundled cable TV subscriptions for the bulk of their revenues, these numbers present a bleak outlook.

UTOPIA, a fiber-based broadband network financed by a group of 11 Utah cities, provides a grim preview. After failing to reach the threshold of customers needed to pay the debt on construction, the project was turned over to Australia-based Macquarie Capital. As part of the agreement for Macquarie funding completion of the network, the UTOPIA cities proposed assessing all residents a monthly $20 utility surcharge for the next 30 years (Dunn 2014). Five of the UTOPIA cities rejected the plan, but six approved it. In those towns, residents will still be paying for 2010-era technology in the 2040s.

Something similar is playing out in Cedar Falls, Iowa, home of another celebrated municipal broadband system. The economic benefits of the system have been vastly oversold (see Bast 2005). In January 2015, while touting the 10 GBs fiber-to-the-home service provided by the city, Obama neglected to mention the service costs $275 a month

(Bauters 2013). That is hardly the economical alternative municipal broadband promised.

Recommended Readings: Charles M. Davidson and Michael J. Santorelli, *Understanding the Debate over Government-Owned Broadband Networks: Context, Lessons Learned, and a Way Forward for Policy Makers* (New York, NY: Advanced Communication Law & Policy Institute at New York Law School, 2014); Steven Titch, "Lessons in Municipal Broadband from Lafayette, Louisiana," *Policy Study* No. 424, Reason Foundation, 2013.

4. Reform carrier of last resort and buildout obligations.

Incumbent telephone companies and cable companies should not be burdened by regulatory obligations that make it difficult for them to innovate.

A now-obsolete way to provide high-quality, affordable telecommunication services to all consumers in a monopoly environment was to award an exclusive franchise to one service provider and require it to extend service to all consumers at similar prices. The monopoly made it easy for the service provider to subsidize high-cost customers through rate averaging.

The 1996 Telecommunications Act prohibited exclusive franchises, but the obligation remains on incumbent telephone companies to be carriers of last resort (COLR), providing service throughout the existing service territory at similar rates with their losses covered by distributions from federal and state universal service funds. Similarly, even though cable markets are now competitive in all places, many cities still impose buildout requirements on new entrants, requiring them to submit plans to serve the entire community by some deadline.

Forced Subsidies

The problem with both COLR and buildout requirements is that without a monopoly, customers who can be served at low cost no longer can be forced to subsidize customers whose connections require a much higher investment by the service provider. Low-cost customers can sign up with a competing service provider that serves only low-cost customers and therefore can offer lower rates.

The incumbent, meanwhile, is still required to serve everyone else. But because of competition, there are fewer low-cost customers to generate a subsidy for the high-cost customers, so the incumbent has to be able to recover its costs from the remaining customers through rate increases, or policymakers have to find ways to distribute equitably among competing providers the cost of providing subsidized service to high-cost customers.

One element of the solution is to eliminate the telephone rate averaging requirement. It can be replaced with a competitively neutral subsidy mechanism in which all providers participate, with retail prices in rural areas set no higher or lower than prices in urban areas.

Incumbent phone companies should not be required to act as a COLR where the market is competitive and consumers can choose among multiple providers. In a competitive market, rivals sometimes sign exclusive deals with property developers or landlords. If the incumbent has a COLR obligation, it may be required to build costly facilities to serve a single customer in an office park, shopping mall, or housing development. The revenue may be inadequate to cover the cost without rate averaging. Regulation that imposes costs on some carriers but not others is anti-competitive.

Telephone Service

Indiana addressed the COLR problem facing phone companies in part by protecting an incumbent from having to provide communications service to occupants of multitenant nonresidential real estate if the owner, operator, or developer of the property does any of the following to benefit another provider: (1) permits only one provider to install communications facilities or equipment on the premises, (2) accepts incentives from a provider in exchange for allowing the provider the exclusive right to provide service to the premises, (3) collects charges from occupants for communications service, or (4) enters into a prohibited agreement with a provider.

Florida ended all COLR obligations on phone companies as of January 1, 2009. Previously, it automatically relieved a carrier of last resort of its obligation to provide basic local telecommunications service to any customer in a multitenant business or residential property when an owner or developer permitted only one communications service provider to install its facilities or equipment and under other circumstances.

Cable and Internet Access

The situation for cable service is similar to that of phone service. Incumbent cable companies often operate under mandates in their franchise agreements to provide universal service to the community. A "level playing field" could require competitors be subject to the same requirement—that they "build out" their network to cover the entire community by some deadline. But there is no social purpose served by requiring every customer be served before a single customer is given a second, third, or even fourth choice of cable provider.

The level playing field goal can better be met by relieving both the incumbent and new competitors from buildout requirements (Skorburg *et al.* 2007). In high-cost areas where a carrier of last resort is necessary to deliver basic service, the provider should be allowed to choose the most efficient technology, such as voice over internet protocol (VoIP) or a wireless technology. Indiana takes this approach to telephone service, relieving the carrier of having to offer costly service using outmoded network facilities and then find a way to subsidize it.

Finally, competitors should be given the opportunity to become carriers of last resort. Any provider ought to be allowed to bid for contracts to provide essential service in high-cost areas and receive adequate and equitable support from an explicit funding mechanism if it wins the contract. Incumbent providers that currently provide subsidized service should not be under any legal obligation to continue to serve areas where other providers have won the contracts.

Recommended Reading: John Skorburg, James Speta, and Steven Titch, "The Consumer Benefits of Video Franchise Reform in Illinois," *Policy Study* No. 112, The Heartland Institute, April 4, 2007.

5. Reform inter-carrier access charges and interconnection fees.

The current system of high intrastate access charges and low interstate charges ought to be replaced with parity and technology neutrality.

Inter-carrier access charges and interconnection fees—the payments service providers pay each other for the connection and completion of calls that originate on their networks—form another subsidy mechanism that supports service in high-cost areas. Such cross-subsidies cannot be maintained in a competitive market if competitors can choose to serve profitable customers and ignore everyone else.

Since competitors are free to choose their customers, cross-subsidies discourage competitive entry in high-cost areas when the incumbent is charging a lower price than a competitor would need to charge to cover its costs plus earn a reasonable profit. In the low-cost areas, competitive entry is extremely profitable when the incumbent's services are priced high enough to subsidize other customers. Competitors can profitably underprice the incumbent in low-cost areas while the incumbent is helpless to match the price decreases.

Consumers suffer the consequences. High-cost consumers are deprived of competitive choices and ultimately of the heavily subsidized service they need. Low-cost consumers are harmed, even if they have a choice of providers, because the inflated price charged by the incumbent acts as an umbrella guaranteeing competitors also can maintain a high price without fear the incumbent will cut its prices below theirs.

Indiana Reforms Show the Way

Reforming voice call termination rates and removing the remaining implicit subsidies from intrastate access charges would spread the benefits of competition in both urban and rural areas.

In Indiana, the cost of intrastate access does not exceed the cost of interstate access. This policy of "parity" makes sense because interstate access charges are fully compensatory and a telephone company does not incur a separate set of costs when it provides intrastate versus interstate access. Reducing intrastate access charges does not necessarily mean forcing rural and residential consumers to pay higher prices for basic service. Indirect subsidization through intrastate access charges can be replaced with an explicit funding mechanism into which all competitors must contribute equitably and out of which any competitor who wishes to serve a high-cost area may receive adequate funding.

In some cases, reducing access charges would spur the deployment of broadband in rural areas without sacrificing consumer choice. Access charges were originally set to reflect the cost of analog phone service, which is more expensive to deliver than wireless or VoIP phone services. Smaller rural providers are still under "rate of return" or "cost-plus" regulation entitling them to recover their costs plus a reasonable return of approximately 10 percent to 15 percent. Since the return is defined as a percentage of the costs they incur, profits rise as costs rise.

Moreover, since VoIP often deprives smaller rural providers and new entrants of access charges, current policies discourage rural phone companies from marketing VoIP services. States should consider reducing intrastate access charges for smaller rural providers and new entrants to remove a disincentive to market less-expensive phone services, such as wireless and VoIP.

Parity and Technology Neutrality

It is not possible to preserve the status quo, nor is it desirable to postpone reform. If wired and wireless phone companies are forced to charge or pay inflated call termination rates, they will lose customers to lower-priced VoIP offerings. If they are required to reduce intrastate access charges at least to the same level as interstate access charges, they can provide a more competitive offering.

Policymakers could reduce intrastate long-distance charges for most consumers and promote the availability of flat-rate long-distance plans by reducing intrastate access charges. Ideally, the current system of high intrastate access charges and low interstate charges ought to be replaced with parity and technology neutrality in call-termination fees generally.

Recommended Reading: Mark Jamison, *Methods for Increasing Competition in Telecommunications Markets* (Gainesville, FL: Public Utility Research Center University of Florida, 2012).

6. Repeal discriminatory taxes and fees on telecom services.

Policymakers should repeal discriminatory taxes and fees to encourage investment in telecom services.

A standard policy rule is: If you want less of something, tax it, and if you want more of something, don't tax it. If elected officials want to encourage investment in telecom services, the first step they should take is to repeal discriminatory taxes and fees on these services.

Telecom Taxes Are Too High

According to a 2014 report, Americans pay an average of 17 percent in combined federal, state, and local taxes and fees on wireless service (Mackey and Henchman 2014). The average rates of taxes and fees on wireless telephone services are more than two times higher than the average sales tax rates that apply to most other taxable goods and services.

Cable television services, which support internet and VoIP phone service, continue to be subject to state and local sales taxes, franchise fees, and state and federal universal service fees. A 2007 study found taxes and fees on cable TV and telephone subscribers averaged 13.4 percent, twice as high as the national average retail sales tax of 6.6 percent (Tuerck *et al.* 2007).

Taxes also vary from one communication service to another and according to the technology used to deliver otherwise-similar services. A typical pay-per-view movie ordered through a cable TV box is often taxed as part of the overall consumer cable bill, so the download could carry a levy of as much as 10 percent to 12 percent, depending on jurisdiction. The same movie downloaded over the internet using a service such as iTunes may be subject only to sales tax.

Communications taxes and fees are regressive with respect to income. Cell phones are increasingly the sole means of communication and connectivity for many low-income Americans. At the end of 2013, according to surveys by the Centers for Disease Control, more than 56 percent of all poor adults had only wireless service, and nearly 40 percent of all adults were wireless-only (Mackey and Henchman 2014). Public officials seeking to close the so-called digital divide can lower the price of communication services by repealing discriminatory taxes and fees.

High and discriminatory taxes and fees are legacies of an era when cable and telephone companies had near-monopolies and could pass the cost of taxes and fees along to their then-captive ratepayers. Today, competition allows consumers to choose less-taxed alternatives, causing taxes and fees to distort buying and investment decisions. Policymakers should bring public policy up-to-date with the following changes.

Policy Agenda

Local governments can:

- Reduce cable franchise fees, making sure they do not exceed the true economic cost of using public rights-of-way;

- Repeal or avoid regulations that impose costs on cable companies and their new competitors from the phone and wireless sectors.

State governments can:

■ Lower and streamline communication taxes as Ohio and Virginia have done;

■ Preempt local franchise laws that impose excessive fees or restrict new entry by competitors, following the example of such states as Indiana, Ohio, and Wisconsin;

■ Allow cable companies to operate under the same franchise agreements as their competitors.

The national government, having phased out a 3 percent national excise tax on all wireless and wired long-distance calls (a positive and long-overdue step), can improve on that by prohibiting states and cities from adopting discriminatory sales, use, or business taxes on communication services.

Recommended Readings: Scott Mackey and Joseph Henchman, "Wireless Taxation in the United States 2014," *Fiscal Fact* No. 441, Tax Foundation, 2014; Scott Mackey and Joseph Henchman, "Record High Taxes and Fees on Wireless Consumers in 2015," *Fiscal Fact* No. 490, Tax Foundation, 2015.

7. Prohibit the collection of sales taxes on online purchases that cross state lines.

States should see e-commerce as an opportunity to boost their economies by welcoming internet enterprises instead of treating them, and their customers, as just another cash cow.

As many states struggle to balance their budgets, their elected officials look ever more covetously at the $385 billion in online sales in 2016 that largely escaped taxation (BI Intelligence 2016). Sometimes they are aided and abetted by local business owners who feel it is unfair they must collect sales taxes at their bricks-and-mortar stores while online sellers do not.

That is why many states have thrown their support behind congressional efforts to force "remote sellers," meaning internet and catalog merchants, to calculate and collect sales taxes from out-of-state consumers. Thankfully, the principal legislation toward this end, the Marketplace Fairness Act (MFA), introduced in 2013 and reintroduced in 2015, 2016, and 2017, has failed to gain traction.

Taxing Internet Sales Is Unconstitutional

MFA would undo two U.S. Supreme Court decisions that predate the internet yet undergird its sales-tax-free character: *Quill Corp.* v. *North Dakota* (504 U.S. 298 (1992)) and *National Bellas Hess* v. [Illinois] *Department of Revenue* (386 U.S. 753 (1967)).

Quill Corporation and National Bellas Hess were mail-order catalog merchants. Both Court decisions held that a business had to have a "nexus," or specific physical presence within a state, before it could be forced to collect sales taxes in that state. Both decisions said forcing a remote seller to collect sales taxes from customers in tax jurisdictions across the country—there are some 9,600 taxing jurisdictions in the United States today—constitutes an undue burden on interstate commerce, the regulation of which is constitutionally assigned to Congress. The *Quill* decision left the door open for a congressional override of the Court's decision.

Supporters of MFA say the bill will close a "loophole" that allows internet purchases to escape taxation (Editorial Board 2012). That is inaccurate. *Quill* and *Bellas Hess* sharpened and affirmed the U.S. Constitution's Commerce Clause, which prevents one state from taxing residents of another. Hardly a loophole, the Commerce Clause was included by the Founders to prevent states from plundering each other's residents and enterprises with taxes.

MFA ignores the constitutional underpinnings of the *Quill* and *Bellas Hess* decisions and treats the internet sales tax issue as a procedural issue, when in fact the constitutional bar is set much higher. MFA puts great stock in the idea that software and technology can relieve the burden state and local tax compliance places on out-of-state business. But sales tax complexity cannot be solved with the click of a mouse. More than the 9,600 sales tax jurisdictions that need to be considered, tax rules differ from state to state, city to city, and town to town. Sometimes a candy bar is taxed, sometimes it's not. Every August, some states declare a "sales tax holiday weekend" in hopes of boosting back-to-school business. Dates can vary.

Bottom line: There is no reliable plug-and-play software for this. Overstock.com's CEO Patrick Byrne told Congress the company spent

$300,000 and months of man-hours writing compliant sales tax software (U.S. House Hearing 2011).

Better Alternatives

MFA is the wrong response to the rise of internet sales. Bricks-and-mortar store owners are free to also sell their goods online, and the market is plainly telling them many consumers prefer that avenue. These "main street" merchants also are free to not collect sales taxes from people who can show they live outside their state. States such as Texas and Virginia have reached compromises with online retailers, designating distribution hubs as nexuses under *Quill*.

Consumers and businesses would be much better off if states looked at e-commerce as an opportunity to boost their economies by welcoming internet enterprises instead of treating them, and their customers, as just another cash cow.

Recommended Reading: Joseph Henchman, "The Marketplace Fairness Act," *Background Paper* No. 69, Tax Foundation, 2014.

8. Strengthen privacy and Fourth Amendment protections.

Legislators should not overlook constitutionally protected civil liberties in an attempt to stop domestic terrorism.

The nation was stunned in June 2013 when the news media began reporting on the National Security Agency (NSA) PRISM program, which allows for the interception and collection of data from wireless phones to track contact between U.S. citizens and foreign nationals. NSA's infiltration into the electronic communications and transactions of American and foreign users extended into demanding U.S. ISPs turn over customer data and forcing U.S. infrastructure manufacturers to build software "back doors" into the servers built for private companies, to facilitate NSA spying.

Other NSA programs, such as MUSCULAR and "Tailored Access Operations," were aimed at defeating the encryption protocols and firewalls internet companies use to safeguard user data. NSA justified these programs as necessary to fight the "war on terror," yet at least one study has shown these sweeping surveillance initiatives resulted in little or no intelligence or prevention of terrorism (Bergen *et al.* 2014).

The Costs of Spying

NSA spying extracted a great cost from the U.S. economy. The Information Technology and Innovation Foundation, a research institute promoting public policies that advance technological innovation and productivity, in 2013 estimated international concern and mistrust of U.S. tech companies could cost the industry between $21.5 billion and $35 billion through 2016 (Castro 2013). The author of that study has since said economic fallout will "likely far exceed" that figure (Groden 2015). Forrester Research, which provides analysis for financial firms and investors, estimates the potential global industry cost could be much more: $180 billion worldwide over the same period (Staten 2013).

More recently, the Court of Justice of the European Union invalidated the Safe Harbor Arrangement that has existed between the European Commission and the U.S. Department of Commerce since 2000, concerning the protection and use of data about consumers in European Union countries. Essentially, the Safe Harbor Agreement sets data protection principles U.S. companies agree to follow, with enforcement handled by the U.S. Department of Commerce. If the companies are compliant with these principles, they are deemed compliant with EU privacy directives. The court's primary reason for invalidating the Safe Harbor Agreement was its concern about NSA's nearly unrestricted power to demand information from the private sector.

Protecting Privacy

Faced with a national consensus concerning NSA's activities as a large-scale violation of citizen privacy and a court ruling declaring PRISM unconstitutional, bipartisan efforts in Congress to scale back these efforts have gained ground. In November 2015, the USA Protection Act ended NSA's collection of cell phone calling data.

Earlier in 2015, U.S. Sens. Patrick Leahy (D–VT) and Mike Lee (R–UT) reintroduced a bill they had cosponsored previously offering revisions of the Electronic Communications Privacy Act (ECPA) to extend Fourth Amendment protections to private data stored on servers on the internet or in the "cloud." Among the legal weaknesses NSA had been able to exploit was ECPA's silence on internet-related communications. ECPA, which sets rules for law enforcement agencies that want to tap phone conversations, became law 30 years ago when there was no concept of e-commerce, cloud storage, web searching, or other routine internet-based applications people now use daily.

The House took a major step toward reform in February 2017, passing the Email Privacy Act (H.R. 387). The baseline bill updates ECPA and requires the government to obtain a warrant before it may access emails, social media posts, and other online content stored in the cloud. The bill also eliminates the provision in ECPA that allowed warrantless seizures of stored communications after 180 days. As of July 2017, H.R. 387 was awaiting action in the Senate.

Some states also are taking action. In July 2015, Montana became the first state to enact a comprehensive law requiring police to obtain a search warrant before obtaining location information generated by personal electronic devices, such as cell phones. In October 2015, California Gov. Jerry Brown signed CalECPA, a bipartisan bill requiring police to get a warrant before searching online accounts or personal communications devices.

These actions come none too soon. In addition to NSA's surveillance activities, state and local police are using devices called Stingrays, which mimic cell phone reception towers to trick phones into revealing identifying information and location data. The American Civil Liberties Union and other groups have called for more transparency on their use (ACLU n.d.). Congress, along with legislatures in states such as New York, South Carolina, and Utah, has introduced bills that would require search warrants for Stingray use. In September 2015, the Department of Justice made it policy that federal law enforcement agencies obtain a search warrant before using Stingrays.

The lack of specific Fourth Amendment protection is partly responsible for the massive scope of the government's use of the internet to violate citizens' privacy. NSA hid behind judicial interpretations suggesting cloud data have no explicit legal protection, but this is use of a technicality to evade the principle of the law. The intent of ECPA was to prevent the very sort of fishing expeditions NSA has been conducting.

Had there been appropriate judicial and legislative oversight, it is difficult to imagine these surveillance programs would have grown as large and intrusive as they became. After the December 2015 attack in San Bernardino, California by two Islamic terrorists, some, including presidential candidate Sen. Marco Rubio (R-FL), questioned the wisdom of curtailing warrantless NSA surveillance—even though the program failed to alert the government to those attackers or their plan.

Policy Agenda

Legislators should avoid a rush to overlook constitutionally protected civil liberties in an attempt to police domestic terrorism. Any future surveillance programs should be subject to strict oversight from lawmakers and an independent judiciary. Those safeguards should recognize:

- the right of internet companies to be notified when their infrastructure is being used for surveillance;

- the right of internet companies to disclose instances when they have been asked to assist with surveillance and turn over information;

- the necessity of due process;

- domestic civilian surveillance is within the purview of conventional courts, not Foreign Intelligence Surveillance Court or secret military courts; and

- requests for data should be held to the same standard as other search warrants: The requester must identify the suspect, the probable cause, the data to be searched, and the specific information being sought.

In a free society, individuals are not automatically assumed to be suspects requiring or justifying constant surveillance. Citizens have the right to go about their business without answering to the state for every thought, act, purchase, or social media comment.

Recommended Readings: Steven Titch, "Has the NSA Poisoned the Cloud?," *Policy Study* No. 17, R Street Institute, 2014; Daniel Solove, "Sunken Safe Harbor: 5 Implications of Schrems and US-EU Data Transfer," *LinkedIn Pulse*, October 6, 2015.

9. Prohibit government regulation of content.

Content freedom must be protected. Censorship of speech we don't like may be counterproductive, keeping ideas underground and hence free from direct rebuttal.

Calls for censorship, often in the name of "civil discourse" or "safe spaces," have become increasingly common in recent years, at least in part because the internet, with its global reach, can amplify the most repulsive of statements as easily as it can the most attractive.

"Fairness" as Censorship

Most people do not seek to intentionally and gratuitously offend others. However, offensive speech, even hate speech, is a by-product of a society that has agreed to tolerate all forms of expression. As tempting as it might be to place limits on speech we don't like, such bans may actually foster the very ideas they are intended to suppress by keeping them underground and hence free from direct rebuttal.

A recent Anti-Defamation League study found in France, where Holocaust denial has been illegal for more than 20 years, the percentage of Holocaust deniers plus skeptics increased 21 percent during that period, whereas in other European countries and the United States, which place no limits on such statements, the relatively low level of skeptics and deniers has remained constant (Shulman 2015).

Although the repression of political speech first comes to mind when the word "censorship" is invoked, the right to free speech is rarely attacked so directly. Instead, there are demands that content providers allow for expression of all points of view. This was the thinking behind FCC's Fairness Doctrine, which required broadcasters to furnish an alternative point of view to any editorial statement they made. As with hate speech, the effect was the opposite of what was intended. Instead of stimulating debate, stations backed away from any editorial discourse whatsoever, choosing not to be liable to give airtime to all comers. It wasn't until the Reagan administration scrapped the Fairness Doctrine that politically oriented programming, as seen in Fox on the right and CNN, MSNBC, and PBS on the left, became common in the broadcast media.

The failure of the Fairness Doctrine in broadcast media has not stopped calls from some circles for an internet fairness doctrine, although how such a thing would be enforced is almost impossible to imagine. Would conservative blogger Michelle Malkin be required to publish postings from liberal blogger Markos Moulitsas Zúniga's *Daily Kos* site (without sardonic rebuttal) and vice versa? And these are high-profile writers. Is it really a good use of resources for the federal government to micromanage the tens of thousands of tiny WordPress blogs on the internet to determine whether they are adequately providing equal time to opposing points of view?

The potential for political abuse of a new Fairness Doctrine is considerable. During the Obama administration, the Internal Revenue Service (IRS) was "weaponized" and used against conservative groups seeking nonprofit status (Washington Times 2016). What would keep future administrations from weaponizing FCC?

FCC as "Ministry of Truth"

In an October 2014 blog entry, FCC Chairman Thomas Wheeler floated the idea of regulating internet video content, a step any future FCC chairman could take now that the internet has been classified a Title II regulated utility (Wheeler 2014). Wheeler was vague about how such regulation would take shape, but there was immediate speculation this could mean applying network must-carry rules, franchise fees, subsidies, and even content ratings to internet video.

Again, how this could be enforced fairly and without a huge layer of bureaucracy and costs is difficult to imagine. When we think of internet video, services such as Netflix come to mind, but YouTube hosts thousands of content providers with their own "channels" that have anywhere from a handful of regular viewers to millions. Will FCC claim to have the authority to determine the truthfulness of statements on all these sites?

One area of explosive growth in online opinion-sharing is user reviews and comment fields, which have become an integral part of most websites. Most retailing, travel, and dining sites allow consumers to provide feedback on specific products and properties. To date, website owners, not federal or state regulators, have decided whether negative reviews or critical comments can be posted on a website. If FCC becomes a "Ministry of Truth," it could inject itself into these decisions. How could that possibly be a good idea?

Gag Clauses and Right to Yelp

Negative online reviews on a website such as Yelp can hurt a business, and if the review is posted anonymously the business may have little or no recourse, even if the review is inaccurate or malicious. To discourage such reviews, some businesses are including negative internet reviews in "non-disparagement" clauses in purchase agreements, specifying penalties or litigation may result if consumers publish negative comments in online reviews (Nadolenco 2014).

Some consumer advocates oppose non-disparagement clauses, calling them "gag clauses" and saying they attempt to silence legitimate criticism and stifle free speech. Businesses can usually respond online to anonymous negative reviews, or use libel laws to prosecute especially malicious reviews. Small business advocates, however, point out that many small businesses can't afford to hire lawyers and may not survive the months or years a libel case requires to go through the courts, all the while the malicious review is still available to be viewed online (Bergal 2016).

Yelp has led a coalition of businesses and trade associations to press for "Right to Yelp" laws at the state and national level. The effort bore fruit in January 2017 when Obama signed the Consumer Review Fairness Act of 2016. The act …

> [M]akes a provision of a form contract void from the inception if it: (1) prohibits or restricts an individual who is a party to such a contract from engaging in written, oral, or pictorial reviews, or other similar performance assessments or analyses of, including by electronic means, the goods, services, or conduct of a person that is also a party to the contract; (2) imposes penalties or fees against individuals who engage in such communications; or (3) transfers or requires the individual to transfer intellectual property rights in review or feedback content (with the exception of a nonexclusive license to use the content) in any otherwise lawful communications about such person or the goods or services provided by such person (Congress.gov 2017).

Only California and Maryland had passed legislation aimed at barring gag clauses before the federal action, and the federal law appears to supersede or duplicate their bans. Prohibiting one kind of freedom—in this case the freedom to put a negative-review gag provision in a contract—in order to protect another—the freedom to write and post online a negative review of something you purchased—is rarely a good idea. Despite the federal law, businesses will find ways to combat negative reviews and Yelp will defend its right to post negative reviews and protect the anonymity of its reviewers. We ultimately see no value in passage of "Right to Yelp" laws.

Recommended Readings: Milton Mueller, "Internet Content Regulation and the Limits of Sovereignty," *World Politics Review,* September 1, 2009; Rikke Frank Jørgensen, *Internet and Freedom of Expression* (Netherlands: International Federation of Library Associations and Institutions, 2001).

10. Don't thwart expansion of internet applications and e-commerce.

Lawmakers should avoid regulating innovative applications of the digital economy that consumers want but may compete with established businesses.

The same lawmakers who routinely promote technology policies in hopes of stimulating the local digital economy often are the first to create obstacles when entrepreneurs make those policies bear fruit. This is especially true when new applications threaten entrenched businesses and attitudes.

The Sharing Economy

When talk turns to stimulating local technology jobs, state and local legislators often envision incubating the next Google or Facebook, businesses that employ engineers and software coders. To be sure, these are attractive and high-paying twenty-first century jobs. But in their quest to land the next large tech employer, local lawmakers should not overlook innovators who are using the internet to fashion new ways to deliver everyday services. This is the real digital economy.

The best example is ridesharing services, or transportation network services (TNCs), as they are more recently described. Companies such as Lyft, Sidecar, and Uber sign up drivers willing to use their own vehicles as taxis and work their own hours in return for paying a share of their fares to the TNC. Another is homesharing services, such as Airbnb. (The name Airbnb is a playful combination of "airbed" and "bed and breakfast." It is pronounced "Air bee and bee.") Airbnb connects travelers seeking a short-term stay to people with a vacant home or bedroom. Other sharing services on the rise include DogVacay (petsitting), GetAround (peer-to-peer car renting), and TaskRabbit (household chores and office help).

Such sharing opportunities are revolutionizing their respective industries, dramatically reducing costs and expanding access to widely used services. They also pose significant competition for established businesses. Ridesharing threatens taxicab companies, which operate under heavy regulations in return for what once was a monopoly or duopoly in the short-distance car rental market. Many cities cap the size of taxi fleets, creating an artificial market scarcity that protects incumbent companies and keeps fares high. TNC drivers, often working part-time, cannot afford the insurance, special inspections, and licensing fees and background checks the large, politically protected firms can afford to bear.

Airbnb threatens conventional hotels and motels, which must comply with zoning, parking, and noise ordinances that don't apply in many residential areas. Hotels and motels also often pay extra taxes to finance sports stadiums, arenas, airports, and convention facilities intended to draw tourism. The chief complaint against Airbnb in New York, for example, was not over safety or cleanliness of the rooms being offered, but the tax revenues being lost. The state attorney general declared the service illegal and warned residents anyone sharing an apartment through Airbnb could be fined for operating an illegal hostel. In contrast to the resistance in New York State, San Francisco legalized Airbnb fairly quickly after it entered the market there (Streitfeld 2014).

Road Navigation Apps

A road navigation app named "Waze" has come under fire from law enforcement agencies because it pinpoints the location of speed traps and police checkpoints. Waze allows multiple users to input information about traffic conditions, accidents, detours, road closures—and police presence—in real time. Police departments have begun pushing Google, which purchased Waze in 2013, to drop the feature that lets drivers alert others to police locations, arguing criminals could use this feature to target police for killings.

Although lawmakers should be sympathetic to concerns for police officers' safety, forcing Waze to prohibit postings about police presence would be a violation of free speech. In addition, when drivers are aware of a police presence on the highway, they are more likely to comply with speed limits. In this way, applications like Waze support the safety goals behind these laws, even if fewer speeding tickets ensue.

Seasoned travelers might point out Waze makes it more difficult for towns to accumulate traffic fines from questionable traps—short stretches of a major highway through a small town that has lowered speed limits by 15 to 20 mph in hopes of netting speeding fines from drivers who fail to observe the change. Such tactics earn the ire of law-abiding motorists who feel more like victims of a shakedown, and apps that make such activities less viable could be seen as a public good.

Online Sales of Beer, Wine, and Liquor

In many states it is legal for residents to drive to a winery within their own state, purchase a case of their favorite varietal, and drive back home to serve it at dinner. It is illegal, however, for the same consumer to order a case of that same varietal over the internet and have it shipped to his home.

Online sales of beer, wine, and liquor are caught in a legal web dating back nearly 100 years to Prohibition. Today, many states still regulate the sale, transportation, and distribution of alcoholic beverages so online sales are murky. Reports suggest that since the Eighteenth Amendment was repealed, no American has been prosecuted for illegally receiving wine for personal consumption (Taylor 2014). Many wine lovers have violated their state's wine-shipping laws without realizing it.

Online sales of alcoholic beverages are far from the only internet commerce lawmakers have tried to prevent. When automaker Tesla launched a sales campaign allowing buyers to purchase its cars online directly from the factory, the North Carolina state legislature, in what was seen as a bid to protect car dealerships, introduced a bill to make such orders illegal. The effort failed, but it did not stop lawmakers in Minnesota, New Hampshire, New Jersey, and Texas from mounting similar efforts.

Online Gambling and Fantasy Sports

The popularity of daily fantasy sports (DFS) has reignited the debate over online gambling, pitting a specialized carve-out in federal legislation against the traditional right of states to regulate gambling within their borders. This is another area where the simple rule of "hands off the internet" ought to prevail.

According to the Fantasy Sports Trade Association, 57.4 million people in the United States and Canada played some sort of fantasy sports game for money in 2015 (Gouker 2016). Although there are legal semantics to consider, it is difficult to dispute that DFS is gambling. Players pay a pooled entry fee. Winning players are paid cash prizes from the pool in much the same way as a poker tournament or lottery.

DFS companies have capitalized on two aspects of the law. The first is a carve-out for fantasy sports wagering in the Unlawful Internet Gambling Enforcement Act (UIGEA), which otherwise prohibits U.S. banks from conducting transactions with foreign online gambling sites. Second is that law in most U.S. jurisdictions is written so the gambling definition applies largely to games of chance, such as dice and slot machines. DFS operators claim, with a certain legitimacy, that fantasy sports is a game of skill.

Despite the UIGEA carve-out, several states have begun to view DFS as online gambling and have attempted to regulate it. The debate offers a chance for the federal government and states to revisit prohibitions on online gambling. The federal government has never been involved in gambling regulation save for enforcing the Wire Act, which the Department of Justice has stated does not apply to intrastate online gambling, and it should not be involved in DFS. States should consider the popularity of the game and whether prohibitions or regulations truly reflect the will of the constituents they represent (Titch 2012).

Let Innovation Flourish

These are just a few examples of the forms the digital economy is taking. Disruption is to be expected but not feared. Lawmakers should be wary of pursuing any e-commerce bans, including those that seek to protect current businesses or outlaw immoral or morally ambiguous behavior such as drinking and gambling. Instead, state and local governments should work in tandem with those adding value to the internet, resulting in more and better goods and services at lower costs. That benefits everyone.

Recommended Readings: Logan Albright, "Regulating the Mobile App Market," *Regulation*, Fall 2014, p. 13; Seth Stevenson, "Think of the Children!," *Slate*, September 29, 2015.

References

ACLU (American Civil Liberties Union). n.d. "Stingray Tracking Devices" (website).

Albright, Logan. 2014. "Regulating the Mobile App Market." *Regulation* **37** (3): 13.

Anthony, Sebastian. 2013. "Microsoft Now Has One Million Servers – Less Than Google, But More Than Amazon, Says Ballmer." *Extreme Tech*.

Bagchi, Sutirtha, and Jagadeesh Sivadasan. 2015. "Barriers to Entry and Competitive Behavior: Evidence from Reforms of Cable Franchising Regulations." *Ross School of Business Paper* No. 1195.

Bast, Joseph. 2004. "Municipally Owned Broadband Networks: A Critical Evaluation." *Heartland Policy Study*. Chicago, IL: The Heartland Institute.

_____. 2005. "A Second Look at Cedar Falls, Iowa's Municipal Telecommunications Network." Chicago, IL: The Heartland Institute.

Bauters, Fred. 2013. "Cedar Falls Residents Can Join Iowa's First Gigabit Network For $275/Month." *Silicon Prairie News*.

Bergal, Jenni. 2016. "The Right to Gripe: States Seek to Protect Negative Online Reviews." *Stateline* (website). The Pew Charitable Trusts. June 16.

Bergen, Peter, David Sterman, Emily Schneider, and Bailey Cahill. 2014. "Do NSA's Bulk Surveillance Programs Stop Terrorists?" New American Foundation. January.

BI Intelligence. 2016. "Retail Forecast: U.S. Consumers Will Spend $632 Billion Online by 2020." *Business Insider* (website). November 3.

Castro, Daniel. 2013. *How Much Will PRISM Cost the U.S. Cloud Computing Industry?* Washington, DC: Information Technology and Innovation Foundation.

Congress.gov. 2017. "H.R.5111 – Consumer Review Fairness Act of 2016, Summary."

Davidson, Charles M., and Michael J. Santorelli. 2014. *Understanding the Debate over Government-Owned Broadband Networks: Context, Lessons Learned, and a Way Forward for Policy Makers*. New York, NY: Advanced Communication Law & Policy Institute at New York Law School.

Dunn, Scott. 2014. "Plan to 'Save' UTOPIA Advances in WVC." KSL.com (website).

Editorial Board. 2012. "Taxing Online Purchases." *Washington Post*. July 15.

Eisenach, Jeffrey A., and Thomas M. Lenard. 2003. *Telecom Deregulation and the Economy: The Impact of 'UNE-P' on Jobs, Investment and Growth*. Washington, DC: Progress & Freedom Foundation.

Experian Marketing Services. 2014. "Cross-Device Video Analysis: Engaging Consumers in a Multi-Screen World."

FCC (Federal Communications Commission). 2017. "Accelerating Wireline Broadband Deployment by Removing Barriers to Infrastructure Investment." Notice of Proposed Rulemaking, WC Docket No. 17-84.

Goodman, Ted. 2017. "The FCC Did NOT Vote to Roll Back Net Neutrality." *Daily Caller* (website). May 18.

Gouker, Dustin. 2016. "Study: Growth Of Fantasy Sports Participation Flattens Out, Little Growth For DFS." *Legal Sports Report* (website). June 14.

Groden, Claire. 2015. "NSA Spying Is Going To Cost The Tech Sector Much More Than We Thought." *Fortune Tech*. June 9.

Hazlett, Thomas W. 2011. *The Fallacy of Net Neutrality*. New York, NY: Encounter Books.

Henchman, Joseph. 2014. "The Marketplace Fairness Act." *Background Paper* No. 69. Washington, DC: Tax Foundation.

Hill, Judson. 2014. "State Wireless Facility Reforms Promise Jobs and Economic Benefits." *Congress Blog* (website). July 9.

Hovis, Joanne, and Andrew L. Afflerbach. 2014. *Gigabit Communities*. Kensington, MD: CTC Technology and Energy.

Huther, Cristopher S., and Thomas B. Magee. 2013. "Determining Joint Use Utility Pole Rates: What's Fair?" *Western Energy Magazine* Fall: 14–17.

Hyman, Elizabeth, and Matt Starr. 2017. "An Easy Way for the FCC to Boost Wireless Competition." *Washington Examiner*. July 26.

Jamison, Mark. 2012. *Methods for Increasing Competition in Telecommunications Markets*. Gainesville, FL: Public Utility Research Center University of Florida.

Jørgensen, Rikke Frank. 2001. *Internet and Freedom of Expression*. Netherlands: International Federation of Library Associations and Institutions.

Katz, Diane S. 2006. "Assessing the Case for Cable Franchise Reform." *Policy Brief*. Mackinac Center for Public Policy. September 19.

Lakely, Jim. 2009. "Neutralism: The Strange Philosophy Behind the Movement for Net Neutrality." *Policy Study* No. 122. The Heartland Institute. October 5.

Lennett, Benjamin, and Sascha Meinrath. 2009. "Building a 21st Century Broadband Superhighway: A Concrete Build-out Plan to Bring High-Speed Fiber to Every Community." New American Foundation. January.

Litan, Robert, and Hal Singer. 2014. "Outdated Regulations Will Make Consumers Pay More for Broadband." *Policy Brief*. Washington, DC: Progressive Policy Institute.

Mackey, Scott, and Joseph Henchman. 2014. "Wireless Taxation in the United States 2014." *Fiscal Fact* No. 441. Washington, DC: Tax Foundation.

———. 2015. "Record High Taxes and Fees on Wireless Consumers in 2015." *Fiscal Fact* No. 490. Washington, DC: Tax Foundation.

McSherry, Corynne. 2015. "Dear FCC: Rethink the Vague 'General Conduct' Rule." *Electronic Frontier Foundation* (blog). February 24.

Mueller, Milton. 2009. "Internet Content Regulation and the Limits of Sovereignty." *World Politics Review*. September 1.

Nadolenco, John, Richard M. Assmus, and Maximillian Del Rey. 2014. "California Approves Consumer Law Protecting Right to Leave Negative Online Reviews." *Mayer Brown Legal Update* (website).

Pressman, Aaron. 2016. "More Than One in Five Households Have Dumped the Cable Goliath." *Fortune Tech*. April 5.

Protalinski, Emil. 2015. "Streaming Services Now Account for Over 70% of Peak Traffic in North America, Netflix Dominates with 37%." *VentureBeat* (website). December 7.

Shulman, Sam. 2015. "The Great Free Speech Experiment." *Weekly Standard*. January 26.

Skorburg, John, James Speta, and Steven Titch. 2007. "The Consumer Benefits of Video Franchise Reform in Illinois." *Policy Study* No. 112. The Heartland Institute. April 4.

Solove, Daniel. 2015. "Sunken Safe Harbor: 5 Implications of Schrems and US-EU Data Transfer." *LinkedIn Pulse* (website). October 6.

St. John, David C. 2013. "State and Local Government Role in Facilitating Access to Poles, Ducts, and Conduits in Public Rights-of-Way." Fiber to the Home Council.

Staten, James. 2013. "The Cost of PRISM Will Be Higher Than ITIF Projects." *Forbes*. August 15.

Stevenson, Seth. 2015. "Think of the Children!" *Slate* (website). September 29.

Streitfeld, David. 2014. "Airbnb Listings Mostly Illegal, New York State Contends." *New York Times*. October 15.

Taylor, Robert. 2014. "U.S. Wine Shipping Laws, State by State." *Wine Spectator*. July 14.

Titch, Steven. 2012. "Internet Gambling: Keys to a Successful Regulatory Climate." *Policy Study* No. 408. Reason Foundation.

———. 2013. "Lessons in Municipal Broadband from Lafayette, Louisiana." *Policy Study* No. 424. Reason Foundation.

———. 2014. "Has the NSA Poisoned the Cloud?" *Policy Study* No. 17. R Street Institute.

———. 2014. "Alternatives to Government Broadband." *Policy Study* No. 27. R Street Institute.

Tuerck, David, Paul Bachman, Steven Titch, and John Rutledge. 2007. "Taxes and Fees on Communication Services." *Policy Study* No. 113. The Heartland Institute.

U.S. House Hearing. 2011. *Constitution Limitation on States' Authority to Collect Sales Taxes in E-Commerce*: *Hearing Before the Comm. on the Judiciary, House of Representatives*. 112th Congress, 1st Session.

Washington Times. 2016. "IRS Finally Reveals List of Tea Party Groups Targeted for Extra Scrutiny." Editorial. June 5.

Wheeler, Tom. 2014. "Tech Transitions, Video, and the Future." *Federal Communications Commission Blog*. October 28.

Zelnick, Bob, and Eva Zelnick. 2013. *The Illusion of Net Neutrality: Political Alarmism, Regulatory Creep and the Real Threat to Internet Freedom*. Stanford, CA: Hoover Institution Press.

Additional Resources

Additional information about telecommunications and information technology policy is available from The Heartland Institute:

- PolicyBot, The Heartland Institute's free online clearinghouse for the work of other free-market think tanks, contains more than 2,000 documents on telecommunications issues. It is on Heartland's website at https://www.heartland.org/policybot/.

- https://www.heartland.org/topics/infotech-telecom/ is a website devoted to the latest research, news, and commentary about info tech and telecom policy. Read headlines, watch videos, or browse the thousands of documents available from PolicyBot.

- *Budget & Tax News* is The Heartland Institute's monthly newspaper devoted to government regulation, spending, and tax issues. It regularly covers the sharing economy, discriminatory taxation of wireless services, and internet sales tax proposals, among other infotech and telecom topics. Subscriptions with digital delivery are free, print subscriptions are $36/year for 10 issues.

Directory

The following national organizations offer valuable resources about information technology and telecommunications issues:

American Civil Liberties Union, https://www.aclu.org/issues/national-security/privacy-and-surveillance

Cato Institute, https://www.cato.org/research/telecom-internet-information-policy

Discovery Institute, http://www.discovery.org/

Electronic Frontier Foundation, https://www.eff.org/

Heartland Institute, https://www.heartland.org/

Institute for Policy Innovation, http://www.ipi.org/ipi_issues/cf/detail/technology--communications

Less Government, http://lessgovernment.org/

Precursor LLC, http://www.precursor.com/

Reason Foundation, http://reason.org/areas/topic/telecommunications

R Street Institute, http://www.rstreet.org/

Tax Foundation, https://taxfoundation.org/

U.S. Telecom: The Broadband Association, https://www.ustelecom.org/

Chapter 8
State Fiscal Policy

Matthew Glans and Timothy Benson

---

10 Principles of State Fiscal Policy

1. Keep taxes low.
2. Avoid progressive income taxes.
3. Reduce reliance on excise taxes.
4. Create a transparent and accountable budget process.
5. Stop corporate welfare.
6. Remove regulatory barriers to prosperity.
7. Reform public pension and health care programs.
8. Fund school children, not schools.
9. Fix, don't expand, Medicaid.
10. Cap taxes and expenditures.

Introduction

State fiscal policy has grown in importance in step with the rise in state and local government spending. That rise has been rapid:

■ State governments spent $1.77 trillion and local governments spent $1.71 trillion in 2016 (usgovernmentspending.com 2017).

■ From 1990 to 2014, state government spending grew 277 percent in nominal dollars, by about $1.1 trillion (*Ibid.*).

■ Per-capita state spending in current dollars climbed 60 percent from 2001 to 2014, rising from $3,282 to $5,457 (*Ibid.*).

■ State and local government revenues grew from about 1.8 percent of national gross domestic product (GDP) in 1960 to 7.8 percent in 2014 (*Ibid.*).

Due to this growth, state fiscal policy now plays a major role in determining which states prosper—as reflected in rising population, strong job creation rates, and rising per-capita income—and which do not. States with unsound fiscal policies also waste money and deliver government services poorly, doing a disservice to their taxpayers and often imposing a burden on taxpayers in other states.

Each state is different and faces unique challenges, but certain sound principles concerning budgets, taxes, economic development, and other policies apply coast to coast. In this chapter we present 10 such principles.

1. Keep taxes low.

Low taxes and tax cuts spur economic growth, while high or rising taxes stunt growth.

American independence was born of a tax revolt. The great American statesman Daniel Webster was right when he argued in a 1819 Supreme Court case, "An unlimited power to tax involves, necessarily, a power to destroy" (17 U.S. 327 (1819)).

During the first century of the country's existence, except in times of war, low taxes and government spending were the American way. The effective tax rate imposed by all levels of government in the United States seldom rose above 5 percent prior to 1916 (Rabushka 2002).

During the past century, however, the nation has moved far from its low-tax tradition. According to Scott Greenberg of the Tax Foundation, in 2016 American taxpayers handed over $3.3 trillion in taxes to the federal government and an additional $1.6 trillion to state and local government. This tax bill of almost $5.0 trillion represents approximately 31 percent of the nation's total GDP. The typical taxpayer must work nearly four months—114 days—a year just to pay his taxes (Greenberg 2016).

High Taxes Stunt Economic Growth

Advocates of raising taxes offer an endless litany of benefits they promise will come about if only taxes were raised "just a little." Sometimes they claim higher taxes will produce more jobs or prosperity by financing needed infrastructure or essential public services. Behind every tax increase proposal stand special-interest groups hoping to benefit from the new revenues.

But there is no such thing as a free lunch. Experience has shown the price of higher taxes almost invariably is slower economic growth. Higher taxes discourage work and risk-taking, reduce demand for goods and services, and distort economic decisions. This means less private investment, fewer jobs, less income, and more demand for welfare spending.

Hundreds of studies have examined the relationship between taxes and economic growth. Here is a brief survey of recent studies with a focus on those looking at taxes and economic growth in U.S. states:

- In 2012, the Tax Foundation's William McBride reviewed 26 studies on the relationship between taxes and economic growth in developed countries around the world, at the national level in the United States, and among the 50 states since 1983. All but three studies found taxes had a negative effect on economic growth, including every one of the studies conducted in the 15 years prior to 2012 (McBride 2012).

- In 2006, W. Robert Reed, an economist at the University of Canterbury in New Zealand, studied the relationship between taxes and income growth from 1970 to 1999 in the 48 continental U.S. states and found "taxes used to fund general expenditures are associated with significant, negative effects on income growth. This finding is generally robust across alternative variable specifications, alternative estimation procedures, alternative ways of dividing the data into 'five–year' periods, and across different time periods and Bureau of Economic Analysis (BEA) regions, though state–specific estimates vary widely" (Reed 2006).

- In 2006, economist J. Scott Moody of the Maine Heritage Policy Center reported the effect of total tax burden for all 50 states from 1994 to 2004 (Moody 2006). Low-tax states saw population growth rates nearly three times greater than population growth rates in high-tax states (17.5 percent versus 6.4 percent); personal income growth rates 32 percent greater (75.6 percent versus 57.3 percent); and employment growth rates 79 percent greater (23.3 percent versus 13.0 percent).

- In 2005, Ohio University economist Richard Vedder found that between 1957 and 1997, real personal income growth was more than twice as high in the states that did not raise their income taxes (or increased them only minimally) as in the states with the biggest increases in income taxes (Vedder 2005).

- In an earlier study published in 2001, Vedder examined a number of measures of taxes and spending in the years 1957, 1977, and 1997. He found, "In every single case, without exception, the results are consistent: High or rising taxes are associated with lower amounts of economic growth. The use of more sophisticated statistical models produces the same sort of result: higher taxes, lower growth" (Vedder 2001).

- In seminal research published in 1991, economists Robert Genetski and John Skorburg found low-tax states that raise their taxes faster than other states experience slower economic growth, even if their total tax burden remained lower than their neighbors'. Change in tax burden *relative* to other states has a greater impact on economic growth than *absolute* tax burden (Genetski and Skorburg 1991).

Research on the impact of national taxes on economic growth in the United States and taxes and economic growth in other developed countries has by and large found the same relationships. Harvard University economists Robert Barro and Charles J. Redlick looked at national income tax and economic growth rates in the United States from 1912 to 2006 and found reducing the average marginal tax rate by one percentage point raised the following year's per-capita GDP by 0.5 percent (Barro and Redlick 2011). A study by the International Monetary Fund (IMF) of 15 developed countries over 30 years found a 1 percent tax increase on average reduced GDP by 1.3 percent after two years (IMF 2010). And in *Rich Nation/Poor Nation: Why Some Nations Prosper While Others Fail*, Genetski examines data on prosperity in 40 countries over many decades and finds they are highest and/or grow fastest in countries that adhere to the classical liberal principles of free markets, private property rights, and limited government (Genetski 2017).

The North Carolina Example

Tax cuts at the state level have led to more rapid economic growth. In 2013, the North Carolina General Assembly passed a pro-growth flat-rate income tax, eliminated the estate tax, and lowered the corporate income, franchise, and sales taxes while broadening the latter tax to include other services. Since the reforms were implemented, the state's economy has grown 30 percent faster than the national average and created a projected $400 million revenue surplus for the 2014–15 fiscal year (Clancy 2015).

A key component of the reform was lowering the corporate income tax rate from 6.9 percent to 5 percent in 2015. Further decreases are scheduled if revenue continues to meet targets. The North Carolina Department of Commerce reports the state's unemployment rate fell from 8.1 percent in July 2013 to 5.4 percent in December 2016. Since those tax cuts, more than 188,000 new jobs have been created in the state. North Carolina also has seen improvements in every category of private-sector employment (Berger 2015).

Policy Agenda

The record is clear: Lower tax burdens and falling tax rates produce more rapid economic growth. State lawmakers should resist the temptation to raise taxes to deal with budget deficits that are usually a problem of overspending. High taxes only make fiscal challenges worse. America's low-tax heritage and the negative economic effects of high taxes confirm the first principle of fiscal policy all legislators should follow: Keep taxes low.

Recommended Readings: W. Richard Reed, "The Robust Relationship Between Taxes and U.S. State Income Growth," *Working Paper* No. 13/2006, University of Canterbury, 2006; William McBride, "What Is the Evidence on Taxes and Growth?" *Special Report* No. 207, Tax Foundation, 2012.

2. Avoid progressive income taxes.

"Progressive" tax systems are really punitive tax systems that punish many productive efforts and retard economic development.

Progressive taxes, such as income taxes, target the highest earners who tend also to be individuals who produce the most economic value. These taxpayers often are highly educated, technologically sophisticated, and increasingly mobile, and so are able to "vote with their feet" by moving to states with lower taxes. In the 1990s, nearly three million native-born Americans left the 41 states with general income taxes for the nine states without income taxes (Vedder 2001, 2005).

Maryland's tax experience is a case in point. In 2009, Maryland created a millionaire tax projected to raise an additional $106 million. Instead of providing the expected new revenue, by the next year, the number of people in the state reporting incomes of $1 million or more fell by one-third (*Wall Street Journal* 2009). Maryland took in $100 million *less* from millionaire earners than the previous year; the state allowed the tax to expire in 2010.

Failure to Raise Revenue

By increasing taxes on higher-income individuals, progressive tax systems de-incentivize critical economic activities—investment, entrepreneurship, and financial risk-taking—that are the engines of economic growth and more commonly undertaken by those with higher incomes (McBride 2012). The adverse economic effects of progressive taxes appear to be universal. A 2008 Organisation for Economic Co-operation and Development (OECD) working paper reported progressive income tax systems around the world have a negative effect on economic growth (Arnold 2008).

"Soak the rich" progressive taxes often fail in their principal aim to raise more revenue. A study by David A. Hartman found between 1957 and 1997, the tax share paid by those in the top 10 percent of reported income was inversely related to the after-tax income share of the other 90 percent. "In other words, when tax share of the top 10 percent goes up, the after-tax income share of the other 90 percent goes down," wrote Hartman (2002).

Because progressive tax systems rely on a small percentage of higher-income taxpayers for a larger percentage of revenues, large budget gaps can result during economic recessions (Glans 2013). As the economy waxes and wanes, tax revenue received, especially from those in the upper brackets, rises and falls as individuals and corporations move between higher and lower tax brackets. This makes it difficult for policymakers to predict tax revenues and prepare state budgets. Flat tax systems are not as vulnerable to such fluctuations.

Crippling Capital

Taxes on capital gains—generally speaking, the increase in the value of a capital asset (investment or real estate) realized when the asset is sold—also harm economic growth. Capital gains taxes discourage investments and business transactions that make job creation and economic growth possible (Cai and Gokhale 1997; Kotlikoff 1993).

Some states have particularly oppressive taxes on capital gains. California has a 33 percent rate and New York a 31.5 rate (Pomerleau and Borean 2014). An increase in the capital gains tax rate, especially when combined with a hike in dividend taxes and high inflation, dramatically increases the effective tax rates paid by many taxpayers.

According to a study by the Institute for Research on the Economics of Taxation (IRET), "Higher taxes on capital retard capital formation and reduce wages across the board" (Entin 2009). In 2006, IRET Executive Director Stephen J. Entin wrote, "When a tax is imposed on capital, the quantity of capital employed falls until the rate of return rises to cover the tax, leaving the after-tax return about where it was before the tax. The tax is largely shifted to users of capital and those who work with it" (Entin 2006). According to Entin, reducing taxes on capital by 1 percent increases private-sector GDP by about 1.5 percent, with about two-thirds going to labor income and about one-third going to capital income.

Dividend taxes—a tax on money paid regularly (typically quarterly) by a company to its shareholders—also discourage investment and economic growth. Policymakers also should take note that raising the dividend tax doesn't necessarily target the wealthy. A study by Ernst and Young found 65 percent of the 27.1 million tax returns in 2007 that reported dividend income showed total incomes of less than $100,000. Senior citizens would be disproportionately affected by such a tax hike because they make up the majority of dividend-reporting taxpayers (Ernst and Young 2010).

Policy Agenda

All taxes have distorting effects on work, consumption, and investment decisions, but progressive income taxes have the worst effects on economic growth. Higher-income taxpayers are highly motivated by state tax policies to change the locations of their businesses, the banks that hold their savings and may manage their investments, and the locations of their investments. This means policymakers should avoid tax policies that penalize earnings and investment.

Recommended Readings: Walter J. Blum and Harry Kalven Jr., *The Uneasy Case for Progressive Taxation* (Chicago, IL: University of Chicago, 1952); George Will, "Try as They Might, Progressives Can't Make the Case for Progressive Taxation," *National Review,* December 5, 2015.

3. Reduce reliance on excise taxes.

Taxes on specific goods and services, called excise or "sin" taxes, are often unfair, unreliable, and regressive.

Excise taxes are a type of sales tax applied to specific goods, such as alcohol, motor fuels, and tobacco products. They typically are not calculated as a percentage of the price of the product, but instead are based on ounces, gallons, or some other product measure. Some governments apply these taxes to soda and other sugary beverages, plastic bags, e-cigarettes, tanning beds, hotels, car rentals, and even Netflix rentals.

States have become increasingly reliant on sin taxes (Maciag 2015). According to the National Association of State Budget Officers (NASBO 2015), between the years 2000 and 2015, states enacted 111 tax increases on tobacco products and another 23 on alcohol. In 2014 alone, states collected approximately $32 billion in tobacco, alcohol, and gambling taxes. Delaware, Nevada, New Hampshire, Rhode Island, and West Virginia rely the most on sin tax revenues as a percentage of total state tax revenues.

Elected officials often impose these taxes because they generally are not paid by a majority of their constituents, and thus are generally less visible than broad-based taxes. Two justifications legislators claim for sin taxes are to combat what they deem unhealthy or immoral behavior, and to increase tax revenues. These goals are contradictory, and those taxes often fail to accomplish either.

Excise Taxes Harm Businesses

Excise taxes originated centuries ago when government revenue needs were smaller, interstate commerce was minimal, and local enforcement was typically easier (Wagner 2005). Today's integrated mass economy makes them problematic and obsolete.

Targeted taxes on specific retail products have a significant detrimental effect on local small businesses. Retailers and wholesalers experience decreased sales because consumers avoid the tax by buying products online or outside the state, city, or county imposing the tax. Increased consumer mobility, thanks to improvements in cars, highways, and ridesharing breakthroughs such as Uber and Lyft, mean the harm to small businesses caused by high excise taxes is much higher than it once was.

Philadelphia's experience with its soda tax should serve as a cautionary tale for state and local governments. John Buhl of the Tax Foundation points out that thanks to a new levy, a 12-pack of flavored sports drinks is more expensive than a 12-pack of beer (Buhl 2017). In less than one year, sales of sports drinks have fallen significantly, and Philadelphia city officials have watched as numerous companies have planned to lay off workers. Canada Dry Delaware Valley planned to cut 30 of its 165 workers. PepsiCo, a major beverage company in the region, also plans layoffs related specifically to the Philadelphia tax.

That tax has harmed small retail businesses as well. Brown's Super Stores, which tend to serve otherwise underserved inner-city communities, have experienced a 50 percent drop in soda sales. Jeff Brown, the chain's CEO, said, "In 30 years of business, there's never been a circumstance in which we've had a sales decline of any significant amount," adding that the result of this decline is "nothing less than devastating." His stores have cut 5,000 to 6,000 hours of employment per week, the equivalent of about 280 jobs (Kaplan 2017).

Excise taxes often encourage illegal activity. Cigarette smuggling from low-tax to high-tax states, for example, is a big business (Drenkard and Borean 2015). Black markets create opportunities for organized crime and can endanger people's health by leading to the circulation of products that have not been inspected for safety. The Washington State Department of Revenue estimated $376 million in tax revenue was lost in 2012 through tobacco tax evasion (Blair 2014).

Most revenue projections for new or increased excise taxes are never met. The National Taxpayers Union Foundation found tobacco tax collections failed to meet initial revenue targets in 72 of 101 recent tax increases (Oprinescu 2013). This is partly because high taxes often lead to tax evasion and, if the tax rate is sufficiently high, to underground markets and counterfeiting.

Unfair and Regressive

Excise taxes often are imposed based on the argument that certain lifestyle choices—smoking, drinking, poor diets—impose costs on taxpayers and the rest of society. In some cases this may be true, but excise taxes are mostly paid by people whose use of these substances does not cause any social harms; for example, social drinkers and people who only occasionally smoke. Excise taxes in such cases are a blunt tool to achieve a social objective.

Excise taxes often bear no relationship to actual social costs, making them unfair. Economist W. Kip Viscusi examined the costs smokers impose on society and concluded, "a comprehensive assessment of these costs suggests that on balance smokers do not cost society resources because of their smoking activities, but rather save society money"

(Viscusi 1994). Note this analysis was conducted *before* major increases in state and national taxes on cigarettes.

The "social costs" arguments fails even worse as lawmakers extend cigarette taxes to e-cigarettes and other vapor products, which are known to be less harmful than traditional cigarettes (Rodu *et al.* 2017). Taxing a less-harmful vapor product the same as traditional cigarettes can mean fewer people will give up traditional cigarettes for this less harmful alternative. The tax on vaping thus can harm public health and impose unnecessary burdens on state budgets. In a report for State Budget Solutions, economist J. Scott Moody wrote, "45 states and D.C. stand to gain more from potential Medicaid savings than through lost cigarette tax collections and tobacco settlement payments" if they do not discourage smokers from switching to vapor products (Moody 2015).

Excise taxes unduly burden moderate- and lower-income individuals since consumption makes up a larger part of their budgets than is the case with persons with higher incomes. A Tax Foundation study, for example, found "from 2010 to 2011, smokers earning less than $30,000 per year spent 14.2 percent of their household income on cigarettes, compared to 4.3 percent for smokers earning between $30,000 and $59,999 and 2 percent for smokers earning more than $60,000" (Callison and Kaestner 2014).

Policy Agenda

Excise taxes are an inefficient, unreliable, and unfair revenue source for state and local governments. They require regular rate increases to keep pace with inflation, whereas income, sales, and property taxes all rise with inflation and economic growth. Instead of trying to hide taxes by creating and increasing excise taxes, states should repeal or lower excise taxes and rely instead on uniform broad-based taxes.

Recommended Readings: Adam J. Hoffer, William F. Shughart II, and Michael D. Thomas, "Sin Taxes: Size, Growth, and Creation of the Sindustry," *Working Paper* No. 13-04, Mercatus Center, 2013; W. Kip Viscusi, "Cigarette Taxation and the Social Consequences of Smoking," *Working Paper* No. 4891, National Bureau of Economic Research, October 1994.

4. Create a transparent and accountable budget process.

A state's budget process should enable policymakers and the public to identify core functions and measure the performance of state agencies.

Budget debates in many states are confusing and unproductive because the public and even elected officials do not have the information they need to make informed decisions. Budgets are often presented as huge tomes with almost-impossible-to-decipher tables and appendices, usually presented to the public after the fact or too late to inform public debate.

Elected officials need to have accurate estimates of total revenues and how they are forecast, the liabilities of public pensions, and public debt and how it is paid for. Often, these key pieces of information are controlled by a governor or by a few legislative leaders and are manipulated or hidden in order to advance their political agendas. In short, few states have budget processes in place that enable legislators and the public to perform their duties.

The good news is that guidelines and models exist for creating a transparent and accountable budget. The American Legislative Exchange Council (ALEC) published a "State Budget Reform Toolkit" in 2011 that offered 25 specific tools for improving budget systems (ALEC 2011). Among its recommendations are the following:

- Define core-governing principles.

- Require nonpartisan revenue forecasts and independent certification of budgets.

- Pass a strong, balanced budget requirement.

- Adopt an effective state spending limit.

- Require preparation of agenda mission statements.

- Adopt performance assessment and management.

- Create a transparent budget website.

- Adopt activity-based costing.

- Adopt a sunset review process for state agencies, boards, and commissions.

In 2012, the Oklahoma Council on Public Affairs offered a state budget reform plan with 10 key recommendations many states could follow:

- Statutorily prohibit budget/spending bills in the last five days of session, just like the constitutional prohibition against passage of revenue-raising measures.

- Statutorily require all budget/spending bills be made available for public review for five legislative days before passage of a budget bill.

- Statutorily require all budget/spending bills have a public hearing with recorded votes for approval in the subcommittee and committee with jurisdiction over that particular spending area.

- Lawmakers should make the commitment to vote on budget and spending bills individually (by agency), rather than as omnibus spending packages.

- Lawmakers should amend statutes to require that any funds specifically directed (in a lump sum without a clear statement for reimbursement of direct and performance-measured services to the state) toward any non-state entity be specifically and plainly written or "earmarked" in the bill providing the funding. Bills containing spending provisions should also include an intent statement, clearly stating that the (or a) purpose of the bill is to provide funding for all intended recipients of the funding.

- Lawmakers should create an oversight committee specifically to review and make recommendations for all state programs utilizing federal funds.

- Lawmakers should begin work on the budget at the beginning of session and pass funding bills for the core functions of government before non-core functions, and weeks prior to the end of session.

- Lawmakers should focus on core functions, reducing non-core efforts and limiting time spent on non-core issues.

■ Lawmakers should remove unproductive deadlines.

■ Reforms should be adopted to encourage better coordination and reporting of financial data between the House fiscal staff, the Senate fiscal staff, and executive budget staff (Small 2012).

Dealing with Public Pensions

A uniquely troubling part of state and local government budgets involves public pension funds. Lack of transparency and accountability has resulted in gross mismanagement of those funds. According to Bob Williams, president of State Budget Solutions, "Unfunded pension liabilities today are pushing many cities close to bankruptcy; state pension plans are similarly in dubious fiscal health" (Williams 2017). According to ALEC, state public pension funds are now underfunded by nearly $5.6 trillion, a $900 billion increase from a comprehensive report by State Budget Solutions in 2014. The combined price tag for all unfunded public pension liabilities in the United States is $17,427 for every man, woman, and child.

Proposals to reform public pensions are presented later in this chapter (Principle 8). The point to be made here is that many elected officials have little or no idea how large public pension liabilities are. They are fed misleading information by fund managers, bond houses, and union leaders who all have incentives to conceal shortfalls in current fund balances, project unrealistic rates of return on investments, and fail to acknowledge just how unaffordable promised benefits are likely to be.

Policy Agenda

Until a transparent and accountable budget process is put in place, taxpayers and conscientious lawmakers are at a huge disadvantage in their efforts to rein in spending and make their state and local governments more efficient. Lacking information and sufficient advance notice, they cannot ask the right questions or propose the right solutions. For this reason, fixing broken budget processes should be high on the list of priorities for patriots.

Recommended Readings: American Legislative Exchange Council, *State Budget Reform Toolkit* (Washington, DC: ALEC, 2011); Jonathan Small, "10 Steps for Improving the State Budget Process," *OCPA Memorandum*, Oklahoma Council of Public Affairs, November 8, 2012.

5. Stop corporate welfare.

Subsidies or tax incentive programs for businesses do not create jobs or promote economic growth.

State legislators spend between $40 billion and $50 billion a year using their influence over taxes and spending to entice businesses to relocate to their state or to reward businesses already present for creating jobs and not leaving (Peters and Fisher 2004). Research by *The New York Times* in 2012 that included county- and city-level spending produced an estimate of annual spending of $80 billion (Story 2012). This massive spending on selective tax abatement and subsidies to businesses goes under the name of "economic development," but research suggests it is better called "corporate welfare."

According to a 2014 report from Good Jobs First, 514 economic development programs in the 50 states and the District of Columbia granted more than 245,000 awards since 1976, the first year of the study (Mattera 2014). Three-quarters of all state economic development subsidies went to just 965 corporations, and Fortune 500 corporations alone accounted for approximately 16,000 subsidy awards, primarily in the form of tax breaks, at a cost to taxpayers of $63 billion.

How Effective?

Economists have long been skeptical of selective tax abatements and other state economic development efforts (Beck 1987). A 1999 review of state economic performance found "the states that spent the most on economic development programs were more likely to experience slow job and/or income growth than states with the lowest economic development expenditures" (Gulibon 1999). A 2001 review of more than 300 scholarly papers on economic development programs found "studies of specific taxes are split over whether incentives are effective, although most report negative results" (Buss 2001, p. 99).

An examination published in 2002 of the effect of state economic development incentives on 366 Ohio businesses that began large expansions between 1993 and 1995 found the incentives had little or no impact on expected employment growth; the possible small impact was negative (Gabe and Kraybill 2002).

A 2004 survey article by University of Iowa economists concluded:

The upshot of all of this is that on this most basic question of all—whether incentives induce significant new investment or jobs—we simply do not know the answer. Since these programs probably cost state and local governments about $40–$50 billion a year, one would expect some clear and undisputed evidence of their success. This is not the case. In fact, there are very good reasons—theoretical, empirical, and practical—to believe that economic development incentives have little or no impact on firm location and investment decisions (Peters and Fisher 2004).

In 2012, urbanologist Richard Florida used the numbers produced by the *New York Times* investigation, mentioned above, and compared them to economic growth rates in individual states. He found "there is virtually no association between economic development incentives and any measure of economic performance. We found no statistically significant association between economic development incentives per capita and average wages or incomes; none between incentives and college grads or knowledge workers; and none between incentives and the state unemployment rate" (Florida 2012).

Why Tax Incentives Don't Work

Even if robust evidence of a positive effect of targeted financial incentives were to be found, it would not tell us if the tax dollars given away would have produced better returns if put toward new roads, schools, or crime prevention, or left in the pockets of taxpayers. All of these activities have been shown by at least some researchers to have a positive impact on economic growth.

Tax abatements don't work for a number of reasons. First, state elected officials are unlikely to know which businesses are the most promising ones to subsidize or selectively exempt from tax or regulatory burdens. There is little reason to believe elected officials are better at picking winners than private investors, who have "skin in the game" and probably have more experience in making investments.

The presence of economic development programs encourages private firms to allocate their resources to lobbying efforts rather than to market analysis or productive efforts. This effort, called "rent seeking" by economists, can consume millions of dollars directly, in the form of paying lobbyists and making campaign contributions, and billions of dollars indirectly, by distracting investors and business owners from what they ought to be doing, which is coming up with ways to satisfy customers.

Location decisions are distorted because private firms locate on the basis of subsidy rather than markets, meaning inefficient enterprises are favored at the expense of efficient ones. This might produce some jobs in the short term, but in the long term it can only destroy jobs by putting business in the wrong places, or propping up companies that should probably have failed or been forced to innovate to survive.

Policy Agenda

Instead of offering corporations tax abatements, low-interest loans, subsidies, and the like, policymakers should focus on keeping general taxes low and providing public services efficiently. As the John Locke Foundation notes:

> Unlike the maintenance of low across-the-board tax rates or the provision of core public services such as education, highways, and public safety, corporate welfare doesn't benefit everyone. It requires public officials to intervene in private markets to decide which businesses or regions are worthy of support. This sets the stage for increased special-interest lobbying, strings-attached campaign contributions, and unethical behavior in public office (John Locke Foundation 2004).

The Pew Charitable Trusts has been working with state legislatures to better manage their economic development programs (Pew Charitable Trusts 2017). It recommends states "put processes in place to regularly evaluate the results of major tax incentives," use "high-quality evaluations [to] carefully assess the results of incentives for the state's budget and economy," and adopt "a formal process that ensures lawmakers will consider the results—for example, by holding legislative hearings on evaluations."

According to Pew, "27 states and the District of Columbia have made progress in gathering evidence on the results of their economic development tax incentives" and 10 are leaders in tax incentive evaluation: Florida, Indiana, Iowa, Maine, Maryland, Minnesota, Mississippi, Nebraska, Oklahoma, and Washington.

Recommended Readings: Richard Florida, "The Uselessness of Economic Development Incentives," *CityLab* (website), 2012; Pew Charitable Trusts, *How States are Improving Tax Incentives for Jobs and Growth: A National Assessment of Evaluation Practices* (Philadelphia, PA: Pew Charitable Trusts, May 3, 2017).

6. Remove regulatory barriers to prosperity.

State governments enforce many regulations that erect barriers to investment, job creation, and prosperity. When in doubt, repeal.

Next to taxes, state regulatory policy has the greatest impact on investment, job creation, and prosperity. Many current regulations were first implemented decades ago and were designed for a world that no longer exists. New technologies, institutions, and experience require some regulations be revised and others repealed entirely. Four most promising areas for regulatory reform are forced unionization (or Right to Work), prevailing wage laws, minimum wage laws, and lawsuit abuse.

Increase Worker Freedom

A good place to start using regulatory reform to expand prosperity is to adopt right to work (RTW) laws. These laws are popular and fair, and they have a proven record of promoting economic growth.

Passage of the Taft-Hartley Act in 1947 enabled states to adopt laws prohibiting "closed shop" arrangements whereby union leaders and employers agree to force workers to join a union and pay dues as a condition of employment. Opposition to this practice, on the grounds that it gave unions too much power relative to employers and the workers they claimed to represent, led many states to adopt RTW laws banning closed shops. In 2017, 22 states were not yet right to work states (NRTW 2017).

Opponents claim RTW laws, by making it more difficult for unions to organize, force wages down and lower people's standard of living, but this is unlikely. Labor economist James Sherk explains, "Economic theory holds that unions operate as labor cartels. Unions only raise wages for their members by raising prices and reducing job opportunities for nonunion workers. Few economists believe unions increase overall living standards" (Sherk 2015).

Researchers have found RTW laws affect union organizing activities, plant location decisions, manufacturing employment, and the rate of business formation (Tannenwald 1997). Surveys find employers and investors prefer to locate new facilities in states with RTW laws (see references in footnotes 11, 12, and 13 of Sherk 2015).

Researchers also find a positive impact of RTW on wages and economic growth, although the analysis is often complicated by when states adopted RTW laws and their level of prosperity and growth rates prior to doing so. New Zealand economist W. Robert Reed controlled for those differences and found:

> Using state-level data, I estimate that, *ceteris paribus,* RTW states have average wages that are significantly higher than non-RTW states. This result is robust is [sic] across a wide variety of specifications. An important distinctive of this study is that it controls for state economic conditions at the time states adopted RTW. States that adopted RTW were generally poorer than other states. Failure to control for these initial conditions may be the reason that previous studies have not identified a positive wage impact for RTW (Reed 2013).

More anecdotally, a study by the Mackinac Center for Public Policy found, "right-to-work states showed a 42.6 percent gain in total employment from 1990 to 2011, while non-right-to-work states showed gains of only 18.8 percent" (LaFaive and Hicks 2013). The study also found inflation-adjusted gross personal income in right-to-work states increased 86.5 percent between 1990 and 2013, versus 51.3 percent for forced-unionization states.

Repeal Prevailing Wage Laws

Repealing prevailing wage laws is a second way to promote prosperity. The national Davis-Bacon Act of 1931 requires contractors and subcontractors working on federal construction contracts, or federally assisted contracts in excess of $2,000, to pay workers no less than the currently "prevailing wage" paid in the area in which the construction project is carried out. Thirty-two states have their own prevailing wage laws, which affect state taxpayer-funded projects. According to the U.S. Department of Labor, 20 states do not have prevailing wage laws, and 11 states have repealed such laws by legislative action or court decision (DOL 2017a).

The federal government and many state governments use voluntary surveys to determine the wage that "prevails" (DOL 2017b). Those surveys tend to produce results skewed in favor of the higher wages paid to union contractors. Union contractors have a strong incentive to respond to wage surveys, while nonunion or smaller contractors have little reason to do so. As a result, the prevailing wage is most often equal to the union wage, even though only a few construction workers are union members.

Prevailing wage laws are really "super minimum wage" laws. They are used by elected officials to purchase political support from unions rather than to purchase the best bargains in road construction, bridges, schools, and other infrastructure for the taxpayers whose money they are using in the first place.

State prevailing wage laws impose a huge and unnecessary cost on taxpayers and consumers. The additional cost attributable to the prevailing wage has been estimated at 22 percent of labor costs and 9.91 percent of overall construction costs, for an annual excess expense to taxpayers of $8.6 billion a year (Glassman *et al.* 2008). A 2013 study by Anderson Economic Group estimated Michigan's prevailing wage law increased expenditures for construction of K–12 and higher-education facilities in the state an average of $224 million per year (Anderson Economic Group 2013). When Ohio exempted public school construction projects from its prevailing wage law in 1996, it saved nearly $500 million, about 10.7 percent of school construction costs, in the first five years alone (Lundell 2002). A 2011 study by the Nevada Policy Research Institute estimated the state's prevailing law increased the cost of public works projects by $625 million in 2009 and $346 million in 2010 (Lawrence 2011).

Oppose Minimum Wage Laws

A third way to promote economic growth and prosperity is to resist proposals to mandate a higher legal minimum wage. Having the government order businesses to pay their workers more might sound like a good way to promote prosperity, but the real world doesn't behave this way. Very few people rely on the government to guarantee their wages, and raising the minimum wage destroys jobs and opportunities for those who need both.

The minimum wage is the lowest hourly wage employers may legally pay employees. With passage of the Fair Minimum Wage Act of 2007, the national minimum wage was raised gradually, from $5.15 an hour to $7.25 an hour in 2010. Only Georgia and Wyoming have set minimum wages below the national minimum, while six states set no minimum wage (NCSL 2017).

Proponents of minimum wage laws say they protect workers from exploitation by employers and reduce poverty. But in a 2010 study, economists at Cornell University and American University found no reduction in poverty in the 28 states that raised their minimum wages between 2003 and 2007 (Burkhauser and Sabia 2010). This can hardly be surprising, since although governments can set minimum wages, a worker's compensation is largely determined by his or her productivity.

Most people earn more than the minimum wage—not because a government law requires people to be paid more, but because businesses compete vigorously for workers. The Bureau of Labor Statistics reported in April 2015 that only 2.3 percent of the nation's 131.5 million wage and salary workers earned at or below the minimum wage in 2014 (BLS 2015). A worker who produces significantly more value to a company than he or she is being paid has a strong incentive to work for other companies willing to pay more, and those companies will see the opportunity to profit by hiring that worker at a higher wage.

Raising minimum wages destroys jobs at the bottom of the employment ladder, those requiring the fewest skills and most likely to be filled by young people and new immigrants (Balis 2007). Economists at the University of California–Irvine and the Federal Reserve Board examined the body of work on the subject and found 85 percent of credible studies demonstrate minimum wage laws cause job losses for less-skilled employees (Neumark and Wascher 2007). Without a way to enter the workforce, these people remain unemployed and may place greater demands on welfare and other social services.

End Lawsuit Abuse

A fourth way to promote prosperity is to reform a state's tort system to discourage lawsuit abuse. Lawsuit abuse imposes billions of dollars of unnecessary costs on businesses and citizens every year and can be a major job killer.

A state's tort system—the subset of laws governing questions of liability in the event of injury—helps protect the safety of individuals, but its cost influences the competitiveness of businesses operating within its borders. Importantly, in an increasingly global economy, American firms must compete with businesses in other countries that operate under different tort systems. "European courts," wrote Northwestern University law professor Stephen Presser (2002), "are much less likely to hand out unpredictable and disproportionate damage judgments—unlike American courts, where ruinous verdicts are a potential in too many lawsuits."

During the 1980s and 1990s, many states reformed their tort systems to discourage lawsuit abuse. Ten states—Arizona, California, Florida, Georgia, Indiana, Louisiana, Oklahoma, Rhode Island, Tennessee, and West Virginia—adopted reforms in the past several years. Of this group, Oklahoma was the most successful, adopting reforms in 16 areas of tort law (ATRA 2009).

States can implement several common-sense tort reforms states to limit lawsuit abuse:

- Establish a limit on noneconomic tort damages, such as pain and suffering, which are a major source of lawsuit abuse.

- Limit punitive damages or ban them altogether. Like noneconomic damages, this is an area of frequent abuse, and it creates a windfall for trial lawyers.

- Limit contingent fees. Lawyers, as fiduciaries for their clients, should have a legal duty to turn over to their clients any attorneys' fees in excess of amounts that are reasonable and risk-based (Horowitz 2001).

- Move away from the "American rule" of litigation where each side bears its own legal fees, win or lose, and toward the "English rule," under which the loser pays the other side's legal fees.

- Establish stiffer sanctions against frivolous claims. In many states, the prevailing parties in cases found to have been frivolous can recover their legal fees. State legislatures can give judges the authority to levy additional monetary sanctions against parties, lawyers, and law firms that file frivolous claims.

Recommended Readings: U.S. Chamber of Commerce, *2015 Lawsuit Climate Survey*, September 2015; Brian M. Johnson and Todd Hollenbeck, *2009 Index of Worker Freedom: A National Report Card*, Alliance for Worker Freedom, 2009; Ryan Balis, "Employment: Do Minimum Wage Increases Benefit Workers and the Economy?" National Center for Public Policy Research, 2007.

7. Reform public pension and health care programs.

> Reform public pension and health care programs to make them financially sustainable and fair to taxpayers and retirees.

State and local government workers routinely are able to retire in their 50s, a decade or more earlier than can most private-sector workers, with pension and health insurance benefits exceeding what most private sector workers receive. The burden on taxpayers to fund public-sector retirement programs is skyrocketing, forcing elected officials to consider raising taxes, borrowing, cutting other government services, or using a combination of those strategies. According to Moody's Investors Service, states' adjusted net pension liabilities totaled $1.25 trillion in fiscal year 2015 and are likely to increase by an additional $500 billion in the two next years (Kilroy 2016).

Unfunded and Abused Pensions

Under many traditional defined-benefit plans retirees receive a predetermined monthly benefit based on their earnings history and years on the job, regardless of returns on money invested in their pension funds. Such plans contain key flaws and are open to abuse.

Many public-sector employees enrich themselves through "double-dipping" by taking another public-sector job after retirement and working toward a second pension. Public-sector employees also can engage in "benefit spiking," when an employer dramatically increases an employee's salary at the end of his or her career, thus increasing the pension payout, which is often based on a salary average for the final few years of employment. A Milken Institute study found if pension payouts were based on employees' compensation over five years or a whole career, instead of the abuse-prone final year, the overall cost of funding pension plans could be 30 percent lower (Zeidman *et al.* 2010).

Another major expense for public pension plans is automatic cost of living adjustments (COLAs). Such increases are supposed to reflect inflation and higher living costs. But in many state pension systems, COLAs are implemented automatically without regard to the government's ability to pay for them or the condition of the economy.

State policymakers and regulators often overestimate the future rates of investment into pension funds and the rate of return on those investments. Optimistic assumptions of strong investment returns allow them to reduce yearly government contributions to the funds and buy labor peace by promising more generous retirement benefits. But when these estimates prove wrong, the level of unfunded obligations increases.

Defined Contribution Approach

Lawmakers should begin the process of replacing defined-*benefit* pension plans with defined-*contribution* plans, under which retirees receive benefits based on the actual investment returns on contributions they and their employers make. Newly hired public-sector workers should be automatically enrolled in a defined-contribution plan; current workers should be given the option of transferring into one.

Workers with defined-contribution plans own and control their pensions and can change employers without losing their accrued benefits. Defined-contribution plans also benefit taxpayers: The pension plan burden does not rise automatically because of COLAs and is more transparent, avoiding the accounting gimmicks governments currently use to hide the true liability.

Unhealthy Health Care Plans

Public-employee health care costs have also grown quickly out of control. The Cato Institute estimates state and local governments spent $117 billion on health insurance in 2010, up from $70 billion in 2001 (in 2012 dollars). Cato found the real increase amounted to roughly $2,400 per state and local government employee, or $150 per U.S. resident (Clemens and Cutler 2014).

In a study of public-employee health care costs in Michigan, the Mackinac Center found the average family health plan cost school districts $17,692 in 2011, whereas the average private-sector plan cost businesses $10,988 (Hohman 2013).

The small share public employees contribute to their own health insurance coverage is a major part of the problem. According to the American Enterprise Institute, state and local government employees pay 13 percent of their total health care premiums on average, compared to 20 percent for private-sector workers in establishments of more than 100 employees. The study also found 30 percent of state and local government employees make no contribution to their health care coverage at all, compared to only 13 percent for private-sector employees (Biggs and Richwine 2014).

Indiana offers a model for how states can bring their public-employee health care spending under control. Indiana offers public employees a traditional health insurance plan with a health savings account (HSA) tied to it. The health insurance plan has a deductible of $2,500 for individual coverage and $5,000 for a family, and preventive services are not subject to the deductible. State employees pay nothing toward the plan premium, and Indiana deposits $1,500 for individuals and $3,000 for families into the employee's HSA annually. The employee can add to the account tax-free (Cheplick 2009).

State officials estimate the HSA program had saved the state more than $42 million from 2005 to 2009. According to an evaluation of Indiana's HSA plan by Mercer Consulting, the reforms have helped reduce the state's total health care costs for employees by 11 percent (Cheplick 2016).

Policy Agenda

In the short term, pension finances can be stabilized by capping per-year pension payouts, raising retirement ages, prohibiting double-dipping and benefit spiking, requiring realistic rate of return assumptions, and protecting pension systems from borrowing and fund raids (Nothdurft

2013). In the longer term, public employees should be moved from defined-benefit to defined-contribution pension plans.

To address escalating public-employee health care spending, states should consider implementing an HSA-based health care plan similar to Indiana's.

Recommended Readings: John Nothdurft, "The Municipal Debt Crisis," *Policy Brief,* The Heartland Institute, June 2013; Dan Liljenquist, *Keeping the Promise: State Solutions for Government Pension Reform,* American Legislative Exchange Council, 2013; Richard Dreyfuss, "Fixing the Public Sector Pension Problem: The (True) Path to Long-Term Success," *Civic Report* No. 74, Manhattan Institute, February 2013.

8. Fund school children, not schools.

States intent on improving the quality of K–12 education and getting more value for taxpayers must embrace parental choice in education.

Spending on elementary and secondary schools is second only to Medicaid programs in most states. When that investment fails to produce an educated citizenry able to be self-sufficient and productive members of society, prosperity suffers.

An earlier chapter of this book (Chapter 2) addressed the need for transforming education in the United States, so we won't repeat it here. Suffice it to say that per-pupil spending is at historically high levels while the academic achievement of U.S. students is below that of their counterparts in many developed countries.

An Antiquated Model
The current system of public education in the United States is built on a nineteenth-century model emphasizing seat time rather than mastery of subject matter. For the most part, students progress from one grade to the next merely by attending classes for the school year, not by proving they've learned grade-level content. This focus on seat time rather than subject mastery means educators teach to the middle, preventing the

accelerated learner from reaching his or her potential and leaving behind those with greater needs.

Societies, economies, and technologies have changed dramatically since the nineteenth century. In the twenty-first century, we expect to be able to make choices narrowly tailored to meet our individual wants and needs. Compared to our nineteenth-century ancestors, today we choose relatively easily where to live, what occupation to work in, and what transportation we use.

To respond to the new circumstances of the twenty-first century, K–12 education needs to be transformed. Parents must be empowered to choose the schools their children attend. They should be given the information they need to make wise choices, and schools must compete for their loyalty. Choices, not uniformity, and accountability, not top-down mandates from distant bureaucracies, ought to define how K–12 schooling is organized today.

Successful Choice Alternatives

The 1990 adoption of the Milwaukee Parental Choice Program marked the beginning of the modern "school choice" movement. All forms of school choice—including charter schools, private scholarship programs, tax-credit scholarships, voucher programs, education savings accounts (ESAs), and homeschooling—have grown since then. EdChoice reports there are now 52 school choice programs in 28 states and the District of Columbia, commanding $2 billion in public financing and offering three million scholarship opportunities (EdChoice 2017). According to EdChoice, approximately 446,000 students will utilize vouchers, tax-credit scholarships, and ESAs in the United States in the 2016–17 school year (*Ibid.*).

School choice improves educational outcomes for all children, even those who remain in traditional public schools. In Milwaukee, for example, competition from the choice schools is forcing the Milwaukee public schools to improve. Research conducted by Patrick J. Wolf (2009) at the University of Arkansas shows the Milwaukee Parental Choice Program "has led to increased achievement for the children who remain in Milwaukee's public schools while saving the state millions of dollars."

Education Savings Accounts

Twenty-one years after the Milwaukee voucher program was adopted, Arizona in 2011 became the first state to pass an education savings account (ESA) program. ESA programs for students with special needs went into effect in Florida in 2014, in Mississippi and Tennessee in 2015, and in North Carolina in 2017 (Benson 2017).

By the end of February 2016, nearly all students in Nevada were eligible for an ESA program that pays at least $5,000 per pupil for educational expenses. While a Nevada Supreme Court decision upheld the program's constitutionality, the court required the state to find a different way to fund the program (*Schwartz* v. *Lopez* 2016). Nevada lawmakers were unable to achieve that in 2017, and the thousands of families who signed up for ESAs will have to wait until the legislature reconvenes in two years to learn of the program's fate (Mull 2017).

ESAs enable families to customize their children's education. The state establishes an individual account for each child who qualifies for the program, and it funds that account with 80 to 90 percent of what the state would otherwise spend to educate that child in a public school. Parents control their child's ESA and can use the money for any approved educational expenses such as tuition, tutoring, books, class enrollment fees, and computers. They must submit receipts to document their expenses, and the accounts are subject to quality control audits. An EdChoice survey conducted in 2013 by Jason Bedrick and Jonathan Butcher found "65 percent of parents [in Arizona] used the accounts for private school tuition, 41 percent accessed education therapy, and more than one-third of respondents used the accounts for a tutor for their child" (Bedrick and Butcher 2013).

Tailored to Students

ESAs are the ultimate "funding-follows-the-student" reform. They allow parents great flexibility in designing their children's education portfolio. Some providers might be conventional, such as tutors or foreign language instructors, but others might be unconventional, such as entrepreneurship training or local businesses that arrange foreign travel for language immersion. Providers could team up with each other or with schools to provide students a portfolio of services offering a full learning experience (Bast 2005).

Research shows parents who have school choice options tend to be more satisfied with their children's education, which leads to more parental involvement in student learning. Seventy-one percent of Arizona parents whose children participate in the ESA program reported being "very satisfied" with their children's education. The remaining 29 percent of parents were either satisfied or somewhat satisfied, and no parents reported being unsatisfied (Bedrick and Butcher 2013).

ESAs are especially valuable to low-income families, whose educational options in the traditional public school system are generally limited to the failing neighborhood public school. Not only are ESAs more empowering for parents, they are also a more cost-effective way to educate children.

Policy Agenda

States intent on improving the quality of K–12 education and getting more value for taxpayers must expand parental choice in education. See Chapter 2, on transforming education, for best practices and other guidance for expanding parental choice.

Recommended Readings: EdChoice, *The ABCs of School Choice: 2017 Edition* (Indianapolis, IN: EdChoice, 2016); Greg Forster, *A Win-Win Solution: The Empirical Evidence on School Choice: Fourth Edition* (Washington, DC: American Federation for Children, 2016); Tim Benson, "Education Savings Accounts: The Future of School Choice Has Arrived," *Policy Brief*, The Heartland Institute, June 2017.

9. Fix, don't expand, Medicaid.

Medicaid, the largest single item in state budgets, delivers low-quality care. The program needs to be fixed, not expanded.

Medicaid accounts for 26 percent of all state spending, ahead of K–12 education, postsecondary education, transportation, public assistance, and corrections. Total state spending on Medicaid reached more than $475 billion in fiscal year 2014, 71 percent higher than it was a decade earlier (Sigritz 2015). By 2025, that number is expected to grow to $588 billion (Congressional Budget Office 2015).

Medicaid is an expensive program on an unsustainable fiscal path that provides poor quality care (Blase 2011). Yet the Affordable Care Act (ACA), also known as Obamacare, gives states an incentive to expand their Medicaid programs by offering a large federal subsidy for opening eligibility to all individuals with incomes between 133 and 138 percent of the federal poverty level. The allure of federal dollars has proven difficult for most states to resist, with 31 having signed on to expansion as of early 2016.

Contrary to expansion supporters' depiction of the new federal funds as "free money," Medicaid expansion is expensive, creating new costs not only for the federal government but also for states. The states that have expanded Medicaid have seen enrollment numbers much higher than they anticipated, exceeding maximum projections by 61 percent.

Not a single state had enrollment numbers below its maximum projection (Ingram and Horton 2015). This inundation of enrollees threatens to swamp state budgets once the federal government starts dropping its matching rate.

Block-granting Medicaid

The failure of Congress to repeal and replace Obamacare offers states the opportunity to take the initiative on Medicaid. Specifically, they can seek from the Secretary of Health and Human Services (HHS) waivers from the current federal program and a block-grant of Medicaid funds. This would give states flexibility in how they run the program and manage its costs. States would receive a set, finite grant from the national government to spend on Medicaid. Although the state programs would have to abide by several guidelines, the states would be allowed to customize their programs to fit their needs and goals. If a state decided to expand its Medicaid program to a larger population, it would be able to do so, but if the costs of the program exceeded the grant, the state would pay the difference.

To encourage states to support the block-grant reforms, the federal block grants could incorporate the funds Obamacare promised to states that expanded their Medicaid programs. Such a block-grant proposal would likely be scored by the Congressional Budget Office as a sharp reduction in federal Medicaid costs. According to Peter Ferrara, senior fellow for budget and entitlement policy at The Heartland Institute:

> States could then use their new control over Medicaid to provide benefits in the form of health insurance vouchers the poor could use to help buy the health insurance of their choice, including health savings accounts. That would vastly improve health care for the poor, who today cannot get timely, essential health care through Medicaid because the government so badly underfunds payments to doctors and hospitals for health care provided under the program. Private insurers, by contrast, must adequately compensate doctors and hospitals in order to attract health insurance customers in the competitive marketplace (Ferrara 2015).

The Rhode Island Approach

Since January 2009, Rhode Island has been experimenting with a Medicaid block grant initiated under a waiver from HHS. Highlights of that experiment include the following (Alexander 2010):

- The traditional federal matching grant for Medicaid was replaced by a grant capped at $12.075 billion through 2013. In exchange for accepting the capped grant, the state was given more flexibility in administering its Medicaid program and an incentive to keep its costs down.

■ The state requires able-bodied people with incomes above 150 percent of the poverty level to contribute toward their health coverage. The state helps pay all or part of the cost of employer-sponsored health insurance for Medicaid-eligible families who have access to employer plans.

■ The program brought impressive reductions in spending: By 2010, the state's Medicaid spending was $1.34 billion below the budget-neutral target of $2.4 billion.

■ The state also reduced waiting times for long-term care services and provided additional home care and physical therapy services.

The Florida Approach

Florida also has a pilot program that can address the problems with Medicaid. Known as the "Medicaid Cure" (Bragdon 2011), the program provides Medicaid recipients with a range of health insurance plans and premiums from which to choose, dramatically improving health care competition and consumer choice.

The results have been promising: a 64 percent improvement in health outcomes over managed care and an 83 percent satisfaction rate among enrollees. The program saved $118 million a year in the five counties where it was implemented (Florida Agency for Health Care Administration 2012).

Avoid *Faux* Free-market Reforms

Legislatures in some states, including Indiana, Tennessee, Utah, and Wyoming, have attempted to address the concerns of their conservative legislators and constituents by adding "free-market" components to Medicaid expansion proposals, such as using Medicaid funds to purchase private insurance or imposing premiums or copays to ensure recipients have "skin in the game."

Many of these so-called free-market models have shortcomings. The programs still represent an expansion of the failed Medicaid system, where multiple aspects of the insurance plan are dictated by the federal government and the beneficial elements of real market competition are lost. Although many of the models proposed by the states included more substantive reforms, such as copays and employment requirements, the

Centers for Medicare and Medicaid Services largely rejected those reforms.

Policy Agenda

Without significant reforms, Medicaid will remain fiscally unsustainable, costly, deliver subpar health care, and shift more power to the national government. State lawmakers should not expand a failing program. Instead, they should focus on reform options like those piloted in Florida, which reduce costs and offer better care. See Chapter 1, on health care, for a detailed reform agenda.

Recommended Readings: Peter Ferrara, *The Obamacare Disaster* (Chicago, IL: The Heartland Institute, 2010); Katherine Baicker, *et al.* "The Oregon Experiment—Effects of Medicaid on Clinical Outcomes," *The New England Journal of Medicine* **368**: 1713–22.

10. Cap taxes and expenditures.

States should adopt constitutional tax and expenditure limitations as a way to avoid excessive spending during good economic times and hardship in bad times.

As a matter of basic fiscal responsibility, every state should consider adopting a tax and expenditure limitation (TEL). This is a sound way to protect elected officials from public pressure to raise spending during good economic times instead of conserving revenues for use in the inevitable downturns.

The Spending Temptation

During good economic times, elected officials come under enormous pressure to spend every available tax dollar. Rising property values, strong retail sales, and other factors that drive up government revenues are often used as an excuse to expand government. During bad economic times, the beneficiaries of new programs oppose any spending cuts. Thus state and local governments across the country struggle to balance their budgets when the economy slows.

Other forces also push up government spending. Government's powers to tax and regulate can be used to concentrate benefits on a small number of beneficiaries while spreading the cost across large numbers of taxpayers, without much protest (Olson 1971). The legislative practice of "logrolling"—trading votes for one another's favorite projects—also results in more spending being approved than any individual elected official might otherwise support (Buchanan and Tullock 1962).

Government spending is not free, however. An additional dollar of government spending increases GDP by significantly less than one dollar. The National Bureau of Economic Research has found government spending has a "multiplier effect" on total GDP of approximately 0.5 (Ramey 2013). That is, an increase in government spending does not generally stimulate the economy but instead results in half as much economic activity as a dollar spent by the private sector. As a result, high taxes reduce economic output and, as noted in Principle 1, states with lower taxes outperform those with higher taxes.

Cutting Spending

In response to mounting debt, lawmakers are increasingly considering tax and expenditure limitations, pension reforms, privatization (see Chapter 5), and other cost-cutting measures to fix their short- and long-term budget problems. Since 1978, 30 states have enacted formal limitations on taxes, budgets, or outlays to strengthen their fiscal discipline (Zycher 2013). Several approaches have proven effective:

■ Require supermajority votes for tax increases and spending.

■ End expensive economic development schemes such as selective tax abatement and subsidies to favored industries (Nothdurft 2009).

■ Privatize public services.

■ Adopt public-sector workforce reforms.

Expensive and excessive government workforces are putting great pressure on state budgets. Long-term solutions must focus on reforming public-sector pensions and health care systems, which now constitute a trillion-dollar unfunded liability states clearly cannot afford. Necessary reforms to these and other areas of state government spending appear in other principles in this chapter and in other chapters of this book.

A Constitutional Cap

The surest way to counteract the spending-cycle problem is a constitutional provision limiting growth of taxes and spending to the sum of inflation and population growth, so the public sector grows no faster than the private sector. Any revenue collected above this limit is either saved in a rainy day fund or returned to taxpayers. Colorado's Taxpayer

Bill of Rights—TABOR—passed in 1992, offers a good model of such a limitation.

A tax and expenditure limitation (TEL) breaks the spending cycle because voters and lobbyists cannot force elected officials to spend money they cannot constitutionally collect or spend. Thus, it effectively keeps more money in the pockets of families and job creators. The best TELs are enshrined in the state's constitution, because lawmakers can evade statutory limitations. TELs also should apply to local governments to avoid cost-shifting from the states to local governments. TELs typically allow voters to override the limit in a special election, to address emergency situations.

Lew Uhler, president of the National Tax Limitation Committee, and Independence Institute Senior Fellow Barry Poulson report successful TELs have four key features:

- Annual increases in expenditures are limited to the growth in inflation and population.

- Tax revenues in excess of allowable expenditures must be refunded to taxpayers as soon as possible.

- The government is required to create an emergency fund equal to some share of the state's total personal income.

- The TEL establishes limits on local property tax rates to prevent local governments from simply filling the perceived expenditure gaps created by the state-level limitations (Uhler and Poulson 2004).

Policy Agenda

Legislators as well as civic and business leaders must reexamine their habits in setting budget priorities. Spending should be limited to the amount of money lawmakers can realistically expect to have—and lower than that, if possible. John Nothdurft recommends starting by totaling up the required spending and matching it to revenue. "What's left over should go not to new projects outside the core functions of government but to a rainy day fund or tax relief. That's the way to set spending priorities, consolidate agencies, get rid of redundant programs, eliminate non-core programs, etc.," he wrote (2009). Implementing a constitutional tax and expenditure limitation is a key part of this plan.

Recommended Readings: Barry Poulson, *Tax and Spending Limits: Theory, Analysis, and Policy*, Independence Institute, 2004; Lewis K. Uhler and Barry Poulson, *How to Limit Taxes and Spending*, Oklahoma

Council of Public Affairs, 2003; John Nothdurft, "The Best And Worst Ways To Eliminate A Budget Deficit," *Research & Commentary*, The Heartland Institute, February 2009.

References

Alexander, Gary D. 2010. *Rhode Island Global Consumer Choice Compact Medicaid Waiver: A National Model for Medicaid Reform*. Alexandria, VA: Galen Institute.

ALEC (American Legislative Exchange Council). 2011. *State Budget Reform Toolkit*. Washington, DC: ALEC.

ATRA (American Tort Reform Association). 2009. *Tort Reform Record*. December 23.

Anderson Economic Group. 2013. *The Impact of Michigan's Prevailing Wage Law on Education Construction Expenditures*. East Lansing, MI: Anderson Economic Group.

Arnold, Jens. 2008. *Do Tax Structures Affect Aggregate Economic Growth? Empirical Evidence from a Panel of OECD Countries*. Paris: Organisation for Economic Co-operation and Development.

Baicker, Katherine, *et al*. 2013. "The Oregon Experiment—Effects of Medicaid on Clinical Outcomes." *The New England Journal of Medicine* **368**: 1713–22.

Balis, Ryan. 2007. "Employment: Do Minimum Wage Increases Benefit Workers and the Economy?" National Center for Public Policy Research.

Barro, Robert, and C.J. Redlick. 2011. "Macroeconomic Effects of Government Purchases and Taxes." *Quarterly Journal of Economics* **126**: 51–102.

Bast, Joseph. 2005. "A Short History of Education Savings Accounts." *Policy Brief*. Chicago, IL: The Heartland Institute.

Beck, John H. 1987. "Selective Tax Abatements: Do They Work?" *Policy Study* No. 14. The Heartland Institute. March 16.

Bedrick, Jason and Jonathan Butcher. 2013. *Schooling Satisfaction: Arizona Parents' Opinions on Using Education Savings Accounts*. Indianapolis, IN: EdChoice.

Benson, Tim. 2017. "Education Savings Accounts: The Future of School Choice Has Arrived." *Policy Brief*. The Heartland Institute. June.

Berger, Phil. 2015. "North Carolina's Tax Cuts Really Have Helped the State." *The Wall Street Journal*. June 30.

Biggs, Andrew G., and Jason Richwine. 2014. *Overpaid or Underpaid? A State-by-State Ranking of Public-Employee Compensation*. Washington, DC: American Enterprise Institute.

Blair, Paul. 2014. "Update: Proposal to Tax E-Cigarettes at 95% in Washington State Up for Debate in House." Americans for Tax Reform.

Blase, Brian. 2011. *Medicaid Provides Poor Quality Care: What the Research Shows*. Washington, DC: The Heritage Foundation.

BLS (Bureau of Labor Statistics). 2015. "Characteristics of Minimum Wage Workers." *BLS Reports* Report No. 1054. April.

Blum, Walter J., and Harry Kalven Jr. 1952. *The Uneasy Case for Progressive Taxation*. Chicago, IL: University of Chicago Press.

Bragdon, Tarren. 2011. *Florida's Medicaid Reform Shows the Way to Improve Health, Increase Satisfaction, and Control Costs*. Washington, DC: The Heritage Foundation.

Buchanan, James M., and Gordon Tullock. 1962. *The Calculus of Consent*. Ann Arbor, MI: University of Michigan.

Buhl, John. 2017. "The Case Against Soda Taxes" (website). Tax Foundation. March 15.

Burkhauser, Richard V., and Joseph J. Sabia. 2010. *Why Raising the Minimum Wage Is a Poor Way to Help the Working Poor: An Analysis of Senators Kerry and Kennedy's Minimum Wage Proposal*. Washington, DC: Employment Policies Institute.

Buss, Terry F. 2001. "The Effect of State Tax Incentives on Economic Growth and Firm Location Decisions: An Overview of the Literature." *Economic Development Quarterly* **15** (1): 90–105.

Cai, Jinyong, and Jagadeesh Gokhale. 1997. "The Welfare Loss from a Capital Income Tax." *Federal Reserve Bank of Cleveland, Economic Review* **33** (1): 2–12.

Callison, Kevin, and Robert Kaestner. 2014. "Cigarette Taxes and Smoking." *Regulation* **37** (4–7): 42–6.

Cheplick, Thomas. 2009. "Indiana HSA Success a Lesson for Other States." *Health Care News*. November.

———. 2016. "Indiana Government Workers, Taxpayers Saving Big Through HSAs." *Health Care News*. May.

Clancy, Kaitlyn. 2015. "North Carolina Tax Reform, a Model for Other States." *Research & Commentary*. The Heartland Institute.

Clemens, Jeffrey, and David M. Cutler. 2014. *Who Pays for Public Employee Health Costs?* Washington, DC: Cato Institute.

Congressional Budget Office. 2015. *The Budget and Economic Outlook: 2015 to 2025*. Washington, DC: Congressional Budget Office.

DOL (Department of Labor). 2017a. "Wage and Hour Division (WHD). Dollar Threshold Amount for Contract Coverage" (website).

———. 2017b. "Wage and Hour Division (WHD). Government Contracts, Wage Surveys" (website).

Drenkard, Scott, and Richard Borean. 2015. "How Many Cigarettes Are Smuggled Into Your State Each Year?" (website). Tax Foundation. February 9.

Dreyfuss, Richard. 2013. "Fixing the Public Sector Pension Problem: The (True) Path to Long-Term Success." *Civic Report* No. 74. Manhattan Institute. February.

Dubay, Curtis, and Scott A. Hodge. 2006. *America Celebrates Tax Freedom Day*. Washington, DC: Tax Foundation.

EdChoice. 2017. *The ABCs of School Choice: 2017 Edition*. Indianapolis, In: EdChoice.

Entin, Stephen J. 2006. *Exploring the Effects of a Flat Federal Income Tax for the District of Columbia*. Washington, DC: Institute for Research on the Economics of Taxation.

————. 2009. *The Effect of the Capital Gains Tax Rate on Economic Activity and Total Tax Revenue*. Washington, DC: Institute for Research on the Economics of Taxation.

Ernst and Young LLP. 2010. *The Beneficiaries of the Dividend Tax Rate Reduction: A Profile of Utility Shareholders*. Washington, DC: Edison Electric Institute.

Ferrara, Peter. 2010. *The Obamacare Disaster*. Chicago, IL: The Heartland Institute.

————. 2015. "A Strategy for Obamacare after the Supreme Court Rules." *Washington Times*, April 20.

Florida Agency for Health Care Administration. 2012. *Comprehensive Medicaid Managed Care Enrollment Report*. Tallahassee, FL: Florida Agency for Health Care Administration..

Florida, Richard. 2012. "The Uselessness of Economic Development Incentives." *CityLab* (website).

Forster, Greg. 2016. *A Win-Win Solution: The Empirical Evidence on School Choice*. Fourth Edition. Washington, DC: American Federation for Children.

Gabe, Todd M., and David S. Kraybill. 2002. "The Effect of State Economic Development Incentives on Employment Growth of Establishments." *Journal of Regional Science* **42** (4): 703–30. doi: 10.1111/1467-9787.00278.

Genetski, Robert J. 2017. *Rich Nation/Poor Nation*. Campbell, CA: Fastpencil Publishing.

Genetski, Robert J., and John W. Skorburg. 1991. *The Impact of State & Local Taxes on Economic Growth: 1975–1987*. Chicago, IL: Chicago Association of Commerce and Industry.

Glans, Matthew. 2013. "Progressive Taxation." *Research & Commentary*. The Heartland Institute.

Glassman, Sarah, Michael Head, David G. Tuerck, and Paul Bachman. 2008. *The Federal Davis-Bacon Act: The Prevailing Mismeasure of Wages*. Boston, MA: Beacon Hill Institute at Suffolk University.

Greenberg, Scott. 2016. "Tax Freedom Day 2016 is April 24." The Tax Foundation. April 6.

Gulibon, Grant R. 1999. *Growing Pennsylvania's Economy: Tax Cuts vs. Economic Development Programs*. Harrisburg, PA: Commonwealth Foundation.

Hartman, David A. 2002. "Does Progressive Taxation Redistribute Income?" *The Road Map to Tax Reform Series* No. 162. Irving, TX: Institute for Policy Innovation.

Hoffer, Adam J., William F. Shughart II, and Michael D. Thomas. 2013. "Sin Taxes: Size, Growth, and Creation of the Sindustry." *Working Paper* No. 13-04. Arlington, VA: Mercatus Center at George Mason University.

Hohman, James M. 2013. *Benefits in Balance: Benchmarking Public Sector Employee Benefits in Michigan*. Midland, MI: Mackinac Center for Public Policy.

Horowitz, Michael. 2001. "Can Tort Law Be Ethical? A Proposal to Curb Ill-Gotten Gains." *Weekly Standard*. March 19.

IMF (International Monetary Fund). 2010. "Will It Hurt? Macroeconomic Effects of Fiscal Consolidation," in *World Economic Outlook: Recovery, Risk, and Rebalancing*. Washington, DC: International Monetary Fund.

Ingram, Johnathan, and Nicholas Horton. 2015. *The ObamaCare Expansion Enrollment Explosion*. Naples, FL: Foundation for Government Accountability.

John Locke Foundation. 2004. *Agenda 2004: A Candidate's Guide to Key Issues in North Carolina Public Policy*. Raleigh, NC: John Locke Foundation.

Johnson, Brian M., and Todd Hollenbeck. 2009. *2009 Index of Worker Freedom: A National Report Card*. Washington, DC: Alliance for Worker Freedom.

Kaplan, Jennifer. 2017. "Philadelphia's Soda Sellers Say Tax Has Reduced Sales by as Much as 50%." *Bloomberg Markets* (website).

Kilroy, Meaghan. 2016. "Moody's: State Pension Liabilities Set to Balloon to $1.75 Trillion." *Pensions & Investments*. October 7.

Kotlikoff, Laurence J. 1993. "The Economic Impact of Replacing Federal Income Taxes with a Sales Tax." *Policy Analysis* No. 193. Cato Institute.

LaFaive, Michael D., and Michael J. Hicks. 2013. "Right-to-Work Laws Improve Economic Well-Being." Mackinac Center for Public Policy.

Lawrence, Geoffrey. 2011. *Who Really Prevails Under Prevailing Wage? Nevada Governments Waste Billions in Subsidies to Union Labor*. Nevada Policy Research Institute.

Liljenquist, Dan. 2013. *Keeping the Promise: State Solutions for Government Pension Reform*. American Legislative Exchange Council.

Lundell, Allan. 2002. "The Effects of the Exemption of School Construction Projects from Ohio's Prevailing Wage Law." *Staff Research Report* No. 149. Ohio Legislative Service Commission.

Maciag, Mike. 2015. "States Turn to Smokers for Band-Aid Budget Fixes." *Governing*. August.

Mattera, Philip. 2014. *Subsidizing the Corporate One Percent: Subsidy Tracker 2.0 Reveals Big-Business Dominance of State and Local Development Incentives*. Washington, DC: Good Jobs First.

McBride, William. 2012. "What Is the Evidence on Taxes and Growth?" *Special Report* No. 207. Tax Foundation.

Moody, J. Scott. 2006. "Higher Taxes Lower Economic Performance." *Maine Issue Brief* No. 3. Maine Heritage Policy Center.

———. 2015. *E-Cigarettes Poised to Save Medicaid Billions*. Charleston, SC: State Budget Solutions.

Mull, Teresa. 2017. "Nevada Legislature Fails to Fund State's ESA Program." *School Reform News*. The Heartland Institute. September.

NASBO (National Association of State Budget Officers). 2015. *State Expenditure Report: Examining Fiscal 2013–2015 State Spending*. Washington, DC: National Association of State Budget Officers.

NRTW (National Right to Work Legal Defense and Education Foundation). 2017. "Right to Work States" (website).

NCSL (National Conference of State Legislatures). 2017. "State Minimum Wages/2017 Minimum Wages by State" (website). January 5.

Neumark, David, and William L. Wascher. 2007. "Minimum Wages and Employment." *Foundations and Trends in Microeconomics* **3** (1–2): 1–182. doi: 10.1561/0700000015.

Nothdurft, John. 2009. "The Best And Worst Ways To Eliminate A Budget Deficit." *Research & Commentary*. The Heartland Institute.

_____. 2013. "The Municipal Government Debt Crisis." *Policy Brief.* The Heartland Institute. June.

Olson, Mancur. 1971. *The Logic of Collective Action*. Cambridge, MA: Harvard University Press.

Oprinescu, Diana. 2013. "Tobacco Taxes: Problems, Not Solutions, for Taxpayers and Budgets." National Taxpayers Union.

Peters, Alan H., and Peter S. Fisher. 2004. "The Failures of Economic Development Incentives." *Journal of the American Planning Association* **70** (1): 27–37.

Pew Charitable Trusts. 2017. "How States are Improving Tax Incentives for Jobs and Growth: A National Assessment of Evaluation Practices." May 3.

Pomerleau, Kyle, and Borean, Richard. 2014. "How High are Capital Gains Tax Rates in Your State?" (website). Tax Foundation.

Poulson, Barry. 2004. *Tax and Spending Limits: Theory, Analysis, and Policy*. Golden, CO: Independence Institute.

Presser, Stephen B. 2002. "How Should the Law of Products Liability be Harmonized? What Americans Can Learn from Europeans." *Global Liability Issues* **2**. Center for Legal Policy at the Manhattan Institute.

Rabushka, Alvin. 2002. "The Colonial Roots of American Taxation, 1607–1700." *Policy Review*. Hoover Institution. August 1.

Ramey, Valerie A. 2013. "Government Spending and Private Activity." In Alberto Alesina and Francesco Giavazzi (editors). *Fiscal Policy after the Financial Crisis*. Chicago, IL: University of Chicago Press, pp. 19–55.

Reed, W. Richard. 2006. "The Robust Relationship Between Taxes and U.S. State Income Growth." *Working Paper* No. 13/2006. Department of Economics, College of Business and Economics, University of Canterbury, Christchurch, New Zealand.

Reed, W. Robert. 2013. "How Right-to-Work Laws Affect Wages." *Journal of Labor Research* **24** (4): 713–30.

Rodu, Brad, Matthew Glans, and Lindsey Stroud. 2017. *Vaping, E-Cigarettes, and Public Policy Toward Alternatives to Smoking*. The Heartland Institute. February.

Schwartz v. *Lopez*. 2016. 132 Nev. Adv. Op. No. 73. September 29.

Sherk, James. 2015. *How Unions and Right-to-Work Laws Affect the Economy: Testimony before Committee on Labor and Government Reform, Wisconsin Senate*. The Heritage Foundation.

Sigritz, Brian. 2015. "State Budgets in 2014 and 2015: Spending and Revenue Growth Remains Limited, As States Experience Slow Growth." Council of State Governments.

Small, Jonathan. 2012. "10 Steps for Improving the State Budget Process." *OCPA Memorandum*. Oklahoma Council of Public Affairs. November 8.

Story Louise. 2012. "As Companies Seek Tax Deals, Governments Pay High Price." *New York Times*.

Tannenwald, Robert. 1997. "State Regulatory Policy and Economic Development." *New England Economic Review* (March/April 1997): 83–99.

Uhler, Lewis K., and Barry Poulson. 2003. *How to Limit Taxes and Spending*. Oklahoma Council of Public Affairs.

———. 2004. "State Budget Problems Lead to Renewed Interest in TELs." *Budget & Tax News*. January 1.

USCB (United States Census Bureau). 2014. "Population Estimates; State Totals: Vintage 2014" (website). United States Census Bureau.

U.S. Chamber of Commerce. 2015. *2015 Lawsuit Climate Survey*. September.

Usgovernmentspending.com. 2017. "Total Budgeted 2017 Government Spending" (website).

Vedder, Richard K. 2001. *Taxes and Economic Growth*. Green Bay, WI: Taxpayers Network.

———. 2005. "Taxes Fuel Historic American Migration." *Budget & Tax News*. December 1.

Viscusi, W. Kip. 1994. "Cigarette Taxation and the Social Consequences of Smoking." *Working Paper* No. 4891. National Bureau of Economic Research. October.

Wagner, Richard E. 2005. "State Excise Taxation: Horse-and-Buggy Taxes in an Electronic Age." *Background Paper* No. 48. Tax Foundation.

Wall Street Journal. 2009. "Millionaires Go Missing." Editorial. May 27.

Will, George. 2015. "Try as They Might, Progressives Can't Make the Case for Progressive Taxation." *National Review* (website). December 5.

Williams, Bob. 2017. "The Time for Pension Reform Is Now." *HuffPost* (website). June 26.

Wolf, Patrick J. 2009. *Research: School Choice in Milwaukee Benefits Some Students, Saves Money*. Fayetteville, AR: University of Arkansas, College of Education and Health Professions.

Zeidman, Betsy, Rick Palacios Jr., and Robert E. Litan. 2010. *Ensuring State and Municipal Solvency*. Santa Monica, CA: Milken Institute.

Zycher, Benjamin. 2013. "State and Local Spending: Do Tax and Expenditure Limits Work?" American Enterprise Institute.

Additional Resources

Additional information about state fiscal policy is available from The Heartland Institute:

■   PolicyBot, The Heartland Institute's free online clearinghouse for the work of other free-market think tanks, contains thousands of documents on state fiscal policy issues. It is on Heartland's website at https://www.heartland.org/policybot/.

■ https://www.heartland.org/topics/government-spending/ is a website devoted to the latest research, news, and commentary about government spending, taxes, and related fiscal policy matters. Read headlines, watch videos, or browse the thousands of documents available from PolicyBot.

■ *Budget & Tax News* is The Heartland Institute's monthly newspaper devoted to government regulation, spending, and tax issues. Subscriptions with digital delivery are free, print subscriptions are $36/year for 10 issues.

Directory

The following national organizations offer valuable information and resources concerning state fiscal policy.

Alliance for Worker Freedom, http://www.atr.org/authors/alliance-worker-freedom

American Legislative Exchange Council, https://www.alec.org/

Institute for Research on the Economics of Taxation, http://iret.org/

Heartland Institute, https://www.heartland.org/

John Locke Foundation, https://www.johnlocke.org/

NASBO – National Association of State Budget Officers, http://www.nasbo.org/home

NBER – National Bureau of Economic Research, http://www.nber.org/

NCPPR – National Center for Public Policy Research, http://www.nationalcenter.org/

NRTWF – National Right to Work Foundation, http://www.nrtw.org/

NTLC – National Tax Limitation Committee, http://limittaxes.org/

NTU – National Taxpayers Union, http://www.ntu.org/

Oklahoma Council of Public Affairs, http://www.ocpathink.org/

Pew Charitable Trusts, http://www.pewtrusts.org/en

State Budget Solutions (a project of the American Legislative Exchange Council), https://www.facebook.com/StateBudgetSolutions/

Tax Foundation, https://taxfoundation.org/

Truth in Accounting, http://www.truthinaccounting.org/

U.S. Chamber of Commerce, Institute for Legal Reform, http://www.instituteforlegalreform.com/

Chapter 9
Federal Tax Policy

Daniel J. Pilla

---

10 Principles of Federal Tax Policy

1. Tax codes should be simple and understandable.
2. Collect taxes in the least invasive manner.
3. Tax collection should be efficient.
4. The tax code should be stable and predictable.
5. Taxes should not be hidden from taxpayers.
6. The tax code should be neutral.
7. Taxes profoundly affect economic growth.
8. The broader the tax base, the better.
9. Everyone should pay the same income tax rate.
10. Perhaps it is time to repeal the income tax.

Introduction

> "Of all the powers conferred upon government
> that of taxation is most liable to abuse."

Loan Association v. *Topeka* (87 U.S. 655 (1874))

The power to tax is the most dangerous and far-reaching of all government powers. It reaches directly or indirectly to all people, all industries, and all elements of society. Taxes always place burdens on businesses, individuals, and the economy. They are a necessary evil. However, patriots should never tolerate unlawful taxes, administered unfairly, or taxes used to punish some individuals or interests while favoring others.

Policymakers and legislators are responsible for adhering to sound constitutional and economic principles when levying taxes, and citizens are responsible for holding legislators accountable if they violate these principles. Abdicating these duties can seriously threaten liberty and justice. The Supreme Court warned in *Loan Association* v. *Topeka*:

> It must be conceded that there are such [private] rights in every free government beyond the control of the State. A government which recognized no such rights, which held the lives, the liberty, and the property of its citizens subject at all times to the absolute disposition and unlimited control of even the most democratic depository of power, is after all but a despotism (87 U.S. 655 (1874)).

The Internal Revenue Service (IRS) has abused its powers in the past and continues to do so. President Richard Nixon famously used the IRS to harass perceived enemies of his administration. During the Obama administration, the IRS delayed or denied approval of tax-exempt status for more than 100 new organizations whose names included "Tea Party," "Patriots," "We the People," and other conservative-sounding words (Terry 2016). Some experts believe this illegal activity by the IRS was responsible for Obama's reelection in 2012 (Veuger *et al.* 2012).

Misconduct by the IRS under Obama marked a bold and disturbing departure from past abuses of power. Whereas past abuses were typically committed by a small number of IRS agents or officials and aimed at specific individuals or possibly violent or criminal groups, under Obama the offenses were "systematically committed by officials in multiple offices across the country over a long period of time against representatives of a grassroots political movement supported by major portions of the American electorate" (*Washington Examiner* 2013). The threat to democracy could not be more apparent.

Thankfully, adherence to sound principles of tax policy can protect liberty and justice, make the administration of taxes less burdensome and unfair, and meet government's revenue needs while not hindering dynamic economic growth. Some of these principles were presented in the previous chapter on state fiscal policy. Here are 10 more principles patriots and honest elected officials should embrace.

Recommended Reading: Peter Ferrara and Lewis Uhler, "Roadmap for the 21st Century: Budget and Tax," *Policy Brief*, The Heartland Institute and National Tax Limitation Committee, December 5, 2016.

1. Tax codes should be simple and understandable.

> The national tax code's overwhelming complexity and ambiguity make it impossible to administer fairly, impose a heavy burden on workers and entrepreneurs, and pose a threat to basic liberties and justice.

The Supreme Court in its 1926 *Connally* v. *General Construction Co.* decision recognized a fundamental right to know what legislation means, especially legislation that creates an affirmative duty to act. The majority wrote, "[A] statute which either forbids or requires the doing of an act in terms so vague that men of common intelligence must necessarily guess at its meaning and differ as to its application, violates the first essential of due process of law" (269 U.S. 385 (1926)).

Overwhelming Complexity

The current tax code is the epitome of a vague statute. In April 2017, Nina E. Olson, the National Taxpayer Advocate, told Congress, "The compliance burdens the current tax code imposes are overwhelming for taxpayers and the IRS alike. ... The tax code, which runs several million words, contains more than 200 tax deductions, credits, exclusions, and similar tax breaks. ... As the National Taxpayer Advocate, I believe the most effective and comprehensive way to reduce taxpayer burden is for Congress to vastly simplify the Internal Revenue Code" (Olson 2017).

In 2016 alone, nearly 41 million citizens faced IRS collection actions, as shown in the table below (IRS 2016, pp. 41–2).

Nearly 41 Million Citizens Faced IRS Collection Actions in 2016	
Type of Action	*Number of Taxpayers Affected*
Penalty assessments	39,573,561
Wage and bank levies	869,196
Tax liens	470,602
Property seizures	436

These figures do not include tens of millions notices the IRS mails annually. Nor do they include the IRS's so-called "soft contacts"; that is, a letter the IRS uses to explain you "might" have done something wrong and you "should" examine your own tax return and records to make the correction before the IRS does.

The tax code's "overwhelming" complexity undermines people's willingness to voluntarily comply with the law, especially when they believe, not without reason, they are being taxed unequally. The President's Advisory Panel on Federal Tax Reform reported in 2005:

> [T]axpayers think that with the myriad of targeted exclusions, deductions, and credits, others may not be paying their fair share—so why should they? Some call this "the cheat or chump syndrome." In addition, clever tax advisors mine the complexity of the tax code to develop and market tax shelters and other schemes clearly designed to manipulate the tax code's hidden loopholes for their clients' exclusive benefit. The perception that the tax code is unfair and easily manipulated undermines voluntary compliance—the foundation of our tax system (p. 4).

Difficulty complying with a complex tax code and decreasing motivation to comply voluntarily are putting millions of Americans in the crosshairs of IRS enforcement actions. The number of civil tax penalties increased from about 14 in 1955 to 170 in 2014 (Olson 2016, p. 324), meaning the possible consequences of an IRS audit are much worse today than they were in the past.

How to Simplify the Tax Code

Nina Olson, the National Taxpayer Advocate, rightly urged the elimination of the many exclusions, deductions, and other breaks in her 2016 annual report to Congress. She recommended a "zero-based budgeting" approach whereby every tax break is eliminated unless lawmakers specifically decide to keep it, "if, on balance, … the public policy benefits of running the provision or program through the tax code outweigh the tax complexity burden that the provision creates for taxpayers and the IRS" (Olson 2016, p. 319). That proposal also was endorsed by the National Commission on Fiscal Responsibility in its 2010 report (p. 29).

Olson admitted eliminating tax breaks is probably politically impossible, since elected officials are beholden to special interests who benefit from the current tax code. The failure by Congress to enact the recommendations of the National Commission on Fiscal Responsibility and Reform was evidence to that effect. So Olson recommended nine more modest reforms:

- Repeal the Alternative Minimum Tax (AMT) for individuals.

- Consolidate the family status provisions that now appear in filing status, personal and dependent exemptions, the child tax credit, the earned income tax credit, the child and dependent care credit, and the separated spouse rule under IRC §7703(b).

- Improve other provisions relating to taxation of the family unit.

- Consolidate 12 existing education savings tax incentives.

- Consolidate 15 existing retirement savings tax incentives.

- Simplify worker classification determinations to minimize employee-versus-independent contractor disputes.

- Eliminate (or reduce) procedural incentives for lawmakers to enact tax sunsets. The tax code contains at least 71 provisions scheduled to expire between 2016 and 2025.

- Eliminate (or simplify) phase-outs.

- Streamline the penalty regime.

These reforms would certainly help simplify the tax code, but the history of past tax reform efforts suggests they are insufficient. Two more promising solutions are the flat-rate income tax and replacing the income tax with a consumption tax, such as the so-called FairTax. These alternatives are discussed in Principle 2, next, and will often come up in discussions of other principles in this chapter.

Policy Agenda
Complexity and ambiguity allow politicians to use the tax code to reward friends and punish opponents. They undermine voluntary compliance and impose a heavy compliance load on workers and employers. Lawmakers should radically simplify the tax code, starting with the National Taxpayer Advocate's nine recommendations.

Recommended Readings: Nina Olson, *National Taxpayer Advocate's 2016 Annual Report to Congress* (Washington, DC: Internal Revenue Service, 2016); Chris Edwards, "Our Complex Tax Code Is Crippling America," *Time* (website), April 11, 2016.

2. Collect taxes in the least invasive manner.

Government has a duty to collect revenue in the least invasive manner. The current federal tax code is the most invasive part of the entire body of federal law.

Federal tax laws affect almost everything we do. The code rewards or penalizes us depending on the choices we make; for example, whether we get or stay married, have children, buy a home, make charitable gifts, change employment, obtain personal and professional education, buy health insurance, save for retirement, make gifts to our children and others, leave an inheritance, and even when and how we die. Businesses are required to file with the IRS information returns that report any payment of $600 or more to a "person" in a year (IRS 1099-MISC).

The tax code requires that *we report to the government* the choices we make on the most important and most personal matters of our lives. Often, we must provide details we do not share even with close friends and family members. Can we trust the government to keep this information confidential? Might it be used against us?

Invasions of Privacy

We can start with what is called "IRS browsing," employees peeking into taxpayers' files for their own purposes. The IRS calls this UNAX, for "unauthorized access," and reported 521 such cases in 2007 alone (Paulson 2008). IRS employees caught "browsing" are typically subjected to only light disciplinary measures such as unpaid leave. Only 185 offenders were prosecuted from 1998 to 2007 under the 1998 Taxpayer Browsing Protection Act and the Computer Fraud and Abuse Act, and offenders typically received probation (*Ibid.*).

A second risk to privacy is outsiders hacking IRS databanks. In 2005, the Government Accountability Office released a report titled "Internal Revenue Service Needs to Remedy Serious Weaknesses over Taxpayer and Bank Secrecy Act Data" (GAO 2005). It found, "in addition to the remaining 21 previously reported weaknesses for which IRS has not completed actions, 39 newly identified information security control weaknesses impair IRS's ability to ensure the confidentiality, integrity, and availability of its sensitive financial and taxpayer data and FinCEN's Bank Secrecy Act data" (p. 2). The report cites IRS's failure to implement access controls over its mainframe computers and "other information security controls relating to physical security, segregation of duties, and service continuity at the facility. Collectively, these weaknesses increase the risk that sensitive taxpayer and Bank Secrecy Act data will be inadequately protected from unauthorized disclosure, modification, use, or destruction" (*Ibid.*).

The report concludes on this sober note: "Until IRS fully implements a comprehensive agencywide information security program, its facilities and computing resources and the information that is processed, stored, and transmitted on its systems will remain vulnerable" (*Ibid.*).

Data Mining

"Data mining"—using a software program to conduct pattern-based queries, searches, or other analyses of databases to find a predictive pattern or anomaly indicative of illegal conduct—poses a third threat to privacy. According to a 2016 U.S. Department of the Treasury report, the IRS uses five data-mining programs:

- Investigative Data Examination Application (IDEA), formerly known as Investigative Data Analytics

- Lead and Case Analytics (LCA)

- Electronic Fraud Detection System (EFDS)

- Return Review Program (RRP)

- FinCEN Query

The report describes IDEA as follows: "By using the IDEA application, special agents and investigative analysts can proactively identify patterns indicative of illegal activities. This tool enhances investigation selection and supports investigative priorities in tax law enforcement, counterterrorism, and other high-priority criminal investigations. The IDEA application uses data for both reactive and proactive queries. Reactive queries are a result of specific, targeted investigations; proactive queries are the result of pattern matching to generate leads" (Department of the Treasury 2016, p. 23).

The report says the purpose of data mining is "to detect suspicious financial transactions indicative of money laundering, terrorism, and other financial crimes" (*Ibid.*, p. 24). The programs may succeed in this, but the possibility that IDEA and other data-mining programs will mistake innocent financial transactions or investment decisions for illegal or criminal activities, triggering audits and investigations, is very real.

This threat to privacy is compounded when the IRS shares its data-mining results with other government agencies or non-federal entities conducting their own investigations or research. All taxpayer data are supposed to be private and confidential under 26 U.S.C. §6103, but subsections (c) through (o) of §6103 contain more than a dozen exceptions to this general rule. Examples include disclosures to state tax officials and certain state and local law enforcement agencies, to certain committees of Congress, to the president and certain other persons, to federal employees and the courts for tax administration purposes, for "statistical purposes," and to contractors for tax administration purposes. In other words, §6103 falls well short of guaranteeing the confidentiality of information we share with the IRS.

Foreign Account Tax Compliance Act (FATCA)

A fourth privacy threat is the Foreign Account Tax Compliance Act, or FATCA. The act compels foreign bankers, brokers, insurers, and mutual funds to collect U.S. Social Security numbers and report account balances to the IRS or risk being assessed a 30 percent withholding tax. Willful failure to file a foreign bank account report could lead to a penalty of 50 percent of the value of the account or $100,000, whichever is greater.

In a lawsuit filed in 2015, U.S. Senator Rand Paul and five U.S. citizens living abroad called the law "a sweeping financial surveillance program of unprecedented scope that allows the Internal Revenue Service to peer into the financial affairs of any U.S. citizen with a foreign bank account" (Crawford *et al.* 2015, p. 2). According to a summary of the suit produced for Courthouse News Service, the plaintiffs say "FATCA allows the Internal Revenue Service to collect information about U.S. citizens' account balances and transactions, information it cannot collect on U.S. citizens living domestically. The law requires foreign banks to report citizens' account information to the IRS even when the agency has no reason to suspect that citizen of violating U.S. tax laws" (Bailey 2015).

FATCA was enacted during the Obama administration in an effort to crack down on wealthy Americans thought to be hiding their wealth in foreign accounts. Like so many other laws and regulations, it has the effect of violating the privacy rights of millions of Americans who are not wealthy and not guilty of violating any tax laws.

Less Invasive Taxation

The national government could raise tax revenues sufficient to meet its spending needs without requiring taxpayers to surrender to the IRS massive amounts of personal information. Two alternatives have been proposed, studied, and publicly debated for many years. They are the flat tax and a national sales tax. The most popular national sales tax proposal is the FairTax, introduced in Congress as H.R. 25 and S. 18.

The Flat Tax

The case for replacing the current tax code with a flat-rate income tax has been made by many authors since the 1980s. The idea is to collapse current tax brackets into a single rate and abolish some or all exemptions, credits, and deductions so that the single tax rate can be as low as 10 percent, more often 15 percent to 20 percent. Such a tax code would be so simple most taxpayers could file their taxes using a postcard. The IRS would no longer be necessary or, if it remains, could be a small fraction of its current size.

Flat tax plans have been proposed by Robert E. Hall and Alvin Rabushka (19 percent), Steve Forbes (17 percent), presidential candidate Ben Carson (10 percent, later raised to 15 percent), and U.S. Senators Ted Cruz and Rand Paul (10 percent on personal income, 16 percent on corporate income). Although they all share the goal of radically simplifying the tax code, these plans differ in how they treat corporate income, the personal deduction, payroll taxes, the death tax, and more.

One flat tax plan that is unique is the "Freedom Tax" written and explained by Washington, DC-based tax attorney James K. Jeanblanc on the website www.thefreedomtax.org. Jeanblanc's plan would tax all income (whether business or individual) at the same 10 percent rate; there would be no personal deductions, exemptions, or tax credits, and most interesting, the tax "would be collected at the source of payment in the case of salaries and wages, interest, dividend, and retirement income. Once received, this income would be fully taxed" (Jeanblanc 2017). The result would be no tax return filing by individuals.

There is a lively debate about what the single tax rate should be, how much revenue it would generate, and whether a flat tax can be designed that would survive the natural inclinations of politicians to add brackets and raise the rate and of bureaucrats to impose more reporting requirements on filers. But one thing seems certain: Any of these plans would make the federal income tax much less intrusive. They all merit the attention and perhaps support of patriots and policymakers.

The FairTax

The FairTax is a proposal to replace the federal personal income tax, corporate income tax, payroll (FICA) tax, capital gains, alternative minimum, self-employment, and estate and gifts taxes with a single-rate federal retail sales tax. Every person living in the United States would pay a sales tax on purchases of new goods and services, excluding necessities, of approximately 23 percent. Every household would receive a "prebate" set to offset any taxes on spending up to the poverty level (Tuerck et al. 2007).

By replacing virtually all income-based taxes at the national level,

the FairTax would end the invasions of privacy due to the current tax
code. It would even abolish the IRS. By dramatically reducing the
number of entities charged with collecting the tax, it would reduce
administrative costs and opportunities for tax evasion. According to the
Beacon Hill Institute and other researchers, the national sales tax could
be set at 23 percent and still raise sufficient revenue to meet the national
government's spending needs.

The website of Americans For Fair Taxation, www.fairtax.org,
provides extensive background and commentary on the FairTax.

Policy Agenda

The complexity of the current tax code makes it invasive and a threat to
privacy. A less invasive system would benefit taxpayers by reducing
compliance costs and protecting their privacy. Tax administrators would
need fewer resources to manage a system that does not attempt to
monitor every aspect of the financial lives of all taxpayers. Less
enforcement action would mean fewer collectors spending fewer hours
tracking down bank accounts, paychecks, and other assets to levy and
seize.

The Flat Tax and FairTax are two tax systems that would be much
less invasive and could raise the revenue needed for legitimate
government functions without placing revenue officers in the homes and
offices of Americans.

Recommended Readings: Robert E. Hall and Alvin Rabushka, *The Flat
Tax* (Stanford, CA: Hoover Institution Press, second edition, 2007);
Daniel J. Pilla, *How to Fire the IRS: A Plan to Eliminate the Income Tax
and the IRS* (Stillwater, MN: Winning Publications, 1993).

3. Tax collection should be efficient.

> The federal tax code imposes collection and compliance
> costs of 65 cents for every dollar of revenue collected.
> That is a massive and unnecessary burden on society.

The IRS regularly asserts it is extremely efficient in collecting taxes. In
2016, the agency reported collecting gross tax revenue of more than
$3.3 trillion with a work force of 80,825 employees. Given the agency's
budget of approximately $11.7 billion, the cost of collecting $100 of tax

was just 36 cents (IRS 2016, pp. 63, 65, 68). However, these numbers are misleading.

Spending $2.1 Trillion to Raise $3.3 Trillion

The IRS's estimate does not take into account the costs *borne by the public* to comply with income tax laws. In April 2017, Nina Olson, the National Taxpayer Advocate, told Congress, "My staff analyzed IRS data for 2015 and determined that individuals and businesses spend about six billion hours a year complying with the tax code's filing requirements—not including the millions of additional hours they spend responding to IRS audits or notices. If tax compliance were an industry, it would be one of the largest in the United States. To consume six billion hours, the 'tax industry' requires the equivalent of three million full-time workers" (NTA 2016, p. 310).

In 2008, the National Taxpayer Advocate estimated that the out-of-pocket cost associated with tax return filing alone was approximately $193 billion annually: "This is a staggering 14 percent of aggregate income tax receipts" (NTA 2008, p. 4). Even the NTA did not address the whole picture. It ignored the cost of challenging penalty assessments and responding to the tens of millions of annual notices and letters, as well as millions of annual audits and appeals, tax litigation, enforced collection, economic disincentives, and tax evasion and avoidance.

When all these factors are accounted for, the cost of compliance is close to 65 percent of the amount collected (Pilla 1993, p. 204; Payne 1993). That is to say, for every dollar of tax paid to the Treasury, it costs citizens and businesses 65 cents to get it there. Given that $3.3 trillion was paid to the IRS in 2016, society incurred a collection cost of nearly $2.1 trillion. That is nearly $18,000 per household in the United States, a staggering cost that produces no social benefit.

Making Federal Tax Collection More Efficient

All of the recommendations to simplify the federal tax code made by the National Taxpayer Advocate and listed previously (see Principle 1) would make tax collection more efficient. Many of the recommendations made to make tax collection less invasive (Principle 2) would have the same effect, though the IRS may argue that reining in data-mining could hinder collection enforcement efforts.

Moving to a flat tax would dramatically reduce compliance and enforcement costs. Most tax policy experts writing about the flat tax estimate it would lower the cost of compliance by 90 percent or more. Reducing the number of tax brackets and eliminating deductions reduces the need to call the IRS to answer questions or to hire accountants or lawyers to file tax returns. Enforcement becomes vastly easier when the incentives to misstate income or spending or hide the sources of income are removed by taxing all income at a single low rate.

Trading in the income tax for a single-rate national consumption tax, like the FairTax, would likely reduce compliance costs even more than changing to a flat tax. The FairTax would dramatically reduce the number of collection points needing to collect information and tax dollars and submit them to the government. Back in 1999, this author calculated the savings to a single state, Minnesota, of moving from an income tax to a broad-based sales tax as the principal means of collecting the state's revenue. The state could have expected to achieve a reduction of 82 percent in the number of collection points, 88 percent in the number of taxpayer questions, 63 percent in the state tax return filing obligation of the average business, and about $38 million overall in the state's administrative costs. Also, there could have been an annual savings of at least $4.96 million in return processing costs (Pilla 2000).

Policy Agenda

At a time when both taxpayers and governments are straining to find ways to save money, ways to improve the efficiency of tax collection need to be on the table. Two ways are the flat tax and the FairTax.

Recommended Readings: James L. Payne, *Costly Returns: The Burdens of the U.S. Tax System* (Oakland, CA: Institute for Contemporary Studies Press, 1993); Joshua D. McCaherty, "The Cost of Tax Compliance," Tax Foundation, September 11, 2014.

4. The tax code should be stable and predictable.

> A tax code that is unstable and unpredictable makes planning difficult or impossible, imposing uncertainty and huge costs on businesses and individuals.

Frequent changes to a tax code make financial planning difficult or even impossible. The efficiency of markets is adversely affected because the passage of a change in the tax code can turn financially sound investment decisions into bad ones and bad ones into seemingly good ones. Because the current federal tax code affects so much of our personal lives, an unstable tax code also affects everything from our marriages to our retirement plans, and many other decisions in between.

The Constantly Changing Code

Congress is constantly changing the tax code and the IRS is constantly releasing new rules and instructions on how to comply with a sprawling and vague tax code. On its website in 2017, the National Taxpayer Advocate reported, "according to a tally compiled by a leading publisher of tax information, there have been approximately 4,428 changes to the tax code over the past 10 years, an average of more than one a day, including an estimated 579 changes in 2010 alone" (NTA 2017).

Some changes to the tax code have resulted in retroactive tax increases. Critics were appalled the Supreme Court seemed to violate the clear meaning and foundational principle in Article I, Section 9, Clause 3, that "no ex post facto Law shall be passed," when in 1994 the Court approved, in *United States* v. *Carlton* (512 U.S. 26 (1994)), a decision by Congress to repeal a tax deduction retroactively, thereby increasing an estate's tax liability by more than $600,000.

Parts of the tax code also come and go without any action by Congress or the courts. In 2009 and 2010, 24 tax laws expired, and six more expired by 2012 (Joint Committee on Taxation 2008). In 2016, the National Taxpayer Advocate said the tax code contains at least 71 provisions that are scheduled to expire between 2016 and 2025 (Olson 2016).

The Cato Institute's Chris Edwards, writing at *Time* magazine's website in 2016, noted, "the latest layer of complexity was added by the Affordable Care Act, which manipulates our health choices through the tax system. If you don't have health insurance, you calculate how much you get penalized. If you do have individual insurance, you calculate the tax credits you receive. If you get advance credits during the year, then you recalculate your benefits when you file. And so on" (Edwards 2016). The IRS is trying to be helpful: It offers a 24-page Affordable Care Act overview, a 19-page guide for penalties, and a 71-page guide to credits. But the Affordable Care Act (a.k.a. Obamacare) may not even exist in 2018.

Making Planning Impossible

Changes in the tax code interfere with people's ability to plan their personal and business affairs. Between 1986 and 2000, Congress changed the requirements for making estimated tax payments seven times (IRS 2000, p. 34). Changing the law on estimated taxes every other year is one reason IRS assesses the penalty for failure to pay estimated taxes so often. In 2009, the IRS assessed that penalty against 7.6 million individuals and more than 243,000 businesses (IRS 2009, p. 42).

The President's Advisory Panel on Federal Tax Reform observed the expiring provisions and phase-ins and phase-outs of various provisions "are a nuisance at best, and a negative force at worst, in the daily economic lives of American families and businesses" (2005, 5, p. 5). The panel concluded:

> The tax system is both unstable and unpredictable. Frequent changes in the tax code, which often add to or undo previous policies, as well as the enactment of temporary provisions, result in uncertainty for businesses and families. This volatility is harmful to the economy and creates additional compliance costs (*Ibid.*, p. xiii).

Why the Tax Code Changes

Why is the federal tax code changed so frequently? One reason is the assumption by policymakers and much of the public that the tax code can be used to achieve non-revenue ends. It is commonly agreed the tax code should encourage home ownership, marriage, raising children, and so on and so on. If social engineering is the goal and changing the tax code is the means, then there is no limit to the number of times the code should be changed.

The demand for changes to the code is very high since even small changes can produce millions of dollars in benefits for a small number of taxpayers or businesses. Economists recognize this as the familiar problem of "concentrated benefits and dispersed costs": Government programs often produce large benefits for small numbers of people, who can readily organize to lobby for them. The costs are widely dispersed, perhaps amounting to only a few pennies per person, and such large groups are difficult or costly to organize.

Elected officials are vulnerable to constituents, especially campaign donors, asking for their help in getting changes made to the tax code to advantage them. The code is so complex already, what is the harm in making one more change? And perhaps the current code is "unfair" to the campaign donor, making the change a positive "reform."

Well-intended bureaucrats working inside the IRS and other government agencies often change how the tax code is administered to address contradictions and uncertainties in the code. Given the code's enormous size and thousands of rules and policies, an endless number of "corrections" could be made.

Policy Agenda

A more stable and predictable tax code is possible only if it addresses all these reasons for constant change. Policymakers and the public must be persuaded the tax code should be used only to raise revenue, and not to achieve other social goals. There should be so few rules and regulations in the code that special-interest groups, campaign donors, and bureaucrats are not tempted to add more or "fix" those that still exist. Parts of the code should not be scheduled to "sunset."

A stable tax code is likely to resemble a flat tax or national consumption tax, since they address the reasons why the current tax code changes so frequently. However, as noted earlier, both of those alternatives can still be vulnerable to the natural tendency of politicians and bureaucrats to meddle in the operation of government programs. There is no sure solution.

Recommended Readings: Tax Foundation, *Options for Reforming America's Tax Code* (Washington, DC: Tax Foundation, June 6, 2016); David R. Burton, "A Guide to Tax Reform in the 115th Congress," *Backgrounder*, The Heritage Foundation, February 10, 2017.

5. Taxes should not be hidden from taxpayers.

> Americans generally have no idea how much they pay in taxes because taxes are taken out of their paychecks by their employers.

When asked how much money they paid in federal income taxes the prior year, many people reply, "I didn't pay anything. I got a refund!" They do not remember the thousands of dollars employers withheld from their paychecks for federal and state tax payments. That is a big problem because taxes hidden from taxpayers can be raised without their knowledge or unfairly imposed or avoided.

Automatic Income Tax Withholding

About 85 percent of the income earners in America do not write a check to the government for their taxes. Since the tax is taken out of their paychecks by their employers, they do not even see the money. As a result, Americans generally don't appreciate how much they are paying. The 1996 report of the National Commission on Economic Growth and Tax Reform called attention to the danger of this arrangement:

The history of hidden taxes, rapidly rising rates, and perpetual budget deficits proves that what you don't know can hurt you. The current system hides the cost of government behind a chronic deficit and a maddening multiplicity of taxes—many of which are virtually invisible to the taxpayer who pays them. How much did we pay in payroll taxes last year? What excise taxes were hidden in the prices of the products we bought? What [is] the tax cost of exclusions, deductions, and corporate income taxes? Few of us know the answers (p. 85).

Our system of automatic income tax withholding by employers arose in the 1940s as a temporary war-time expedient to help meet the country's urgent need for tax revenue. (Withholding of Social Security and Medicare taxes started sooner, in the 1930s.) Milton Friedman, at the time working for the Treasury Department, proposed it. He would go on to become the most influential economist of the twentieth century, and he always regretted having made that fateful suggestion. In his 1998 memoir coauthored with his wife, Rose, he wrote, "It never occurred to me at the time that I was helping to develop machinery that would make possible a government that I would come to criticize severely as too large, too intrusive, too destructive of freedom. Yet, that was precisely what I was doing" (Friedman and Friedman 1998, p. 123).

Social Security and Medicare

In addition to withholding income taxes, employers are required by the Federal Insurance Contributions Act (FICA) to withhold three other taxes from the wages they pay employees: a 12.4 percent Social Security tax, a 2.9 percent Medicare tax, and beginning in 2013 as part of Obamacare, a 0.9 percent Medicare surtax when the employee earns more than $200,000. Like the income tax, these taxes are deducted from workers' paychecks as the income is earned. It then becomes the responsibility of the employers to pay the money to the IRS.

Unlike the income tax, employees never file a Social Security tax return, never write a check to the IRS for this tax, and never keep records to correctly figure the tax. They are never subject to an audit or to enforced collection if the tax is not paid by their employers. The money simply disappears from their paychecks. (This is not true of the self-employed. They must calculate their Social Security taxes on Schedule SE and include the tax on Form 1040. Since the tax is figured as a flat percentage of business profit, they are subject to audit as to the amount of tax and collection if the tax is not paid.)

As "easy" as all this sounds, it means most taxpayers never know the true cost of Social Security—or, for that matter, government in general.

Make Taxes Crystal Clear

Taxes that are highly visible are more stable, tend to stay low, and are not generally subject to tinkering. The best example of this is retail sales taxes imposed by state governments. Just compare the number of changes in a state's sales tax laws to changes made in the Internal Revenue Code during the past 10 years. The contrast is staggering. In Minnesota, one can practically count on one hand the number of sales tax law changes that occurred since the sales tax began in 1963.

One way to make taxes crystal clear to taxpayers is to eliminate the requirement that employers withhold taxes from the paychecks of employees. For example, workers paid $1,000 per week would receive a check or a notice of a direct deposit into their bank account of $1,000. They would then need to pay the IRS themselves the amount their employer would normally withhold. Or those employees could keep their entire $1,000 and the rest of the money they earn during the year, but be required by April 15 to pay what they owed for the entire year. This would make it crystal clear to every worker just how much the government takes from them (Vance 2005).

Another way to make taxes more visible is to shift from the national income tax to a national consumption tax, such as the FairTax. Such a substantial tax (possibly 23 percent) paid at the point of sale is noticeable, and opposition to raising the tax is likely to be widespread. This is in contrast to another kind of sales tax, the value-added tax or VAT, which is imposed on the "value added" at each stage of the production process and so is largely invisible to buyers. A VAT fails the transparency test (Mitchell 2005).

Policy Agenda

Letting people see how much they are being forced to pay in taxes every time they are paid or when making every retail purchase would lead to considerable public support for cutting everyone's taxes. In fact, ending tax withholding by employers would likely cause a tax revolt of a size not seen since the Boston Tea Party rebellion of 1773. But maybe that is the point of talking about it now. Does the country need another Boston Tea Party?

Recommended Readings: Laurence Vance, "The Curse of the Withholding Tax," The Mises Institute, 2005; Daniel Mitchell, "Beware the Value-Added Tax," *Backgrounder,* The Heritage Foundation, May 16, 2005.

6. The tax code should be neutral.

Selectively targeting some businesses for heavier tax burdens while giving other businesses tax breaks is an illegitimate use of the taxing power of government.

Chief Justice John Marshall, in the 1819 case *McCulloch* v. *The State of Maryland,* wrote that the power to tax is "the power to destroy" (17 U.S. 316 (1819)). The case dealt with the 10 percent excise tax Congress imposed on the circulation of all bank notes other than those issued by the national bank. Within two years of its passage, the tax drove out of circulation every state bank note.

Destruction through Taxation

In her 2016 testimony to Congress, NTA Nina Olson reported, "the Treasury Department has estimated that tax expenditures [i.e., lost revenue due to exemptions, deductions, or credits] in FY 2016 came to about $1.4 trillion—more than the $1.2 trillion Congress appropriated to fund the entire federal government. Put simply, Congress now spends more money each year through the tax code than it spends through the appropriations process" (Olson 2016).

Governments should not interfere with the ability of legitimate businesses to compete in the marketplace on equal footing with one another. Otherwise, the only businesses with a chance to succeed are those that are able and willing to pay the lobbyists and peddlers who influence Congress and state legislatures. Research on the negative effects of corporate welfare was summarized in Principle 5 of Chapter 8, on state fiscal policy, and need not be repeated here.

Citizens across the political spectrum are disgusted by what they rightly understand to be a corrupt, crony system in which raw political power, especially the power to punish or reward selectively with taxes, determines who gets what. The 1996 National Commission on Economic Growth and Tax Reform summarized well the essential elements of sound tax policy:

> The tax code should be used to raise revenue to run the government while doing the least possible damage to the economy. This means leaving individuals free to make decisions and to set priorities based on economic reality—not on the bureaucratic whims of Washington, D.C. ... The result of the biases and distortions in the current system is to make the market

less free, the system less fair, and families less financially secure (p. 20).

The 2010 National Commission on Fiscal Responsibility similarly concluded, "corporate tax reform should eliminate special subsidies for different industries. By eliminating business tax expenditures—currently more than 75—the corporate tax rate can be significantly reduced while contributing to deficit reduction. A lower overall tax rate will improve American business competitiveness. Abolishing special subsidies will also create an even playing field for all businesses instead of artificially picking winners and losers" (p. 33).

The Supreme Court condemned the selective targeting of industries for heavier taxation in *Loan Association* v. *Topeka*, referenced above, involving the use of government bonds to finance railroads and the taxes imposed to pay for the bonds. Referring to government's power to impose selective taxes, the Court stated:

> This power can as readily be employed against one class of individuals and in favor of another, so as to ruin the one class and give unlimited wealth and prosperity to the other, if there is no implied limitation of the uses for which the power may be exercised. To lay with one hand the power of the government on the property of the citizen, and with the other to bestow it upon favored individuals to aid private enterprises and build up private fortunes, is none the less a robbery because it is done under the forms of law and is called taxation (87 U.S. 655, 664 (1874)).

The IRS versus Guns and Bitcoin

Operation Choke Point and the IRS's recent targeting of the alternative currency called Bitcoin are two very recent examples of how the IRS, working with other government agencies, is using its power to discriminate against specific industries and individuals.

Operation Choke Point was another Obama administration effort to bypass Congress and achieve its political agenda through regulations, in this case by pressuring banks to withhold lines of credit, freeze assets, and prohibit online sales by companies selling products opposed and demonized by the administration, such as guns, pornography, drug paraphernalia, and payday loans. The Justice Department, working with other government agencies including the IRS through a collaboration called the Financial Fraud Enforcement Task Force, urged banks and payment processors to cut their ties with companies in the targeted industries even though the companies were selling legal products and had valid licenses and good credit histories.

Peter Weinstock, a lawyer at Hunton & Williams LLP, was quoted in

The Washington Times saying "this administration has very clearly told the banking industry which customers they feel represent 'reputational risk' to do business with ... so financial institutions are reacting to this extraordinary enforcement arsenal by being ultra-conservative in who they do business with: Any companies that engage in any margin of risk as defined by this administration are being dropped" (Riddell 2014).

The same article quoted Richard Riese, a senior vice president at the American Bankers Association, saying, "We're being threatened with a regulatory regime that attempts to foist on us the obligation to monitor all types of transactions. All of this is predicated on a notion that the banks are a choke point for all businesses" (*Ibid.*).

Another example of IRS targeting is its campaign against Bitcoin, a novel type of digital currency. In November 2016, the IRS filed a "John Doe" summons seeking to require U.S. Bitcoin exchange Coinbase to turn over records about every transaction of every user from 2013 to 2015. Jim Harper, writing for the Cato Institute's *Cato at Liberty* blog, observed: "That demand is shocking in sweep, and it includes: 'complete user profile, history of changes to user profile from account inception, complete user preferences, complete user security settings and history (including confirmed devices and account activity), complete user payment methods, and any other information related to the funding sources for the account/wallet/vault, regardless of date'" (Harper 2016).

Harper notes the IRS summons violates Fourth Amendment protections against search and seizure without evidence of probable guilt, is spectacularly over-reaching in the information it seeks, and seems intended to frighten away investors in the currency. While this is done in the name of battling "tax cheats," it seems clear the real target is digital currencies, opposed by the Obama administration because they allow financial transactions to occur without federal agencies monitoring them.

Policy Agenda

A good tax code, like the administration of justice itself, must be blind to the identities of the individuals or interests that come before it. Choosing winners is bad economic policy and deeply corrosive to justice. The current federal tax code invites this abuse, another reason it must be replaced.

Recommended Readings: Jim Harper, "The IRS Believes All Bitcoin Users Are Tax Cheats," *Cato at Liberty,* November 18, 2016; Robert Carroll, John E. Chapoton, Maya MacGuineas, and Diane Lim Rogers, "Moving Forward with Bipartisan Tax Policy," *Working Paper* No. 5, Tax Foundation, 2009.

7. Taxes profoundly affect economic growth.

The current federal tax code has profoundly negative effects on economic growth. A sound tax system should be pro-economic growth.

Two presidential commissions on taxes highlighted how the complex and ever-changing federal tax code harms the U.S. economy. The 1996 National Commission on Economic Growth and Tax Reform declared,

> Our country is poised to help lead the world into a new era of economic growth fueled by an information-age technological revolution that can yield unparalleled expansion in jobs, productivity, innovation, and prosperity. We must embrace this opportunity and challenge. However, such an embrace will prove difficult, perhaps impossible, if we remain saddled with our current tax code. The current system is indefensible. It is riddled with special interest tax breaks, and it overtaxes both labor and capital. We must construct a tax system that reflects our highest values and unleashes our greatest potential (p. 3).

In 2010, the National Commission on Fiscal Responsibility similarly found, "the tax code is rife with inefficiencies, loopholes, incentives, tax earmarks, and baffling complexity. We need to lower tax rates, broaden the base, simplify the tax code, and bring down the deficit. We need to reform the corporate tax system to make America the best place to start and grow a business and create jobs" (p. 12).

High Taxes Impede Economic Growth

In 2001, economist Richard Vedder at Ohio University examined several dozen measures of taxes and spending in the years 1957, 1977, and 1997. He found, "In every single case, without exception, the results are consistent: High or rising taxes are associated with lower amounts of economic growth. The use of more sophisticated statistical models produces the same sort of result: higher taxes, lower growth" (Vedder 2001, p. 9).

Other researchers, including J. Scott Moody (2006) at the Maine Heritage Policy Center and Scott A. Hodge at the Tax Foundation, have found the same thing: High taxes lead to slower economic growth. According to Hodge, "Taxes are an important cost to business, as important as the cost of labor and raw materials. ... Nearly all of the best states raise sufficient revenue without imposing at least one of the three major state taxes: sales taxes, personal income taxes, and corporate income taxes" (Stanek 2006).

The Founding Fathers had the wisdom and foresight to know imposing direct taxes on the determinants of economic growth would inhibit growth. That is why they rejected imposing direct taxes on incomes, savings, and investments. Instead, they favored indirect taxes on consumption. The nation's first treasury secretary, Alexander Hamilton, observed that taxing the "articles of our own growth and manufacture are more prejudicial" to economic growth than excise taxes (Morris 1957, p. 258).

Progressive Taxes Slow Economic Growth

While high taxes contribute to slow economic growth and low taxes make faster economic growth possible, the type of tax also matters. Extensive research finds progressive taxation has a greater negative impact on economic growth than other types of taxation.

William McBride, an economist with the Tax Foundation, conducted a survey of academic literature on taxes and economic growth in 2012 and reported finding 26 studies "going back to 1983, and all but three of those studies, and every study in the last fifteen years, find a negative effect of taxes on growth. Of those studies that distinguish between types of taxes, corporate income taxes are found to be most harmful, followed by personal income taxes, consumption taxes and property taxes" (McBride 2012). McBride explains why progressive taxes have the greatest negative effect on economic growth:

> These results support the Neo-classical view that income and wealth must first be produced and then consumed, meaning that taxes on the factors of production, i.e., capital and labor, are particularly disruptive of wealth creation. Corporate and shareholder taxes reduce the incentive to invest and to build capital. Less investment means fewer productive workers and correspondingly lower wages. Taxes on income and wages reduce the incentive to work. Progressive income taxes, where higher income is taxed at higher rates, reduce the returns to education, since high incomes are associated with high levels of education, and so reduce the incentive to build human capital. Progressive taxation also reduces investment, risk taking, and entrepreneurial activity since a disproportionately large share of these activities is done by high income earners (*Ibid.*, p. 2).

Negative Impacts on Workers and Entrepreneurs

The complexity and ambiguity of the tax codes also harm businesses and entrepreneurs, resulting in slower economic growth. In 1987, for example, the IRS issued a list of 20 factors employers should consider when deciding whether a worker is an employee or an independent contractor. (See Revenue Ruling 87-41, 1987-1 C.B. 296.) According to Nina Olson, the list is "complex, subjective, and does not always produce clear answers. The potential for errors and abuse is high in those gray areas where not all factors yield the same result, particularly because there are no weighting rules" (Olson 2016).

In 2015, the Department of Labor issued a memo in which it adopted its own more expansive interpretation of the definition of "employees" under the Fair Labor Standards Act. (See United States Department of Labor, Administrator's Interpretation No. 2015-1, July 15, 2015.) Employers and workers are often bewildered by the conflicting requirements.

If the IRS reclassifies a worker after an audit, the employer may be liable for employment taxes for a number of years, interest, penalties, and potential disqualification of employee benefit plans. The worker may have to pay self-employment taxes and lose the ability to take certain business-related deductions. Workers have no right to petition the classification determination to the U.S. Tax Court.

Innovators and entrepreneurs find the tax code especially burdensome. A survey conducted in 2016 of members of the National Association for the Self-Employed (NASE) found 34 percent of those who reported earning income in the sharing economy (i.e., individuals typically using the internet to borrow or rent from each other assets such as cars and homes) did not know they needed to file quarterly estimated tax payments, 36 percent did not understand what records they would need to maintain as a small business for tax purposes, and 43 percent did not set aside money to meet their tax obligations or know how much they owed (Bruckner 2016). Many of these entrepreneurs will be subject to penalties or worse because the tax code is just too complicated for them to understand or has never been explained to them.

Corporate Taxes

Corporations pay a federal corporate income tax of 35 percent on net earnings plus additional state and local levies that average 4 percent, for a total tax rate of 39 percent. Investors pay an additional tax of up to 23.8 percent on dividends paid out by the corporation to its shareholders. A capital gains tax (a tax on the increased value of a stock or asset while in the possession of the taxpayer) ranging from 15 percent to 20 percent (depending on the taxpayer's income tax bracket) is yet another tax on top of those. As a result, corporations are taxed more in the United States than companies in any other developed country.

In 2010, the National Commission on Fiscal Responsibility described the U.S. corporate income tax as "a patchwork of overly complex and inefficient provisions that creates perverse incentives for investment." It found

> the corporate income tax ... hurts America's ability to compete. On the one hand, statutory rates in the U.S. are significantly higher than the average for industrialized countries (even as revenue collection is low), and our method of taxing foreign income is outside the norm. The U.S. is one of the only industrialized countries with a hybrid system of taxing active foreign-source income. The current system puts U.S. corporations at a competitive disadvantage against their foreign competitors. A territorial tax system should be adopted to help put the U.S. system in line with other countries, leveling the playing field (p. 28).

The commission recommended creating a single corporate tax rate set at between 23 percent and 29 percent, eliminating all tax "expenditures" for businesses, and moving to a territorial tax system.

Policy Agenda

Americans want an economy that is diverse, dynamic, and growing. Such an economy requires rising employment, savings, investments, and productivity. Today's tax system imposes heavy and unnecessary burdens on these factors. To minimize the negative effect of taxes on job creation, income tax rates must be reduced, the tax code made less complex and progressive, and corporate taxes must be reduced significantly.

Recommended Readings: National Commission on Economic Growth and Tax Reform, *Unleashing America's Potential: A Pro-growth, Pro-family Tax System for the 21st Century* (Washington, DC: U.S. Government Printing Office, 1996); Chris Edwards, "Options for Tax Reform," *Policy Analysis* No. 536, Cato Institute, 2005.

8. The broader the tax base, the better.

A broad tax base is pro-growth, makes lower tax rates possible, and fosters equal treatment of taxpayers.

A tax base is the sum of the values of all the financial streams or assets on which a tax is imposed. An income tax draws revenue from earnings but not from other sources. Similarly, a sales tax draws revenue from consumption but not earnings or savings.

Politicians delight in manipulating the tax bases of existing taxes and proposing new taxes on previously untaxed activities or assets. They do this because such alterations of the tax code are often hidden from most taxpayers, allowing politicians to grant favors or punish rivals without most voters knowing. But over time the tax base becomes riddled with exceptions, deductions, and credits, making it necessary to raise the tax rate in order to collect the same amount of revenue as before.

A good rule of thumb for a sound tax system is: The broader the tax base, the better. A broad tax base is pro-growth, makes lower tax rates possible, and fosters equal treatment of taxpayers.

Dangerous Shrinking Base

The National Taxpayer Advocate's 2016 report to Congress reports, "Based on all the comments we receive every year in the Taxpayer Advocate Service and our experience in handling hundreds of thousands of taxpayer cases a year, we believe that lowering rates in exchange for broadening the tax base would be an excellent bargain for U.S. taxpayers" (p. 324). Unfortunately, Congress didn't get the message.

As previously reported in this chapter, the federal tax code is riddled with tax breaks, deductions, credits, and loopholes, each reducing the base of the tax and requiring a higher putative tax rate on most taxpayers. Tax "expenditures"— i.e., lost revenue due to exemptions, deductions, or credits—in 2016 exceeded by $200 billion the entire amount Congress appropriated to fund the national government. Business tax breaks numbered more than 75 in 2010.

As lawmakers add more tax breaks for lower-income citizens and limit those for higher-income citizens, the tax burden is being disproportionately loaded onto an increasingly smaller segment of income earners. In 2014, the oft-demonized top 1 percent of income earners accounted for 40 percent of income tax revenue. The top 5 percent of earners accounted for 60 percent of revenue, and the top 10 percent of earners contributed 70 percent. By contrast, the bottom

50 percent of income earners paid only 2.75 percent of federal income taxes (Greenberg 2017, p. 9).

As more people are removed from the tax rolls through credits, deductions, exemptions, and the like, the burden on the remaining taxpayers must necessarily increase, increasing incentives to invest in lobbyists to obtain even more tax breaks and lawyers to find ways to qualify for existing tax breaks. High marginal tax rates distort investment decisions and reduce the incentive to work and take risks. The motive to comply voluntarily with tax rules diminishes as more and more people decide to cheat rather than be "chumps."

Power without Paying

One problem created by the disproportionate distribution of the burden is that a growing portion of the population pays little or no taxes, yet has the electoral power to dictate spending policy at the ballot box. This problem is real, although perhaps too complicated for elected officials and candidates for public office to comment on.

In 2012, presidential candidate Mitt Romney responded to a question during what he thought was a private meeting with campaign supporters that "there are 47 percent of the people who will vote for the president [Obama] no matter what" because they don't pay federal income taxes. The number was accurate, but it referred only to the federal income tax: Many Americans pay payroll taxes (Social Security and Medicare) and virtually all Americans pay federal excise taxes as well as state and local taxes. So most Americans do pay taxes, and a candidate promising to reduce taxes or make them more fair can still compete for their votes.

Still, elected officials can raise campaign funds and win votes by pandering to constituents wanting expanded entitlement programs, just as they can by pandering to businessmen and -women seeing tax breaks and subsidies for their businesses. The evidence that this occurs is overwhelming: Entitlement programs and the massive deficits and national debt they cause threaten the solvency of the national government and many states and local governments.

Even before passage of the Obamacare health care entitlement program and any of the recent stimulus packages, and bailouts, our entitlement programs were on a path to bankrupt America. In 1995, the Bipartisan Commission on Entitlement and Tax Reform stated:

> The Commission's Interim Report graphically displays the need to address our future fiscal imbalance. The conclusion of the Report is clear and inescapable: If we do not plan for the future, entitlement spending promises will exceed financial resources in the next century. The current spending trend is unsustainable (p. 8).

Similar warnings can be found in the 1996 report by the National Commission on Economic Growth and Tax Reform and the 2010 report of the National Commission on Fiscal Responsibility, showing the concern is bipartisan as well as long-standing. Rather than make the systemic changes needed to control the problem, Congress and every president since 1995 have caused or allowed entitlement programs and spending to grow.

Ways to Expand the Tax Base

The tax base for federal taxation can be expanded in several ways. First, and the focus of previous principles in this chapter, is to end tax exemptions, deductions, and credits that are currently in the tax code. Ending these "tax expenditures" is clearly the low-hanging fruit in the national tax and budget debate, just waiting for a political leader willing to rally taxpayers and voters to the cause.

Second, the tax base also can be expanded by adopting pro-growth policies. Recall that a tax base consists of the values of all the financial streams or assets on which tax is imposed. Increase that value, and revenue grows without any changes to the tax code. Economic growth can be encouraged through deregulation, entitlement reform, improving the efficiency with which public services are provided, and many other methods, many of them described in other chapters of this book. Like the proverbial "rising sea that lifts all ships," economic growth expands the tax base and makes tax rate reductions possible.

Third, shifting from an income tax to a consumption-based tax, such as the FairTax, also would expand the tax base. While income can be hidden or reduced by high taxation, consumption is (at least arguably) more difficult to hide and, since the national retail sales tax is a single fixed rate, it is unlikely to change consumption in ways that cause economic inefficiency and waste. Taxing consumption may encourage a higher rate of saving, which increases economic growth and consequently increases the tax base.

A fourth way to expand the tax base is maintaining a diverse portfolio of taxes rather than relying heavily on only one or two. Such an approach is usually defended by appealing to fairness, since taxing both income (with an income tax) and consumption (with a sales tax) means everyone pays some taxes even if they are retired or independently wealthy and report no income. A diverse tax base promises to generate more stable revenues, since too much reliance on a single tax, say a property tax, can result in a major drop in revenue when housing markets tumble. A third justification is economic competitiveness: Consumers will cross state lines to buy groceries and other products if the sales tax differential is large enough. Another justification is that taxes ought to reflect the value of public goods and services a taxpayer receives, something unlikely to be captured by either a retail sales tax or a personal income tax.

While the portfolio approach to taxes is popular in the public finance literature, it has shortcomings. It requires administrative infrastructures to handle each tax system, making collection less efficient. It is less transparent to taxpayers, since the total taxes paid are never reported. If some forms of taxation are known to be anti-growth, such as income taxes, then they arguably should not be in the portfolio at all, a choice made by seven states. Their superior economic performance suggests they made the right choice.

Policy Agenda

A broad tax base is beneficial because it makes lower tax rates possible, resulting in less evasion and less distortion of incentives to work and invest wisely. Eliminating deductions, credits, and the like is one way to expand the tax base but it is not the only way. Promoting economic growth, changing from taxing income to taxing consumption, and diversifying the tax base are other ways. All these ways would mark an improvement over the current federal tax code.

Recommended Readings: Scott Greenberg, "Options for Broadening the U.S. Tax Base," Tax Foundation, November 24, 2015; Curtis Dubay and David Burton, "A Tax Reform Primer for the 2016 Presidential Candidates," *Backgrounder* No. 3009, The Heritage Foundation, April 2015.

9. Everyone should pay the same income tax rate.

> It ought to be morally and legally unacceptable that some people are singled out to pay a higher rate of tax on their income than others pay.

Most Americans do not believe the federal tax code is moral. It was reported as early as 1977 that as many as 60 percent of Americans felt the federal tax system was either "somewhat unfair or quite unfair" (Pilla 2001, p. 12). Thirty years later, in a report titled *Reducing the Federal Tax Gap*, the IRS stated, "Special rules, subtle distinctions in the tax law and complicated computations add to this complexity and foster a sense of unfairness in our tax system, which ultimately discourages compliance" (IRS 2007, p. 50).

Unequal Treatment

The public widely perceives the federal income tax as unfair because the law *is* unfair. A 2005 report by the President's Advisory Panel on Federal Tax Reform stated:

> Taxpayers with the same income, family situation, and other key characteristics often face different tax burdens. Such differing treatment creates a perception of unfairness in our tax code. For example, taxpayers in states with high state and local income and property taxes receive higher deductions than taxpayers who live in lower-tax states with fewer state-provided services. Taxpayers with substantial employer-provided health insurance benefits receive in-kind compensation that is not taxed, while taxpayers who buy the same health insurance on their own usually pay tax on the income used to purchase the insurance. And Social Security benefits are taxed at a higher rate for married seniors than for those not married. How much or little taxpayers pay in tax is sometimes dependent on where they happen to live, the choices made by their employers, and whether they are married (p. 5).

Note none of these reasons why some people pay a higher tax rate than others has to do with the income they earn. We will address that basis for tax discrimination in a moment, but it is a different kind of concern. The problem described so well by the President's Advisory Panel on Federal Tax Reform is that the tax code, having been altered so many times by elected officials seeking to achieve social objectives other than raising revenue, has become profoundly inequitable in its impacts today.

By attempting to reward homeowners, the tax code penalizes renters; by rewarding marriage it discriminates against the single and divorced; by rewarding employers who provide health insurance to their employees it punishes the self-employed and self-insured. When tax breaks and credits to corporations are included, we discover people who live in certain areas, buy a certain kind of car, or purchase their electricity from a certain company, benefit at the expense of others. We find employees of some industries benefit at the expense of others.

How do we justify this disparate impact of the federal income tax on millions of people? Is it enough to say "it is in the national interest" that there should be 75 specific tax exemptions, deductions, and credits for some businesses but not others? Or thousands of different combinations of duties and privileges that make it virtually impossible to know how much any taxpayer truly owes?

Unacceptable in Law

The touchstone of American liberty is found in the Declaration of Independence, which declared "that all men are created equal, that they are endowed by their Creator with certain unalienable rights, that among these are Life, Liberty, and the Pursuit of Happiness." In the Founders' vocabulary, the "pursuit of happiness" was synonymous with the right to private property. How can this commitment to *equal treatment under the law* be squared with a tax code that has such a disparate impact on people and their rightfully earned property?

The Founders never would have approved federal income taxation, much less a progressive income tax. They prohibited any such tax in Section 9 of the Constitution, and they believed that by preventing the national government from having its own source of revenue, it would be forced to rely on the states for much of its funding and the execution of necessary public works programs. That prohibition stood until passage of the Sixteenth Amendment in 1913, the year that marked the beginning of the national government's unchecked growth.

The invidious discrimination manifest in the income tax would be unacceptable in any other area of law. Who would suggest that groups of people whether rich or poor should be more or less liable under, say, the fraud statutes, merely because of their social standing? In tax law, not only is this tolerated, it is embraced. Politicians and policymakers present it as though it were a noble, high-minded pursuit. But the power of law cannot and should not be used as a sword to attack the lawful and peaceful pursuits of entire segments of the population, perhaps as a means for the "masses" to get even with high income earners.

Taxing Only the Rich

The definition of "progressive" income taxation is marginal tax rates that rise with income. This means people with more reportable income don't only pay *proportionately* more than people with lower incomes, they pay *disproportionately* more.

Progressive income taxation ought to be much more controversial in America than it is today. It was number two in the 10-plank proposal put forth by Karl Marx and Frederick Engels in 1848 in *The Communist Manifesto* "to wrest, by degrees, all capital from the bourgeois, to centralize all instruments of production in the hands of the state."

The Sixteenth Amendment was approved amid promises that the tax would be levied only on the very rich. At that time, the bottom tax bracket was 1 percent on incomes more than $20,000 and the top bracket was just 6 percent on incomes more than $500,000. James   A.   Dorn, writing for the Cato Institute, reports, "When the first income tax was passed by Congress in 1894, the *New York Times* called the legislation, 'a vicious, inequitable, unpopular, impolitic, and socialistic act,' and the *Washington Post* added, 'It is an abhorrent and calamitous monstrosity'" (Dorn 1996). Alas, sentiments changed and today we tolerate and even celebrate such a law.

Policy Agenda

The arbitrary nature of the tax code makes clear why Alexander Hamilton, America's first treasury secretary, argued consumption taxes "have, upon the whole, better pretensions to equality than any other" (Morris 1957, pp. 259–60). Lawmakers today would do well to heed his wisdom and end progressive taxation of income.

Recommended Readings: Daniel J. Pilla, "A Monument of Deficient Wisdom: The Constitutional Conflict in the Federal Income Tax Law Enforcement," *Road Map to Tax Reform Series* No. 165, Institute for Policy Innovation, 2001; James A. Dorn, "Ending Tax Socialism," Cato Institute, December 13, 1996.

10. Perhaps it is time to repeal the income tax.

> The only constitutional purpose of the tax code is to raise revenue. The federal income tax violates that purpose. Maybe it is time to repeal it altogether.

The only constitutional purpose of the tax code is to raise revenue. Tax laws should not be used by politicians to compel behavior or to reward their friends and punish their opponents. Saying this begs a question: Is it time to repeal the income tax?

The federal income tax no longer operates primarily to raise revenue. The Earned Income Tax Credit, Child Tax Credit, and First-Time Homebuyers Credit are just a few of the dozens of personal and business credits in the code, but they are especially important because they are *refundable* credits. This means even citizens who owe no taxes can get cash from the government. This is not how a just tax operates.

Refundable credits are welfare programs, transfer payments used for social purposes. While the value of these credits has fluctuated in recent years, the Congressional Budget Office estimates the value of these credits is roughly $150 billion (CBO 2013, p. 1).

Ignoring the Constitution

Article I, Section 8 of the United States Constitution authorizes the federal government to collect taxes for just three narrow purposes: to pay the debts of the nation, to provide a national defense, and to ensure the "general welfare" of the nation. This latter term was understood narrowly as limiting the use of the powers enumerated in that section to such programs as benefited the nation as a whole, not its individual inhabitants or locales, and certainly not classes of citizens at the expense of others (Pilla 2001, pp. 8–12). And yet, a great portion of the national government's budget finances transfer payments imposed for the purpose of social engineering. The income tax enables many of those payments.

The Bipartisan Commission on Entitlement and Tax Reform hit the issue head-on when it said, "Government does not create wealth by distributing entitlement benefits; rather, it is engaging in a willful choice to take dollars from one segment of the population and to distribute that money in the form of benefits for others" (1995, p. 37).

Redistribution through Taxation

In a 1933 case titled *United States* v. *Butler,* the Supreme Court addressed the government's claim that redistribution is justifiable under the General Welfare Clause of the Constitution. The Court ruled: "a tax, in the general understanding of the term, and as used in the Constitution, signifies an exaction for the support of the government. The word has never been thought to connote the expropriation of money from one group for the benefit of another" (297 U.S. 1, 61 (1933)). Today, contrary to the principle expounded by the Court, Congress engages in just such expropriation.

In *Loan Association* v. *Topeka,* discussed earlier under Principle 6 (neutrality), the Supreme Court ruled using taxes to transfer wealth is a wholly illegitimate use of governments' taxing authority. The Court correctly labeled the practice "robbery." By this understanding, the tax code enforced as the law of the land today can be considered such "robbery." Thomas Jefferson condemned the practice as an attack upon the idea of liberty. He stated:

> To take from one, because it is thought his own industry and that of his father has acquired too much, in order to spare to others who (or whose fathers) have not exercised equal industry and skill, is to violate arbitrarily the first principle of association, the *guarantee* to everyone a free exercise of his industry and the fruits acquired by it (Ellis 1973, p. 94, italics in the original).

Immoral Taxation

There is simply no legal or moral authority in a free society that justifies using the power of government to take from some what they have legally and peacefully acquired and give it to others who have not earned it.

Frederic Bastiat (1801–1850)—a French economist, statesman, and author—called the practice of using the power of taxation to take from producers and give to non-producers "legal plunder." In the strongest terms, he called for the elimination of any such law because "it is not only an evil itself, but it is a fertile source for further evils because it invites reprisals. If such a law—which may be an isolated case—is not abolished immediately, it will spread, multiply, and develop into a system" (Bastiat [1850] 1977, p, 21).

So long as such laws permeate the tax culture in America, there will never be enough money to satisfy government. No tax system can produce sufficient revenue to provide for the social programs formulated by those seeking more ways to spend money they have not earned. Tax burdens for the producers will grow to confiscatory levels while the non-producers have further incentive to remain non-producers. The only hope of controlling the burden is to hold government strictly accountable to the constitutional limitations on its taxing authority.

Is the Income Tax Necessary?

In a column written in 2001, then Congressman Ron Paul wrote, "You may be surprised to know that the income tax accounts for only approximately one-third of federal revenue. Only 10 years ago, the federal budget was roughly one-third less than it is today. Surely we could find ways to cut spending back to 1990 levels, especially when the Treasury has single year tax surpluses for the past several years. So perhaps the idea of an America without an income tax is not so radical after all" (Paul 2001).

Eliminating the federal income tax would cost the national government about $3.3 trillion in lost revenue but would reduce overall compliance costs by $2.1 trillion. The effect of lifting the combined burden of $5.4 trillion off the nation's taxpayers, businesses, and consumers is difficult to imagine. Gross Domestic Product (GDP) in 2016 was $18.5 trillion, so the economic stimulus would be an incredible 29 percent of the value of all the goods and services produced in the nation that year.

As Paul argues, eliminating the federal income tax in 2001 would have left the budget deficit unchanged, provided spending was reduced to its level in 1991. The calculation is probably similar today. Regrettably, no one in public office today, in 2017, can imagine returning the national government to the size it was in 2007, even though many of those same elected officials campaigned for office and got elected *in 2008* saying government was too big.

Paul ended his column by asking,

> Is it impossible to end the income tax? I don't believe so. In fact, I believe a serious groundswell movement of disaffected taxpayers is growing in this country. Millions of Americans are fed up with the current tax system, and they will bring pressure on Congress. Some sidestep Congress completely, bringing legal challenges questioning the validity of the tax code and the 16th Amendment itself. Ultimately, the Liberty Amendment could serve as a flashpoint for these millions of voices (*Ibid.*).

Ron Paul introduced the Liberty Amendment in 1998, 1999, 2003, 2005, 2007, and 2009. Section 4 of the four-part amendment reads: "Three years after the ratification of this amendment the sixteenth article of amendments to the Constitution of the United States shall stand repealed and thereafter Congress shall not levy taxes on personal incomes, estates, and gifts."

Recommended Readings: Frederic Bastiat, *The Law,* Foundation for Economic Education, (1850) 1977; Ron Paul, "The Case Against the Income Tax," *Texas Straight Talk*, May 7, 2001.

Policy Agenda

Convention wisdom says it is impossible to repeal the federal income tax. Even President Donald Trump, the iconoclastic outsider who seems willing to champion unpopular causes, has not called for abolishing the income tax. But the case for doing so—on moral, political, and economic grounds—is strong. This may be an idea whose time has come.

References

Bailey, L. 2015. "Rand Paul Suit Blasts Foreign Banking Rules." *Courthouse News Service* (website). July 15.

Bastiat, Frederic. (1850) 1977. *The Law.* Irvington, NY: Foundation for Economic Education.

Bipartisan Commission on Entitlement and Tax Reform. 1995. *Final Report to the President.* Washington, DC: The Commission.

Bruckner, Caroline. 2016. *Shortchanged: The Tax Compliance Challenges of Small Business Operators Driving the On-Demand Platform Economy*. Washington, DC: American University.

Burton, David R. 2017. "A Guide to Tax Reform in the 115th Congress." *Backgrounder* No. 3192. The Heritage Foundation. February 10.

Carroll, Robert, John E. Chapoton, Maya MacGuineas, and Diane Lim Rogers. 2009. "Moving Forward with Bipartisan Tax Policy." *Working Paper* No. 5. Tax Foundation.

CBO (Congressional Budget Office). 2013. *Refundable Tax Credits*.

Crawford, Mark, *et al.* 2015. *Verified Complaint for Declaratory and Injunctive Relief.* Filed in the United States District Court for the Southern District of Ohio. July 14.

Department of the Treasury. 2016. *2016 Annual Privacy Act and Data Mining Report*.

Dorn, James A. 1996. "Ending Tax Socialism" (website). Cato Institute. December 13.

Dubay, Curtis, and David Burton. 2015. "A Tax Reform Primer for the 2016 Presidential Candidates." *Backgrounder* No. 3009. The Heritage Foundation. April.

Edwards, Chris. 2005. "Options for Tax Reform." *Policy Analysis* No. 536. Cato Institute.

_____. 2016. "Our Complex Tax Code Is Crippling America." *Time* (website). April 11.

Ellis, Richard E. 1973. "The Political Economy of Thomas Jefferson." In Lally Meymouth, editor. *Thomas Jefferson, The Man, His World, His Influence*. New York, NY: G.P. Putnam's Sons.

Ferrara, Peter, and Lewis Uhler. 2016. "Roadmap for the 21st Century: Budget and Tax." *Policy Brief*. The Heartland Institute and National Tax Limitation Committee. December 5.

Friedman, Milton, and Rose Friedman. 1998. *Two Lucky People: Memoirs*. Chicago, IL: University of Chicago Press.

GAO (Government Accountability Office). 2005. "Internal Revenue Service Needs to Remedy Serious Weaknesses over Taxpayer and Bank Secrecy Act Data."

Greenberg, Scott. 2017. "Summary of Latest Tax Data, 2016 Update." Washington, DC: The Tax Foundation.

Hall, Robert E., and Alvin Rabushka. 2007. *The Flat Tax*. Second Edition. Stanford, CA: Hoover Institution Press.

Harper, Jim. 2016. "The IRS Believes All Bitcoin Users are Tax Cheats." *Cato at Liberty* (blog). November 18.

IRS (Internal Revenue Service). 2000. *Annual Report from the Commissioner of IRS on Tax Law Complexity*. Washington, DC: Internal Revenue Service.

————. 2007. *Reducing the Federal Tax Gap: A Report on Improving Voluntary Compliance*. Washington, DC: U.S. Department of Treasury.

————. 2009. *Data Book, 2009*. Washington, DC: Internal Revenue Service.

————. 2016. *Data Book, 2016*. Washington, DC: Internal Revenue Service.

————. N.d. Form 1099-MISC.

Jeanblanc, James K. 2017. "Not Just Another Flat Tax." *The Freedom Tax* (website). July 10.

Joint Committee on Taxation. 2008. *List of Expiring Federal Tax Provisions, 2007–2020.* Washington, DC: U.S. Government Printing Office.

McBride, William. 2012. "What Is the Evidence on Taxes and Growth?" *Special Report* No. 207. Tax Foundation.

McCaherty, Joshua D. 2014. "The Cost of Tax Compliance" (website). Tax Foundation. September 11.

Mitchell, Daniel. 2005. "Beware the Value-Added Tax." *Backgrounder* No. 1852. The Heritage Foundation. May 16.

Moody, J. Scott. 2006. "Higher Taxes Lower Economic Performance." *Maine Issue Brief* No. 10. Maine Heritage Policy Center.

Morris, Richard B. 1957. *The Basic Ideas of Alexander Hamilton.* New York, NY: Pocket Books.

National Commission on Economic Growth and Tax Reform. 1996. *Unleashing America's Potential: A Pro-growth, Pro-family Tax System for the 21st Century.* Washington, DC: U.S. Government Printing Office.

National Commission on Fiscal Responsibility. 2010. *The Moment of Truth.* Washington, DC: The White House. December.

NTA (National Taxpayers Advocate). 2008. *National Taxpayer Advocate's 2008 Annual Report to Congress.* Washington, DC: Internal Revenue Service.

———. 2016. *National Taxpayer Advocate's 2016 Annual Report to Congress.* Washington, DC: Internal Revenue Service.

———. 2017. "Most Serious Problem #1" (website). Accessed August 20, 2017.

Olson, Nina E. 2016. "Statement of Nina E. Olson, National Taxpayer Advocate Hearing on 'The Sharing Economy: A Taxing Experience for New Entrepreneurs' Before the Committee on Small Business." U.S. House of Representatives. May 26.

———. 2017. "Statement of Nina E. Olson, National Taxpayer Advocate Hearing on 'IRS Oversight' before the Subcommittee on Financial Services and General Government Committee on Appropriations." U.S. House of Representatives. May 23.

Paul, Ron. 2001. "The Case Against the Income Tax." *Texas Straight Talk* (website). May 7.

Paulson, Kevin. 2008. "Five IRS Employees Charged With Snooping on Tax Returns." *Wired* (website). May 13.

Payne, James L. 1993. *Costly Returns: The Burdens of the U.S. Tax System.* San Francisco, CA: Institute for Contemporary Studies Press.

Pilla, Daniel J. 1993. *How to Fire the IRS: A Plan to Eliminate the Income Tax and the IRS.* Stillwater, MN: Winning Publications.

———. 2000. *Freedom to Prosper: Analyzing the Merits of Replacing Minnesota's Income Tax System with a Broad-Based Sales Tax.* Stillwater, MN: Tax Freedom Institute.

———. 2001. "A Monument of Deficient Wisdom: The Constitutional Conflict in the Federal Income Tax Law Enforcement." *Road Map to Tax Reform Series* No. 165. Institute for Policy Innovation.

President's Advisory Panel on Federal Tax Reform. 2005. *Simple, Fair and Pro-Growth: Proposals to Fix America's Tax System.* Washington, DC: U.S. Treasury Department.

Riddell, Kelly. 2014. "'High Risk' Label from Feds Puts Gun Sellers in Banks' Crosshairs, Hurts Business." *The Washington Times* (website). May 18.

Stanek, Steven. 2006. "Lowest Business Tax States Have Best Economies: Study." *Budget & Tax News*. The Heartland Institute. December.

Tax Foundation. 2016. *Options for Reforming America's Tax Code.* Washington, DC: Tax Foundation. June 6.

Terry, Miles. 2016. "President Obama's IRS Scandal: Seven Years & Counting" (website). American Center for Law and Justice.

Tuerck, David G., *et al.* 2007. *A Comparison of the FairTax Base and Rate with Other National Tax Reform Proposals.* Boston, MA: Beacon Hill Institute. February.

Vance, Laurence. 2005. "The Curse of the Withholding Tax" (website). The Mises Institute. April 21.

Vedder, Richard. 2001. *Taxes and Economic Growth.* Green Bay, WI: Taxpayers Network.

Veuger, Stan, *et al.* 2012. "Do Political Protests Matter? Evidence from the Tea Party Movement." *AEI Economic Policy Working Paper* No. 2012–05. American Enterprise Institute. December 18.

Washington Examiner. 2013. "IRS Targeting of Tea Party Is No Mere Political Scandal." Editorial. June 4.

Additional Resources

Additional information about tax policy is available from The Heartland Institute:

■ PolicyBot, The Heartland Institute's free online clearinghouse for the work of other free-market think tanks, contains thousands of documents on tax policy issues. It is on Heartland's website at https://www.heartland.org/policybot/.

■ https://www.heartland.org/Center-Budget-Taxes/ is The Center for Budgets and Taxes website, devoted to the latest news and commentary about budget and tax issues. It often addresses local, state, and federal tax policy issues. Read headlines, watch videos, or browse the thousands of documents available from PolicyBot.

■ *Budget & Tax News*, a monthly publication from The Heartland Institute, is available for free online at the websites described above, or subscribe to the print edition for $36 a year (ten issues).

Directory

The following national organizations are among the many that support sound tax policies.

Americans for Fair Taxation, https://fairtax.org

Americans for Tax Reform Foundation, http://www.atr.org/

American Legislative Exchange Council (ALEC), https://www.alec.org/

Beacon Hill Institute, http://www.beaconhill.org/

Cato Institute, https://www.cato.org/

Center for Strategic Tax Reform, http://www.cstr.org/

Council on State Taxation (COST), http://www.cost.org/

Dan Pilla's TaxHelpOnline.com, http://taxhelponline.com/

Freedom Tax, http://thefreedomtax.org/

Heartland Institute, https://www.heartland.org/

Heritage Foundation, http://www.heritage.org/

John Locke Foundation, https://www.johnlocke.org/

Pacific Research Institute, http://www.pacificresearch.org/

Small Business & Entrepreneurship Council (SBEC), http://sbecouncil.org/

Tax Foundation, https://taxfoundation.org/

Tax Freedom Institute, www.taxfreedominstitute.com

Taxpayer Advocate Service, https://taxpayeradvocate.irs.gov

Winning Publications, Inc., http://taxhelponline.com/

Chapter 10
Constitutional Reform

Roman Buhler and Peter J. Ferrara

---

10 Principles of Constitutional Reform

1. The national government is out of control..
2. Constitutional reform is the solution.
3. Fear of a runaway convention is unfounded.
4. Choose amendments carefully.
5. Agree on convention procedures ahead of time.
6. Require Congress to balance its budget.
7. Consider the Compact approach.
8. Require congressional approval of major regulations.
9. Require due process for all administrative law proceedings.
10. States can refuse to enforce federal laws.

Introduction

Limits on the size and power of the national government intended by the Founding Fathers and placed in the Constitution have been violated repeatedly and with devastating consequences. The national government has grown to the point that it is now a clear and present danger to American life, liberty, and happiness.

The national debt currently stands at nearly $19.8 trillion. National entitlement programs are all on paths to bankruptcy, some as soon as this year. Many states and cities face their own impending financial cliffs. Government debt is a "ticking time bomb" that threatens to destroy people's savings, the economy, and America's leadership in the world. The regulatory state is similarly out of control.

The U.S. Supreme Court and Congress are unable or unwilling to protect the Constitution from these assaults. The strategy used by concerned patriots of confronting Leviathan issue-by-issue or program-by-program has produced many successes, but it has failed spectacularly to rein in *total national government spending, borrowing, and regulating*. While we rightly celebrate victories at the state level or blocking one or two national programs and repealing one or two regulations, countless other programs expand and regulations get enacted. We win some battles but we are clearly losing the war.

Fortunately, Article V of the U.S. Constitution defines a process by which both Congress and the states themselves can offer amendments to deal with crises and challenges that are beyond the scope of the existing political regime. Since Congress today will not act to limit its own power, the states should call for a convention for the purpose of amending the Constitution. There are several active campaigns proposing balanced budget amendments as well as other changes that would rein in abuses by the national government and place the country back on sound fiscal footing.

Recommended Readings: Friedrich A. Hayek, *The Constitution of Liberty* (Chicago, IL: University of Chicago Press, 1960); John R. Vile, *The Constitutional Convention of 1787: A Comprehensive Encyclopedia of America's Founding* (Santa Barbara, CA: ABC-CLIO, Inc., 2005).

1. The national government is out of control.

The system created by the Founders to rein in the national government is now broken. The national government has unlimited power to tax, regulate, and borrow.

The Founders thought they had created a federal system of government in which the national government would be small and the states would conduct most of the nation's government business (Buckley 2015). That system has failed to keep the growth of the national government in check.

The Founders' Plan

The Constitution enumerated the national government's powers in Article 1, Section 8 and reserved, in the Tenth Amendment, all other powers to the people or to the states. Language in the preamble to the Constitution and again in Article 1, Section 8 limited the national government to using its power to "promote the general Welfare," not the narrow interests of specific groups of individuals or regions.

By forbidding direct taxation in Article 1, Section 9 (repealed by the Sixteenth Amendment in 1913), the Founders envisioned a national government with too little of its own revenue to take over the duties reserved to the states. The grant to Congress of the power to tax in Article 1, Section 8 specifies taxes can be used only to "to pay the Debts and provide for the common defense and general Welfare of the United States." Redistribution of income and other social engineering goals are prohibited by their exclusion from this grant of power. By arranging for the states to appoint Senators (Article 1, Section 3, repealed by the Seventeenth Amendment in 1913), the Founders thought they were creating a branch of Congress that would act out of self-interest to resist attempts to expand the national government.

This system of constitutional prohibitions and checks and balances worked well during the nation's first century. In 1913—the fateful year that saw the Sixteenth and Seventeenth Amendments adopted—national government expenditures were only 2.5 percent of Gross National Product (GNP). Real per-capita expenditures by the national government, in 1990 dollars, were only $79.56 in 1895.

A Government Out of Control

Freed by the Sixteenth and Seventeenth Amendments from constitutional checks and balances, and by Supreme Court rulings that removed other important prohibitions on its use of power, the national government started to grow. Today, it is a government out of control.

After a brief spike during World War I, per-capita spending fell again during the 1920s, but spending has soared since the 1930s. Writing in 2014, the Mercatus Center's Veronique de Rugy reported, "After adjusting for population and inflation, federal outlays have, with a few exceptions, grown at a staggering pace since 1945. The first Truman budget spent $5,039 per capita. Government spending per capita decreased for the next two years and in 1948 hit a historic low of $2,214—a low that has not been matched in six decades. Today's spending per capita is more than five times this amount, at $10,970" (de Rugy 2014).

In 1900, the federal government consumed less than 5 percent of the nation's total output of goods and services. By 2009 it had reached

24.4 percent, its highest level since the height of World War II in 1945. In 2016, its share was about 21 percent (Federal Reserve Bank of St. Louis 2017).

During the 55 years between 1961 and 2016, Congress chose to balance the budget only five times. In 2009, the federal deficit hit a record high of $1.419 trillion, more than three times the previous record of $458 billion. The $458 billion all-time record high before the Obama years is now the new normal. Congressional overspending at least through 2021 is still projected to be well over $400 billion annually (CBO 2017).

In the last fiscal year under President George W. Bush, the country's debt was just under $10 trillion. With the Obama spending requests passed by Congress, that debt more than doubled, reaching $20 trillion, now surpassing the country's GDP. Obama added more to America's national debt than all prior presidents combined, from George Washington to George W. Bush (Boyer 2015).

The Regulatory State

The dysfunction of the national government also can be seen in the uncontrolled growth of the regulatory state. The National Association of Manufacturers (NAM) put the burden of federal regulations alone at more than $2 trillion in 2012 (Crain and Crain, 2014). If the regulatory compliance burden were lifted, NAM found 63 percent of manufacturers would use funds they save for investment—growing the economy—and 22 percent would put those funds into employee initiatives.

It has increasingly become the habit of Congress to pass vague and contradictory laws, and leave it to the executive branch to work out the details. While there is a process for promulgating new rules, many times the regulations are not subject to that process. Worse, the runaway regulatory regime is often insulated from effective legal checks. Citizens do not have the right to challenge many regulations in the courts.

The Root of the Problem

The root of the problem lies in the Constitution itself, a magnificent document without any doubt "the most wonderful work ever struck off at a given time by the brain and purpose of man," as William Gladstone wrote in 1878. But it is not immune to the contrivances of generations of men and women set on finding ways to evade its restrictions on their power, prestige, and access to the wealth of others. As Thomas Jefferson warned, "the natural progress of things is for liberty to yield and government to gain ground."

The system created by the Founders to rein in the national government is now broken. The national government has unlimited power to tax, regulate, and borrow. The courts have failed to interpret and enforce key provisions of the Constitution that limit the powers of Congress and the executive branch. State governments, no longer represented in the U.S. Senate, have become addicted to "revenue sharing," losing their independence and hence their ability to check the growth of the national government.

Recommended Readings: Peter Ferrara, *America's Ticking Bankruptcy Bomb* (Washington, DC: Broadside Books, 2011): F.H. Buckley, *The Once and Future King: The Rise of Crown Government in America* (Washington, DC: Encounter Books, 2015).

2. Constitutional reform is the solution.

Anticipating that the national government would attempt to slip the bonds they had placed on it in the Constitution, the Founders created two roads to constitutional reform.

The Founders never intended for the national government to grow so large that it would challenge the states for leadership in so many arenas. James Madison wrote in *Federalist 45*, "The powers delegated by the proposed Constitution to the federal government are few and defined. Those which are to remain in the State governments are numerous and indefinite. The former will be exercised principally on external objects, as war, peace, negotiation, and foreign commerce; with which the last the power of taxation will, for the most part, be connected" (Hamilton *et al.* 2014).

Anticipating the national government would attempt to slip the bonds they had placed on it in the Constitution, the Founders created two roads to constitutional reform. A new social movement is arising across the nation calling for the use of these tools to rein in an out-of-control national government. Legitimate and increasingly successful groups that exist solely for the purpose of pursuing constitutional reform include the Assembly of State Legislatures, Balanced Budget Amendment Task Force, Compact for America, Convention of States, Friends of Article V Convention, and State Legislators Article V Caucus.

Congressional Amendments

Throughout our country's history, constitutional amendments have been enacted with the purpose of curbing the power of the national government. Indeed, the first 10 amendments, the Bill of Rights, is a landmark attempt in human history to limit the power of government and to protect individual liberty.

The Eleventh Amendment forbids the federal courts from adjudicating lawsuits against any state government brought by citizens of another state or foreign country. The Fourteenth Amendment provided equal protection of the law for former slaves after the Civil War. Over time, the equal protection clause has been the basis of many court cases limiting government power and abuses. The Twenty-Second Amendment provided a two-term limit for presidents, in response to President Franklin Delano Roosevelt winning four terms in office (Annenberg Classroom, n.d.).

Passing amendments through Congress is the primary method of amending the Constitution. Constitutional amendments proposed by Congress are introduced through a joint resolution. Both the House and the Senate must approve the resolution by a two-thirds vote. The National Archives and Records Administration (NARA) then receives a copy for processing. Staff at NARA's Office of the Federal Register (OFR) process the resolution before distribution to the states. Legislative history notes are added to the amendment during processing.

Amendments proposed by Congress do not take effect unless approved by the states. OFR delivers to each governor a letter describing the proposed constitutional amendment. Governors introduce the amendment to their respective legislatures for consideration. Both houses of a state's legislature must approve a joint resolution in order for the proposed amendment to be considered for ratification. Three-fourths of the state legislatures must approve a proposed amendment in order to achieve full ratification. Although the U.S. Constitution does not expressly require the states be given a deadline within which to approve proposed amendments, the U.S. Supreme Court has ruled Congress has the authority to establish a deadline. Seven years is common; the deadline must be stated either in the body of the amendment or in the resolution proposing it.

OFR receives a copy of the amendment from each state after approval; it is OFR's responsibility to determine the sufficiency of the states' approval of the amendment. An amendment goes into effect as soon as it reaches the three-fourths of the states threshold. Once certified by the Archivist of the United States, it officially becomes an article of the Constitution.

All 27 of the amendments to the U.S. Constitution have taken this path. The last amendment—the 27th, prohibiting any law that increases or decreases the salary of members of Congress from taking effect until the start of the next set of terms of office for Representatives—was ratified on May 18, 1992. It was originally submitted by Congress to the states for ratification on September 25, 1789. The ratification period thus took 202 years, seven months, and 10 days.

Article V Convention of the States

In today's highly partisan political environment, it is unlikely Congress will ever consider constitutional amendments meant to curb its own power. This places the task in the hands of state elected officials.

Article V states in full:

The Congress, whenever two thirds of both Houses shall deem it necessary, shall propose Amendments to this Constitution, or, on the Application of the Legislatures of two thirds of the several States, shall call a Convention for proposing Amendments, which, in either Case, shall be valid to all Intents and Purposes, as Part of this Constitution, when ratified by the Legislatures of three fourths of the several States, or by Conventions in three fourths thereof, as the one or the other Mode of Ratification may be proposed by the Congress; Provided that no Amendment which may be made prior to the Year One thousand eight hundred and eight shall in any Manner affect the first and fourth Clauses in the Ninth Section of the First Article; and that no State, without its Consent, shall be deprived of its equal Suffrage in the Senate.

In a 1920 case title *Hawke* v. *Smith*, which concerned voter approval of the Eighteenth Amendment (Ohio History Central n.d.), and a 1921 case titled *Dillon* v. *Gloss* (FindLaw n.d.(a)), which concerned time limits for ratifying constitutional amendments, the U.S. Supreme Court affirmed the authority of the states to call amendment conventions. Similarly, in a 1931 case titled *United States* v. *Sprague*, which dealt with whether the Eighteenth Amendment had been properly ratified, the Court was emphatic that "[A]rticle 5 is clear in statement and in meaning, contains no ambiguity and calls for no resort to rules of construction. ... It provides two methods for proposing amendments. Congress may propose them by a vote of two-thirds of both houses, or, on the application of the legislatures of two-thirds of the States, must call a convention to propose them" (FindLaw n.d.(b)).

Once dismissed as too impractical or too risky, constitutional reform under Article V has emerged as a valid and even indispensable tool for the kind of changes to public policy that are needed. Six states passed a total of seven Article V resolutions or bills in 2015, and all 50 states either saw bills introduced or recently adopted Article V resolutions. The Constitution requires Congress to call a convention if 34 states submit matching applications, and 38 states would have to ratify the proposed amendment for it to become part of the Constitution.

Alaska, Arizona, Georgia, Mississippi, and North Dakota have passed the Compact for a Balanced Budget (Guldenschuh 2017). The measure, spearheaded by Compact for America, calls for an Article V convention to vote on a proposed amendment requiring a balanced federal budget, through an interstate compact agreement that simplifies the procedures for calling a convention. Twenty-nine states have passed single-subject applications for an Article V convention calling for a balanced federal budget (*Ibid.*).

Ten states have passed a multiple-subject resolution sponsored by Convention of States calling for an Article V convention (*Ibid.*). The proposal includes term limits for Members of Congress and reducing federal regulations in addition to a balanced budget amendment. As of April 2017, 15 state legislatures were actively considering this resolution (*Ibid.*).

Three times in American history, pressure from states forced Congress to propose amendments states wanted, because Congress wanted to avoid an Article V convention. The three cases were the Bill of Rights itself, the Seventeenth Amendment (popular election of senators), and the Twenty-Second Amendment (presidential term limits). National lawmakers fear such conventions might lead to even greater control over Congress and its current spending and regulatory habits, and so endorse constitutional amendments as a way to preempt them (American Opportunity Project 2017).

Policy Agenda

The most promising and permanent way to deal with the current spending and regulatory abuses of the national government is in the Constitution. Amending the Constitution by a joint resolution of Congress or by an Article V convention of the states could restore the original bonds on the national government—for example, by repealing the Sixteenth and Seventeenth Amendments—or by creating new ones, such as a balanced budget amendment or an amendment imposing term limits on members of Congress. In America's current situation, this seems the only way to confine government to its limited powers and stop runaway spending and regulations.

Recommended Readings: Alexander Hamilton, John Jay, and James Madison, *The Federalist Papers and Other Essays* (Mineola, NY: Dover Publications, 2014); Thomas E. Brennan, *The Article V Amendatory Constitutional Convention: Keeping the Republic in the Twenty First Century* (Landover, MD: Lexington Books, 2014).

3. Fear of a runaway convention is unfounded.

Patriots should not hesitate to use the tools the Founders gave them to restore the constitutional order the Founders thought they were creating for posterity.

What if a convention of states is held for the purpose of voting on a specific constitutional amendment, but its delegates decide to rewrite the entire Constitution instead? What if the convention is taken over by "fake delegates" recruited by reclusive billionaires, whether conservative or liberal or otherwise, who vote to remove from the Constitution protections for cherished rights such as the First Amendment (freedom of speech) and Second Amendment (firearms ownership)? These fears of a "runaway convention" helped defeat the balanced budget amendment in the past and are being circulated by opponents of constitutional reform today.

A Convention Can Be Limited

The principal reason a "runaway convention" scenario is highly unlikely is because the call for the convention can be limited to proposing a single or few amendments. Virtually all campaigns now underway for constitutional reform propose such limited conventions. One effort, the Compact for America, was designed very specifically to confront and extinguish fears of a "runaway convention."

How do we know states can limit a convention to proposing one or only a few amendments? First, the plain language of Article V does not exclude single-amendment conventions, and a common-sense inter-pretation of the language would say the Founders intended to create an avenue for consideration of single amendments. The Founders were aware of conventions of states preceding the writing of the Constitution and assumed future ones would follow their precedents. (If they didn't assume this, they would have specified nontraditional procedures in the

Article, and they did not.) The conventions of states the Founders knew of were invariably limited to one or only a few subjects and their delegates were faithful to pledges to limit their deliberations to those subjects. (For more about those conventions, see Principle 6.)

Constitutional scholars see a second reason to believe the courts would rule states have the right to limit the call for a convention to one or only a few amendments. Robert Natelson explains, "the central purpose of the state application and convention procedure—to grant state legislatures parity with Congress in the proposal process—would be largely defeated unless those legislatures had the same power Congress does to define an amendment's scope in advance" (Natelson 2014). The Founders would have opposed an interpretation of Article V that placed a large procedural obstacle in front of the states but not Congress.

A third reason we know a convention can be limited to one or a few amendments is historical practice *after* ratification of the Constitution. Nearly all of the Article V applications made by the states in the past were limited to a particular subject. (See the Article V Library 2017.) All of those state legislators over all of those years believed they had the authority to call for conventions on a single or few amendments. It seems highly unlikely they were all wrong.

The fate of these applications is also significant. Why didn't Congress call a convention when 34 applications were received? If a convention cannot be limited, the fact that the applications call for different amendments would not have stopped them from combining disparate applications. A convention of the states hasn't already been called only because Congress and the courts believe a convention of the states can be limited to one or a few amendments.

Finally, writings at the time of the founding make it clear the Founders intended for the Article V convention route to be a relatively easy way to amend the Constitution. In *Federalist* No. 43, James Madison wrote Article V "guards equally against that extreme facility, which would render the Constitution too mutable; and that extreme difficulty, which might perpetuate its discovered faults." In *Federalist* No. 85, Alexander Hamilton wrote there was "no comparison between the facility of affecting an amendment, and that of establishing in the first instance a complete Constitution."

The Federalists sold the Constitution to the public by saying Article V conventions could be used routinely to fix any problems found in the Constitution after ratification. During the New Jersey ratification debates, the *New Jersey Journal* wrote the Constitution included "an easy mode for redress and amendment in case the theory should disappoint when reduced to practice" (cited by Dranias 2016). Similarly, during the Connecticut ratification debates, Roger Sherman wrote, "If, upon experience, it should be found deficient, [the Constitution] provides an easy and peaceable mode of making amendments" (*Ibid.*).

After the Convention

The biggest restriction on the power of a convention of states is not how it can be called or whether it can or cannot be limited to proposing one or a small number of amendments. It is that its power is only to *propose* and not to enact. The plain language of Article V makes this clear: A convention may be held for the purpose of "proposing Amendments" to the Constitution, but no more.

Whatever a convention proposes must be "ratified by the Legislatures of three fourths of the several States, or by Conventions in three fourths thereof" before it can take effect. In other words, nothing a convention of states does can take effect unless approved by legislators or voters in 38 states. It is inconceivable today that voters or legislators in 38 states would agree to give up essential liberties such as those of free speech or firearms ownership. On the contrary, surveys show high levels of popular support, often at levels greater than 80 percent, for a balanced budget amendment, term limits, and better protection of private property rights.

Policy Agenda

More than a few well-intentioned and thoughtful patriots oppose constitutional reform out of fear of a "runaway convention." Love of the Constitution quite rightly leads to opposition to attempts to change it except for the most urgent reasons and through mechanisms the Founders would have approved. The Founders approved of amending the Constitution following proposals adopted through joint resolution by Congress or approved by conventions of states followed by approval by voters in 38 states. Patriots should not hesitate to use the tools the Founders gave them to restore the constitutional order the Founders thought they were creating for posterity.

Recommended Readings: Edwin Meese II, *et al., The Heritage Guide to the Constitution* (Washington, DC: The Heritage Foundation, 2005); Michael Farris, *Answering the John Birch Society Questions about Article V*, Convention of States, May 2016.

4. Choose amendments carefully.

The surplus of good ideas for amendments makes a focused and sustained effort difficult.

Many writers have been composing and vetting their ideas for constitutional amendments for many years. One of the challenges the constitutional reform movement faces is a surplus of good ideas, which makes a focused and sustained effort difficult. Patriots are advised to do their homework, to find out if an organization already exists that has worked through the details of drafting an amendment and sharing it with legislators and activists. Some of the best groups working in this area are identified in the directory at the end of this chapter.

It's Not a Constitutional Convention

For years, opponents of an Article V convention have called it a "constitutional convention" and claimed it would put the current Constitution in jeopardy and perhaps replace it (Newman 2015). This is inaccurate. As the previous principle makes clear, a convention of states is not a constitutional convention. It is an "amendments convention," a constitutional way to bypass Congress and propose amendments to the Constitution directly to the people.

Organizations that support an Article V convention should avoid using the term "constitutional convention," since this fans fears that the entire Constitution might be subject to changes. Legislators should understand the difference between the two terms in order to improve communication with constituents and facilitate a stronger working relationship with organizations that promote such legislation.

Convention supporters should be alert especially for distorted language in the media and public forums that confuse and frighten citizens about the convention's purpose. Such distortions are commonplace in the legacy media and were even on display in the *Washington Post* and *New York Times* some five decades ago (Natelson 2017a).

Composing Amendments

In *Article V: A Handbook for Legislators,* Natelson argues legislators should evaluate a proposed amendment by these measures: Does it return America to its founding principles? Will it promote a significant effect on public policy? Is the amendment proposal widely popular? Is it a subject most legislators, regardless of political party, can understand and appreciate? (Natelson 2013b).

Natelson discourages states from issuing a single convention application with multiple subjects, since applications for a convention with multiple subjects will win the approval of only as many states as support the least popular of the multiple subjects. This makes it less likely to meet the 34-state threshold (Natelson 2013b). "One at a time" should be the rule. After the first convention of states takes place, the next one will be much easier and faster to convene ... and then the next, and the one after that.

Natelson also suggests a "correspondence committee" be formed, composed of a representative from each legislature that issues an application for a convention, so they can communicate regularly on the status of the amendment and help supporters in other states get their applications approved. State legislators are keenly interested in hearing from their peers on the consequences, positive or negative, of endorsing legislation or taking controversial stands. A correspondence committee can help make sure the message they hear is accurate and positive.

Guidelines for Writing Amendments

In a more recent publication, Natelson (2017b) suggested the following guidelines for drafting a constitutional amendment:

- The proposal should be written in a manner consistent with the Constitution's text as currently understood. One should not draft as if one were writing a new, free-standing document.

- The Constitution is fairly concise, so complying with its style requires the amendment not be too long. Moreover, lengthy amendments face obstacles to ratification by feeding public suspicion and offering more targets for attack.

- To the extent possible, the amendment's central terms should consist of words and phrases appearing elsewhere in the Constitution.

- The language should minimize opportunities for manipulation to evade or otherwise thwart the intent behind them.

- The wording of exceptions (e.g., "emergencies") should not be such as to allow exceptions to become the norm.

- Although all parts of the Constitution may come under judicial scrutiny, the amendment should minimize the chances of judicial intervention.

- The amendment should not prejudice the outcome of unrelated constitutional controversies.

- The amendment should not contain ineffective or counterproductive provisions.

- The amendment should not include irrelevant material that impedes creation of the coalition necessary to ratify.

Recommended Readings: Mark R. Levin, *The Liberty Amendments* (New York, NY: Threshold Editions, 2014); Robert G. Natelson, *Article V: A Handbook for State Lawmakers* (Washington, DC: American Legislative Exchange Council, 2013).

5. Agree on convention procedures ahead of time.

If a convention is to be successful, states must cooperate in the application process and planning convention operations.

There is no specific language in the Constitution defining how an Article V convention of states should be conducted, but constitutional scholars say agreement on procedures can be achieved by looking at the proceedings of past conventions.

A History of Conventions

Since the adoption of the Constitution in June 21, 1788, when New Hampshire became the ninth state to ratify the Constitution, the Constitution has been amended 17 times (not counting the original 10 Amendments proposed at the constitutional convention itself), but never via an Article V convention of states. While this has sometimes been raised as a reason to oppose calling a convention today, it overlooks a long history of state conventions that offers legal and procedural precedents for patriots to learn from.

Robert Natelson has identified 21 inter-governmental conventions that took place before Independence, 11 after Independence but before ratification, and five that occurred after ratification, for a total of 37 conventions (Natelson 2016). According to Natelson,

> Universally-accepted protocols determined multi-government convention procedures. These protocols fixed the acceptable ways of calling such conventions, selecting and instructing delegates, adopting convention rules, and conducting convention proceedings. The actors involved in the process—state legislatures and executives, the Continental and Confederation Congresses, and the delegates themselves—each had recognized prerogatives and duties, and were subject to recognized limits.
>
> These customs are of more than mere Founding-Era historical interest. They governed, for the most part, multi-state conventions held in the nineteenth century as well—notably but not exclusively, the Washington Conference Convention of 1861. More importantly for present purposes, they shaped the Founders' understanding of how the constitutional language would be interpreted and applied (Natelson 2013c).

Guidelines for Successful Conventions

Based on his studies of past conventions, Natelson identified six important rules of organization for any document outlining convention operations:

- *Identification of the presiding officers of a convention and how they will be selected.* Who will be responsible for the overall operation of the convention, calling it to order, ensuring the debate moves smoothly, and administering oversight of committees?

- *Selection of delegates and limitations on their conduct.* How many delegates will be selected from each state and who is responsible for selecting the delegates?

- *Voting rules.* Each state will have one vote on amendments. If states appoint more than one delegate, will the state's vote be based on a majority vote or a supermajority of its delegates?

- *Order of business and conduct of debate.* What agenda will guide the state delegations in properly carrying out their business on the convention floor? What are the rules of debate?

■ *Payment of expenses for delegates attending the convention.* Should the delegates themselves, their sponsoring organizations, or each state cover their convention expenses?

■ *Standing committees.* What issues should they cover? The Assembly of State Legislatures, which promotes a convention, suggests standing committees cover administration, convention research, communications to Congress and the states, credentials, printing and publications, rules, and style (Assembly of State Legislatures, 2015). Citizens for Self-Governance calls for six: administration, credentials, rules, federal jurisdiction, fiscal restraints, and term limits.

In *Article V: A Handbook for Legislators,* Natelson notes legislative instructions come from the legislature or the legislature's designee, such as a committee, the executive, or another person or body. Although state convention applications should not specify exact wording for an amendment, a state could instruct its commissioners not to agree to any amendment that did not include particular language (Natelson 2013b).

In a manner somewhat similar to Natelson, David Long, writing for the National Conference of State Legislatures in 2013, identified eight key concepts legislatures should address, either in the convention application itself or in specific legislation, concerning delegates (Long 2013):

■ *Legislative instructions.* Each state must provide official instructions to convention delegates, outlining the official procedures from the state before, during, and after the convention.

■ *Delegate selection.* Each state must outline qualifications for convention delegates in addition to the procedures for selecting them. Some important provisions to consider are minimum age, residency, and registered voter requirements. The qualifications also should specify who, if anyone, is prohibited from serving as a delegate. Georgia, for example, enacted a delegate selection bill in 2014 prohibiting registered lobbyists and federal elected officials from being considered as delegates (Georgia 2014).

■ *Recall of delegates.* Each state should enact procedures for recalling delegates who fail to follow the legislative instructions they receive after their appointment.

■ *Selecting alternate delegates when regular delegates are being chosen.* This ensures a replacement delegate can be provided in a timely manner in the event of a recall.

■ *Ban on delegates proposing unauthorized amendments.* This provision is designed to prevent a "runaway convention" scenario. The instructions to delegates must limit them to consideration of authorized amendments only (ALEC 2013).

■ *Require all delegates to take an official oath.* Legislators are required to take an oath of office, and the same requirement should apply to delegates to a convention.

■ *Civil or criminal penalty for any delegate who violates the delegate instructions.* States will differ on whether civil or criminal sanctions should be applied for violating official legislative instructions, with each state referring to its official criminal codes to determine appropriate penalties and sanctions.

■ *Advisory committees.* Each state should form an advisory group to help delegates navigate whether their actions fall within the scope of the convention. Such advisory groups typically are a three-judge panel, usually consisting of the chief justice of the state supreme court, the chief judge of the state's intermediate appeals court, and a chief judge of a circuit or district court.

Recommended Readings: Russell L. Caplan, *Constitutional Brinksmanship: Amending the Constitution by National Convention* (Oxford, England: Oxford University Press, 1988); William Fruth, *Ten Amendments for Freedom* (Palm City, FL: POLICOM, 2010); Robert G. Natelson, "The Article V Convention Process and the Restoration of Federalism," *Harvard Journal of Law & Public Policy* **36** (3): 955–60.

6. Require Congress to balance its budget.

> High on the list of possible amendments should be one requiring Congress to balance its budget.

High on the list of possible amendments should be one requiring Congress to balance its budget. The Balanced Budget Amendment Task Force (BBATF) has been leading this effort for decades and has garnered the support of 29 of the 34 state legislatures needed for a convention to consider its amendment (BBATF 2017).

Call for an Amendment Convention

BBATF worked with the American Legislative Exchange Council (ALEC) to produce the following model application for states calling for a convention to propose a balanced budget amendment (ALEC 2015):

Application for a Convention of the States under Article V of the Constitution of the United States:

WHEREAS, the Founders of our Constitution empowered State Legislators to be guardians of liberty against future abuses of power by the federal government; and

WHEREAS, the federal government has created a crushing national debt through improper and imprudent spending; and

WHEREAS, the federal government has invaded the legitimate roles of the states through the manipulative process of federal mandates, most of which are unfunded to a great extent; and

WHEREAS, the federal government has ceased to live under a proper interpretation of the Constitution of the United States; and

WHEREAS, it is the solemn duty of the States to protect the liberty of our people— particularly for the generations to come—by proposing Amendments to the Constitution of the United States through a Convention of the States under Article V for the purpose of restraining these and related abuses of power;

BE IT THEREFORE RESOLVED BY THE LEGISLATURE OF THE STATE OF _____:

SECTION 1. The legislature of the State of _____ hereby applies to Congress, under the provisions of Article V of the Constitution of the United States, for the calling of a convention of the states limited to proposing amendments to the Constitution of the United States that impose fiscal restraints on the federal government, limit the power and jurisdiction of the federal government, and limit the terms of office for its officials and for members of Congress.

SECTION 2. The secretary of state is hereby directed to transmit copies of this application to the President and Secretary of the United States Senate and to the Speaker and Clerk of the United States House of Representatives, and copies to the members of the said Senate and House of Representatives from this State; also to transmit copies hereof to the presiding officers of each of the legislative houses in the several States, requesting their cooperation.

SECTION 3. This application constitutes a continuing application in accordance with Article V of the Constitution of the United States until the legislatures of at least two-thirds of the several states have made applications on the same subject.

Language of a BBA
Constitutional scholars disagree on how a balanced budget amendment should be phrased. The phrasing recommended by the Compact for a Balanced Budget campaign appears in Principle 7. Robert Natelson (2017b) has offered the following model language:

Section 1. Every measure that shall increase the total of either the public debt of the United States or the contingent public debt of the United States shall, after complying with the requirements of the seventh section of the first article of this Constitution, be presented to the legislatures of the several states; and before the same shall take effect, it shall be approved by a majority of legislatures in states containing a majority of the population of the United States as determined by the most recently completed decennial enumeration pursuant to the third clause of the second section of the first article. Each state legislature shall have power to determine its own rules for considering such measures.

Section 2. "Contingent public debt" means the secondary public liabilities of the United States. Any measure to increase total contingent public debt shall be presented to the state legislatures separately from any measure to increase total public debt.

Section 3. Any purported increase in total public debt or contingent public debt after the effective date of this article not approved in compliance with this article shall not be deemed money borrowed on the credit of the United States pursuant to the second clause of the eighth section of the first article nor valid public debt under the fourth section of the fourteenth article of amendment.

Section 4. This article shall be inoperative unless it shall have been ratified as an amendment to the Constitution within seven years from the date of its submission to the state legislatures or conventions in accordance with the fifth article of this Constitution. This article shall become effective six months after ratification as an amendment to the Constitution.

Other Efforts

In addition to a balanced budget amendment (BBA), the Convention of States project calls for term limits on members of Congress, reduction of federal regulations, a redefinition of the "General Welfare clause," and procedures for overturning unconstitutional decisions by federal judges (Convention of States n.d.).

One interesting BBA approach comes from Congress itself. Sens. Chuck Grassley (R-Iowa) and Mike Lee (R-Utah) in 2017 introduced Senate Joint Resolution 7, which would prohibit "total outlays for a fiscal year from exceeding total receipts for that fiscal year or 18% of the U.S. gross domestic product unless Congress authorizes the excess by a two-thirds vote of each chamber. The prohibition excludes outlays for repayment of debt principal and receipts derived from borrowing. The amendment requires a two-thirds vote of each chamber of Congress to levy a new tax, increase the rate of any tax, or increase the debt limit" (U.S. Congress 2017a).

Recommended Readings: Lewis K. Uhler, *Setting Limits: Constitutional Control of Government* (Washington, DC: Regnery Publishing, 1989); Robert Natelson, "A Proposed Balanced Budget Amendment," *Policy Brief,* The Heartland Institute, July 17, 2017.

7. Consider the Compact approach.

One approach to constitutional reform differs from the rest and deserves special attention.

One approach to constitutional reform differs from the rest and deserves special attention. It is the Compact for a Balanced Budget, the work of attorney and legal scholar Nick Dranias and his organization, Compact for America (CFA) (Dranias 2016).

Faster, Safer, Better

CFA's Compact for a Balanced Budget uses an interstate agreement to make the Article V convention process faster, safer, and better. It is *faster* because without it the process for calling a convention of states requires at least 100 legislative enactments and five years of legislative sessions. It is *safer* because the interstate agreement contains provisions that even convention skeptics admit would minimize the chances of last-minute obstacles or a "runaway convention." It is *better* because it can be used over and over again to propose amendments without having to build each amendment effort from the ground up.

Dranias points out the non-compact Article V approach requires at least two-thirds of state legislatures pass resolutions applying for a convention (34 enactments), a majority of states must pass laws appointing and instructing their delegates (26 enactments), Congress must pass a resolution calling the convention, the convention must meet and propose an amendment, Congress must pass another resolution to select the mode of ratification (either by state legislature or in-state convention), and finally, three-fourths of the states must pass legislative resolutions or successfully convene in-state conventions that ratify the amendment. All of this takes time, often multiple legislative sessions, and all the while, opponents of the constitutional reform effort are lobbying to slow down approvals or rescind applications already in hand.

The Compact approach to Article V consolidates everything states do in the Article V convention process into a single agreement among the states that is enacted once by three-fourths of the states. Everything Congress needs to do is consolidated in a single concurrent resolution passed just once with simple majorities and no presidential presentment.

The Compact is able to pack the Article V convention process into just two overarching legislative vehicles by using something called "conditional enactments." For example, using a conditional enactment, the Article V application contained in the Compact goes "live" only after three-fourths of the states join the compact (three-fourths, rather than two-thirds, is the threshold for activating the Article V application because the Compact is designed to start and complete the entire amendment process). The Compact also includes a "nested" legislative ratification of the contemplated balanced budget amendment, which goes live only if Congress selects ratification by state legislature rather than in-state convention.

Of particular interest to constitutional reform skeptics, the Compact approach identifies and specifies in advance the authority of the delegates from its member states, establishes, the convention ground rules, limits the duration of the convention to 24 hours, and requires all member state delegates to vote to establish rules that limit the agenda to an up-or-down vote on a specific, pre-drafted balanced budget amendment. It disqualifies from participation any member state—and the vote of any member state or delegate—that deviates from that rule. It further bars all member states from ratifying any other amendment that might be generated by the convention.

The Compact's Balanced Budget Amendment

While the Compact approach could work for any constitutional amendment, Dranias started with a balanced budget amendment because it tops the list in surveys of what constitutional amendments people are likely to support. The amendment in its entirety reads:

> *Section 1.* Total outlays of the government of the United States shall not exceed total receipts of the government of the United States at any point in time unless the excess of outlays over receipts is financed exclusively by debt issued in strict conformity with this article.

> *Section 2.* Outstanding debt shall not exceed authorized debt, which initially shall be an amount equal to 105 percent of the outstanding debt on the effective date of this article. Authorized debt shall not be increased above its aforesaid initial amount unless such increase is first approved by the legislatures of the several states as provided in Section 3.

> *Section 3.* From time to time, Congress may increase authorized debt to an amount in excess of its initial amount set by Section 2 only if it first publicly refers to the legislatures of the several states an unconditional, single subject measure proposing the amount of such increase, in such form as provided by law, and the measure is thereafter publicly and unconditionally approved

by a simple majority of the legislatures of the several states, in such form as provided respectively by state law; provided that no inducement requiring an expenditure or tax levy shall be demanded, offered or accepted as a quid pro quo for such approval. If such approval is not obtained within sixty (60) calendar days after referral then the measure shall be deemed disapproved and the authorized debt shall thereby remain unchanged.

Section 4. Whenever the outstanding debt exceeds 98 percent of the debt limit set by Section 2, the President shall enforce said limit by publicly designating specific expenditures for impoundment in an amount sufficient to ensure outstanding debt shall not exceed the authorized debt. Said impoundment shall become effective thirty (30) days thereafter, unless Congress first designates an alternate impoundment of the same or greater amount by concurrent resolution, which shall become immediately effective. The failure of the President to designate or enforce the required impoundment is an impeachable misdemeanor. Any purported issuance or incurrence of any debt in excess of the debt limit set by Section 2 is void.

Section 5. No bill that provides for a new or increased general revenue tax shall become law unless approved by a two-thirds roll call vote of the whole number of each House of Congress. However, this requirement shall not apply to any bill that provides for a new end user sales tax which would completely replace every existing income tax levied by the government of the United States; or for the reduction or elimination of an exemption, deduction, or credit allowed under an existing general revenue tax.

Section 6. For purposes of this article, "debt" means any obligation backed by the full faith and credit of the government of the United States; "outstanding debt" means all debt held in any account and by any entity at a given point in time; "authorized debt" means the maximum total amount of debt that may be lawfully issued and outstanding at any single point in time under this article; "total outlays of the government of the United States" means all expenditures of the government of the United States from any source; "total receipts of the government of the United States" means all tax receipts and other income of the government of the United States, excluding proceeds from its issuance or incurrence of debt or any type of liability;

"impoundment" means a proposal not to spend all or part of a sum of money appropriated by Congress; and "general revenue tax" means any income tax, sales tax, or value-added tax levied by the government of the United States excluding imposts and duties.

Section 7. This article is immediately operative upon ratification, self-enforcing, and Congress may enact conforming legislation to facilitate enforcement.

* * *

The Compact has been adopted by five states: Alaska, Arizona, Georgia, Mississippi, and North Dakota (Guldenschuh 2017). The Compact for a Balanced Budget Commission—an interstate agency dedicated to organizing a convention for proposing a balanced budget amendment composed of representatives from the first three states to join the compact—has been meeting since 2015 (Dranias 2016). In March of that year, it introduced House Concurrent Resolution 26, calling on Congress to fulfill its role in the amendment process (*Ibid.*).

Recommended Readings: Nick Dranias, "Introducing Article V 2.0: The Compact for a Balanced Budget," *Policy Study* (second edition), The Heartland Institute, March 2016; Harold R. DeMoss Jr. *et al.,* "Clearly Constitutional: The Article V Compact," *Policy Brief* No. 11, Compact for America, August 22, 2016.

8. Require congressional approval of major regulations.

> Congress should have to vote to approve regulations that impose heavy burdens on businesses and taxpayers.

The federal regulatory process is out of control. Federal regulators now have the power to dictate regulations by reinterpreting laws in ways never intended by Congress. Regulators are developing a new style of government: Instead of governing democratically through the legislative process, regulators rule undemocratically through edicts issued by bureaucrats in Washington. President Barack Obama epitomized this approach when he declared he would use his pen and his phone to rule when Congress declined to approve his agenda.

Enormous Costs

Government regulations impose an enormous burden on people and the economy. A 2014 study by the National Association of Manufacturers estimated,

> Federal regulations cost a whopping $2.028 trillion in 2012. While the average American company pays $9,991 per employee, per year, to comply with these federal rules, the average manufacturer pays even more: $19,564 per employee each year. The costs are even higher for small manufacturers (those with less than 50 employees), who spend $34,671 per employee, per year, complying with federal regulations (Crain and Crain 2014).

"Tip of the Costberg," a report issued in December 2014 by the Competitive Enterprise Institute, estimates the annual cost of regulations at $1.885 trillion a year. According to the report,

> Unmeasured costs, and in particular, "regulatory dark matter," the "costs of benefits" and citizens' loss of liberty imply that if we're missing regulation, we are missing the biggest part of government's role in the economy, perhaps society itself. In addition to the burden of specific regulations is the uncertainty created by the capricious nature of the regulatory process. Regulatory uncertainty seriously lowers the rate of economic growth and the creation of new jobs (Crews 2014).

Federal spending and workers devoted to developing and administering regulations also reveal the growth in the regulatory state. Susan Dudley and Melissa Warren give a historical perspective: "In the final year of the [President] Dwight D. Eisenhower administration (FY 1960), regulatory agencies employed a little more than 57,000 people and spent $533 million (equivalent to $3 billion in 2009 dollars)." But Obama's final budget "proposes expenditures of $70.0 billion ($61 billion in 2009 dollars) on regulatory activities in FY 2017, and a staff of almost 279,000. In the 58 years tracked in this report, fiscal outlays for administering regulation have increased more than 20-fold (after adjusting for inflation) and staffing has increased by a factor of five" (Dudley and Warren 2016).

Reining in Regulation

Regulations, like laws, should have the consent of the governed. The Regulations of the Executive In Need of Scrutiny (REINS) Act, passed by the House of Representatives in 2017, would require major new federal regulations be approved by Congress before going into effect (U.S. Congress 2017b). The REINS Act would be an excellent first step, but passage is by no means certain. Even if passed and signed into law, it could be undone or repealed by future Congresses. A clear constitutional limit on the abuse of regulatory power is required (Hamburger 2014).

The Regulation Freedom Amendment, backed by more than 500 state legislators, provides, "Whenever one quarter of the Members of the U.S. House or the U.S. Senate transmit to the President their written declaration of opposition to a proposed federal regulation, it shall require a majority vote of the House and Senate to adopt that regulation" (American Opportunity Project 2017). Any regulation would be subject to review and approval by Congress if at least 109 members of the House or 25 Senators call for such a review. It also can cover regulations that threaten all liberties, like free speech or religious freedom.

As of March 2017, 21 state legislative chambers had passed resolutions urging Congress to propose the Regulation Freedom Amendment (Yack 2017). A 2014 survey conducted by McLaughlin and Associates showed more than two-to-one voter support for a constitutional amendment to require major new federal regulations not take effect unless explicitly approved by Congress (McLaughlin and Associates 2014).

As the public's discontent with federal regulatory abuses increases, states should take action to support constitutional regulatory reform to help restore the checks on executive branch power intended by the authors of our Constitution.

Recommended Readings: Philip Hamburger, *Is Administrative Law Unlawful?* (Chicago, IL: University of Chicago Press, 2014); Susan Dudley and Melinda Warren, "Regulator's Budget from Eisenhower to Obama: An Analysis of the U.S. Budget for Fiscal Years 1960 Through 2017," The Regulatory Studies Center with the Weidenbaum Center on the Economy, Government, and Public Policy, May 2016.

9. Require due process for administrative law proceedings.

Constitutional clarification is needed to ensure all citizens can fully challenge regulations restricting their liberty.

The suffering of citizens at the hands of regulators begs for a second amendment solution, one that protects U.S. citizens' rights to due process, promised under the Fifth Amendment, during administrative law proceedings (Justia n.d.).

Lawmakers at the national and state levels have increasingly relinquished their authority to government agencies. The rules, regulations, and laws by which citizens must abide are often imposed bureaucratically rather than legislatively. The Founders did not foresee such law-making by unelected bureaucrats, and the Fifth Amendment does not clearly provide for due process in matters of agency rule-making (EPIC 2015).

Few Rights in Non-judicial Proceedings

The Administrative Procedure Act of 1946 outlines the process of challenging administrative rules of the national government and affords the right to judicial review (Cornell University Legal Information Center n.d.). Any agency decision is subject to judicial review, but the statute of limitations is a mere six years. In addition, the burden of proof to determine whether an agency action is unconstitutional is very high: The court must find an agency action was "unlawfully withheld or unreasonably delayed" and must also deem the action to have been arbitrary, capricious, an abuse of discretion, contrary to constitutional rights, in excess of statutory jurisdiction without proper observance of procedure required by law, and unsupported by substantial evidence in the Code of Federal Regulations (EPIC 2015).

Three court decisions in particular have given national and state government agencies broad, expansive power to make decisions without judicial review:

- In 1877, the Supreme Court in *McMillen* v. *Anderson* found judicial review is not required for administrative proceedings (U.S. Supreme Court 1877).

- In 1941, the Court in *Railroad Commission of Texas* v. *Rowan & Nichols Oil Co.* found administrative proceedings for state agencies that promulgate new rules do not require judicial review (U.S. Supreme Court 1941).

- In 1978, the Ninth Circuit Court of Appeals ruled in *Moore* v. *Johnson* that it is not unconstitutional to deny judicial review for administrative proceedings. The court ruled the Department of Veterans Affairs could reassign patients to different facilities without the need for judicial review (Google Scholar n.d.).

Needed Reforms

Heritage Foundation Research Fellow Robert Moffitt has suggested the national government return to oral proceedings governed by an administrative law judge and create a congressional Office of Regulatory Review to ensure regulations promulgated by federal agencies are subject to judicial review (Moffitt 2011). Moffitt describes failed attempts in the past by Congress and the president to gain control of the administrative rulemaking process. Such reform attempts can be blocked by the court.

Congress was turned away twice by the nation's highest court in asserting its power in the administrative rulemaking process. In *Buckley* v. *Valeo*, the Court found the Federal Elections Commission is authorized to issue administrative rules on campaign finance and election activities without congressional oversight (Case Briefs 1976). In *Bowsher* v. *Synar,* the Court found the Comptroller General of the United States violated the separation of powers clause of the U.S. Constitution by executing laws to control the budget deficit during the Reagan era (Oyez 1985).

Constitutional protection of due process rights can prevent politicians from changing laws and policies regarding administrative rules and non-judicial proceedings at will. A constitutional amendment also could check the power of independent agencies by allowing full congressional oversight. Our system of government is built on the fundamental principle of checks and balances. A constitutional guarantee of due process for administrative law proceedings would restore that critical check on administrative rule-making by Congress and government agencies.

Recommended Readings: Robert A. Levy and William Mellor, *The Dirty Dozen: 12 Cases that Gave the Supreme Court Expansive Power* (Washington, DC: Cato Institute, 2010); Mark R. Levin, *Plunder and Deceit* (New York, NY: Threshold Editions, 2015).

10. States can refuse to enforce federal laws.

States need to understand when they can stand up for the Constitution against the national government.

Throughout America's history, there have been conflicts between the national and state governments over which level of government properly has authority over various issues (Chumley 2014). The Founders anticipated this and viewed it as an important check on the abuse of power by both levels of government. However, During President Barack Obama's two terms in office, his administration used the power of administrative rules and executive orders to impose its agenda in such areas as environmental regulation, K–12 and higher education, and health care without congressional oversight or the consent of the states.

States can fight back, but only to a limited degree. Constitutional scholar and Cato Institute chairman Robert Levy explains, "State officials need not enforce federal laws that the state has determined to be unconstitutional; nor may Congress mandate that states enact specific laws." He cites as an example the 1997 case of *Printz* v. *United States*, in which the Supreme Court ruled the federal government could not command state law enforcement authorities to conduct background checks on prospective handgun purchasers (Levy 2013).

Levy warns "states may not block federal authorities who attempt to enforce a federal law unless a court has held that the law is unconstitutional." This principle goes back to the *Marbury* v. *Madison* case of 1803, in which the Supreme Court ruled "It is emphatically the province and duty of the judicial department to say what the law is." Further, Levy explains "individuals are not exempt from prosecution by the federal government just because the state where they reside has legalized an activity or pronounced that a federal law is unconstitutional."

Recent State Actions

An example of using the state legislative process to reassert constitutional rights is the Firearms Freedom Act, legislation designed to give state law enforcement officers the authority not to enforce any new gun control laws from the national government (Firearms Freedom Act 2015). The legislation arose in response to the Sandy Hook school shooting in 2012, when many citizens feared the national government would pass stricter gun control laws or otherwise violate Second Amendment rights. Eight states have enacted the Firearms Freedom Act as of 2015, and the legislation has been introduced in 26 additional states.

Citizens of the states are also beginning to use popular referenda to instruct their own governments when not to enforce federal laws. For example, in 2014 Arizona voters approved Proposition 122, an amendment to that state's constitution prohibiting all state and local governments from using taxpayer resources to fund administration, cooperation, or enforcement of any action or program of the national government the Arizona legislature or voters deem unconstitutional (Ballotpedia 2014). In 2016, North Dakota could have become the second state to consider such a state constitutional amendment, but the measure was not approved by the state Senate and thus did not make it to the ballot (Ballotpedia 2016).

States using amendments to their own constitutions to refuse to cooperate in enforcing federal laws and regulations that their legislatures or voters deem unconstitutional should aim for one of two goals: to empower state government officials to opt out of such federal laws and regulations; or to give the state legislature the authority to decide which federal laws and regulations are to be treated as unconstitutional.

Nullification

While states can refuse to enforce laws they deem unconstitutional, this is not the same as the theory of nullification, which claims the states have the power to declare federal laws unconstitutional and therefore null.

The idea that states can nullify federal laws was first introduced in the Kentucky and Virginia resolutions in response to the Alien and Sedition Acts. It had the support of Thomas Jefferson, a leading Founder, but it was not part of the ratification debate and receives no support in the text of the Constitution. James Madison, in *Federalist* No. 46, wrote the people have the natural right to revolt against a government and establish another, but that this is an extraconstitutional step that amounts to revolution and should not be invoked unless all constitutional remedies had been exhausted (Dranias 2016).

Today, nullification refers to a state law declaring one or more federal laws void within the boundaries of the state. The state may or may not make the nullification ordinance conditional. It may or may not impose criminal or civil penalties on persons attempting to enforce the nullified law. Robert Natelson wrote in a February 3, 2014 article titled "Struggling with Nullification," "Once the pure state compact theory falls, it is very hard to justify nullification (narrowly defined) as a constitutional remedy. It remains instead a remedy reserved by natural law for when the Constitution has wholly failed—in other words, in situations justifying revolution."

* * *

Governors and state legislators have a duty to fight back against the expansion of national government authority beyond its proper constitutional bonds. In past years, the states have surrendered too much authority and responsibility to the national government, allowing it to grow out of control. States can refuse to enforce federal laws they consider unconstitutional, but they cannot nullify those laws outright. That is the province of the U.S. Supreme Court.

Recommended Readings: Robert A. Levy, "Yes, States Can Nullify Some Federal Laws, Not All," *Investor's Business Daily,* March 18, 2013; Robert Natelson, "Struggling with Nullification?" Tenth Amendment Center, February 5, 2014.

References

ALEC (American Legislative Exchange Council). 2013b. "Resolution for Limitations on Authority of State Delegates to a 'Convention for Proposing Amendments' under Article V of the US Constitution" (website).

_____. 2015. "ALEC Model Legislation for an Article V Convention Faithful Delegate Act."

American Opportunity Project. 2017. "Regulation Freedom Amendment" (website). January.

Annenberg Classroom. n.d. "The Twenty Second Amendment: What it Says." In Donald J. Ritchie and JusticeLearning.org (editors). *Our Constitution.*

Assembly of State Legislatures. 2015. "Proposed Convention Rules" (website).

BBATF (Balanced Budget Amendment Task Force). 2015. *Balanced Budget Amendment Convention Handbook* (website).

_____. 2017. "Campaign Report" (website).

Ballotpedia. 2014. "Arizona Rejection of Unconstitutional Actions Amendment" (website).

_____. 2016. "North Dakota Rejection of Unconstitutional Actions Amendment" (website).

Boyer, Dave. 2015. "$20 Trillion Man: National Debt Nearly Doubles During Obama Presidency." *The Washington Times.* November 1.

Brennan, Thomas E. 2014. *The Article V Amendatory Constitutional Convention: Keeping the Republic in the Twenty First Century*. Landover, MD: Lexington Books.

Buckley, F.H. 2015. *The Once and Future King: The Rise of Crown Government in America*. Washington, DC: Encounter Books.

Caplan, Russell L. 1988. *Constitutional Brinksmanship: Amending the Constitution by National Convention*. New York, NY: Oxford University Press.

Case Briefs. 1976. *Buckley* v. *Valeo*.

Chumley, Cheryl. 2014. "Frustrated States Fight Federal Overreach." *Newsmax* (website). March 3.

Citizens for Self-Governance. n.d. (website).

Compact for America. n.d. "The Solution" (website).

CBO (Congressional Budget Office). 2017. "Budget" (website).

Convention of States. n.d. "The Strategy" (website).

Cornell University Legal Information Center. n.d. *Administrative Law* (website).

Crain, W. Mark, and Nicole V. Crain. 2014. *The Cost of Federal Regulation to the U.S. Economy, Manufacturing and Small Business*. National Association of Manufacturers.

Crews, Clyde Wayne. 2014. *Tip of the Costberg: 2015 Edition*. Competitive Enterprise Institute.

DeMoss, Harold R. Jr., *et al.* 2016. "Clearly Constitutional: The Article V Compact." *Policy Brief* No. 11. Compact for America. August 22.

de Rugy, Veronique. 2014. "The Rise in Per Capita Federal Spending" (website). Mercatus Center.

Dranias, Nick. 2016. "Introducing Article V 2.0: The Compact for a Balanced Budget." *Policy Study* (second edition). The Heartland Institute.

Dudley, Susan, and Melinda Warren. 2016. *Regulator's Budget from Eisenhower to Obama: an Analysis of the U.S. Budget for Fiscal Years 1960 Through 2017*. Washington, DC: The Regulatory Studies Center. St. Louis: The Weidenbaum Center on the Economy, Government, and Public Policy.

EPIC (Electronic Privacy Information Center). 2015. *The Administrative Procedure Act (APA)* (website).

Farris, Michael. 2016. *Answering the John Birch Society Questions about Article V*. Convention of States. May.

Federal Reserve Bank of St. Louis. 2017. "Federal Net Outlays as Percent of Gross Domestic Product (FYONGDA188S)" (website).

Ferrara, Peter. 2011. *America's Ticking Bankruptcy Bomb*. Washington, DC: Broadside Books.

FindLaw. n.d.(a). *United States Supreme Court, Dillon* v. *Gloss* (website).

FindLaw. n.d.(b). *United States Supreme Court, United States* v. *Sprague* (website).

Firearms Freedom Act. 2015. "State by State" (website).

Fruth, William. 2010. *Ten Amendments for Freedom*. Palm City, FL: POLICOM.

Georgia General Assembly. 2014. "2013–2014 Regular Session - HB 930. General Assembly; adopt standards and instructions for Article V convention delegates; provisions" (website).

Google Scholar. n.d. *Moore* v. *Johnson*, 582 F. 2d 1228 - Court of Appeals, 9th Circuit 1978 (website).

Guldenschuh, David. 2017. "Article V Convention Legislative Report Card."

Hamburger, Philip. 2014. *Is Administrative Law Unlawful?* Chicago, IL: University of Chicago Press.

Hamilton, Alexander, John Jay, and James Madison. 2014. *The Federalist Papers and Other Essays*. Mineola, NY: Dover Publications.

Hayek, Friedrich A. 1960. *The Constitution of Liberty*. Chicago, IL: University of Chicago Press.

Justia. n.d. *The Requirements of Due Process* (website).

Levin, Mark. 2013. *The Liberty Amendments*. New York, NY: Threshold Editions.

_____. 2015. *Plunder and Deceit*. New York, NY: Threshold Editions.

Levy, Robert A. 2013. "Yes, States Can Nullify Some Federal Laws, Not All." *Investor's Business Daily*. March 18.

Levy, Robert A., and William Mellor. 2010. *The Dirty Dozen: How Twelve Supreme Court Cases Radically Expanded Government and Eroded Freedom*. Washington, DC: Cato Institute.

Long, David. 2013. *Amending the U.S. Constitution by State-Led Convention: Indiana's Model Legislation*. National Conference of State Legislatures.

McLaughlin and Associates. 2014. "National Omnibus (survey)." January 20.

Meese, Edward II, *et al.* 2005. *The Heritage Guide to the Constitution*. Washington, DC: The Heritage Foundation.

Moffitt, Robert. 2011. "How to Roll Back the Administrative State." *Discussion Paper* No. 1. Center for Policy Innovation at The Heritage Foundation. February 17.

Natelson, Robert G. 2013a. "The Article V Convention Process and the Restoration of Federalism." *Harvard Journal of Law & Public Policy* **36** (3): 955–690.

_____. 2013b. *Article V: A Handbook for State Lawmakers*. Washington, DC: American Legislative Exchange Council.

_____. 2013c. "Founding-Era Conventions and the Meaning of the Constitution's 'Convention for Proposing Amendments'." *Florida Law Review* **65** (3): 615–710.

_____. 2014. "Struggling with Nullification?" (website). Tenth Amendment Center. February 5.

_____. 2016. "The 37th 'Convention of States' Discovered!" (website). Independent Institute. August 21.

_____. 2017a. "Fake News: How Two Leading Newspapers Spread the 'Runaway Convention' Story in the 1960s & 1970s" (website). Article V Information Center.

_____. 2017b. "A Proposed Balanced Budget Amendment." *Policy Brief*. The Heartland Institute. July 27.

Newman, Alex. 2015. "Con-Con Backers Deploy False Attacks on the John Birch Society." *The New American*. March 25.

Ohio History Central. n.d. *Hawke* v. *Smith*.

Oyez. 1985. *Bowsher* v. *Synar*.

Uhler, Lewis K. 1989. *Setting Limits: Constitutional Control of Government*. Washington, DC: Regnery Publishing.

U.S. Congress. 2017a. "S.J.Res.7 - A Joint Resolution Proposing an Amendment to the Constitution of the United States Requiring that the Federal Budget Be Balanced."

_____. 2017b. "H.R.26 - Regulations from the Executive in Need of Scrutiny Act of 2017."

U.S. Supreme Court. 1877. *McMillen* v. *Anderson*.

_____. 1941. *Railroad Commission of Texas* v. *Rowan and Nichols Oil Co.*

Vile, John R. 2005. *The Constitutional Convention of 1787: A Comprehensive Encyclopedia of America's Founding*. Santa Barbara, CA: ABC-CLIO, Inc.

Yack, Austin. 2017. "Proposed Constitutional Amendment Would Accelerate Regulatory Reform." *National Review*. March 1.

Additional Resources

Additional information about constitutional reform is available from The Heartland Institute:

- The Heartland Institute's Center for Constitutional Reform was created to highlight individuals and organizations working to find solutions to our nation's constitutional problem. It does not endorse one particular path to constitutional reform, but supports and seeks constructive debate on all efforts to restore constitutional order. Its website at http://www.heartland.org/constitutional-reform/ provides the latest news and commentary about constitutional reform and links to key allies. Read headlines, watch videos, or participate in the conversation using Twitter (@usconstreform) and Facebook.

- PolicyBot, The Heartland Institute's free online clearinghouse for the work of other free-market think tanks, contains thousands of documents on constitutional reform issues. It is on Heartland's website at https://www.heartland.org/policybot/.

- *Budget & Tax News*, *Environment & Climate News*, *Health Care News*, and *School Reform News*—all monthly publications from The

Heartland Institute—cover constitutional reform issues as they relate to those specific topics. Print subscriptions are available at store.heartland.org; subscribe to the digital editions at www.heartland.org/subscribe.

Directory

The following national organizations offer additional resources about constitutional reform. This list continues to grow; for the most up-to-date list, visit the website of Heartland's Center for Constitutional Reform at http://www.heartland.org/constitutional-reform/.

American Legislative Exchange Council, http://www.alec.org

American Opportunity Project,
http://www.americanopportunityproject.org/

Article V Legislators Caucus, http://www.articlevcaucus.com

Assembly of State Legislatures, http://www.theasl.org

Balanced Budget Amendment Task Force , http://www.bba4usa.org

Ballotpedia, http://www.ballotpedia.com

Citizens for Self-Governance, http://www.selfgovern.org

Compact for America, http://www.compactforamerica.org

Convention of States, http://www.conventionofstates.com

Convention USA, http://www.conventionusa.org

Goldwater Institute, http://www.goldwaterinstitute.org

Heartland Institute, https://www.heartland.org/

Independence Institute's Article V Info Center,
http://www.articleVinfocenter.com

National Federation of Independent Businesses, http://www.nfib.org

Our American Constitution, http://robnatelson.com/

Tenth Amendment Center, http://www.tenthamendmentcenter.com

U.S. Term Limits, http://www.termlimits.org

About the Authors and Contributors

Lead Authors/Editors

Herbert J. Walberg is distinguished visiting fellow at Stanford University's Hoover Institution and chief scientific advisor to the Center on Innovation and Improvement. He has written and edited more than 65 books and written some 350 articles on such topics as school choice, educational testing and evaluation, and exceptional human accomplishments. He served as a professor at Harvard University and the University of Illinois at Chicago after earning a Ph.D. in educational psychology at The University of Chicago. Walberg has given invited lectures in Australia, Belgium, China, England, France, Germany, Israel, Italy, Japan, the Netherlands, South Africa, Sweden, Taiwan, the United States, and Venezuela. He has frequently testified before congressional committees, state legislatures, and federal courts. He is the only American to have served on the National Assessment Governing Board, which oversees the National Assessment of Educational Progress, and the presidentially appointed National Board for Educational Sciences. He has served on seven boards, including that of the California-based Foundation for Teaching Economics. He currently chairs the boards of the Beck Foundation and The Heartland Institute.

Joseph L. Bast cofounded The Heartland Institute in 1984, served as president and CEO until July 2017, and currently is CEO. He is the author or editor of 21 books, including *Why We Spend Too Much on Health Care* (1992), *Eco-Sanity: A Common-Sense Guide to Environmentalism* (1994), *Education & Capitalism* (2003), *Rewards* (2014), and *Why Scientists Disagree About Global Warming* (2015). His writing has appeared in the *Phi Delta Kappan, Economics of Education Review, Wall Street Journal, Investor's Business Daily, The Cato Journal, USA Today*, and many of the country's largest-circulation newspapers. He has been recognized many times for his contributions to public policy research and debate, including being named one of "The 88 to Watch in 1988" by the Chicago Tribune and being awarded the 1994 Roe Award from the State Policy Network, the 1996 Sir Antony Fisher International Memorial Award, the 1998 Eagle Award from Eagle Forum, the 2004 Champion of Liberty Award from the Libertarian National Committee, and the 2014 Edward Teller Award from Doctors for Disaster Preparedness. He was commissioned a Kentucky Colonel by Gov. Paul E. Patton in 1996, elected a member of the Philadelphia Society in 2002, and served on the board of directors of the American Conservative Union from 2007 to 2016.

Contributors

Vicki E. Alger is a research fellow at the Independent Institute in Oakland, California, and author of the book *Failure: The Federal Misedukation of America's Children*. She holds senior fellowships at the Fraser Institute, headquartered in Vancouver, British Columbia, and the Independent Women's Forum in Washington, DC. Alger is also president and CEO of Vicki Murray & Associates LLC in Scottsdale, Arizona. She is the author of more than 40 education policy studies, co-author of *Lean Together: An Agenda for Smarter Government, Stronger Communities, and More Opportunities for Women*; *Short-Circuited: The Challenges Facing the Online Learning Revolution in California*; and *Not as Good as You Think: Why the Middle Class Needs School Choice*, as well as associate producer of the documentary "Not as Good as You Think: Myth of the Middle Class School."

Timothy Benson is a policy analyst at The Heartland Institute. Prior to joining Heartland, Benson worked for the Foundation for Government Accountability as an editor and writer. He also wrote a regular column for Scripps Treasure Coast Newspapers. His work has appeared in *Investor's Business Daily*, *National Review Online*, *The Hill*, *The Washington Times*, *Crain's Chicago Business*, *The American Spectator*, and many other publications across the country. He is author of the *Heartland Policy Brief* "Education Savings Accounts: The Future of School Choice Has Arrived," and coauthor of the *Heartland Policy Brief* "Saving Chicago Students: Strike Vouchers and SOS Accounts."

Roman Buhler is national director of the Madison Coalition, working to restore a balance of state and federal power and curb the authority of abusive federal regulators. He served as Newt Gingrich's first Committee Counsel and from 1989 to 2003 and again in 2007 as Elections Counsel to the Committee on House Administration, handling election issues for

House Republicans. Prior to his service in the House, Buhler worked as an attorney and political consultant in California. He graduated from Stanford University, the University of Southern California Law School, and the Harvard University Program for Senior Managers in Government.

Joshua Distel is an executive assistant and office manager at the Buckeye Institute, a Columbus, Ohio-based research institute. Previously, he was an administrative assistant at the Center for College Affordability and Productivity. The author of studies on Winston Churchill, Distel is a graduate of Ashland University and has a master's degree from Hillsdale College.

Peter J. Ferrara is senior fellow for entitlement and budget policy at The Heartland Institute and a senior fellow at the Social Security Institute. He served in the White House Office of Policy Development under President Ronald Reagan and as associate deputy attorney general of the United States under President George H.W. Bush. He is a graduate of Harvard College and Harvard Law School. Ferrara is author of several books, including *President Obama's Tax Piracy* and *America's Ticking Bankruptcy Bomb: How the Looming Debt Crisis Threatens the American Dream – and How We Can Turn the Tide Before It's Too Late.* Ferrara's latest book (Heartland Institute, 2015) is *Power to the People: The New Road to Freedom and Prosperity for the Poor, Seniors, and Those Most in Need of the World's Best Health Care.*

George Gilder is chairman of Gilder Group, Inc. and a senior fellow at Seattle's Discovery Institute, where he directs Discovery's program on high technology and democracy. Gilder is a contributing editor of *Forbes* magazine and a frequent writer for *The Economist, The American Spectator, Harvard Business Review, The Wall Street Journal,* and other publications. He wrote the classic *Wealth and Poverty* (1981), a book widely credited with setting the free-market agenda for the Reagan era. Other books include *Microcosm* (1989), *Life After Television* (1990), *Telecosm* (2000), *The Silicon Eye* (2005), *The Israel Test* (2008), *Knowledge and Power* (2013), and *The Scandal of Money* (2016).

Leonard Gilroy is director of government reform at Reason Foundation, researching privatization, public-private partnerships, pension reform, infrastructure and urban policy issues. Gilroy has worked closely with legislators and elected officials in Texas, Arizona, Louisiana, New Jersey, Utah, Virginia, California and several other states and local governments in efforts to design and implement market-based policy approaches, improve government performance, enhance accountability in government programs, and reduce government spending. Gilroy is the editor of the *Privatization & Government Reform Newsletter* and the widely read *Annual Privatization Report*, which examines trends and chronicles the experiences of local, state, and federal governments in bringing competition to public services.

Matthew Glans joined the staff of The Heartland Institute in November 2007 as legislative specialist for insurance and finance. In 2012, Glans was named senior policy analyst. He is a member of the American Legislative Exchange Council's Commerce, Insurance and Economic Development Task Force. His work has appeared in several publications, including the *Chicago Tribune, Milwaukee Journal-Sentinel, Los Angeles Times, USA Today*, and *St. Louis Post Dispatch*. Glans is the co-author of The Heartland Institute's "Ten Principles of Property and Casualty Insurance Regulation" booklet and *Policy Briefs* on credit scoring and Medicaid reform. Glans earned a master's degree in political studies from the University of Illinois at Springfield and a Bachelor of Arts degree in political science from Bradley University.

Hance Haney is director and senior fellow of the Technology & Democracy Project at the Discovery Institute, in Washington, DC. He spent ten years as an aide to former Senator Bob Packwood (OR) and advised him in his capacity as chairman of the Senate Communications Subcommittee during the deliberations leading to the Telecommunications Act of 1996. He subsequently held various positions with the United States Telecom Association and Qwest Communications. He earned a B.A. in history from Willamette University and a J.D. from Lewis and Clark Law School in Portland, Oregon.

Adrian Moore is vice president of policy at Reason Foundation. Moore leads Reason's policy implementation efforts and conducts his own research on topics such as privatization, government and regulatory reform, air quality, transportation and urban growth, prisons and utilities. Moore has testified before Congress and regularly advises federal, state and local officials on ways to streamline government and reduce costs. In 2008 and 2009, Moore served on Congress' National Surface Transportation Infrastructure Financing Commission. Since 2009 he has served on California's Public Infrastructure Advisory Commission. He is co-author of *Mobility First: A New Vision for Transportation in a Globally Competitive 21st Century* (2008) and *Curb Rights: A Foundation for Free Enterprise in Urban Transit* (1997), as well as dozens of policy studies.

Isaac Orr is a research fellow for energy and environment policy at The Heartland Institute. He specializes in hydraulic fracturing, frac sand mining, agricultural, and environmental policy issues. He graduated from the University of Wisconsin Eau Claire with studies in political science and geology, winning awards for his undergraduate geology research before taking a position as an aide in the Wisconsin State Senate. He has written a series of *Heartland Policy Studies* on fracking and frac sand mining. His writing has appeared in many print and online publications, and his work on fracking is featured in the *Alternative Energy and Shale Gas Encyclopedia* (John Wiley & Sons, Inc., 2016).

Daniel J. Pilla is a tax litigation consultant and executive director of the Tax Freedom Institute, a national association of tax professionals. He is admitted to practice before the United States Tax Court. He is the author of 14 books, hundreds of articles, and dozens of research reports on IRS problems resolution and taxpayers rights issues. His book *The IRS Problem Solver* was ranked by *The Wall Street Journal* as the number one tax book in America. His book *How to Fire the IRS* started the national debate on abolishing the IRS that took place throughout the 1990s. He was on the editorial board of the Institute for Policy Innovation's "Road Map to Tax Reform Project" and was a consultant to the National Commission on Restructuring the IRS. He has two websites, at www.taxhelponline.com and www.taxfreedominstitute.com. He speaks nationwide to tax professional associations, trade associations, and citizens' groups on taxpayers' rights and tax policy issues.

Publius is a professor at a United States university. His work on gun control and other topics has appeared in many scholarly journals. He coauthored Chapter 6 with Joseph Bast but prefers to remain anonymous.

Justin Strehle is completing a master's degree in financial economics from Ohio University, from which he earned his bachelor's degree. He has coauthored several studies and articles, including one on higher education that appeared in *The Wall Street Journal*.

Austill Stuart is a policy analyst at Reason Foundation. Prior to joining Reason, he worked with policy in a variety of settings—nonprofits, on Capitol Hill, and in fundraising—where areas of focus included small business regulation, privatization, health care, and labor. Before moving to the D.C. area in early 2009, he worked for five years in the financial services industry, mostly in wealth management.

James M. Taylor is president of the Spark of Freedom Foundation and a senior fellow for environment and energy policy at The Heartland

Institute. He is the former managing editor (2001–14) of *Environment & Climate News* and writes a column for the Forbes.com website. He has presented environmental analysis on CNN, CNN Headline News, CBS Evening News, MSNBC, Fox News Channel, and several national radio programs. His analysis has been published in virtually every major newspaper in the United States. He studied atmospheric science and majored in government at Dartmouth College and obtained his Juris Doctorate from Syracuse University.

Steven Titch is a journalist-turned-policy analyst focusing on tele-communications, internet, and information technology. He is a policy advisor to The Heartland Institute and an associate fellow at the R Street Institute. He is a former policy analyst at the Reason Foundation. He has published research reports on cybersecurity, network neutrality, and municipal broadband. His columns have appeared in *Investor's Business Daily*, the *Washington Examiner*, *ComputerWorld*, and the *Houston Chronicle*. Follow him on Twitter @stevetitch.

Richard Vedder is distinguished professor of economics emeritus at Ohio University, an adjunct scholar of the American Enterprise Institute, and founding director of the Center for College Affordability and Productivity. A graduate of Northwestern University and the University of Illinois, Vedder is the author of *Going Broke By Degree* and numerous other books and journal articles on higher education and other topics in public policy and economic history, and he writes frequently for the popular press, including *The Wall Street Journal*, *New York Times*, *Washington Post*, *Investor's Business Daily*, *Forbes*, and *National Review*.